Henry Stewart

Our Redcoats and Bluejackets

War pictures on land and sea: forming a continuous narrative of the naval and military history of England from the year 1793 to the present time, including the Afghan and Zulu campaigns

Henry Stewart

Our Redcoats and Bluejackets

War pictures on land and sea: forming a continuous narrative of the naval and military history of England from the year 1793 to the present time, including the Afghan and Zulu campaigns

ISBN/EAN: 9783337012151

Printed in Europe, USA, Canada, Australia, Japan

Cover: Foto ©ninafisch / pixelio.de

More available books at **www.hansebooks.com**

OUR REDCOATS AND BLUEJACKETS.

Ballantyne Press
BALLANTYNE, HANSON AND CO.
EDINBURGH AND LONDON

OUR REDCOATS AND BLUEJACKETS

OUR REDCOATS AND BLUEJACKETS:

War Pictures on Land and Sea.

FORMING A CONTINUOUS NARRATIVE

OF THE

NAVAL AND MILITARY HISTORY OF ENGLAND

FROM THE YEAR 1793 TO THE PRESENT TIME.

Interspersed with Anecdotes and Accounts of Personal Service.

BY

HENRY STEWART,

AUTHOR OF "HIGHLAND REGIMENTS AND THEIR BATTLES,"
"THE ROMANCE OF THE SEA," ETC.

WITH TWO COLOURED PLATES.

"Where heroes war, the foremost place I claim,
The first in battle, and the first in fame."—*Pope.*

LONDON:
JOHN HOGG, PATERNOSTER ROW.
1879.
[*All rights reserved.*]

PREFACE.

THE object of this volume is to present, in one view and in a short compass, an account of the principal achievements of the British arms, both by land and by sea, since the opening of the Great War with France in 1793. During that war, the British arms reached the highest pinnacle of renown, and ever since they have maintained the same high character. The naval and military history of England has been well written already; but the general reader—the young reader especially—cannot be expected to wade through the numerous bulky volumes of such writers as James, Napier, and Kinglake.

The narrative is invariably based upon the standard historians of each period—such as James, Brenton, and Yonge, among naval writers; Wilson, Stewart, Napier, Creasy, Gleig, Kinglake, Wellesley, and Stanley, among military writers. To give vividness and variety, anecdotes and short accounts of personal service have been introduced.

The wars of the British in India form a branch of the subject almost quite distinct; but the Mutiny stands apart, and has received a fair share of attention. A short account of the Conquest of India is prefixed to the story of the Mutiny.

The book will, it is believed, be found specially interesting to the young, some of whom will become Redcoats and Bluejackets themselves, and will do their duty all the better for a knowledge of the gallant deeds done by their predecessors. At the same time, the greatest care has been taken with facts and dates, and it is hoped that the older or the professional reader will not find the work altogether uninteresting or unworthy of perusal.

A chronological list of engagements has been added, to increase its usefulness as a handy book of reference.

CONTENTS.

| | PAGE |

CHAPTER I.—THE GREAT FRENCH WAR.
THE NATIONAL CONVENTION—1793-1795.

Campaign in the Low Countries—Toulon—Corsica—Lord Howe's Victory off Ushant on the First of June—Admiral Hotham's Action in the Mediterranean—Admiral Cornwallis's masterly Retreat—Lord Bridport's Victory—The Quiberon Expedition—First Capture of the Cape of Good Hope 11

CHAPTER II.—THE GREAT FRENCH WAR.
THE DIRECTORY—1796-1799.

French Expeditions to Ireland—Cape St. Vincent—The French land in Pembrokeshire—Nelson's Attempt on Santa Cruz—Camperdown—The Nile—Anglo-Russian Expedition to Holland—Sir Sidney Smith foils Napoleon at Acre—Successes of Troubridge in Italy 27

CHAPTER III.—THE GREAT FRENCH WAR.
NAPOLEON FIRST CONSUL—1800-1802.

Battle of the Baltic—Aboukir—Mandora—Alexandria—Attempt on the Gunboats at Boulogne 49

CHAPTER IV.—THE GREAT FRENCH WAR.
FROM AMIENS TO TRAFALGAR—1802-1805.

Projected Invasion of England—Commodore Dance's Action—Seizure of the Spanish Treasure Frigates—Sir Robert Calder's Action—Trafalgar—Sir Richard Strachan's Action off Cape Ortegal . 65

Chapter V.—The Great French War.

FROM TRAFALGAR TO ROLIÇA—1806-1807.

Second Capture of the Cape of Good Hope—Sir Home Popham at Buenos Ayres—Sir John Duckworth's Victory at St. Domingo—Maida—Capture of Monte Video by Sir Samuel Achmuty—Sir John Duckworth forces the Dardanelles—Egypt—General Whitelocke capitulates at Buenos Ayres—Surrender of the Danish fleet to Britain 79

Chapter VI.—The Peninsular War.

ROLIÇA TO CORUNNA—1808-1809.

Roliça—Vimiero—Sir John Moore's March into Spain—The Retreat to Corunna—Battle of Corunna—Lord Cochrane in the Basque Roads 95

Chapter VII.—The Peninsular War.

DELIVERANCE OF PORTUGAL—1809-1811.

Passage of the Douro—Wellington's First March into Spain—Talavera—The Walcheren Expedition—Busaco—Barosa—Fuentes d'Oñoro 109

Chapter VIII.—The Peninsular War.

THE SALAMANCA CAMPAIGN—1811-1812.

Albuera—Arroyo dos Molinos—Frigate Action off Lissa—Ciudad Rodrigo—Badajos—Almaraz—Wellington's Second March into Spain—Salamanca—Wellington enters Madrid—Retreat from Burgos 129

Chapter IX.—The Peninsular War.

LIBERATION OF SPAIN—1813.

Vitoria—Battles of the Pyrenees—Storming of San Sebastian . . 157

Chapter X.

CAMPAIGN IN THE SOUTH OF FRANCE—1813-1814.

Passage of the Bidassoa—Passage of the Nivelle—Passage of the Nive—Battles before Bayonne—St. Pierre—Orthes—Toulouse . . 173

CONTENTS.

CHAPTER XI.
THE AMERICAN WAR—1812-1814.

	PAGE
The Shannon and the Chesapeake	185

CHAPTER XII.
THE HUNDRED DAYS—1815.

Quatre Bras—Waterloo 193

CHAPTER XIII.
FROM WATERLOO TO SEBASTOPOL—1816-1854.

Bombardment of Algiers—First Burmese War—Navarino—First Chinese War—Second Burmese War—The War in Syria—Kaffir War 217

CHAPTER XIV.
THE RUSSIAN WAR—1854-1856.

Odessa—Bomarsund—Kola—Petropaulovski—The Alma—Bombardment of Sebastopol—Balaclava—Inkerman—Expedition to Kertch Taganrog—Sveaborg—The Malakoff and Redan—Russians evacuate Sebastopol—Kinburn 235

CHAPTER XV.
PERSIA—CHINA—1856-1858.

Bushire—Khooshab—Mahommerah and Ahwaz—Fatshan Creek—Canton—The Peiho Forts 277

CHAPTER XVI.
THE CONQUEST OF INDIA—1600-1857 281

CHAPTER XVII.
THE INDIAN MUTINY—1857-1859.

Siege of Delhi—Massacre of Cawnpore—Defence of Lucknow—Relief of Lucknow by Sir Henry Havelock—Rescue of Lucknow by Sir Colin Campbell—Siege of Lucknow—Bareilly—Victorious March of Sir Hugh Rose—Capture of Jhansi and Gwalior . . 287

Chapter XVIII.

CHINA, NEW ZEALAND, BHOTAN—1859-1866.

Capture of the Taku Forts—The Anglo-French troops enter Pekin—Destruction of the Chinese Emperor's Summer Palace . . 321

Chapter XIX.

THE ABYSSINIAN EXPEDITION—1867-1868.

The March on Magdala—Battle of Aroje—Release of the Abyssinian Prisoners—Capture of Magdala, and Suicide of Theodore . . 329

Chapter XX.

THE ASHANTEE WAR—1873-1874.

Crossing the Prah—Skirmish at Borborassie—Battle of Amoaful—Capture of Becquah—Battle of Ordahsu, and March on Coomassie—Destruction of Coomassie and Return of the Troops—Treaty of Fommanah 347

A Chronological List of the Naval and Military Engagements of England 373

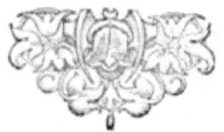

OUR REDCOATS AND BLUEJACKETS.

CHAPTER I.—THE GREAT FRENCH WAR.

THE NATIONAL CONVENTION—1793-1795.

Campaign in the Low Countries—Toulon—Corsica—Lord Howe's Victory off Ushant on the First of June—Admiral Hotham's Action in the Mediterranean—Admiral Cornwallis's masterly Retreat—Lord Bridport's Victory—The Quiberon Expedition—First Capture of the Cape of Good Hope.

THE French Revolution was the trumpet-call which summoned Europe to arms. At first the European Powers refrained from interference with France, and contented themselves with adopting measures for preventing the spread of the revolutionary contagion into their own states. But France was in a warlike mood. War was declared against Austria (April 20, 1792), and the Prussian and Austrian armies, under the Duke of Brunswick, invaded France (July 25). The Republicans, however, were successful at Valmy (Sept. 20) and Jemmappes (Nov. 6), and not only was the most formidable invasion that ever menaced France repelled, but Flanders and Mayence were conquered and captured, and Savoy and Nice were wrested from the King of Sardinia (who had refused to receive an envoy from the Republic), and converted into departments of France.

During the campaign of 1792, Britain preserved a strict neutrality; but the continuance of peace soon became impossible.

Inflamed to frenzy by the overthrow of the throne, the massacres of September, and the victories of Dumourier, the French Convention passed the two famous decrees of the 19th November and the 15th December, declaring that "they would grant fraternity and succour to every people disposed to recover their liberty," and proclaiming in all countries conquered by the Republic, "liberty, equality, the sovereignty of the people, with the suppression of nobility and all exclusive privileges, of all subsisting taxes, and all constituted authorities," and denouncing as enemies "all who refused to accept these benefits." By these decrees the Republic openly declared war with all established governments, and there only wanted some tangible quarrel to plunge France and Britain into war. This was found in the sailing of a French squadron up the Scheldt to co-operate in the reduction of Antwerp (Nov. 30), since by the treaty of Munster the Scheldt had been declared for ever closed. Then came the execution of Louis XVI. (Jan. 20, 1793). On this M. Chauvelin, the French envoy, was ordered to leave England, and the Convention (February 3, 1793) unanimously declared war with Great Britain. This country was thus forced into the coalition arrayed against France. Her vast resources were freely lavished for the common cause, and at the close of the war, which lasted two and twenty years, and deluged all Europe with blood, her arms had acquired a *prestige*, both by land and by sea, which has been maintained, but can scarcely be enhanced.

Britain joined the allies in the Low Countries, whither the Duke of York was sent with 20,000 British troops and 10,000 Hessians and Hanoverians in British pay. It would be tedious to enter into the particulars of this almost forgotten campaign, in which Britain took a comparatively small part, and which ended in Holland being over-run by the French, and the Stadtholder taking refuge in England. It will be sufficient to notice that the Coldstream Guards distinguished themselves at St. Amand (May 8, 1793), routing the French from a strong position from which the Austrians had previously failed to dislodge them. A magazine of the time says that Serjeant-major Darby of the Coldstreams "performed prodigies of valour. He had an arm broken and shattered by a ball, but yet continued fighting with the most animated and determined bravery. . . . He put to death a French officer who made an attack upon him; but at length had his leg broken by another cannon-ball, in consequence of which he fell into the hands of the French." At the siege of Valenciennes (May 25), the forlorn hope consisted of 300 British—150 of the Household Brigade, and an equal number of the line—under Major-general Ralph Abercrombie. "The troops being in readiness," says Corporal Robert Brown, "they rushed on with the greatest impetuosity and jumped over the palisades, carrying all before them at the point of the bayonet. The enemy, after a stout resistance, left the works in possession of the victors." At Lincelles (Aug. 18) the three regiments of guards gained great honour by a spirited attack on a large redoubt, situated on some high ground, and garrisoned by 5000 French troops. "The French," says Corporal Brown, "who had been accustomed to the cold lifeless attacks of the Dutch, were amazed at the spirit and intrepidity of the British; and, not much relishing the manner of our salute, immediately gave way, abandoning all that was in the place, and in their flight threw aside both arms and accoutrements. We took one stand of colours and two pieces of cannon, with two they had taken from the Dutch." The three regiments of Foot Guards carry "Lincelles" on their colours.

The campaign of 1793 was indecisive all along the line—with the British and Austrians in the Low Countries, with the Prussians on the Rhine, and the Sardinians in Savoy. In the Pyrenees, however, the Spaniards had decidedly the advantage. Events of a more important character occurred in the south of France. The fall of the Girondists excited the liveliest discontent in that quarter, and the great towns of Lyons, Marseilles, and Toulon rose in open rebellion. In Lyons and Marseilles the revolt was crushed with the usual atrocities, and a similar fate impended over the Toulonese. In this extremity the citizens entered into negotiations with Admiral Lord Hood and Admiral Gravina, the British and Spanish commanders, offering to surrender the city, with the French fleet in port, to be held in trust for Louis XVII., as the little Dauphin was called. Lord Hood closed with the proposals, and on the arrival of the British fleet, Captain Elphinstone of the *Robust* (afterwards Lord Keith) landed with two regiments and some marines, and took possession of the forts commanding the shipping. The French fleet also submitted, but of the seamen 5000 who professed democratic principles made their escape, and joined the Republican forces in the interior. Lord Hood sent to Genoa and Naples for troops to hold the city, but a large Republican army soon arrived and commenced siege operations. The besiegers were 60,000; the defenders 2000 British and 15,000 Neapolitans and Spaniards; but these last spent the best part of their time in plundering and murdering the inhabitants. All through the summer and autumn the siege went on, the French fighting their way foot by foot. At length (Dec. 17) Fort Mulgrave was captured by the French, and all the posts on the heights of Pharon were carried. The ships were now compelled to retire, and Lord Hood held a council of war, at which it was unanimously resolved to evacuate the place, and destroy the magazines and dockyards and all the French ships that could not be carried off. The execution of this operation was entrusted to Captain Sidney Smith—who afterwards immortalised his name at Acre—and as far as he and the British seamen were concerned nothing could have been more satisfactory. But the Spaniards made a claim to share in the enterprise, the complete success of which was marred by their want of skill and courage. They retreated before completing the task set to them, and in their hurry and confusion set fire to, instead of scuttling, two powder ships, causing the death of several of our men. On the whole, however, the work of destruction was tolerably complete. Of a fleet of 58 vessels which the French had at Toulon, 14 were burnt or otherwise destroyed; 16 were fitted out by the British, and 3 by the allies. Only 25, large and small, were left to the French. The troops and seamen under Captain Elphinstone took advantage of the operations to evacuate the only fort remaining in our possession, and by daylight on the morning of the 19th were on board without the loss of a man. Of the wretched inhabitants 15,000 escaped to the British fleet and were conveyed to England; "but," says the naval historian James, "melancholy was the fate of those left behind. Many on their way to the shore were cut in two by the balls which were falling around them; others, overcome by their fears, fancied the hurried steps they heard behind were those of their pursuers; and some rushed, preferring instant death to infuriated vengeance, with their infants clinging to their breasts, into the waves and perished. Some thousands of others remained in the town, in the hopes that their age, sex, or political insignificance would shield them from the bayonets of the soldiers, their countrymen. Vain hope! a decree of the Committee of Public Safety had doomed the whole of them to destruction; and the Toulonese deputies, Fréron and Moyse Bayle, worthy of such masters, were not to be moved by the entreaties even of Dugommier himself." When the British entered Toulon it contained 28,000 souls, and in a few weeks after they quitted it there were but 7000 left. More than half the population escaped on board the British fleet, but 6000 at least perished by the sword, musket, and guillotine, or, in their despair, by their own hands.

Among Hood's captains at Toulon was Horatio Nelson, and this is the advice he used to give his midshipmen:—"There are three things, young gentleman, which you are constantly to bear in mind. First, you must always implicitly obey orders, without attempting to form any opinion of your own respecting their propriety; secondly, you must consider every man your enemy who speaks ill of your king; and thirdly, you must hate a Frenchman as you do the devil." In the army of General Dugommier was a little captain of artillery, then, like Nelson, commencing his career; a man who would stand "no nonsense." At the attack on Pharon, a commissioner of the National Convention criticised the position of a battery under Buonaparte's orders; he said it would never do, and must be shifted, and in the end gave orders accordingly. Buonaparte had hitherto made no remark, but now he could control himself no longer. "Stick to your *rôle* of representative," he said fiercely, "and leave me to mine of artillerist. That battery shall stand there, sir—there, where it is, and I answer for the success"—*cette batterie restera là, et je réponds du succés.* Just so; and the battery succeeded so well that it was mainly owing to it that the British and Spanish were forced to quit the place. Nelson and Buonaparte were two of the three great heroes of the war; the one on the sea and for England, the other on the land and for France.

In the campaign of 1794, in the Low Countries, the 15th Hussars distinguished themselves at Villiers-en-Couche (April 24), which they bear on their colours; and the Oxford Blues, 1st, 3rd, and 5th Dragoon Guards, 1st Royal Dragoons, and 15th and 16th Light Cavalry decided the day at Caudry (April 25), by charging a brigade of fourteen guns posted on an eminence beyond a steep ravine. But the tide of war went strongly against the allies; and the French were also successful in Savoy and the Pyrenees.

The destruction of the Toulon fleet had totally paralysed the French navy in the Mediterranean, and Paoli and his brave islanders saw an opportunity of driving the French from Corsica. The famous patriot opened a communication with Lord Hood, and help was promised, on the understanding that the island should be delivered up to His Britannic Majesty. San Fiorenzo soon fell before the fire of some of Hood's 74's; and, meanwhile, Nelson was sent with a small squadron to reconnoitre Bastia. He reported that the place could easily be taken by a small force of 1000 men. "With 500 and the *Agamemnon*," he said, "I would attempt it. My seamen are now what British seamen ought to be—almost invincible. They really mind shot no more than peas." General Dundas, who commanded the land forces, was of a different opinion. He characterised the proposed siege as a most visionary and rash attempt, such as no officer would be justified in undertaking, and proposed to wait for a reinforcement of 2000 men, which he expected from Gibraltar. But as time was everything, Lord Hood resolved to undertake the siege with his own resources, and to Nelson he committed the operations on shore. The men were landed (April 4), with some battering guns, mortars, and ammunition, which Lord Hood had begged from Naples. The difficulties arising from the nature of the ground were simply enormous. Batteries had to be placed on rocky elevations which even the natives deemed inaccessible. Guns of 42 cwt. had to be hauled up to these positions with blocks and ropes. There were no roads; only paths which admitted but one person at a time. Above were the beetling crags; below a sheer precipice. But Nelson and his Agamemnons overcame every difficulty. Roads were made, trees cut down, batteries erected; and on the 14th fire was opened on Bastia. The French held out bravely, and their general, La Combe St. Michael, appeared determined to abide by his answer to the first summons to surrender, that "he had shot for our ships and bayonets for our troops; when two-thirds of his men were killed he would trust to the generosity of the English." Nelson redoubled his efforts; new batteries were erected where the guns could never have been put in position, he said, "by any but British seamen;" and (May 22d) the

French colours were hauled down. "I am all astonishment," wrote Nelson, "when I reflect on what we have achieved; 1000 regulars, 1500 National Guards, and a large party of Corsican troops, 4000 in all, laying down their arms to 1200 soldiers, marines, and seamen! I always was of opinion, have ever acted up to it, and never had any reason to repent it, that one Englishman was equal to three Frenchmen."

The *Agamemnon* was now ordered to co-operate with General Sir Charles Stuart in the siege of Calvi. The same difficulties had to be overcome as at Bastia, but Nelson was acting with a man after his own heart, and the enthusiasm with which he inspired his Agamemnons made short work of the enemy. On the 1st August the Governor of Calvi beat a *chamade*, and the island of Corsica, thus freed from the French, became for a time a part of our empire. At the siege of Calvi, Nelson lost the sight of an eye, from some sand and small gravel driven by a shot which fell near.

A still more glorious triumph was to come. France was suffering grievously from a scarcity of grain; a famine was dreaded, and if the people became irritated under the pressure of want, the Revolution might itself be revolutionised. With all Europe hostile, she could look for supplies of grain from no quarter but America; and this necessarily entailed sending a fleet to sea fit to cope with the British. By great exertions, 26 ships of the line were equipped at Brest; and Messieurs Jean-Bon Saint-André and Bréard, the deputies of the National Convention, came down post from Paris to screw the courage of the seamen up to the sticking-point. "You will conquer them!" shouted Jean-Bon Saint-André to the seamen; "yes, you will conquer these eternal enemies of our nation. As to that, you have but to will it, and it is done." Jean-Bon Saint-André and the French in general had yet to learn that seamen cannot be improvised like soldiers; that power at sea must be of gradual formation; that, while almost every nation of Europe has at one time or other suddenly astonished the world with a display of military prowess, naval supremacy has for three centuries belonged to no nation but one. Naval power depends on so many things which must concur: great wealth, a decided taste in a considerable section of the people for a maritime life, and the *prestige* of victory.

B

Lord Howe, having knowledge of these doings at Brest, set sail from St. Helen's (May 2) with the Channel Fleet. His flag was on board the *Queen Charlotte*. Admiral Villaret-Joyeuse, who was in command of the Brest Fleet, did not sail until the 16th. Next day the two fleets passed each other in a dense fog, and so near as to hear each other's signals, but they did not see each other till the 28th. Off Ushant, at half-past six that morning, the wind fresh from south by west, with a very rough sea, the look-out frigates of the British fleet made the signal for a strange fleet to windward. The *Bellerophon* was ordered to reconnoitre, and gave the expected information. Lord Howe made the signal to prepare for battle, and ordered the *Bellerophon* to shorten sail. At ten minutes past eleven the crews were piped down to dinner, and, in their grog, drank "Confusion to the French, and a glorious victory to Old England!"

That day and the next were spent in distant manœuvring, and on the 30th and 31st there was no fighting because of the fog. But at length arrived "the glorious First of June." The two fleets were as equally matched as such mighty armaments can well be. Each had 26 ships of the line, and so far they were equal, but in every other respect the French had the advantage. The aggregate tonnage of the British ships was 46,962 tons, of the French, 52,010; the British crews numbered 18,241 men, the French 19,989; the British had 1087 guns, throwing a broadside of 22,976 lbs., the French 1107 guns, throwing a broadside of 28,126 lbs. So that the French had larger ships, more men, more guns, and these heavier. Still, the two fleets were very fairly matched, for the Revolution had removed many of the best naval officers of France, while Howe's fleet was led by a band of distinguished seamen. Among his captains—to go no higher—were Sir Roger Curtis, one of the heroes of Gibraltar; Cuthbert Collingwood, the friend of Nelson; Duckworth, Gambier, and Stopford, who afterwards commanded at Acre in 1840.

At 7.25 A.M. Lord Howe signalled that he should pass through the enemy's line and engage to leeward. The two fleets were now about four miles apart, and Lord Howe, thinking the crews were in need of some refreshment after sitting up three nights, hove to and sent the men to breakfast. This gave the French an opportunity to think, and to say, that the British were faltering. That distinguished officer, Captain Troubridge, was then a prisoner on board the *Sanspareil*; he was anxiously looking at Lord Howe's line, when the French officers exultingly pointed out the delay that was taking place, and tauntingly said it was evident the British Admiral had no desire for the encounter. "Don't flatter yourselves," said Troubridge; "John Bull does not like fighting on an empty stomach, but see if he does not pay you a visit after breakfast." The officers of the *Sanspareil* had cause to remember these words.

At 8.12 A.M. the British fleet filled and bore down on the enemy, steering about north-west, and going at the rate of very little more than five knots an hour. The breeze was fresh at south by west. The French ships were some of them lying to, and others backing and filling to preserve their stations. About half-past eight Lord Howe threw out a signal for each ship to steer for and independently engage the ship opposed to her in the enemy's line.

The first gun was fired at 9.24 A.M. The action then commenced, and for some hours raged with all the noise, smoke, slaughter, and fury of a great sea-fight. It is thus summarily described by James:—"Between a quarter and half-past nine A.M. the French van opened its fire upon the British van. In about a quarter of an hour the fire of the French became general, and Lord Howe and his divisional flag officers, bearing the signal for close action at their mast heads, commenced a heavy fire in return. A few of the British ships cut through the French line, and engaged their opponents to leeward; the remainder hauled up to windward, and opened their fire, some at a long, others at a shorter and more effectual distance. At 10.10 A.M., when the action was at its height, the French Admiral, in the *Montagne*, made sail ahead, followed by his second astern, and afterwards by such of his ships as, like the *Montagne*, had suffered little in their rigging and sails. At about 11.30 A.M. the heat of the action was over, and the British were left with eleven and the French with twelve more or less dismasted ships. None of the French ships had at this time struck their colours; or, if they had struck, had since rehoisted them: they, for the most part, were striving to escape under a spritsail, or some small sail set on the smallest stump left to them, and continued to fire at every British ship that passed within gunshot. After failing in an attempt on the *Queen*, Admiral Villaret stood on, and succeeded, contrary to all expectation, in covering and cutting off four of his dismasted ships, the *Républicain*, *Mucius*, *Scipion*, and *Jemmappes*; a fifth, the *Terrible*, having previously joined him by fighting her way through the British fleet. At about 1.15 P.M. the general firing ceased; but it was not until 2.30 P.M. that the six dismasted French ships nearest at hand, the *Sanspareil*, *Justo*, *America*, *Impétueux*, *Northumberland*, and *Achille*, were secured."

A seventh French ship, the *Vengeur*, struck at six o'clock, but in so shattered a state that in ten minutes afterwards she went down with upwards of 200 of her crew. Much of the romance of the glorious First of June hangs round this ill-fated *Vengeur*. Her antagonist was the *Brunswick*, Captain John Harvey, Lord Howe's second astern. The two ships ran foul and swung alongside of each other, the muzzles of their guns touching; falling off before the wind, they dropped out of the line, engaging furiously. At eleven o'clock the *Achille* was observed through the smoke bearing down upon the *Brunswick's* larboard quarter, as if with the intention of boarding; but a few well-directed broadsides made her strike her colours. The *Brunswick*, however, was too warmly engaged with the *Vengeur* to be able to take possession. It was a murderous conflict. Captain Harvey was mortally wounded by the crown of a doubleheaded shot, which struck him in the right arm. "Persevere, my brave lads, in your duty," he cried, as he was borne down the ladder. "Continue the action with spirit, for the honour of our king and country, and remember my last words—the colours of the *Brunswick* shall never be struck!" At a quarter to one the *Brunswick* and the *Vengeur* swung clear of each other, after a deadly embrace of three hours, and the *Vengeur* was engaged by the *Ramillies*, a fresh ship, which reduced her to a wreck in a few minutes, and then made sail after the *Achille*, which was endeavouring to escape. Finding herself sinking, the *Vengeur* displayed a Union Jack over the quarter; but all the *Brunswick's* boats being knocked to pieces, she could afford her enemy no assistance. Fortunately, at a quarter-past six, when the *Vengeur* threatened every moment to go down head foremost, the *Alfred*, *Culloden*, and *Rattler* cutter approached, and immediately lowered as many of their boats as would swim, and sent them to the rescue. About 400 of the *Vengeur's* crew were thus saved, but before the work of humanity could be completed, the battered vessel sank with all her dead and wounded, and about 30 or 40 men who were unhurt. Among the rescued were Captain Renaudin, who had so bravely fought his ship, and his son, a boy of twelve. Father and son were taken off by different boats, and each mourned the hapless fate of the other. Imagine their rapturous joy when they met again at Portsmouth, and rushed into each other's arms!

An absurd story got abroad that the *Vengeur* went down with all her colours flying, and her crew rending the firmament with shouts of "Vive la Nation!" "Vive la République!" A model of the ship was suspended under the arch of the Pantheon; the names of the ship's company were inscribed on the column of the Pantheon; and the painters, sculptors, and poets of France were invited to exert their talents in celebration of "this sublime trait of Republican devotion." How the report arose is easily explained. Some of the *Vengeur's* people, as is usual in such cases, had flown to the spirit-room for relief; and, thus inspired, one man, more furiously patriotic than the rest of his drunken companions, waved the tricolour, under which he had so nobly fought, as the ship went down.

In this action the French lost seven fine ships, and about 7000 men in killed, wounded, and prisoners; but they attained the object for which they had risked an engagement; for their American convoy, amounting to 160 sail, and valued at £5,000,000, arrived safe in port a few days afterwards. The British loss was 290 killed and 858 wounded. Showers of honours awaited the home-coming of the victorious fleet.

It is not wonderful to find that that mouther, Jean-Bon Saint-André, proved himself a veritable coward. He accompanied the French Admiral in the *Montagne*, and when that ship was in action with the *Queen Charlotte*, the deputy of the National Convention showed himself in his true colours. "Struck by the spectacle," says a French writer, "he could not overcome the fear he felt, and to escape danger ran with all his might down below." And yet the fellow had the impudence, in his account of the action, to write in such a strain as this—"A number of brave men fell; I envy their fate! I saw them perish on each side, and repine at the decree which doomed me to survive." What a lying hypocrite he must have been! Yet so far do brave words go in this world, that, on the return of the French fleet to Brest, the people threw flowers in the way of—God save the mark!—Jean-Bon Saint André.

The French were so busy at home that they had no time to look after their colonies, which fell an easy prey to the ascendancy of the British navy. In the West Indies, in the course of a few weeks, Tobago, Martinique, St. Lucia, and Guadaloupe were captured by Sir John Jervis and Sir Charles Grey.

The first days of 1795 saw the campaign in the Low Countries at an end. The French were successful at all points. The victorious Pichegru crossed the Waal in force (Jan. 8); the Stadtholder embarked for England; Leyden, Utrecht, and Haarlem opened their gates, and hailed the invaders as deliverers; and "to complete the wonders of the campaign," says Alison, "the Dutch fleet frozen up at the Texel, was captured by a body of French cavalry that had crossed the Zuyder Zee on the ice!"

Unfortunate as was the result of the campaign, the conduct of the British troops was on every occasion all that could be desired. Nor was their behaviour less soldierly in the terrible march through Holland and Westphalia, when retreat became inevitable before the overwhelming invasion of Pichegru; when the cold was so intense that brandy froze in bottles, when the doors of the Dutch boors, for whom they had come to fight, were invariably closed against them, and hundreds of men and women dropped by the wayside and slept to wake no more. In the depth of their misery they made no complaints, and they never failed to stand to their arms at the cry that the enemy was upon them. At Gildermalsen (Jany.), for instance, our outposts were driven in, and a regiment of French Hussars, dressed in a uniform similar to that of the emigrant regiment of Choiseul in our service, pushed forward under cover of this deception, and rode furiously along the road, treacherously crying "Choiseul—Choiseul!" The ruse so far succeeded, that, says General Stewart of Garth, "they were allowed to get close to the advanced company of the 78th Highlanders before the truth was discovered, when they were instantly attacked and checked, but not sufficiently to prevent a part pushing, at full speed, through the intervals between the two wings, towards the village. Here they were met by the light company of the 42d Highlanders, whose fire drove them back, and scattered them in an instant. When the attacking column of the enemy's infantry perceived that their cavalry had got through beyond the first line, they advanced with great boldness, singing the Carmagnole March. The 78th reserved their fire till the enemy nearly closed upon them, when it was opened with such effect that they were driven back in great confusion." At length the shattered army reached Bremen, and the gallant remains of this band of heroes were received on board the transports in the Elbe and Weser, and conveyed to England. "Among them," says Brenton, "were few who had not lost a limb, either from the casualties of war or the inclemency of the weather, and numbers of them were reduced to skeletons. . . . The conduct of our troops in this terrible retreat excited the admiration even of the proud and insolent Republicans."

The conquest of Holland led to the dissolution of the confederacy against France. Prussia and Spain made peace with the Republic, and Holland was compelled to conclude an alliance offensive and defensive with her conqueror. The whole weight of the war thus fell on Britain, Russia, and Austria; but the co-operation of Russia only went the length of sending a squadron to join the North Sea blockading fleet under Admiral Duncan; while Austria, subsidised by Britain, maintained an indecisive contest on the Rhine.

This year the French made an ineffectual attempt to recover Corsica. During the winter they had succeeded in equipping a number of ships of the line at Toulon, and on the 3d March Rear-admiral Martin put to sea with 15 sail of the line and six frigates, together with 5000 men, to effect the re-conquest of the island. Admiral Hotham, who then commanded in the Mediterranean, hearing that the French had been seen standing to the southward, put to sea on the 7th, with 12 British and 1 Neapolitan sail of the line, 4 frigates, 2 ships, and a cutter, in the hope of intercepting them before they reached Corsica. On the 10th the enemy were sighted working back to Toulon. After a three days' chase the British Admiral, finding the enemy had no intention of fighting, again made the signal for a general chase; but none of the enemy's ships could be come up with except the *Ça Ira*, which had lost her main and fore topmasts by running foul of the *Victoire*. The *Inconstant*, Captain Fremantle, a frigate of 36 guns, had the temerity to attack the huge 80-gun ship, but had at length to sheer off with severe loss. Then Nelson came up in the *Agamemnon*, a 64, and fought his ship in so masterly a way that he reduced his huge antagonist to a perfect wreck, killing and wounding 110 of her crew. The *Sans Culotte*, the flag-ship of Admiral Martin, now bore down to the assistance of her consort, and Admiral Hotham signalled to the *Agamemnon* to rejoin the fleet. At daybreak next morning, the 14th, Genoa distant about seven leagues, the *Ça Ira* was observed a long distance astern and to leeward of her fleet, in tow of the *Censeur*. This brought on an engagement, in which some of the French ships suffered so heavily, that Admiral Martin went about and stood away to the westward, leaving the *Ça Ira* and the *Censeur* to their fate. They were taken possession of by the boats of the *Agamemnon*. Nelson urged Hotham to pursue the enemy, but the Admiral had not the energy which burned in the soul of the fiery little captain of the *Agamemnon*. "We must be contented," he said self-complacently; "we have done very well." "Now!" said Nelson, writing to his wife, "had we taken ten sail, and allowed the eleventh to escape when it had been possible to have got at her, I could never have called it well done."

On the 8th June Admiral Cornwallis was cruising off Ushant, with five ships of the line and two frigates, when he fell in with a powerful French fleet under Admiral Villaret-Joyeuse, consisting of one ship of 120 guns, eleven of 74 guns, and eleven frigates. Notwithstanding the immense disparity of force, Admiral Cornwallis succeeded, by superior seamanship, in baffling every attempt of the French, and brought off his squadron safe and sound. His masterly retreat is one of the most memorable occurrences of the year.

On the 22d June Villaret-Joyeuse fell in with the Channel Fleet under Lord Bridport, consisting of fifteen sail of the line, five frigates, and a few smaller vessels. The French Admiral showing no intention of accepting battle, Lord Bridport threw out the signal for a general chase. Little ground was gained, however, and at night it fell calm. Next morning the French fleet was seen in a cluster about three miles ahead, and a light breeze springing up, the British stood in, and a running action ensued. Fighting commenced at six A.M., and by eight, three of the French ships had struck their colours; but by this time the fleet had got so close in with the land, that Lord Bridport judged it prudent to discontinue the chase, and the French Admiral, keeping his wind, anchored with his remaining ships within the Isle of Groix. The three prizes were added to the British navy.

This victory facilitated the expedition of the French emigrants, who had long been soliciting the British Government to assist them in effecting a landing on the western coast of their native country. A force of 2500 *émigrés* was landed at Quiberon Bay, but suffered defeat at the hands of the youthful general Hoche, and Sir J. Borlase Warren, the British naval commander, re-embarked the remnant that fled to the shore.

In August a small expedition, consisting of three 74-gun ships, two 64's, and two sloops of 16 guns, under the command of Vice-admiral Sir George Keith Elphinstone, K.B., and having on board 500 men of the 78th Highlanders, under Major-general Craig, arrived at the Cape of Good Hope, and took possession of Simon's Town. The Dutch regulars and militia showed a bold front on the heights behind the town, and some fighting took place, in which our soldiers and seamen greatly distinguished themselves; but on the arrival of reinforcements under General Alured Clarke, the governor capitulated, and this important colony became ours, with the loss of only a few men.

A new epoch in the war was marked by the revolution of the 3d and 4th October, which resulted in the fall of the Convention, and the concentration of power in the hands of a Directory of Five.

CHAPTER II.—THE GREAT FRENCH WAR.

THE DIRECTORY.—1796-1799.

French Expeditions to Ireland—Cape St. Vincent—The French land in Pembrokeshire—Nelson's Attempt on Santa Cruz—Camperdown—The Nile—Anglo-Russian Expedition to Holland—Sir Sidney Smith foils Napoleon at Acre—Successes of Troubridge in Italy.

LITTLE was done during 1796. The powers now opposed to the French Republic were Russia, Austria, Sardinia, and Great Britain. Russia still kept her squadron with the North Sea blockading fleet under Admiral Duncan, but did no more; Austrian and French armies met each other on the Rhine, with varying success; and Sardinia was almost swept away by the torrent-like advance of Napoleon through Italy. Britain took no part in the campaigns of Europe, but her navy rode triumphant on every sea, while the fleets of France were blockaded in their ports, and her commercial marine was almost entirely destroyed. Our colonial empire was increased by the acquisition of Ceylon, Malacca, and Cochin in the East Indies, and Grenada, St. Vincent, St. Lucia, Essequibo, and Demerara in the West Indies. Spain, jealous of the naval supremacy of Great Britain, concluded a treaty offensive and defensive with France, and declared war against Great Britain (Oct. 2). This necessitated the evacuation of Corsica. Holland made an attempt to recover the Cape of Good Hope, but the whole squadron—two 66's, a 54, two 40's, a 26, a 24, and an 18—surrendered to Sir George Keith Elphinstone (Aug. 17) without firing a shot.

The most important event of the year, as far as this country was concerned, occurred towards its close. Irish officers had represented to the Directory that no better method could be adopted of wounding Britain than by sending an expedition to Ireland, where the natives would receive the French with open arms, as deliverers from the accursed British yoke. Accordingly, a great expedition for the liberation of Ireland was fitted out at Brest. It consisted of 17 ships of the line, 13 frigates, 6 corvettes, 7 transports, and a powder ship—in all, 44 sail of vessels, and had on board an army variously estimated at from 18,000 to 25,000 men. The Commander-in-chief was General Hoche, who had for his lieutenants such men as Grouchy, Borin, and Humbert.

The French fleet sailed on the 16th December, 1796, and next day a disaster occurred, ominous of the fate of the expedition; *Le Seduisant*, a 74, was driven upon the rocks and lost, and all the crew and soldiers, to the number of 1800, perished, with the exception of sixty. The elements fought against the intended invasion. By the 24th most of the ships had reached the rendezvous in Bantry Bay, but before any attempt could be made to disembark the troops, the fleet was driven out to sea and scattered far and wide by a violent gale from the south-south-east. The weather continued tempestuous for many days, and those ships of the French fleet which escaped the fury of wind and wave, and the activity of our cruisers, reached Brest and Rochefort by the middle of January, in a most wretched condition. In this fruitless expedition, the French lost 2 ships of the line, 4 frigates, 2 brig-corvettes, and 5 transports, besides many thousand lives.

While Napoleon and his Republican soldiers were carrying everything before them in Italy, this country was engaged in a fierce struggle to maintain her supremacy at sea. We had in commission 124 ships of the line, 198 50-gun ships and frigates, and 184 sloops; but this great force was scattered over every sea, and could not readily be concentrated in strength on one point; while the naval force of France, swelled by the fleets of Holland and Spain, had again become formidable. If the Spanish fleet could raise the blockade of the French and Dutch harbours, a combined force of 60 or 70 ships of war might be assembled in the Channel, and then—let Britain look to herself!

On the morning of the 13th February 1797, Sir John Jervis was proceeding down the coast of Portugal, under easy sail, when he was joined by the *Minerva* frigate, flying the broad pennant of Commodore Nelson. That distinguished officer reported that on the 11th, soon after quitting Gibraltar, he was chased by two Spanish line-of-battle ships, and that afterwards, when in the mouth of the Straits, he got sight of the Spanish fleet. The Spaniards, then, were at sea. Before sunset signals were made for the British fleet to prepare for battle, and to keep in close order during the night. At 2.30 A.M. next morning the Portuguese frigate *Carlotta*, commanded by Captain Campbell, a native of Scotland, spoke the *Victory*, and gave information that the Spanish fleet was only five leagues to windward. In a few minutes the signal guns of the Spaniards were distinctly heard, and continued to boom at intervals until daybreak.

The morning of the 14th (Valentine's Day) broke dark and hazy. The British were formed in two compact divisions, standing on the starboard tack, with the wind at west by south, Cape St. Vincent bearing east by north, distant eight leagues. The Spanish fleet consisted of 27 sail of the line, including the huge *Santissima Trinidada*, of 130 guns, carrying the flag of Admiral Don Josef de Cordova; the scarcely less huge *Conception*, *Conde de Regla*, *Salvador del Mundo*, *Mexicano*, *San Josef*, and *Principe Asturias*, of 112 guns; the *Neptuno* and *San Nicolas*, of 80 guns; 19 74's, and 12 frigates. Jervis, whose flag was on board the famous *Victory*, had but 15 sail of the line, 3 frigates, 2 18-gun sloops, and a cutter; but he knew that a victory was all-important to England; and he was sure he could rely on the skill of his officers, and the discipline and gallantry of his men, to counterbalance the disparity of force. Most of his captains had already distinguished themselves, and asked nothing better than an opportunity to gather fresh laurels. Among them, and not altogether unknown to fame, were Calder, Foley, Miller, Saumarez, Collingwood, Troubridge, and one whose name was to be greater than all, Horatio Nelson.

The numerical superiority of the Spaniards proved their ruin. Blindly confident in their own strength, they allowed their fleet to separate into two divisions, the main one to windward, and the smaller one of nine ships to leeward. Jervis saw his opportunity, and put in practice the old manœuvre of breaking the enemy's line. At 11 A.M. he ordered his fleet to steer right between the two divisions of the Spaniards, who were thus practically reduced to 18 sail; and so bewildered were the Spaniards by the bold initiative taken by the British, that before they knew where they were, the enemy was upon them.

Troubridge, in the *Culloden*, led in his usual dashing and seamanlike style. "Look," cried Jervis, who stood on the quarter-deck of the *Victory*, and watched him with the intensest interest, "look at Troubridge! Does he not manœuvre as if all England was looking at him?" Then, observing that the *Culloden* had arrived abreast of the van-ships of the Spanish main division, Jervis ordered the signal to be made to open fire. The *Culloden* commenced a cannonade with her starboard guns, receiving replies from such of the Spanish ships as could open their batteries without firing on a friend—for the Spanish line was clustered two or three deep—and the battle soon became general.

Don Josef de Cordova was immediately sensible of his error in allowing his line to be broken, and at a quarter-past one he bore up to pass the rear of the British line to join his ships to leeward. But Nelson caught him in the act. His pennant was flying on board the *Captain*, a 74, which was the third ship from the rear, and had not yet fired a shot. Disregarding the signal still flying on the *Victory*, for the ships to tack in succession, he ordered Captain Miller to wear ship. No sooner said than done, and the *Captain*, passing between the *Diadem* and the *Excellent*, the two rearmost ships of the British line, threw herself in the path of a huge Spaniard, which, from her four tiers of ports, was known to be the *Santissima Trinidada*. Near this leviathan were huddled the *San Josef* and *Salvador del Mundo*, three-deckers of 112 guns, the *San Nicolas* of 80, and the *San Ysidro* of 74.

The other captains in that part of the line saw that Nelson had put his finger on the decisive movement of the day, and hastened to his assistance. First came Troubridge in the *Culloden*, followed by Frederick in the *Blenheim*, Rear-admiral William Parker in the *Prince George*, Saumarez in the *Orion*, and Collingwood in the *Excellent*. The *Salvador del Mundo* and the *San Ysidro* were soon so much battered that they dropped astern and struck their colours. Nelson did not wait for the catastrophe, but plunged into the thickest of the fight in search of another opponent, and engaged the 80-gun ship *San Nicolas*. In a short time the *Captain* was little better than a wreck; her foretopmast had gone over the side, her wheel was shot away, all her sails, shrouds, and running rigging were cut. Incapable of further service in the line or in chase, it was evident that, by all the rules of naval warfare, the *Captain* must drop out of the action. But Nelson was unwilling, after doing so much, to depart without a trophy of the prowess of his seamen, and determined to board his huge opponent. As a preparation he opened his batteries within less than twenty yards. The *San Nicolas* replied with spirit for a few minutes, when the *Captain* suddenly put her helm a-starboard and ran foul of the enemy.

The boarding of the *San Nicolas* cannot be fitly described except in Nelson's own words. "The soldiers of the 69th regiment," he says, "with an alacrity which will ever do them credit, and Lieutenant Pearson, of the same regiment, were almost the foremost on this service. The first man who jumped into the enemy's mizzen chains was Captain Berry, late my first lieutenant (Capt. Miller was in the very act of going also, but I directed him to remain). He was supported from our spritsail-yard, which hooked in the mizzen rigging. A soldier of the 69th regiment having broken the upper quarter gallery window, I jumped in myself, and was followed by others as fast as possible. I found the cabin doors fastened, and some Spanish officers fired their pistols : but, having broken open the doors, the soldiers fired ; and the Spanish brigadier (commodore with a pennant) fell, as retreating to the quarter-deck. I pushed immediately onward for the quarter-deck, where I found Captain Berry in possession of the poop, and the Spanish ensign hauling down. I then passed with my people and Lieutenant Pearson on the larboard gangway to the forecastle, where I met two or three Spanish officers, prisoners to my seamen ; they delivered me their swords."

Still, only half the work was accomplished. The stern of the *San Josef* was directly amidships of the weather-beam of the *San Nicolas;* and from the poop and galleries of the three-decker the enemy kept up a fire of musketry which threatened to force the British to quit their prize. The only other alternative was to board the *San Josef*, and Nelson, confident in the bravery of his seamen, determined to adopt it. Directing an additional number of men to be sent on board the *San Nicolas*, the fiery one-eyed commodore led the way, with a shout of " Westminster Abbey or victory !" Captain Berry assisted him into the main chains. "At this moment," continues Nelson, "a Spanish officer looked over the quarter-deck rail and said they surrendered. From this most welcome intelligence it was not long before I was on the quarter-deck, where the Spanish captain, with a bow, presented me his sword, and said the admiral was dying of his wounds. I asked him, on his honour, if the ship was surrendered. He declared she was; on which I gave him my hand, and desired him to call on his officers and ship's company, and tell them of it, which he did: and, on the quarter-deck of a Spanish first-rate, extravagant as the story may seem, did I receive the swords of the vanquished Spaniards; which, as I received, I gave to William Fearney, one of my bargemen, who put them, with the greatest *sang-froid*, under his arm. I was surrounded by Captain Berry, Lieutenant Pearson of the 69th regiment, John Sykes, John Thompson, Francis Cooke, all old Agamemnons; and several other brave men, seamen and soldiers. Thus fell these ships."

We are all familiar with the picture, which has been extensively engraved, of Nelson standing on the deck of the *San Josef*, surrounded by a small group of soldiers and seamen, in the act of receiving the sword of the Spanish captain. The dejected looks of the vanquished Spaniards are not insulted by the slightest appearance of triumph in the generous countenance of Nelson, but honest William Fearney, who stands by, bedecked in the pigtail of the period, and with a bundle of Spanish swords tucked under his arm, cannot altogether suppress a grim satisfaction.

This achievement of Nelson's, one of the most audacious recorded in naval history, in which a handful of men out of a 74 captured first an 80-gun ship and then a first-rate of 112 guns, practically closed the action. The ships of the lee division of the Spanish fleet were approaching, and the victory could not be further improved. The last gun was fired about five o'clock. Four ships, on whose high and gilded poops the Spanish standard had that morning proudly floated, remained in the hands of the conquerors—the *Salvador del Mundo* and the *San Josef*, of 112 guns, the *San Nicolas*, of 80 guns, and the *San Ysidro*, of 74. Their magnificent architecture and their large size had not been able to save them from the audacity of the British. To build a navy is one thing, but to breed a race of seamen and animate them with the traditions of victory is quite another.

The Spanish loss in men cannot be stated, but it must have been severe. The British had 74 killed and 227 wounded. The four ships that suffered most were those that may be said to have borne the brunt of the action—the *Captain*, the *Blenheim*, the *Culloden*, and the *Excellent*, commanded by Nelson, Frederick, Troubridge, and Collingwood respectively. Great was the joy when news of the memorable action of Valentine's Day reached England, and numerous were the honours with which a grateful country rewarded the victors. Jervis had a peerage and a pension, and Nelson, to whom the victory was more than half due, received the Order of the Bath.

After the battle the Spaniards retreated to Cadiz, which was closely blockaded by Jervis, now Earl St. Vincent, whose fleet was raised to 21 sail of the line. With the ships previously in port, the Spaniards numbered 28 sail of the line, but so cowed were they by their defeat that they would not venture out. A blockade is always a wearisome business; and partly for the sake of a little diversion, partly to provoke Admiral Massaredo to attempt putting to sea, Nelson proposed to bombard Cadiz and the Spanish fleet where it lay.

This little bit of by-play—for it was nothing more—would scarcely be worth mentioning, but for the circumstance that during the progress of the bombardment a desperate boat action occurred, in which Nelson was personally engaged. Commodore Don Miguel Tyrason, the Spanish commandant, laid his boat alongside the barge in which Nelson was as usual pushing into the thickest of the fire. The boat of the Spanish commodore carried 26 men, while Nelson had with him only 10 oarsmen, Captain Fremantle, and his coxswain, John Sykes, an old Agamemnon. The issue was that when 18 of the Spaniards had been killed and all the rest were wounded, Don Miguel Tyrason surrendered his sword to the conqueror. The conflict was the most desperate in which Nelson was ever engaged. He fought like the hero he was, and only escaped death by a miracle. Twice his life was saved by the faithful Sykes, who parried the blows that were aimed at him, and at last interposed his head to receive a Spanish sabre which he had no other means of averting. Such was the love and devotion which Nelson was capable of inspiring in the breasts of his followers!

From Cadiz Nelson led an expedition to Santa Cruz, in the island of Teneriffe, where, it was rumoured, a richly-freighted

Manilla ship had arrived; but his force was too small to enable him to rival the success of the mighty Blake, and after a display of the most heroic and useless bravery, the English were obliged to retire, with a loss of 141 killed and drowned, 105 wounded, and 5 missing—a loss which did not fall very far short of that which won the battle of Cape St. Vincent. It was at Santa Cruz that Nelson lost his right arm.

Scarcely had the guns of the Tower of London and the Castle of Edinburgh ceased firing in honour of Valentine's Day, when England was invaded by a foreign foe. On the morning of the 22d February, two French frigates, a corvette, and a lugger, anchored in Fishguard Bay, on the coast of Pembrokeshire. During the night they landed the *Légion Noire*, a band dressed in black, the scum of the French galleys, and sailed away again. The alarm soon spread, and next morning, on the approach of the militia under Lord Cawdor, the lord-lieutenant of the county, the invaders immediately laid down their arms, and were marched as prisoners to Haverfordwest. Some say they did not even wait the near approach of the militia, but were panic-struck at the sight of the red cloaks worn by the Welsh peasant girls. At any rate they surrendered. What was the object of this silly expedition no one, French or English, seems rightly to have understood. Of the small squadron that brought the troops, one of the frigates and the ship-corvette were captured on their return to France.

Later in the year a second attempt was made to raise the blockade on the French ports, this time by the Dutch. Their fleet consisted of 21 ships and 4 brigs, under De Winter, an admiral of great experience and undoubted courage. For more than two years Admiral Duncan had been watching his foe, like cat watching mouse; but on the 3d October he put into Yarmouth Roads to refit and revictual, leaving a small squadron of observation under Captain Trollope, of the *Russell*, 74. De Winter took advantage of his absence, and on the 7th put to sea with his whole fleet. On the morning of the 9th, the *Black Joke*, hired armed lugger, was seen at the back of Yarmouth Sands, with the signal flying that the Dutch had put to sea.

Admiral Adam Duncan, the hero of Camperdown, will ever occupy a pedestal in the temple of naval fame only lower than that of Nelson himself. The second son of Duncan of Lundie, in Forfarshire, he was born at Dundee in 1731. He seems to have been intended for a commercial life, but the blue waters of the German Ocean perpetually surged in his fancy, and when he was sixteen, his friends were compelled to acquiesce in his entrance into the navy as a midshipman. In 1755, when he had been eight years at sea, he was made a lieutenant, and in 1761 commander of the *Valiant*, a 74, which took part in the famous expedition to Havana. After this, Duncan had little opportunity of distinguishing himself, and in 1795, although he had risen to the rank of Vice-admiral of the Blue, he is said to have meditated retiring from the service altogether, when he was appointed to the command of the North Sea fleet, with the special duty of watching the movements of the Dutch. A Russian fleet was for some time associated with the British in this duty, and the Empress Catherine II. was so much pleased with the conduct of Admiral Duncan as commander-in-chief, that, unsolicited, she conferred on him the Imperial order of Alexander Newski. Duncan's blockade of the Texel was one of the most effective ever made, and the Dutch trade was almost ruined.

In person, Admiral Duncan was, "without exception," says an officer who met him at a public dinner, "the finest man I ever beheld. Imagine a man of six feet two inches in height—I think he was six feet four—with limbs of proportionate frame and strength. His features were nobly beautiful, his forehead high and fair, his hair white as snow. His movements were all stately, but unaffected, and his manner easy, though dignified." In short, he looked the hero he was.

After more than two years of tedious watching, Admiral Duncan at length reaped the fruits of his patience. The moment the *Black Joke* was seen with the signal flying that the Dutch had put to sea, Duncan made the signal for a general chase. Immediately all was bustle and preparation, and before noon the whole fleet had weighed, and was standing towards the Texel, with a fair wind. The Dutch coast was sighted at daybreak on the 11th, and, two hours after, the Dutch were seen about nine miles from the shore, between their own villages of Egmont and Camperdown. De Winter's flag was flying on board the *Vryheid*, and Duncan's on board the *Venerable*, both 74's.

De Winter was desirous above all things to avoid an action,

as his instructions enjoined him to form a junction with the Brest fleet, for the purpose of undertaking a joint invasion of Ireland. But the first glimpse he obtained of the British in the north-north-east showed him this was impossible, and he stood towards the land, to facilitate the junction of his leewardmost ships. As soon as a close line was formed in the direction of north-east and south-west, the Dutch squared their yards and resolutely awaited the approach of the British. While thus drawn up, by keeping their maintopsails shivering and sometimes full, they were fast drawing towards the shore. Their ships were specially built for their own shoaly seas, and Admiral Duncan, fearing they might get so close inshore that he could not follow them, thought there was no time to be lost, and directed all his manœuvres to cut off the enemy's retreat to his own shores. At half-past eleven, the centre of the Dutch line then bearing south-east, distant about four miles, the British fleet bore down, but owing to the disunited state of the ships, in no regular order of battle. Some were stretching across to get into their proper stations; others seemed in doubt where to place themselves; and others again were pushing at all hazards for the thickest of the foe.

As the British bore down they cleared away for action. All the bulkheads and even the cabin chairs were thrown overboard, and everything that might be in the way of working the guns, or occasion splinters. It was only the part of prudence to take every precaution, for De Winter and his people were the descendants of Van Tromp and those brave Dutchmen who so gallantly fought our Blake and his Puritans, and they would fight hard. They would not aim at the masts and rigging, as the French and Spaniards were in the habit of doing, but would try whether the hulls and hearts of their enemies were still made of the famous British oak. The coast was crowded by thousands of spectators, ready to applaud their countrymen if successful; but, as it turned out, they had the mortification of observing the entire destruction of their fleet, without the possibility of affording any relief. Neptune, says the poet-laureate of the navy, was jealous for the honour of our flag, and

> " Bade Duncan's thunder great Britannia's reign
> Proclaim anew, the sovereign of the main."

At seven minutes before noon Admiral Duncan signalled to

his captains to pass through the Dutch line and engage to leeward, so as to get between it and the land, which the Dutch were fast approaching. Unfortunately, owing to the hazy weather, many of the ships were unable to see this signal, which in a quarter of an hour was replaced by the most pleasing of all to British seamen, that for close action. The fourth behind the *Venerable* was the *Belliqueux*, commanded by Captain John Inglis, a veteran Scottish seaman of the old school. Captain Inglis was fairly puzzled by so much signalling; he could not make it out, nor would he try any more; and closing his telescope in disgust, he sung out to the sailing-master, " Damn the thing, Jock, doon wi' the helm, and gang richt intil the middle o't."

Onslow, in the *Monarch*, led the van, bearing down in the most gallant manner upon the Dutch rear. At half-past noon he cut through the enemy's rear, between the *Jupiter* and the *Haarlem*, pouring into each of these ships a well-directed broadside in passing. Then, leaving the *Haarlem* to the *Powerful*, the *Monarch* luffed up alongside the *Jupiter*, and engaged her at close quarters. Meanwhile, Duncan was fast coming down in the *Venerable*, which led the rear. About twenty minutes after Onslow had cut the enemy's rear, Duncan was about to do the same thing to their van, by passing between the *States General* and the *Vryheid*. The *States General* endeavoured to frustrate his intention, by promptly closing up the interval, but Duncan ordered the helm of the *Venerable* to be put a-port, and, running under the stern of the officious *States General*, poured in a broadside which compelled Admiral Storey to bear up. The *Triumph*, Duncan's second astern, found employment for the *Wassenaer*, the second astern of the *States General*, while the *Venerable* ranged up close upon the leeside of the *Vryheid*. At the same time the *Ardent* engaged the *Vryheid* to windward; while three of the Dutch ships, the *Brutus*, *Leyden*, and *Mars*, not being pressed by opponents, advanced to the succour of their Admiral.

It was one of the hardest fights on record. " More than once," says Mr. Yonge, " every flag the *Venerable* hoisted was shot away, and at last one of the men, a native of Sunderland, named James Crawford, nailed the Admiral's colours to the stump of the main-topgallant mast, where during the remainder of the day it braved the battle and the breeze unhurt and triumphant." It must, indeed, have been a warm affair. An officer of the *Ardent*, writing home, said that "one of the men's wives insisted on firing the gun where her husband was stationed, though requested to go below, but she could not be prevailed upon to do so, till a shot carried away one of her legs, and wounded the other."

The Dutch reputation for bull-dog courage suffered nothing from the conduct of De Winter's people, but the superior gunnery of the British began to tell. Soon the *Triumph*, which had compelled the *Wassenaer* to strike, approached to give the *coup de grâce* to the *Vryheid*, which had now to sustain the fire of the *Venerable* to leeward, the *Ardent* to windward, and the *Triumph* and *Dictator* stationed across her bows. One by one her masts fell over the side, and disabled her starboard guns, and the *Vryheid* dropped out of the line an ungovernable wreck. It was useless to fight longer against fortune, and the gallant De Winter, the only man on the quarterdeck who had not been swept away, hauled down the colours with his own hand.

With the surrender of the *Vryheid*, at 3 P.M., the action ceased. The victors were in possession of eleven prizes; and the remnant of the Dutch fleet, which could not be pursued, the land being only five miles distant and the fleet in nine fathoms water, was in full flight towards the Texel.

The battle of Cape St. Vincent was important as a demonstration of the superiority in skill and seamanship of the British navy; but Camperdown was a fair stand-up fight and no favour, and the hardest hitter, holding out longest, had it. The obstinacy of the conflict was attested by the numbers of the killed and wounded, which amounted on the part of the English to 203 killed and 622 wounded, and on the part of the Dutch to 540 killed and 620 wounded. It was also attested by the hulls of the seven British ships that bore the brunt of the action, which were pierced by shot in all directions; and especially by the hulls of the prizes, which were like sieves, and only worth bringing into port as trophies. Three of the prizes, indeed, the *Delft*, and the *Monniekendam* and *Ambuscade* frigates, foundered in a gale which came on the day after the battle.

On the 17th, Admiral Duncan and the rest of his prizes arrived at the Nore. Duncan was created a peer of Great Britain, by the titles of Baron Duncan of Lundie and Viscount Duncan of Camperdown, with a pension of £3000 a year.

In the West Indies, during the course of the year, Trinidad fell to our arms, but an attack on Porto Rico was not so successful.

The danger which had threatened Britain at the beginning of 1797 was very real. Under the name of the Army of England, the French had 150,000 troops collected on the shores of the Channel, and great things were hoped if only "the silver streak of sea" could be crossed. But the battles of St. Vincent and Camperdown relieved this country from apprehension; the fleets off Brest and Cadiz were strengthened; and when Buonaparte, on his return from his brilliant campaign in Italy, was sent by the Directory to take the command of the expedition, a short visit to the coast satisfied him that the project was hopeless.

That restless genius now turned his energies towards an expedition to Egypt. It had long ago been pointed out that the true commercial route to India lay through the country of the Pharaohs; and Buonaparte conceived that, if Egypt were held by French bayonets, and the Mediterranean turned into a French lake, the road to India would be open, the British power might be attacked in its most vulnerable part, and a career of conquest would be offered to himself which would outdo that of Alexander.

Preparations for the expedition were made on a vast scale, but secretly, and on the 19th May, 1798, the armament sailed from Toulon. After the junction of the squadrons from Genoa and Ajaccio, the fleet consisted of 15 sail of the line, 14 frigates, 43 smaller vessels, and 400 transports, bearing 36,000 soldiers. On the 10th June this mighty armament appeared before Malta, which, through cowardice and treachery, was yielded without firing a shot. A garrison of 3000 men was left to maintain the island, and after a delay of nine days the fleet resumed its voyage to Egypt. The low sandy plains of that country were sighted on the 1st July, and the disembarkation of the troops was completed on the following day. After a short resistance Alexandria was carried by assault, and on the 6th the French set out over the desert for Cairo. On the 14th the Mamelukes were routed at Chebreiss, and the decisive battle of the Pyramids was fought on the 21st. The French were now virtually masters of Egypt.

Nelson, meanwhile, was running all up and down the Mediterranean looking for the French. On the night of the 22d June the two fleets had crossed each other's track in a thick fog, and so close that the French could distinctly hear the British signal-guns. What would Nelson not have given to be aware of the fact! He shaped his course for Alexandria, which he felt sure was the destination of the expedition, but found the harbour empty, and immediately sailed away again to pursue his quest. The fact is, he had outsailed the enemy; and on the same day that the British disappeared, the French arrived in sight of the coast.

At length, on the 28th July, the British fleet was cruising off the Morea, and Troubridge of the *Culloden*, looking into Coron, returned with the intelligence that the French fleet had been seen beyond Candia, steering south-east, about four weeks before. Once more Nelson sailed for Alexandria, now sure of his prey. "Before this time to-morrow I shall have gained a peerage or Westminster Abbey," he exclaimed to his officers, after explaining to them his ideas of the different and best modes of attack, so as to make sure of the enemy whatever their situation. There was no possible position which he did not take into consideration, and his officers were lost in admiration at the fertility of his resources. "If we succeed, what will the world say?" cried Captain Berry with transport when he comprehended the full scope of the design. "There is no 'if' in the case," retorted Nelson. "That we shall succeed is certain—who may live to tell the story is a very different question."

On the 1st August, at 10 A.M., the towers and minarets of Alexandria, the Pharos and Pompey's Pillar, made their welcome appearance, and the sight of the tricolour on the walls, showing who were masters of the city, was greeted with a cheer from the whole British fleet. But every visage fell when the *Alexander* and the *Swiftsure*, the two look-out ships, signalled that the enemy's fleet did not form part of the vessels at anchor in the harbour. Stole away! The disappointment, however, was of short duration, for, a little before one o'clock, the *Zealous* signalled the French fleet at anchor in Aboukir Bay.

The bay in which the French were anchored is about twenty miles east-north-east of Alexandria. There is no depth for line-of-battle ships within three miles of the shore, which is fringed to that distance by a long sandbank. Two miles from the Castle of Aboukir, at one end of the bay, is a small island, also surrounded by shoals. Anchored in a convex line towards the sea, supported on one extremity by land batteries, and on the other by shoals, Admiral Brueys considered himself secure, especially as he had the advantage in force. Besides thirteen ships of the line he had four frigates and some gunboats; whereas Nelson, in addition to the same number of ships of the line, had but one 50-gun ship. Besides, Brueys had one 120- and two 80-gun ships, while his opponent had nothing higher than 74's. The French guns were 1196, and their men 11,230; the British guns were 1012, and their men but 8068.

But Brueys had no intention of tempting the fortune of battle, and determined to set sail during the night and give the British the slip. This would have been very well if Nelson had waited till next morning, but nothing was further from his thoughts. At 3 P.M. he made the signal to anchor; at 4 to anchor by the stern; and at 5.30 to form ahead and astern of the Admiral, and attack the enemy's van and centre. His plan was to pass between the outermost French ship and the shoal, each ship opening fire as she ranged inshore. In this way, he calculated, an overwhelming force would be brought to bear on the enemy's van and centre, while their rear was moored at too great a distance to join with effect in the action.

Captain Hood led in the *Zealous*, and was followed by the *Goliath*, *Orion*, *Audacious*, *Theseus*, *Vanguard* (Nelson's flag-ship), *Minotaur*, *Defence*, *Bellerophon*, *Majestic*, *Leander*; the *Culloden* some distance to the northward, and the *Alexander* and the *Swiftsure* at a still greater distance to the westward, but coming up under a press of sail. At six the British hoisted their colours, displaying the Union Jack in various parts of the rigging. Twenty minutes later the French hoisted the tricolour, and opened fire. The broad red disc of the sun began to dip as the first gun was fired, and the most brilliant naval action on record was fought in darkness. Captain Hood had no chart to guide him, but by keeping the lead continually going he safely rounded the shoal off Aboukir Island, and with a favourable breeze from the north-west led the fleet straight on the enemy. The French fire came thick and fast, and many of the British fell, but the survivors maintained a stern silence which boded the enemy no good. The splinters flew in showers, and the smoke curled high amidst the masts and rigging, but the fleet was manœuvred as if it had been at Spithead. Every man was at his post; some at the guns; some out on the yards aloft handling the sails; and some ahead ready to let go the anchors.

Gradually, as the British advanced, their guns opened fire. It was now quite dark, but the flashes from the French port-holes served as excellent guides to the gunners. At length all the ships got into position, the *Majestic* on the outside of the *Heureux*, the ninth ship of the French line. Behind the *Majestic* were the *Bellerophon, Swiftsure, Defence, Minotaur,* and *Vanguard*. The *Alexander, Orion, Theseus, Goliath, Audacious,* and *Zealous* went inside the French line and took the same nine ships on the other side. Greatly to the grief of the gallant Troubridge, the *Culloden* grounded on the reef off the Island of Aboukir, where, in spite of every effort, she stuck fast until two in the following morning, when the action was over. In this position, however, she was able to signal off the *Alexander* and the *Swiftsure*, which would otherwise have gone upon the reef. Thus all the British ships were engaged except the *Culloden*, while the five ships in the rear of the French line were unable to take any part in the action. Nelson's tactics at sea were the same as Napoleon's on land—to overwhelm the enemy in detail.

The action had not become general for more than a quarter of an hour when two of the French ships were dismasted, and the rest so dreadfully mauled that our men looked forward to victory as certain. By half-past eight, three of the enemy had struck their colours. It was about this time that Nelson, who was on the quarter-deck of the *Vanguard*, scanning a rough sketch of the scene of action, was struck on the forehead by a piece of langridge-shot. The torn flesh fell over his eye, and as the other was blind he was in total darkness. He fell back into the arms of Captain Berry, believing himself mortally wounded. Yet, when he was carried down to the cockpit, he would not permit the surgeon to quit the poor fellow who happened to be at that moment under his hands. "No," he said, "I will take my turn with my brave fellows." When, at length, the surgeon came to examine him, the most anxious silence prevailed; and the joy of the wounded men and of the whole crew, when they learned that the hurt was merely superficial, gave Nelson deeper joy than the unexpected assurance that his life was in no danger.

Suddenly, at nine o'clock, a cry arose that the French Admiral's flagship, the huge 120-gun *Orient*, was on fire. The flames spread along the decks and ascended the rigging with terrific and uncontrollable rapidity. It was a spectacle of inconceivable grandeur. Every object became more distinctly visible than in broad daylight. Notwithstanding his wound Nelson was immediately on deck, and with his usual humanity ordered the boats out to the relief of the unfortunate sufferers; but the fierce glow of the flames would not allow them to approach, and Rear-admiral Gantheaume and about 70 men and officers were all that could be saved. Among the many hundreds who perished were Commodore Casa Bianca and his son, a boy of ten. Admiral Brueys had already met a more enviable death. At eight o'clock, as he was descending from the poop to the quarter-deck, wounded in two places, a round shot cut him in pieces. At ten the flames caught the magazine, and the *Orient* blew up with a dreadful explosion. The sea heaved as if troubled by an earthquake; the waves rose high upon the shore, and the batteries and castles around quivered to their foundations. The vibration shook the ships so as to open their seams and threaten the safety of their masts. For full ten minutes not a gun was fired, Englishmen and Frenchmen uniting to pay the homage of dead silence to the awful catastrophe; and not a sound was heard but the wild cries of the wounded and the drowning, and the splash of the burning brands as they fell into the waves.

Next morning the fiery sun of Egypt rose upon a scene of victory such as has never been witnessed in the history of the world. Of the 13 French ships of the line, one had perished in the flames, eight had surrendered, and two were helpless on the shore. As many as 5225 of the French perished in various ways, and 3500 were sent ashore under a flag of truce. Victory, as Nelson said, is not a name strong enough for such a result; he called it a conquest. Indeed, the battle of the Nile electrified the whole world; and the congratulations, rewards, and honours showered upon the naval hero to whom it was due exceeded all previous example. The British Government, however, certainly did not err by excess of generosity; for the most brilliant naval victory on record, the Admiral was only created Baron Nelson of the Nile and Burnham Thorpe, with a pension of £2000.

There is an amusing anecdote told of Nelson, who received Rear-admiral Blanquet and the seven surviving captains of the captured French ships on board the *Vanguard*, and treated them with all the unbounded generosity of his nature. These brave men had all been wounded, and a few days after the action, Nelson, still half blind from the injury to his remaining eye, offered one of them a case of toothpicks. Now, this captain had lost most of his teeth by a musket ball. Mortified at his heedless mistake, which he was afraid might be construed into a covert insult, he hastened to set matters right by offering another his snuff-box. What was his confusion when he observed that this gentleman had had the misfortune to lose his nose!

Nearer home a portion of our troops were engaged in repressing the Irish rebellion, which was practically over with the defeat of the rebels at Vinegar Hill (June 21, 1798). The French made an attempt to revive the contest by landing (August 22) a force of several hundred men under General Humbert at Killala in Mayo. A body of 4000 militia was utterly routed by the discipline of the invaders at Castlebar; but General Humbert was compelled to surrender to a corps of regular soldiers under Lord Cornwallis (Sept. 8). On the 16th of the same month, probably before news of Humbert's surrender could have reached France, Commodore Bompart was despatched from Brest with a small squadron consisting of a 74, three 46's, five 36's, and a schooner, having on board 3000 soldiers destined for a descent on the Irish coast. But the expedition was closely watched by the British cruisers, and on the 11th October it fell in with a British squadron, then cruising off the Donegal coast, under the command of Commodore Sir John Borlase Warren. The issue was the usual one when the contest occurred on the watery element, and of the entire squadron of Commodore Bompart only two ships, a 46 and a 36, got safely back to port.

The other occurrences of the year were not of great importance, with the exception of the reduction of Minorca, which was effected by General Charles Stuart and Commodore Duckworth.

A change in the public mind of Holland, which was said to have veered round to the dethroned Stadtholder, induced the British Cabinet to plan an expedition to Holland. The Czar Paul was to supply 17,593 men, 6 ships of the line, 5 frigates, and 2 transports, on condition of receiving a handsome subsidy from Britain. On the 27th August, 1799, General Sir Ralph Abercrombie landed at Helder Point with 17,000 British troops. General Daendals, a Dutch officer of great experience, and a keen Republican, did not care to oppose him, so skilfully had Admiral Mitchell moored the bomb-vessels and gun-brigs to scour the whole beach. But no sooner did Abercrombie begin to move forward beyond the support of the ships than he found himself in action with his intrepid opponent. The battle lasted from five in the morning till three in the afternoon, when Daendals retired.

This success enabled the British to make preparations for an attack on Helder Point. But the garrison, consisting of 2000 men, did not wait the attack, and during the night retired across the marshes to Medemblick. On the morning of the 28th, the 92d Highlanders and the 2d battalion of the Royal Scots, under Major-General Moore, the future hero of Corunna, took quiet possession of the fortress, with all its numerous train of artillery. At the same time Captain Winthrop of the *Circe* took possession of a squadron of Dutch ships of war at anchor in the Nieuve Diep, consisting of a 64, a 50, six 44's, two 28's, and two 24's, besides three Indiamen and a sheer-hulk, together with the naval magazine at Nieuve Werk, containing a vast quantity of valuable ordnance stores and 97 pieces of cannon. The Texel was now open to Vice-admiral Mitchell, and on the 30th he got under way with his squadron, and sent a summons to the Dutch Admiral Storey, then at moorings in the Texel. That officer would have fought for the honour of his flag, but his seamen had turned politicians and positively refused to support him. He had, therefore, no option but to surrender, and a further naval force, consisting of a 74, five 64's, two 50's, three frigates, and a gun-brig, fell into the hands of the British, who took possession in the name of the Prince of Orange.

While the Dutch fleet was changing hands, General Abercrombie advanced and took post behind the Zype, where, on the morning of the 10th September, our people were attacked by a Gallo-Batavian force of 25,000 men, under General Brune, who was driven back at all points with a loss of from 1000 to 1500 men. On the 13th, the Duke of York landed at the Helder to assume the chief command; and at the same time the Russian troops were disembarked under General Hermann. The force of the invaders now amounted to 35,000, and it was resolved to make an attempt on the lines of General Brune in front of Alkmaar. Twenty thousand men were told off for the service, and divided into four divisions, under the Russian General Hermann, Lieutenant-general Dundas, Sir James Pulteney, and Sir Ralph Abercrombie. The three British divisions were all successful in capturing the posts assigned to them, but General Hermann failed to make good his footing at Bergen, and the whole army was compelled to resume its former position (September 19).

On the 2d October, the Duke of York made a general attack on the Gallo-Batavian line, and General Brune was compelled to retire, leaving the allies masters of the field. On the 6th another bloody battle occurred, not by premeditation, but from the attempt of a Russian column to obtain possession of a height. Neither side gained a decisive advantage.

The winter was now setting in with such severity that it was evident nothing further could be done that season. Nor could the allies re-embark in safety, for General Brune, having been considerably reinforced, pushed forward his posts so as nearly to surround the allied camp. On the other hand, the Duke of York had it in his power to cut the dykes and devastate the whole country by laying it under the ocean. Under these circumstances negotiations were entered into for a suspension of arms, and the unmolested evacuation of Holland by the combined British and Russian forces. Thus terminated the expedition to the Helder. Vice-admiral Mitchell and Sir Ralph Abercrombie received the thanks of Parliament, but the wits said that the chivalry of Britain had been foiled by "a tradesman of Paris and an attorney of Zwolle;" for Brune had been a printer, and Daendals was bred to the law.

The French sustained great reverses in Italy, chiefly by the vigour of Nelson's lieutenants. Troubridge laid siege to St. Elmo, and his batteries, "after much trouble and palaver, brought the vagabonds to their senses." The French garrison of Capua, 3000 strong, capitulated to 1000 British blue-jackets; and Gaeta surrendered to Captain Louis of the *Minotaur*, without firing a shot. Thus the whole kingdom of Naples was for the time delivered from the French. The Russian General Suwarrow was driving the French before him in the north, and nothing now remained to complete the deliverance of Italy but the recovery of Rome. Civita Vecchia yielded to the broadsides of the *Culloden*. Troubridge then sent Captain Louis up the Tiber in his barge, and the Union Jack waved over the Eternal City (September 30).

The battle of the Nile was a great disaster to the French in Egypt, who were thus cut off from all communication with France. But Napoleon would not allow it to interfere with his golden dreams of conquest. A Turkish army was mustering for the attack of Egypt, and he resolved to anticipate it by the invasion of Syria. He expected, by a brilliant victory, to assemble round his nucleus of French veterans an Asiatic army that would enable him to take Constantinople by the way, and march through Persia to the overthrow of the British in India.

On the 11th February he set out with 13,000 infantry and 900 horse—all that could be spared from the army of Egypt. Arish surrendered, but Jaffa held out, and was taken by storm on the 6th March. Four thousand of the Turkish garrison laid down their arms on the promise of quarter, but were afterwards shot in cold blood. It was probably the difficulty of finding food for so many captives that prompted this act of atrocious cruelty.

On the 16th March the French appeared before Acre, where Achmed-Djezzar, Pasha of Syria, had shut himself up with his troops and his treasures. The Turks, excited to a frenzy of unyielding bravery by the massacre at Jaffa, and directed by the skill of Sir Sidney Smith, who had opportunely arrived on the coast with a small squadron, prepared for the defence. Shot and shell were poured on Acre, but without success. At length, on the 51st day of the siege (May 7), the long-expected reinforcements of Turkish troops from Rhodes appeared in the offing. This was the signal to Napoleon for a vigorous assault, in the hope to get possession of the town before the Turks could disembark. Suddenly the French fire increased tenfold. All that day it rained shot on Acre. The Turks replied as well as they could, but the greatest damage to the besiegers was caused by some heavy ship-guns mounted in suitable places and manned by the tars of the *Tiger*. Still the besiegers gained ground, and made a lodgment in the second story of the north-east tower, where they covered themselves with two traverses across the ditch.

Daylight (May 8) showed the French standard planted on the outer angle of the work. It was a critical time, for the Turkish troops had not yet landed, and the place must be preserved for a few hours at all hazards. Sir Sidney Smith, therefore, landed with the ships' boats at the mole, and led on his seamen, armed with pikes, to the breach, which he found defended by a few brave Turks, whose most destructive missiles were stones, which struck the foremost Frenchmen down the slope, and impeded the progress of the rest. Djezzar Pasha, according to ancient Turkish custom, was sitting in his palace, rewarding such as brought him the heads of his enemies, and distributing musket cartridges with his own hands. Hearing that Sir Sidney and his brave shipmates were on the breach, the old man hastily quitted his station, and coming behind the British, pulled them down with violence. "If any harm happens to my English friends all is lost!" This amicable contest as to who should defend the breach occasioned a rush of the Turks to the spot; and thus time was gained for the arrival of the first body of Hassan Bey's troops.

Napoleon was now seen on an elevated piece of ground called Cœur-de-Lion's Mount (after Richard I.), addressing his generals, and making preparations for a renewed assault. To meet this Sir Sidney made a fresh disposition of his ships and gunboats. The attack took place in the evening, but the sabre, with the addition of a dagger in the other hand, proved more than a match for the bayonet, and the French were again driven back with heavy loss. Furious at all his efforts being foiled by an English post-captain, Napoleon sent for General Kleber's division, which was guarding the fords of Jordan; but although thus reinforced he failed again, as he had so often done before. On the night following the last repulse (20th May) he raised the siege in disgust, and made a precipitate retreat, leaving all his battering train behind him.

In after years Napoleon frequently referred to the siege of Acre and Sir Sidney Smith as the event and the man that made him "miss his destiny." His retreat to Egypt was marked by an accumulation of horrors: the British and Arabs hovered continually on his march, the plague broke out in the remains of his army, and a number of sick, whom it was found impossible to remove from Jaffa, are believed to have been poisoned by his orders. Still he did reach Egypt, and defeated with great slaughter a strong Turkish force which disembarked at Aboukir. But the intelligence which reached him of the reverses of the French in Italy and Switzerland determined him to return to Europe. Notwithstanding the very partial success of his expedition, he was received with the greatest enthusiasm by all classes, and seeing things were ripe for a change, he cleared out the effete and unpopular Directory at the point of the bayonet, and lifted himself to the post of First Consul. This event marks the end of the second period in our great struggle with France.

CHAPTER III.—The Great French War.

NAPOLEON FIRST CONSUL.—1800-1802.

Battle of the Baltic—Aboukir—Mandora—Alexandria—Attempt on the Gunboats at Boulogne.

ON mounting the consular throne, Napoleon bent all his energies to the reconquest of Italy. In May, 1800, he crossed the Great St. Bernard, and fought the battle of Marengo (June 14), and the Austrians were driven from Lombardy. Moreau had meanwhile crossed the Rhine, and led a numerous army into the heart of Germany. The decisive battle of Hohenlinden (December 3) completely humbled the Hapsburgs, who gladly welcomed a cessation from arms in the peace of Luneville (February 9, 1801).

As far as we were concerned, the only events of the year (1800) were the surrender of Malta (September 4) and of the Dutch island of Curaçao.

At the beginning of the nineteenth century, a formidable confederacy was formed against us by the States that surround the Baltic. The proposition that neutral ships might, as a matter of right, be searched for contraband of war by the cruisers of the belligerents, was to be set aside for a new maritime code, based on the principle that free ships make free goods, and that the flag covers the merchandise. Frequent collisions took place between British cruisers and neutral vessels, and the capture of the Danish frigate *Freya*, for refusing to allow her convoy to be searched, brought matters to a crisis. A powerful squadron, under Admiral Dickson, anchored off Copenhagen, and the Danes, who were unprepared for resistance, agreed to

D

acknowledge the right of search till further consideration. But the Czar, already won over by the arts of Napoleon, took the passage of the Sound in high dudgeon, and ordered an embargo to be laid upon all British ships in Russian ports, barbarously marching their crews into the interior. Sweden, Prussia, and finally Denmark, entered into his views, and the Maritime Confederacy was formed on the basis of the Armed Neutrality of 1780.

Prompt measures were necessary, for the naval forces of the league were extremely formidable. The Baltic nations could muster among them 88 ships of the line, besides frigates and small craft. If their forces were suffered to unite, they might raise the blockade of the French ports, and ride triumphant in the Channel. What would hinder Napoleon then, from putting his scheme of invasion into effect?

On the 12th March, 1801, our fleet sailed for the Baltic. It consisted of 18 sail of the line, with as many frigates, sloops, bombs, fire-ships, and smaller vessels as made the whole amount to 53 sail. The chief command was entrusted to Sir Hyde Parker, who, although a brave officer and experienced seaman, candidly confessed to feeling "a little nervous about dark nights and fields of ice." Fortunately he had Nelson for his second in command, and the fiery little hero told him to "brace up. These," he said, "are not times for nervous systems."

At the Sound, negotiations were tried, but failed, and Sir Hyde proceeded to force the passage. At 6 A.M. (March 30), with a fine breeze at N.N.W., the fleet advanced into the channel, which is here only three miles wide. The batteries of Elsinore opened with round shot and grape, but as the Swedes did not fire, the ships were able to keep pretty well out of range of the Danish missiles, and the casualties were few. At noon the fleet anchored off Copenhagen.

The delay of the British at the Sound had given the Danes time to prepare defences of the most formidable description. Eighteen ships—frigates, praams, and radeaus—stretched in a line of a mile and a half. At the northern extremity of the line were the two powerful Crown batteries, constructed on piles, fitted with furnaces for heating shot, and commanded by the two-decked block ships, the *Mars* and *Elephant*. The southern extremity of the line was prolonged by gun and mortar batteries on Amak Island. The harbour and docks were protected by a chain thrown across the entrance, and by two 74's, a 40-gun frigate, two 18-gun brigs, and several armed xebecs, besides that they were under the fire of the Crown batteries and some others on the northern shore. There was no want of men to work the guns, for every one, from the Prince-royal to the artisan, had obeyed the call of his country. To increase the difficulties of the attack, too, the Danes had taken up the buoys that marked the navigation in the narrow and intricate channels by which the harbour is approached. At a council of war held that afternoon, some of the British captains looked grave, and spoke of the number of Swedes and Russians they should afterwards have to engage. "The more numerous the better," said Nelson; "I wish they were twice as many—the easier the victory, depend on it!" He undertook to make the attack with 10 ships and all the smaller vessels. Sir Hyde Parker immediately closed with the offer.

A shoal, called the Middle Ground, extends along the whole sea-face of Copenhagen. Between the shoal and the town is the King's Channel, where the Danes had arranged their line of defence, as near to the town as possible. Nelson determined to round the south end of the Middle Ground, and follow this channel. His first care was to buoy it afresh. This occupied the nights of the 30th and 31st. The morning of the 1st April was spent in reconnoitring the defences and the channel; and in the afternoon the attacking squadron coasted along the outer edge of the Middle Ground, and doubled its southern extremity, anchoring about eight o'clock. The headmost ship of the British line was then within two miles of the southernmost Danish ship. Early in the evening Nelson dismissed his captains with the parting toast—"A fair wind and success to-morrow."

At half-past nine next morning (April 2), Nelson, whose flag was on board the *Elephant*, made the signal to weigh in succession. The wind was fair, at south-east, but owing to the ignorance of the pilots, who fancied the water shoaled towards the town, whereas, in fact, it deepened all the way to the enemy's line, the *Agamemnon*, *Bellona*, and *Russell* grounded in weathering the south-east point of the Middle Ground. Even Nelson looked anxious when he saw himself thus deprived of a fourth part of his force. Besides, only one gun-brig succeeded in weathering the point and coming into action, and but two bomb-vessels could reach their station and open their mortars on the arsenal. But the die was cast. The first shot was fired about ten, and by half-past eleven the action was general. For two hours after that time the fire of the Danes never slackened. They knew their king and country were looking on, and that they fought for everything dear to them. On their side alone 1000 guns belched forth fire and smoke. The crash of the shot was tremendous.

> "Again! again! again!
> And the havoc did not slack."

The music of the artillery acted like a charm on Nelson, who soon recovered the high spirits that were natural to him in the hour of action. At one o'clock, when the action was at its hottest, "a shot," says Nelson's biographer Southey—and his words will always be used in describing this portion of the battle —"a shot through the mainmast knocked the splinters about, and he observed to one of his officers with a smile, 'It is warm work, and this day may be the last to any of us at a moment,' and then, stopping short at the gangway, added with emotion, 'But, mark you! I would not be elsewhere for thousands.' About this time the signal lieutenant called that No. 39 (the signal for discontinuing the action) was thrown out by the Commander-in-chief. He continued to walk the deck, and appeared to take no notice of it. The signal officer met him at the next turn, and asked if he should return it. 'No,' he replied, 'acknowledge it.' Presently he called after him to know if the signal for close action was hoisted, and, being answered in the affirmative, said, 'Mind you keep it so.' He now paced the deck, moving the stump of his left arm in a manner which always indicated great emotion. 'Do you know,' said he to Mr. Ferguson, 'what is shown on board the Commander-in-chief? No. 39!' Mr. Ferguson asked what that meant. 'Why, to leave off action.' Then shrugging up his shoulders he repeated the words, 'Leave off action! Now, dam'me, if I do! You know, Foley,' turning to the captain, 'I have only one eye, and have a right to be blind sometimes,' and then putting the glass to his right eye, in that mood of mind which sports with bitterness, he exclaimed, 'I really do not see the signal!' Presently he exclaimed, 'Damn the signal! Keep mine for closer battle flying! That's the way I answer such signals. Nail mine to the mast!'" It is only fair to Sir Hyde Parker to add, that he made the signal in order that Nelson might have an excuse to withdraw, if he felt his force insufficient to maintain the attack.

The signal to "discontinue the action" had no effect on the British line, which looked only to Nelson; but it saved from total destruction the frigate squadron of Riou, which had gallantly filled up the station opposite the Crown batteries, and was nearest the Commander-in-chief. "What will Nelson think of us!" exclaimed Riou, as he reluctantly drew off. He did not live to know. A splinter had wounded him in the head, and he was sitting on a gun encouraging his men. Just as the *Amazon* showed her stern to the Crown batteries his secretary was killed by his side. The *Amazon* having ceased firing, the smoke cleared away, and the Danes were able to take fatal aim. Another shot swept away several marines who were hauling in the main brace. "Come, then, my boys!" cried Riou, "let us all die together." Scarcely were the words out of his mouth when a raking shot struck him in the loins and almost cut him in two. A braver or a better officer there was not in the British navy.

Even the retreat of the frigate squadron could draw from the Danes no more than a feeble cheer. They were now without hope, and without aim, except to die for their country. Their fire began to slacken about half-past one. Their dead lay in ghastly heaps on board the praams and radeaus. The survivors, many of them unacquainted with the rules of warfare, made matters worse by continuing the action after their ships had struck. The Crown batteries and the Isle of Amak fired on friend and foe. Nelson was grieved and angry, and his first impulse was to send in fireships to burn the prizes, but on second thoughts he wrote that letter to the Crown-prince of Denmark which has become so famous:—"Vice-admiral Lord Nelson has been commanded to spare Denmark when she no longer resists. The line of defence which covered her shores has struck to the British flag; but if the firing is continued on the part of Denmark, he must set on fire all the prizes he has taken, without having the power of saving the brave men who have so nobly defended them. The brave Danes are the brothers, and should never be the enemies, of the English." This remonstrance had the desired effect; the firing ceased, and the attacking squadron weighed and joined the reserve force of Sir Hyde Parker in the middle of the straits. The prizes were brought off next day, but were found to be so shattered that it was necessary to destroy them. The *Holstein* alone was carried to England as a trophy. Thus ended the battle of the Baltic, which Nelson considered the most difficult achievement, the hardest fought battle, and the most glorious result that ever graced the annals of our country. " I have been in one hundred and five engagements," he said to the Crown-prince of Denmark, " but this has been the most tremendous of them all." The patriotic valour of the Danes could never have been overcome except by the skill of a Nelson, and that confidence on the part of his seamen which the habit of victory inspires. In their heroic defence the Danes lost 6000 in killed, wounded, and prisoners. The British killed and mortally wounded amounted to 350, and the recoverably and slightly wounded to 850—a greater proportion to their numbers than at the Nile or Trafalgar.

The immediate result of the battle was an armistice with Denmark. The indefatigable Nelson instantly proceeded to follow up the blow at Carlscrona and Cronstadt; but the assassination of the mad Czar Paul rendered further fighting unnecessary. His successor, Alexander, lost no time in letting this country know how much he was her friend. He released the British sailors who had been sent into the interior, and in an autograph letter to His Britannic Majesty, expressed his desire to enter into friendly relations. In due time a convention was signed between England and Russia, by which the English construction of the naval law of nations was acknowledged in all its main points, and Russia agreed to abandon the principles of the Maritime Confederacy. The other Baltic countries followed the lead of Russia. " Thus," says Alison, " in less than six months from its formation, was dissolved the most formidable league ever arrayed against the British maritime power."

Almost at the same time that our seamen were winning fresh laurels in the Baltic, our soldiers were adding to the list of their victories on the sandy plains of Egypt. After Napoleon's departure, Kleber held the country against all the efforts of the Turks, and defeated them with great slaughter, but his career was cut short by the knife of a fanatical assassin. He was succeeded in the command by Menou, who assumed the Mahommedan dress and religion. The British Government could not regard the settlement of the French in Egypt in any other light than a perpetual menace to their Indian Empire, and in concert with the Turks they formed a plan for the expulsion of the invaders. A direct descent was to be made on the coast by Sir Ralph Abercrombie, an officer who had served with distinction in many parts of the world. The Turks were to re-organise their army in Syria, and co-operate by an invasion on that side; while 8000 troops under Sir David Baird, the hero of Seringapatam, were to embark at Bombay for Suez. But the Turks, dispirited by their defeats and decimated by the plague, moved with more than their usual slowness; it was a "far cry" from Bombay to Suez, and the arrival of the Indian auxiliaries was uncertain; so Sir Ralph Abercrombie sailed from Marmorice in the *Levant*, and, with a fleet of 200 transports and other vessels and 17,500 troops, gallantly resolved to make the attempt alone.

On Sunday morning, the 1st March, the coast of Egypt was sighted, and the fleet came to anchor in Aboukir Bay, the scene of Nelson's great victory. But scarcely had the ships come to anchor when a violent gale sprang up, and blew without intermission for six days. No boat could put ashore, and the French had the amplest opportunity of making effectual preparations to resist the landing of our troops, when that should take place. On the low sand-hills which stretch in a semicircular form along the bay, they placed great bodies of cavalry and infantry, and planted twelve heavy pieces of cannon, so as to throw, with the cannon of the castle, a cross fire on every channel of approach. They also brought forward several mortars, and placed them so as to be half-concealed by the inequalities of the ground, in order to pour confusion into our ranks, should they have the temerity to advance up the sand-hills.

The landing was appointed for the morning of the 8th. By two A.M. every man told off for this duty was in the boats. The ascent of a sky-rocket from the admiral's ship was the signal for the boats to shove off, and the seamen bent to their oars, and rowed with a will, to the rendezvous in rear of the *Mondovi*, which was anchored just out of reach of shot from the shore. When the boats arrived at the rendezvous, they were formed so that every brigade, regiment, and company should step on shore in its proper place. On the right were the 23d and the flank companies of the 40th; in the centre the 28th, 42d, and 58th; on the left the 54th, Guards, Royals, and Corsican Rangers—in all, 5230 men. It was eight o'clock before these arrangements were completed, and then the boats shoved off for the shore.

"It would be difficult," says Sir Robert Wilson, the historian of the expedition, "to conceive a situation of deeper or darker interest than that in which the British army was now placed. The men sat erect and motionless; not a sound was heard, except the splash of the oars in the water, while the long line of boats moved rapidly, but in admirable and exact array, towards the shore. Not long, however, was that stern silence permitted to continue unbroken. As if doubting the evidence of their own senses, the enemy gazed for awhile, without offering to the frail armada the slightest molestation; but their astonishment soon gave place to other and more stirring sensations, and they stood to their arms. In a moment the whole of their artillery opened, and the sea hissed and boiled behind and before the boats, with round shot and shells, that fell in showers around them." To the cannonade a hailstorm of musketry was soon added, but the seamen strained every nerve, yet rowed with perfect regularity, till the boats reached the shore.

The four regiments on the right, the 23d, 28th, 40th, and 42d, got under the elevated position of the French batteries, and being thus sheltered from their fire, quietly disembarked and formed in line on the shore. "Forward!" cried General Moore; and with cheers that rang from flank to flank our men commenced the steep ascent, which was so deeply covered with loose sand that they sank back half a pace every step they advanced. When they were half-way up, the French appeared on the summit and poured in a destructive fire. Our men fired not a shot in reply, but, redoubling their exertions, they rushed up the height with almost preternatural energy, and gained the summit before the French could reload their pieces. Though exhausted with fatigue and almost breathless, they charged the enemy at the point of the bayonet, and pursued them till they carried the two hills which commanded the plain on the left, taking three pieces of cannon. Scarcely had the 42d put to the rout that portion of the enemy's infantry immediately opposed to them, when they were attacked by cavalry. The bayonet was again brought into play, and the horsemen galloped off, with many empty saddles, including that of their commander. The Guards, who, in common with the other troops on the left, landed on ground nearly level with the water, were attacked by cavalry the moment they jumped ashore; but a flank fire from the 58th enabled them to form and advance against the enemy.

The engagement of Aboukir was short and decisive, and in a very little time after the first British soldier put his foot on the shore, the French were in full retreat along the road to Alexandria: greatly to their own astonishment, no doubt, if we may judge from the conduct of some of their countrymen, field officers, who were prisoners on board the *Minotaur*. When these officers learned that the British actually intended to land in the face of the French army, they expressed much regret that so many brave men should be sacrificed on a desperate attempt which, in their opinion, could not be successful; and when the boats pushed out for the shore, they went up into the rigging to witness, as they said, the last of their English friends. But when they saw the British land, ascend the heights, and force the French to fly, they burst into tears, ran down below, and did not again appear on deck all that day.

The next three days were spent in landing the stores. On the evening of the 12th the British advanced, and encamped that night near the tower of Mandora. A few miles from the encampment, posted among sand-hills and palm and date trees, three miles to the east of Alexandria, lay the French under Menou—5000 infantry, a column of cavalry, and 32 pieces of cannon. On the morning of the 13th, the British advanced to the attack in three columns of regiments. The 90th (Perthshire Light Infantry) formed the advance of the centre column, and the 92d (Gordon Highlanders) that of the left. The guns were dragged by seamen whom Sir Sidney Smith had landed from the fleet. The sand was so loose and deep that the wheels sometimes sank to the axle. For three or four miles the march lay over the ground covered with date trees; but immediately the two advanced regiments cleared the encumbered ground and deployed into line on the open, the French opened a heavy fire of cannon and musketry, and moved down with great boldness. But the 90th and 92d, though suffering severely, never receded a foot, but bore the whole weight of the enemy until the rest of the line came up to their support. The 92d, indeed, though under the combined fire of infantry and artillery, never paused in their advance, but walked up to the muzzles of the enemy's guns, and captured two field-pieces and a howitzer. Both regiments bear "Mandora" on their colours and appointments.

The French did not wait to receive the attack of the whole British line, but retired to the entrenched position which they had formed before Alexandria. Sir Ralph Abercrombie resolved to force it at all risks, and the next week was spent in bringing forward cannon, provisions, and stores, erecting batteries, and strengthening his position, which had few natural advantages. On his right stretched the blue waters of the Mediterranean, dotted with four cutters stationed close to the shore, on his left Lake Maadie and the canal, and in front a sandy plain. Moore's division (23d, flank companies of the 40th, 42d, 58th, and Corsican Rangers) were placed as an advanced post on the right. The 58th occupied a ruin of vast extent, supposed to have been a palace of the Ptolemies; the 28th a redoubt, close on the left, and a few paces in advance. This redoubt was open to the rear. The 23d, 40th, 42d, and Corsican Rangers were posted 500 yards to the rear of the ruins and redoubt, in support of the 58th and 28th. To the left of the redoubt occupied by the 28th, a sandy plain extended about 300 yards, and then sloped into a valley. Here stood the cavalry of the reserve, a little retired towards the rear. Still farther to the left, on a rising ground behind the valley, were posted the Guards, under General Ludlow, who occupied the centre of the line. Their position was strengthened by a redoubt thrown up on their right, a battery on their left, and a small ditch or entrenchment in front, which connected both. On the left of the Guards the 92d, Queen's Own, 54th, Scots Royals, 8th, 13th, 18th, and 90th regiments, were formed *en échelon*, ready, if necessary, to form on the Guards. The second line consisted (from the left) of the 30th, 89th, 44th, Dillon's, De Rolle's, and Stuart's regiments, and the dismounted cavalry of the 12th and 26th dragoons. Along the whole extent of the line were arranged two 24-pounders, thirty-two field pieces, and a 24-pounder in the redoubt occupied by the 28th. The French were strongly posted on a nearly perpendicular ridge of hills parallel to the British line, and presented a very formidable appearance. A sandy plain divided the armies.

It was Sir Ralph Abercrombie's practice to have the army under arms every morning at three o'clock, and it was well for him that the 21st March proved no exception to the rule. At that hour every man was at his post. For half-an-hour not a sound was heard. Day had not yet begun to break over the sandy plain when the report of a musket was heard on the left of the line, followed by the discharge of some cannon. The

French had begun the action by a false attack, by the dromedary corps, on the British left. Silence again prevailed. It was the stillness that precedes the storm. General Moore, who happened to be the general officer of the right, had galloped off to the left the instant he heard the firing; but, impressed with the idea that this was merely a feint, he galloped back to his brigade on the right. Hardly had he reached it when a wild huzza rising from the plain below, followed by a roar of musketry, announced the real intention of the French, to precipitate their forces on the right and the centre. In the dark, cloudy, close morning the measured tread of the French was distinctly heard, and then the shout with which they met the advanced pickets. The 23d and the flank companies of the 40th were now ordered to move forward to the support of the 58th in the ruins, Major Stirling with the left wing of the 42d to take post in the open space on the left of the redoubt, and Lieutenant-colonel Alexander Stewart, with the right wing, to remain 200 yards in the rear, but exactly parallel with the left wing. These dispositions were scarcely made when the French attacked the ruin, the redoubt, and the left wing of the Highlanders. The darkness was rendered more obscure by the firing; there was not a breath of wind to dispel the smoke, and all objects at arm's length from the eye were totally invisible.

Favoured by the gloom and the noise of the combat in front, a column of French grenadiers—accompanied by a gun—bearing the proud name of "The Invincibles," stole silently along the interval between the left of the 42d and the right of the Guards, from which the cavalry picket had retired; they calculated their distance and line of march so correctly that, wheeling to the left, they marched in between the two wings of the 42d, drawn up in parallel lines 200 yards apart. The instant they were perceived, Lieutenant-colonel Stewart, with the right wing, rushed forward and charged with the bayonet, while the rear-rank of Major Stirling's left wing faced about and charged in the rear. Maddened by this double attack, the Invincibles dashed forward with the intention of pushing into the ruins occupied by the 58th. As they passed the rear of the redoubt occupied by the 28th, that regiment poured in a volley, which quickened their pace. On through the openings of the ruins the shattered and bleeding Invincibles rushed, but only to be met by another withering fire from the 58th and the flank companies of the

40th. Brought to bay here, and hemmed in by the 58th and 40th in front, and the 42d in rear, the Invincibles fought with the courage that is born of despair. It was only after 650 of them had fallen that the survivors, about 250 in number, threw down their arms and surrendered. The standard of the legion was delivered up to Major Stirling of the 42d, who gave it in charge to a sergeant, with orders to remain beside the gun which the regiment had taken. It bore several marks of distinction, such as "Tagliamento," and in the centre was a bugle-horn wreathed with laurel. Bravely had it been borne. The officer who carried it was heard to shout, again and again, "Vive la Republique!" ere he fell, pierced by a shot.

The right wing of the 42d was meanwhile hotly engaged with the enemy in front. Just as the survivors of the Invincibles were laying down their arms, another great body of the enemy was seen advancing on the left of the redoubt. General Moore ordered the right wing of the regiment out of the ruins, and told them to form line in battalion on the flat on the left of the redoubt. Before this formation was complete the French were upon them. It was a critical moment. "My brave Highlanders," cried Sir Ralph Abercrombie, always present in the hottest of the fight, "remember our country, remember your forefathers!" The Highlanders responded with enthusiasm, and soon the French were flying in confusion across the plain. A second and a third attempt on the right of the position met the same fate.

While the battle was thus raging on the right, the Guards in the centre were behaving with their usual coolness and bravery. General Ludlow allowed the French to approach very close to his front, and then gave the order to fire. The French were completely routed. They afterwards tried to turn the left of the position, but were so firmly met by the Scots Royals and the right wing of the 31st, that they desisted from all further attempts on the centre.

By eight in the morning the French were repulsed at all points, only maintaining the combat by a heavy and close cannonade from their great guns, and a straggling fire from their sharpshooters. The British fire had ceased, as those who had been so hotly engaged had expended all their ammunition, and a fresh supply could not be immediately procured, the ordnance stores being at some distance. This was taken advantage of by the

French to advance their sharpshooters close to the redoubt occupied by the 28th; but before they had commenced operations a fresh supply of ammunition arrived. Colonel Duncan of the artillery immediately levelled the 24-pounder in the redoubt, pointing at the sixth file from the right angle of the close column. Bang went the gun, and with so much precision that it levelled with the ground all who stood outward of the file. The second shot plunged into the centre of the column, and before the fourth was ready the French were scampering off in full retreat. The retreat was now general along the whole line, and by ten o'clock the enemy had regained their position in front of Alexandria.

Our loss was 244 killed and 1193 wounded, and a fourth of it fell on the 42d Highlanders, who had 54 killed and 261 wounded. The French loss could not have been less than 4000, for upwards of 1000 of them were buried on the field of battle. But the joy of the victory was dashed by the fall of Sir Ralph Abercrombie. Early in the day, while standing in the hottest of the fight beside the 42d, two of the enemy's cavalry dashed forward and attempted to lead him away prisoner. The old general would not yield, and one of the troopers made a thrust at his breast; but, exerting all his remarkable strength of arm, Sir Ralph seized hold of the sabre and forced it out of the trooper's hand. He then turned to meet his other assailant, but the dragoon was at that moment shot dead by a corporal of the 42d who ran up to Sir Ralph's assistance. Some time after this a musket-ball entered his groin and lodged deep in the hip-joint; but not till the shouts of the British informed him of the enemy's defeat did he yield to exhausted nature, and acknowledge that he required rest. Surrounded by his weeping generals and officers, he was carried on board Lord Keith's ship, the *Foudroyant*, where he expired on the 27th of the month.

The battle of Alexandria paved the way for the re-conquest of Egypt. General Hutchinson, who succeeded Abercrombie in the command, drove the enemy from Damietta and Rosetta. Ramanieh was captured (May 7), and the communication between Alexandria and Cairo cut off. The Turks, directed by British officers, gained a victory near Cairo, and (May 22) Belliard, who commanded there, surrendered with nearly 14,000 troops and 320 guns, on condition of being conveyed to France. Menou refused to be included in the capitulation of Cairo, and proposed to defend Alexandria, but the vigorous measures taken to reduce the place, after the arrival of Sir David Baird, convinced him that resistance was hopeless, and he yielded (August 31). "The total amount of troops that capitulated in Egypt," says Alison, "was upwards of 24,000, all veterans: an astonishing success to have been achieved by a British force which had hardly ever seen a shot fired, and which, even including the Indian auxiliaries, never amounted to the same numerical strength." At London there were great rejoicings; "the humiliation of France, on the element where she had been so long victorious, was hailed as a harbinger of the great triumphs awaiting the British arms, if the enemy should carry into execution their long-threatened scheme of invasion." The expedition to Egypt must always be held in proud remembrance by the British army, for it dates from it that career of success which has continued with rare exceptions to the present time. Dettingen, Minden, and Quebec had shown that the ancient fire was not extinct, but the army had deteriorated sadly from the days of Marlborough. Its reputation had lately been seriously tarnished by the disastrous contest in America, and it was a surprise to all when the battle of Alexandria showed that the British army could, on the open field, cope with the French, the most scientific and the most uniformly successful soldiers of the world.

The only other event of the year—besides the capture of St. Thomas and some of the other West India islands—was Nelson's unsuccessful attempt upon the flotilla at Boulogne. That port had become the head-quarters of swarms of gun-boats, flat-bottomed praams, and other small craft; and it was known that Napoleon, now at leisure from continental affairs, was bending all his energies to the shores of Great Britain. The excitement on our side of the Channel became intense, and in deference to this feeling the hero of Copenhagen was appointed to a command extending from Orfordness to Beachy Head on both shores. Nelson's own opinion was that the main attempt at invasion, if it ever took place, could not be made from Boulogne; but he was content to do something to allay the popular apprehension, and a powerful armament of light vessels was fitted out, and an attack on the Boulogne flotilla fixed for the 15th August. The armament put off about half an hour before midnight, but in the darkness the divisions separated. Those that arrived made the attack gallantly, but the French were fully prepared. Their boats, fortified by strong nettings and projecting pikes, chained by the bottom to the shore and to each other, and crowded with soldiers, were almost impregnable. Still, many were taken possession of, and would have been burnt, since they could not be brought out; but immediately one of their own vessels became a prize, the French opened fire on it, enveloping in common ruin friend and foe. After a desperate conflict of four hours the assailants sheered off. Our loss in this affair was 172 killed and wounded. Meanwhile negotiations for peace were in active progress, and preliminaries were signed at London, on the 1st October, between Great Britain, Holland, France, and Spain.

The treaty, which was signed at Amiens, on March 27th, 1802, provided that "All the colonial conquests of Britain, except Ceylon and Trinidad, should be given up; Egypt was to be restored to the Porte, Malta to the knights of St. John, and the Cape to Holland."

CHAPTER IV.—THE GREAT FRENCH WAR.

FROM AMIENS TO TRAFALGAR.—1802-1805.

Projected Invasion of England—Commodore Dance's Action—Seizure of the Spanish Treasure Frigates—Sir Robert Calder's Action—Trafalgar—Sir Richard Strachan's Action off Cape Ortegal.

THE Treaty of Amiens did not preserve the peace long. The British Government saw that Napoleon was not acting in good faith, and refused to give up Malta. Napoleon insisted on its instant evacuation. The British Government, quite well aware that Napoleon only waited for its evacuation to seize the place for himself, proposed to hold it for ten years, and then restore it to the natives. This ultimatum was rejected, and both sides prepared for war, which was formally declared on the 18th May, 1803. The struggle, it was evident, could only end in the humiliation of one or the other—France, who deemed herself invincible on land, Britain, omnipotent at sea. France saw in the expected conquest of Britain the removal of the last bar to her scheme of universal dominion; Britain boasted, and not in vain, of her wooden walls, and pointed to her recent victories in Egypt as a proof of what she could do if the worst came to the worst. The passions of the people were engaged on both sides; it was no longer a war of governments, but of nations. The departments of France vied with each other in contributing vessels, money, and troops for the great scheme of an invasion of England. The harbour of Boulogne was deepened, extended, and fortified, in order to form a more secure rendezvous for the praams and flat-bottomed boats which were fitted out in every port from Brest to the Texel, and which crept along the shore to the point of assemblage whenever the British cruisers were driven from their stations by contrary winds. At the opportune moment this vast flotilla was to be freighted with an army of 150,000 men, who lay in readiness at Boulogne. The wings of this vast army, extending from Brest on the one side to Antwerp on the other, amounted to 50,000 more. It seemed as if the long-talked-of invasion was about to become a reality. Nothing daunted, Britain collected her energies for the conflict. The regular army was increased by 50,000 men; and in a few weeks 300,000 volunteers were enrolled, armed, and disciplined. Gunboats also clustered along the line of the old Cinque Ports. But, as Nelson had supposed, the Boulogne flotilla was only part of a more extensive scheme. "The squadrons from the Spanish and Mediterranean ports were," says Alison, "to have effected a junction in the West Indies: they were then, returning with combined forces to Europe, to have raised successively the blockade of Rochefort, Brest, &c.; and by their union with the fleets in those harbours, to have formed an irresistible armament, under which the flotilla might effect the passage of the Channel. It will appear in the sequel how nearly this vast design succeeded, and how little the British were aware of the quarter whence danger really threatened them." It would have succeeded had not Nelson, two years later, intercepted the combined French and Spanish fleets at Trafalgar, and there gained his last and crowning victory.

With the threat of invasion hanging over this country, the land forces were in 1804 raised to 300,000 men, besides 340,000 volunteers; and 100,000 seamen and marines were voted for the navy. Still, nothing was done, and the year was spent in conflicts between our cruisers and detachments of the Boulogne flotilla proceeding to the place of assemblage.

On the 14th February this year (1804), a singular action was fought in the Indian Sea, between the China fleet, under Commodore Dance (commodore in the East India Company's maritime service), and a small French naval force, under Admiral Linois. Dance was homeward bound from China to Europe. He had with him 16 Indiamen, mounting between 30 and 36 guns, and 11 country ships. On the 14th February, being off Panlo Auro, he sighted four strange sail to leeward. These were soon made out to be the French ships *Marengo*, 80; *Belle Poule*,

40; *Semillante*, 36; *Berceau*, 22; and the gun-brig *Aventurier*, 16. They had sailed from Batavia for the express purpose of intercepting the China fleet. Commodore Dance accepted the challenge, threw out the signal for a line of battle in close order, disposed his fleet in the best possible arrangement for defence, and hove to for the night. The French Admiral was so puzzled at the bold attitude taken up by trading ships, that it was one P.M. next day before he made any attempt to attack. Edging off the wind, he stood towards the British. Dance, perceiving his rear was threatened, made the signal for his fleet to tack in succession, to edge off the wind to windward of his rear, and to engage the enemy on arriving up. This manœuvre was performed "with the correctness of a well-disciplined fleet." With a light breeze and top-gallant sails set, the *Royal George* approached the enemy, followed in close order by the *Ganges*, *Earl Camden*, *Warley*, *Alfred*, and other ships. The *Marengo* opened fire. The *Royal George* and the *Ganges* replied with spirit, and after an action of forty-three minutes, the French Admiral and his consorts, frightened at the unexpected resistance, ceased firing, hauled to the wind, and made sail away. The *Royal George*, which bore the brunt of the action, had only one man killed and one wounded. On his arrival in England, the gallant Dance received the honour of knighthood.

Spain declared war against Great Britain on the 12th December, 1804. That country was now completely under the influence of the Tuileries, and the rupture would probably have come about sooner or later, but the occurrence that immediately led to it was not a happy one. Spain had commuted her auxiliary force, due by the treaty offensive and defensive with France, into an annual payment of £2,880,000 to Napoleon. Britain looked upon this as a war subsidy to France, and was further alarmed by naval preparations at Cadiz, Ferrol, and Carthagena; and orders were given to Captain Graham Moore to intercept the Spanish treasure frigates, then on their way from Monte Video, to be held as security for the neutrality of Spain. Unfortunately, Captain Moore had only four frigates, and as the Spanish Rear-admiral had as many, he could not submit without a struggle. An action ensued (Oct. 5); one of the Spanish ships blew up, and three, with a freight valued at more than £2,000,000, were captured.

On the 2d December, 1804, Napoleon was crowned, in Nôtre Dame, Emperor of the French; on the 26th May, 1805, he was crowned, in the Cathedral of Milan, King of Italy. One of his first acts was to incorporate Genoa, Parma, and Placentia with France, and to erect Lucca and Piombino into a principality for his sister Eliza. Austria became alarmed, and joined Russia and Sweden in a coalition—the third which Pitt had formed—to meet their common enemy in the heart of Europe. Now or never was the time for Napoleon to put in operation his plan for the invasion of England. A swift blow at England, and a rapid march against the slow-paced Austrians, and all his enemies would be at his feet. The army of invasion still lay at Boulogne —155,000 men, 14,654 horses, and 432 pieces of cannon, with provisions for three months, and munitions of war to an enormous extent. The flotilla of transports consisted of 2293 vessels, 1339 of them armed. The organisation and all arrangements were so complete that, on trial made, it had been found that 25,000 men, drawn up opposite the vessels, could be embarked in ten minutes. Nothing was wanted but the command of the Channel for six hours, and if fortune proved propitious even that might be obtained. "It is only necessary," wrote Napoleon to his Minister of Marine, "to be master of the sea for six hours for England to cease to exist"—*il ne faut être maître de la mer que six heures pour l'Angleterre cesser d'exister.*

In January, Villeneuve had received orders from Napoleon to sail from Toulon, effect a junction with the Spanish Admiral Gravina at Cadiz, and threaten the West Indies with the united fleets. This feint, it was hoped, would draw a large portion of the English fleet from the Channel. Villeneuve was then to elude the vigilance of his pursuers and make a sudden return to Europe; release the 10 Spanish and 5 French ships blockaded at Ferrol; join the Rochefort squadron of 5 sail more; then steer to Brest, where Gantheaume awaited him with 21 sail. Lastly, at the head of this overwhelming force, which would amount to 61 sail of the line, he was to proceed to Boulogne and escort the flotilla to the shores of England.

Villeneuve was in Toulon with twelve sail, where he was blockaded by Lord Nelson with 11 sail of the line. On the 17th January, 1805, while Nelson was watering his fleet at Agincourt Sound, in the Madelena Islands, Villeneuve took the opportunity to put to sea. Lord Nelson went in quest of him, and searched Alexandria, the Gulf of Palma, and Malta, in vain. Villeneuve's fleet had meanwhile been shattered by a gale and forced to return to Toulon, and Lord Nelson waited in Palma Bay with feverish anxiety for his next movement. On the 30th March Villeneuve again successfully eluded the vigilance of Nelson and put to sea; he succeeded in forcing the blockade of Cadiz, which was guarded by only 5 British ships under the command of Sir John Orde; and the combined French and Spanish fleets, amounting to 18 ships of the line and 10 frigates, with 10,000 troops on board, sailed for the West Indies. Lord Nelson, after beating about in the Mediterranean in the teeth of a foul wind, passed the Straits of Gibraltar on the 5th May, and with only 10 sail of the line and 3 frigates boldly followed in pursuit. On the 4th June he arrived at Barbadoes, but the enemy, reinforced by two more ships, had, in obedience to their orders to return to Europe, sailed from Martinique on the 28th May. On the 13th June Nelson received intelligence of this extraordinary movement, and feeling sure that no fleet would retreat before another not half its force without having some ulterior combination in view, he went off in pursuit, and despatched several fast-sailing craft to put the British Government on its guard. One of these reached London on the 9th July, and the Admiralty instantly sent orders to Admiral Stirling to leave his station off Rochefort, and join Sir Robert Calder off Ferrol, to cruise off Finisterre for Villeneuve.

Scarcely had this junction been effected when (July 22) the Franco-Spanish fleet hove in sight. It consisted of twenty sail of the line, a 50-gun ship, and 7 frigates. Sir Robert Calder's fleet numbered but 15 sail of the line, 2 frigates, a lugger, and a cutter; but no sooner did Villeneuve appear than he threw out the signal for action, which, however, was delayed by light airs and a thick fog. In the afternoon the *Sirius* frigate, Captain William Prowse, made an attempt to board the *Siréne*, Spanish galleon, and at five the Spanish ships opened fire. By six the action was pretty general, but the fog was so thick that it was impossible to distinguish any object more than a ship's length a-head, and the firing was distant and not very effective. Nevertheless, the Spanish *Firma*, of 78 guns, and *San Rafael*, of 80 guns, were forced to strike, and the *Espana* and the French *Atlas* would also have fallen into our hands had they not been rescued by their comrades. At

8·25 P.M., the British ships being much scattered, Sir Robert Calder made the signal to discontinue the action, and an hour later the firing ceased. The action was not renewed on the following day, and Villeneuve, after leaving three disabled ships at Vigo, reached Ferrol on the 2d August. Napoleon sent peremptory orders that he should, at all risks, effect a junction with the Brest fleet by the 21st; but Sir Robert Calder had by this time been reinforced to 20 sail, and Villeneuve, in no humour for another encounter, tacked and made sail for Cadiz.

Napoleon was transported with rage at the failure of his plans, and accused Villeneuve of "excessive pusillanimity;" whereas that much-abused admiral had only acted up to his instructions in trying to avoid an engagement, and bring his fleet fresh and entire into the English Channel. On the other hand, so little was Sir Robert Calder's service appreciated by the public, who were ignorant of their real danger, that he found himself compelled to demand a court-martial. The charge brought against him was that he did not do his utmost to renew the battle on the 24th. The British Admiral had, indeed, had every reason to avoid an encounter unless it was forced upon him; for in addition to having a superior fleet in front of him, there lay at Ferrol and Rochefort, within a few hours' sail, a second fleet of 20 sail of the line. This circumstance, however, does not appear to have been regarded as sufficiently exculpatory, and Sir Robert was severely reprimanded.

Nelson, meanwhile, had recrossed the Atlantic, and after cruising along the Spanish and French coasts without meeting the enemy, arrived (July 17) at Portsmouth. From Portsmouth he proceeded to Merton (where he had bought a small estate), to recruit his health, which was dreadfully shattered. He had scarcely been on shore for two years, and required nursing; but he forgot all about his health when he heard that Villeneuve had returned to Europe. Captain Blackwood brought the news home. On his way to the Admiralty he called at Merton. It was but four o'clock in the morning—an early autumn morning (September 1)—but Nelson was already up and dressed. He instantly divined the nature of Blackwood's despatches. "I am sure you bring news of the French and Spanish fleets; I shall have to beat them yet. Depend on it, Blackwood," he repeatedly said, "I shall yet give Monsieur Villeneuve a drubbing." His services were eagerly accepted by Government, and in another fortnight he embarked on board the *Victory* at Portsmouth. The scene which took place there at his departure baffles all description. The whole town turned out to catch a glimpse of the slender little figure, one-eyed and one-armed, whose name was the bulwark of our country, and synonymous with victory. Women loved him for the tenderness of his heart; men respected him as the greatest naval hero the world had ever produced. As he passed along the densely-crowded streets, ancient mariners, who had fought under Hawke and Rodney, stood hat in hand, in reverence to a greater warrior than any under whom they had served. Many were moved to tears; others knelt down on the beach, and implored the blessing of Heaven on his head. The soldiers who had been stationed along the route could not prevent the people from pressing upon the great admiral. It was a triumph such as few men can boast of. Nelson himself was moved to tears of gratitude. "I had their hurrahs before," he said, turning to Captain Hardy; "I have their hearts now."

Sunday the 15th September the *Victory* sailed from Portsmouth, and on the 1st October arrived off Cadiz. The British fleet was inferior to Villeneuve's by several sail; but such was the terror of Nelson's name, that the French Admiral hesitated to put to sea, in spite of Napoleon's positive orders and the threatened scarcity of provisions. At length, by appearing to detach part of his fleet, Nelson overcame Villeneuve's irresolution, and on the 19th and 20th October the combined fleet ventured out. It consisted of 33 sail of the line and 7 frigates; the British fleet of 27 sail of the line and 6 frigates. On the morning of the memorable 21st October, the two fleets were in sight of each other, about twelve miles apart, Cape Trafalgar being distant from the *Victory* twenty-one miles. The wind, from two points to the northward of west, was light, accompanied by a heavy ground swell. At 6.40 A.M. Nelson made the signals to form in order of sailing, to prepare for battle, and to bear up. He himself led the weather division, of 12 ships, in the *Victory;* Collingwood led the lee division, of 15 ships, in the *Royal Sovereign.* The near approach of the British fleet, which was now bearing up to the eastward under all sail, rendered an action unavoidable, and at 8.30 A.M. Villeneuve made the signal for his ships to wear and form a line in close order on the larboard tack, so as to bring Cadiz on his lee bow, and facilitate his escape to that port, if necessary; but the wind was so light, and the swell so heavy, that it was ten o'clock before this movement was performed, and even then the line was not straight, but curved or crescent-like, and instead of the ships being in line a-head, some were to leeward and others to windward of their proper stations. Villeneuve's fleet lay north and south in a curved line, extending nearly five miles.

Nelson's plan of attack was very simple. His fleet was in two lines, with an advanced squadron of eight of the swiftest sailing two-deckers. Collingwood, who led the second line, was to break through the enemy about the twelfth ship from their rear; Nelson himself was to lead through their centre; and the advanced squadron was to cut their van. Nelson frequently explained to his captains his plan of attack, and invariably added this summary note, that in case signals could not be seen or clearly understood, no captain could do wrong if he placed his ship alongside an enemy. It was one of the most momentous hours in the world's history, and both admirals felt equally confident of success. When writing home on the 6th, Nelson said, "I really believe that the country will soon be put to some new expense on my account, either a monument, or a new pension and honours;" and Villeneuve wrote to the French Minister of Marine, that "Napoleon would soon be satisfied, and might reckon on the most splendid success." Still, the enterprising French Admiral began to feel doubtful when he looked on the majestic advance of the British fleet. "These men deserve success," he said to himself: and no one can read the history of his signals on this memorable day, without seeing that he was morally vanquished before a shot was fired.

The wind was so light that, although the British ships had studding-sails set on both sides, they made little more progress than two knots an hour. Between eleven and twelve it occurred to Nelson that the enemy might run for the port of Cadiz, which was at no great distance under their lee, and he signalled to Collingwood, "I intend to pass through the van of the enemy's line to prevent him from getting into Cadiz." Another thing: the shoals of San Pedro and Trafalgar were under the lee of both fleets, so he made the signal for the British fleet to prepare to anchor at the close of the day. This done, he fell to pacing the poop with Captain Blackwood. Suddenly another thought seemed to strike him, and he remarked that he must give the fleet something by way of a fillip. "Suppose we telegraph," he said, after musing a while, "that Nelson expects every man to do his duty?" Blackwood suggested "England." "Certainly, certainly," cried Nelson, rapturously catching at the idea; and at 11.40 A.M. up went to the *Victory's* mizzen topgallant-mast-head the first flag of the celebrated telegraphic message— "ENGLAND EXPECTS THAT EVERY MAN WILL DO HIS DUTY." No sooner were the words communicated to the men at the guns than there burst forth from every ship in the fleet three cheers that gave presage of coming victory.

As Nelson was making more for the van of the enemy than he had originally intended, and was going in a slanting direction, Collingwood was the first to come into action. At 11.50 A.M. the French *Fougeux* fired a shot at the *Royal Sovereign* to try the range of her guns. The British ship hoisted her colours, which were saluted by a heavy fire from the Spanish *Santa Anna* and the ships nearest her. At ten past noon, having reached a position under the stern of the *Santa Anna*, a huge ship of 112 guns, the *Royal Sovereign* fired into her with guns double-shotted; and with such precision, the Spanish officers afterwards acknowledged, that one broadside killed or wounded nearly 400 of their crew. She gave the *Fougeux* her starboard broadside at the same time, but, as the distance was greater, with much less effect. "Rotherham!" cried Collingwood to his captain, after the broadsides were fired, "what would Nelson give to be here?" By a curious coincidence Nelson was just at that moment observing to Captain Hardy, "See how that noble fellow Collingwood carries his ship into action!" The *Royal Sovereign* had far outsailed the rest, and for full fifteen minutes was the only British ship engaged with the enemy. Ranged alongside of her was the huge *Santa Anna*, the flag-ship of Admiral Alava, and so close that the yards were locked and the guns were almost muzzle to muzzle. The *Royal Sovereign*, alone, sustained the fire of this huge vessel, as well as of four others that came to her aid. The *Fougeux* bore up and raked her astern; the *San Leandro* wore and raked her across the bows; the Spanish *San Justo* and the French *Indomptable* were on her starboard bow and quarter, at a distance of less than 300 yards. So incessant was the fire kept up by the five Franco-Spanish ships, that the people of the *Royal Sovereign* frequently saw the balls come in contact with each other. At length the enemy became aware of the injury they were sustaining by their own cross fire, and as the headmost ships of the British lee line (Collingwood's) were fast approaching, they left the *Royal Sovereign* and the *Santa Anna* to settle it between themselves—100 guns to 112. Good gunnery more than counterbalanced the odds. In a few minutes the *Santa Anna* lost her mizzen topmast; at 1.20 P.M. her three masts fell over the side, and at two o'clock she struck her colours. But she had fought well; her shot had sent the *Royal Sovereign's* mainmast toppling over the side, and left her foremast in a falling state.

In the meantime the *Victory* was advancing at the head of the weather line. Nelson was extremely anxious to engage Villeneuve, but as the enemy hoisted no colours until they were required to strike, the French Commander-in-chief could not be made out. There, however, right in front, lay his old acquaintance the *Santissima Trinidad*, and Nelson, correctly divining that Villeneuve was at no great distance, ordered the *Victory* to be steered towards the bows of the huge four-decker, which carried 130 guns and the flag of Rear-admiral Cisneros. The *Victory* had her studding sails set on both sides, but the wind was so light that she was scarcely going a knot and a half an hour through the water. At twenty past noon (ten minutes after the *Royal Sovereign* passed under the stern of the *Santa Anna*) the *Bucentaure*, of 80 guns, the flag-ship of Admiral Villeneuve, fired a shot at the *Victory*. It fell short. Two or three minutes and another shot was fired, and fell alongside. The *Victory* was then about a mile and a quarter distant from the *Bucentaure*. The fifth shot passed through the *Victory's* maintopgallantsail. A minute or two of awful silence, and then, as if by a signal from the French Admiral, the whole of the enemy's van opened upon the *Victory* such a discharge as has seldom been directed at a single ship. This had not continued long when a round shot killed Mr. Scott, Nelson's public secretary, as he was conversing with Captain Hardy. Captain Adair of the Marines, with the help of a sailor, endeavoured to remove the body from Nelson's sight, as he had a great regard for Mr. Scott, but Nelson anxiously asked—"Is that poor Scott that is gone? Poor fellow!" The *Victory* was now within 500 or 600 yards of the enemy's line; her mizzen topmast was shot away, and immediately afterwards her wheel, and she had to be steered by the relieving tackle below. The cannon shot was plunging through the ship, and sweeping the decks in all directions. Two minutes after the wheel was knocked to pieces, a double-headed shot killed eight marines on the poop and wounded several others, and at Nelson's request Captain Adair ordered his men to lie down until they could be employed. In another moment a shot came through the thickness of four hammocks near the larboard chesstree, carried away part of the larboard quarter of the launch as she lay on the booms, struck the forebrace bits on the quarter-deck, and passed between Nelson and Captain Hardy, who were then conversing; a splinter from the bits bruised Captain Hardy's left foot and tore the buckle from his shoe. The friends instantly stopped and looked uneasily at each other, each fearing the other was wounded, and then Nelson smiled—his battle smile—and remarked to Hardy that it was too warm work to last.

As yet the *Victory* had not fired a shot, and she had fifty men killed and wounded, and the sails were torn to ribbons. But her turn was now come. At one P.M. her helm was put a-port, and she passed close to the larboard side of the *Bucentaure;* so close, that the large French ensign trailing at the *Bucentaure's* peak, had there been wind enough to blow it out, might easily have been snatched by the crew of the *Victory*. The 68-pounder carronade on the larboard side of the *Victory's* forecastle contained its usual charge of one round shot and a keg filled with 500 musket balls, and this murderous weapon was discharged right into the cabin window of the *Bucentaure;* and as the *Victory* slowly moved ahead, every gun of the remaining fifty upon her broadside, all double and some of them treble-shotted, was deliberately discharged in the same raking manner. So terrible was the broadside that the French flagship was observed to heel over on receiving it, and it was afterwards ascertained that it struck down 400 of her men and dismounted 20 of her guns. The *Victory* then hauled round close under the stern of the *Bucentaure*, intending to bring her to action to leeward, but came into collision with the *Redoutable*. The two ships engaged with their yard-arms locked, while the *Victory's* larboard guns played upon the *Bucentaure* and the *Santissima Trinidada;* and thus the British flagship continued to engage three antagonists single-handed, until Captain Harvey came up to her assistance in the "grand old *Téméraire.*"

In a few minutes the battle was at its height. The fire from the *Redoutable's* ports was soon silenced, but the marksmen in her tops still kept up a deadly discharge, and erelong a shot from one of them pierced Nelson with a mortal wound, as he was pacing with Captain Hardy the quarter-deck of the *Victory*. The ball entered his left shoulder through the strap of his epaulette, and passing downwards lodged in his spine. Captain Hardy was just about to turn to walk aft when he observed Nelson falling on his knees, with his hand touching the deck, almost on the same spot on which his secretary, Mr. Scott, had received his death wound.

"They have done for me at last, Hardy," said the dying admiral.

"I hope not."

"Yes, my backbone is shot through."

Sergeant Secker, of the Marines, and two seamen carried him down to the cockpit, and laid him on a purser's bed. His fall signed the death-warrant of every soul in the mizzen-top of the *Redoutable;* but nothing could save Nelson, who felt that his life's-blood was ebbing fast. He insisted that the surgeon should attend to the others who were wounded. "For me," he said, "you can do nothing."

The battle continued with unabated fury, the French and Spaniards fighting as they never fought before, and the British exerting all their skill, strong in the *prestige* of victory. At three, ten ships had surrendered. As often as a ship struck, the crew of the *Victory* hurrahed; and at every hurrah an expression of joy gleamed in the eyes of the dying hero. At length the *Redoutable* was carried by boarding by the *Téméraire*, and the *Santissima Trinidada* yielded to the *Prince*. Nelson lived long enough to know that a glorious victory had been gained, and at half-past four he expired without a groan, frequently murmuring, "Thank God, I have done my duty."

When night fell the victory was complete. Eighteen prizes and 20,000 prisoners were in the hands of the victors, whose losses were 1690 killed and wounded. Admiral Gravina escaped to Cadiz with nine sail. Admiral Dumanoir made off with four French ships; but on the 4th November, off Cape Ortegal, he was brought to action by Sir Richard Strachan, who captured his whole squadron. Unfortunately, Nelson's dying order to anchor could not be attended to, and most of the prizes foundered or were wrecked in the heavy gale on the 22d. Only four were brought to Gibraltar in safety. The joy which the country felt at the unprecedented victory was damped by the death of Nelson, who had lived in the hearts of the people. A grave in St. Paul's received the body of the great English sailor.

In the meantime Napoleon had been once more laying the Continent at his feet. Sir Robert Calder's action of the 22d July showed him in a moment that his plans for the invasion of Britain were for ever frustrated, and without wasting a moment in useless regrets, he set about carrying the war from the banks of the Thames to the banks of the Danube. The day before the battle of Trafalgar, the Austrian General Mack surrendered at Ulm (Oct. 20); and the defeat of the Austrians and Russians at Austerlitz (Dec. 2) finally broke the power of the coalition. The peace of Presburg soon followed (Dec. 27).

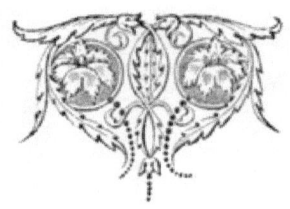

CHAPTER V.—THE GREAT FRENCH WAR.

FROM TRAFALGAR TO ROLIÇA. — 1806-1807.

Second Capture of the Cape of Good Hope—Sir Home Popham at Buenos Ayres—Sir John Duckworth's victory at St. Domingo—Maida—Capture of Monte Video by Sir Samuel Achmuty—Sir John Duckworth forces the Dardanelles—Egypt—General Whitelock capitulates at Buenos Ayres—Surrender of the Danish fleet to Britain.

THE peace of Presburg seemed to have finally subjected the Continent to France. Austria was utterly crushed; the might of Russia was humbled; and Prussia was bribed by the gift of Hanover, which she accepted in exchange for some of her southern possessions ceded to France and Bavaria. Britain alone remained unconquered and unconquerable, and now that she was once and for ever freed from the dread of invasion—for new navies must be built, and a new race of seamen reared before she could again be met on her own element—she began to turn her attention to the enlargement of her colonial empire. The Cape—surrendered to the Dutch by the peace of Amiens—was the first seat of operations, as being necessary to secure the safety of our Indian Empire.

On the 4th January, 1806, the expedition anchored in Table Bay. The naval part of it was under the command of Captain Sir Home Popham. The military part, consisting of about 5000 troops, was under the command of Sir David Baird, the hero of Seringapatam. On the 6th and 7th the landing was effected, and on the 8th General Baird resolved to make the grand attack. The Dutch were drawn up in two lines on a level sandy area between the mountains and the shore. Their strength was 5000 men, and their position was defended by 23 cannon. General Baird divided his troops into two columns, and directed the first towards the right, while the Highland brigade (71st, 72d, 93d) advanced directly on the enemy. The Dutch seemed determined to maintain their post, and opened a smart fire of grape, round shot, and canister, which brought down more than 100 of the advancing Highlanders; but before they could reload, their " formidable array," says Captain Brenton, " was almost instantly borne down by the impetuosity of our troops, headed by Brigadier-general Fergusson. The charge of our infantry was irresistible, and the enemy fled with precipitation, losing in action about 700 men." After completely routing the enemy, and pursuing them for three miles under a burning sun, the Highlanders were ordered to halt, and the first brigade to continue the pursuit. Notwithstanding every one was suffering extreme fatigue from the excessive heat of the sun, no sooner had the Highlanders halted than the grenadier company of the 72d requested the pipers to play them "Cabar Fey," the gathering tune of the regiment, to which they danced a Highland reel, to the utter astonishment of the 59th regiment, which was close in their rear. This smart affair decided the fate of the colony. In a short time a flag of truce came from the Dutch General Janssens, announcing a desire to capitulate; and on the 18th the colony was finally surrendered to the British Crown.

The facility of this conquest inspired Sir Home Popham with the idea that an effective blow might be struck at the Spanish settlements on the Rio de la Plata; and, instead of obeying his orders, and sending on to India all the troops that could be spared from the Cape, he undertook an entirely unauthorised expedition against Buenos Ayres. His forces consisted of the 71st Highlanders, a foreign detachment from the Cape, 200 men from St. Helena, and a party of the Royal Artillery, under the command of General Beresford. The Plata was made on the 10th June, 1806, and on the 25th the troops landed without opposition. The Spaniards were posted behind a morass, and being well supplied with artillery, might easily have offered an effectual opposition; but their whole force gave way before the advance of the 71st. After firing a few shots, they abandoned four cannon, and fled direct to Buenos Ayres, pursued by our people. The result of this affair was that the British colours were hoisted on the walls of Buenos Ayres (June 28); and the strange spectacle was witnessed of a city of 70,000 inhabitants yielding on capitulation to a handful of redcoats. The Spaniards, however, recovered from their panic, and pursued our people so hard that, on the 12th August, being cut off from all supplies and provisions, and seeing no prospect of relief, the British were forced to capitulate. For this unauthorised expedition Sir Home Popham was afterwards tried by court-martial, and severely reprimanded.

The naval war was now practically at an end, and the British flag rode triumphant on every sea; but the Brest fleet, of 11 sail of the line, had not been involved in the catastrophe of Trafalgar, and Napoleon hoped it might be employed with effect against the more remote of the British colonies. One division, consisting of 5 ships, 2 frigates, and a corvette, was sent to St. Domingo, under Admiral Leisseignes. Sir John Duckworth, with 7 ships, 2 frigates, and 2 sloops, pursued him across the Atlantic, and on the 6th February found him lying at anchor off the town of St. Domingo. The French Admiral slipped his cables, and made sail to escape, but without success. At 10 A.M. Sir John Duckworth, in the *Superb*, a 74, engaged the *Alexandre*, of 80 guns; and a few minutes later the *Northumberland*, another 74, the flagship of Rear-admiral Cochrane, gallantly engaged the *Impérial*. This, the flagship of Admiral Leisseignes, was probably the largest vessel then afloat, mounting, as she did, 130 guns, and carrying 1200 men. The other ships singled out opponents, and the action became general, the hostile squadrons running before the wind at the rate of seven knots an hour. By eleven o'clock the *Alexandre* was a wreck, and surrendered. The *Brave* and the *Jupiter* followed suit, and the *Impérial*, worried by the *Northumberland*, the *Superb*, and the *Canopus*, hauled down her colours. The *Diomède* ran on shore and lost her masts; and thus, in less than two hours, the five line-of-battle ships were taken or driven on shore, the frigates alone escaping. Our casualties were 74 killed and 264 wounded; the *Impérial* alone is said to have lost 500 before she surrendered. The other division, under Admiral Villaumez, was scarcely more fortunate. One of his frigates sailed to the Cape of Good Hope, not knowing of its surrender, and was captured by a British squadron lying there. Villaumez sailed to the coasts of

America, where one of his ships, a 74, was driven ashore in a gale, and destroyed by the British, who blockaded three others of the squadron until the crews were obliged to destroy two of them. Only one ship returned in safety. Among many minor disasters which happened to the French naval marine during this year, was the capture of Admiral Linois, with two ships, by Sir John Borlase Warren; and the capture of four out of a squadron of five frigates, bound for the West Indies, by Sir Samuel Hood. The Rochefort fleet alone escaped the vigilance of the British squadrons, and after a cruise of six months returned safe to port.

A few days after the ratification of the peace of Presburg, Napoleon issued a proclamation declaring that "the dynasty of Naples had ceased to reign." An Imperial decree (April 14) raised his brother Joseph to the vacant throne, and the Neapolitan court fled into Sicily. Joseph was supported by 50,000 French bayonets, but Gaeta still held out, and the Calabrian peasants rose in furious revolt. At the earnest solicitation of the exiled Queen, Major-general Sir John Stuart, the British commander in Sicily, determined on an expedition to Calabria, in support of the loyal peasantry; and on the 1st of July he landed in the Bay of St. Euphemia. On the 3d he heard that the French General Regnier was advancing from Reggio, with the intention of giving him battle.

The armies met (July 6, 1806) near the little town of Maida. Regnier had 8000 bayonets; Stuart but 4795. Regnier was posted on the heights. His front was defended by the Amato, a river with muddy and marshy banks, but fordable; and his flanks were protected by thick underwood and laurel groves. Stuart drew up his army with the head of the bay in his rear. Before him stretched a broad and extensive valley, level in the centre, and bounded on both sides by high, wooded hills. It was a bright, clear morning, and the Calabrian reapers were busy in the cornfields.

Regnier was either over-confident in his superior numbers, or afraid that the British might turn his left flank, and place him between them and the sea, where lay the squadron of Sir Sidney Smith. However that may be, he quitted his advantageous position on the hills, and crossing the Amato by fords, advanced into the open plains. This arrangement had at least one advantage, that his dragoons—a force in which Stuart was entirely deficient—could now act with proper effect. Regnier drew up his troops in two parallel lines of equal numbers, with artillery and cavalry on both flanks, and with field pieces placed in different parts of the line. He marched with colours flying and bands playing; the British marched parallel to the sea-shore, in close columns of subdivisions. When the advance commenced, the distance between the armies was nearly three miles. The ground was perfectly level, only intersected by drains to carry off the water in the rainy season, but not so large as to intercept the advance of the field-pieces.

When the two armies were approaching within striking distance, the French were halted by the sound of trumpet, and the British deployed into line. Like their enemies, the British were in two lines; the first composed of the Light Brigade—a provisional battalion formed from our corps in Sicily—on the right, the 78th Highlanders in the centre, and the 81st on the left. The French opened the ball with their field-pieces, but contrary to the usual practice of the French artillery, with little effect, most of their shot passing over the first line, and not reaching the second. The British, on the contrary, made excellent practice, every shot carrying off a file of the enemy's men. Then, when the line came within reach of musketry, the skirmishers were thrown out. Ours, a party of Corsican Rangers, did not behave well. At the first fire of the French *tirailleurs* they fled in great haste, and would have been roughly handled but for the light company of the 20th, who rushed forward, and drove back the party which had advanced on the Corsicans.

In a few minutes the hostile lines came within charge distance, and the field resounded with volleys of musketry. The Light Brigade and the left of the French kept up a close and destructive fire, but all at once, as stated in the despatch, this was suspended " as if by mutual agreement, and in close, compact order, and with awful silence, they advanced toward each other till their bayonets began to cross. At this momentous crisis the enemy became appalled; they broke and endeavoured to fly, but it was too late. They were overtaken with most dreadful slaughter." Nor was it otherwise in the centre and left. When at 300 yards, says General Stewart of Garth, who was present on this part of the field as major of the 78th Highlanders, "the enemy seemed to hesitate, halted, and fired a volley. Our line also halted, and instantly returned the salute, and when the men had reloaded, a second volley was thrown in. The precision with which these two volleys were fired, and their effect, was quite remarkable. When the clearing off of the smoke (there was hardly a breath of wind to dispel it) enabled me to see the French line, the breaks and vacancies caused by the men who had fallen by the fire appeared like a paling, of which parts had been thrown down or broken. On our side it was so different, that, glancing along the rear of my regiment, I counted only fourteen who had fallen from the enemy's fire. As soon as the smoke had cleared off, so that the enemy could be seen, the line advanced at full charge. The enemy, with seeming resolution to stand the shock, kept perfectly steady, till, apparently intimidated by the advance, equally rapid and firm, of an enemy, too, who, they were taught to believe, would fly before them, their hearts failed, and they faced to the right about, and fled with speed, but not in confusion. When they approached within a short distance of their second line, they halted, fronted, and opened a fire of musketry." The 78th again advanced, but the French would not stand the shock, and gave way in greater confusion than at first.

The French cavalry attempted to retrieve the fortune of the day, but could not bring their horses to the charge. Regnier now tried to turn the British left flank. "For this purpose he brought forward some battalions, by an oblique movement, to the British left, and gained so much on the flank that the second line (the grenadier battalion and the 27th regiment, which now came up under General Cole) could not form the line in continuation. Throwing back their left, therefore, they formed an angle of about sixty degrees to the front line, and in this position opened a most admirably directed and destructive fire, which quickly drove back the enemy with great loss."

As a last attempt, Regnier made another desperate push to take our line in flank on the left; but the 20th regiment—which had that morning disembarked from Sicily, and just at this moment reached the field—marched up and formed on the left, nearly at right angles to General Cole's brigade. This reinforcement seemed to destroy all further hopes on the part of the enemy, who lost confidence, and gave way at all points, throwing away their arms and accoutrements to assist them in their flight. Neither the light troops nor the loosely-clad Highlanders could overtake them, and General Stewart had no cavalry to press the pursuit. The loss of the French was almost unprecedented. They left 1300 killed and 1100 severely wounded on the field of battle; and this calculation does not take account of the less severely wounded who had retired to the rear. The loss of the British was 45 killed and 280 wounded.

The battle of Maida, like the battle of Alexandria, is especially memorable because of its moral effect in raising the self-confidence of the British soldiery, and showing them that they were more than equal to the veteran troops of France. Its immediate results were not, however, very important. The French were, for a time, expelled from Calabria, but the fall of Gaeta released their main army under Massena; the British, exposed to the attack of overwhelming numbers, retired to Sicily, and the Calabrian insurrection was suppressed with great cruelty.

Prussia grew restless under her unnatural alliance with France, and when it became known that Napoleon had offered to restore Hanover to Britain, the popular excitement forced the government to declare war. Prussia was promised help from Great Britain, Sweden, and Russia, but before her allies were ready to assist her, her power was destroyed on the field of Jena and Auerstadt (October 14). Napoleon then proceeded against the advancing Russians, and endeavoured to cut off their retreat, but the battles of Pultusk and Golymin (December 26) proved indecisive, and he took up his winter quarters at Warsaw.

Next year (1807) the campaign was commenced by the Russians, who thought to cut off the French left under Bernadotte and Ney. In the bloody battle of Eylau (February 8) the Russians lost 25,000 men, and the French 30,000, besides twelve eagles. The battle of Friedland (June 14) dissolved the confederacy against France, and resulted in the Treaty of Tilsit (June 25). The French Emperor and the Russian Czar divided the world between them; Russia to be master of the East, and France of the West, while both were to join in hostility against this country, and "to summon the three courts of Stockholm, Copenhagen, and Lisbon to declare war against Great Britain."

Though Sir Home Popham was reprimanded for his unauthorised attack on Buenos Ayres, the war in South America was very popular with the public, and Sir Samuel Achmuty was sent out with a fresh force of 3000 men. His operations were directed against Monte Video. A force of 6000 Spaniards endeavoured to oppose his landing, but they were defeated with the loss of a fourth of their number, and the town was taken by assault (February 2, 1807).

This success was highly inspiriting, and orders were sent to General Whitelocke, who now commanded in those parts, to attempt the recovery of Buenos Ayres. The force under his orders numbered 7822 rank and file, including 150 mounted dragoons, with 18 guns. The resistance the Spaniards made outside the walls was easily overcome, and the morning of the 5th July was fixed for the assault. The army was broken up into divisions, and each division was to proceed along the street directly in its front, till it arrived at the last square of houses next the Rio de la Plata. At half-past six in the morning the troops advanced swiftly to the various points assigned to them. Not a sound was heard in Buenos Ayres but the heavy tramp of the invaders and the rumbling of their artillery. "At length," say the records of the 88th Connaught Rangers, a regiment which suffered very severely in this disastrous affair, "a few detached shots seemed to give a pre-arranged signal, at which the entire population of a vast town was to burst from its concealment; and in an instant the flat roofs of the houses swarmed with a mass of musketeers, who poured a deadly and almost unerring aim upon the British soldiers." The British now became aware of the formidable nature of street-fighting, of which Saragossa afterwards furnished so memorable an example. A force of 15,000 men, with 200 cannon, stationed on the flat roofs of the houses, and occupying every point of vantage in the barricaded streets, were great obstacles to progress, and the British troops were shot down without being able to make any adequate return, or cooped up in houses and squares and forced to surrender. When night fell Whitelocke found himself in possession of the great square and the Residentia; but these advantages had cost him 2500 men, and at the instance of the Spanish general, a capitulation was signed (July 7), by which all British prisoners were restored, on condition of the withdrawal of the expedition. As the hope of the public had been high, so its indignation was vehement, and Whitelocke was brought to court-martial and cashiered.

Russia and Turkey had come to blows about the removal, at the instigation of the French Ambassador Sebastiani, of the Hospodars of Wallachia and Moldavia (who by the existing treaties were not to be removed without the consent of Russia), and their replacement by successors in the interest of France; and as Russia was then hard pressed by Napoleon in Poland, an application was preferred to the British Cabinet to make a naval diversion against Constantinople. Accordingly, Sir John Duckworth was instructed to force the passage of the Dardanelles, and threaten the Ottoman capital. His force consisted of 8 sail of the line and 4 frigates. The passage was effected with little loss, and a Turkish squadron in the Sea of Marmora was destroyed by Sir Sidney Smith. Had Constantinople been immediately attacked nothing could have saved it, but the gallant admiral allowed himself to be amused by a show of negotiation, while the whole population laboured at the defences. In a week the Turks had 1000 guns mounted, and a large fleet of 12 sail of the line and 100 gun-boats equipped for the defence of the harbour. Sir John Duckworth resolved to retreat while retreat was still in his power, and (March 3, 1807) the fleet weighed and put down the strait, running the gauntlet of the batteries, which had been repaired and strengthened. The ships suffered severely from the tremendous cannonade of the Turks, some of them being struck with stone shot weighing 800 lbs., and measuring 26 inches in diameter. The squadron reached Tenedos with the loss of 250 men. Scarcely had it taken up its anchorage when a Russian squadron came in sight; the admiral suggested a return, but Sir John Duckworth declined, curtly remarking that "where a British squadron had failed no other was likely to succeed."

Not more successful was a descent on Egypt, undertaken to deprive the Turks of those places which they had received from us six years before. A small expedition sailed from Sicily on the 6th March. The expedition consisted of the 20th Light Dragoons, 31st, 35th, 78th Highlanders, De Rolle's regiment, and the corps of Chasseurs Britanniques. It was under the command of Major-general Mackenzie Fraser, who was accompanied by Major-general Wauchope, and Brigadier-generals the Honourable William Stewart and the Honourable Robert Meade. The naval portion of the expedition, having the troops and transports under convoy, consisted of the *Tiger*, 74 guns, Captain

Hallowell, the *Apollo*, 38 guns, Captain Fellowes, and the *Wizard* sloop-of-war.

Bad weather was encountered on the passage. The *Apollo* and nineteen transports parted company; and when the commodore made the Arab's Tower, off Alexandria, on the 15th, he had only fourteen sail under his convoy. Uncertain how to act with his force so much reduced, the general ordered the transports to stand out to sea, so as not to show themselves within sight of the land, while Captain Hallowell ran in to obtain information. Major Misset, the British Resident, urged him to land immediately, as he knew, he said, that the inhabitants were favourably disposed to the British, and hated the French and Turks. The garrison, he added, did not exceed 500 men. The transports were therefore signalled to stand close in shore, and the squadron came to anchor in the western harbour. On the 17th and 18th, the troops were landed, to the number of about 1000 bayonets, and a summons was sent to the governor of Alexandria to deliver up the fortress. The summons being declined, the general and his force moved forward the same evening, and stormed all the advanced works of the enemy, carrying the whole of the western lines and forts, taking a considerable quantity of artillery, and driving out the Turks. Next morning, General Fraser moved eastward beyond Pompey's Pillar, and took up a position on the ground which our gallant army had occupied in 1801. He then summoned the town, and the governor, seeing the white sails of the *Apollo*, and of the nineteen transports which had parted company in the gale, dotting the horizon, and knowing that the British general would soon receive reinforcements with which he could not expect to cope, surrendered the same day. In the evening the *Apollo* and the nineteen transports anchored in Aboukir Bay, where, on the 22d, they were joined by Duckworth and the fleet from the Dardanelles.

Twice within a few years had our arms been brilliantly successful in Egypt. Twice had the Union Jack been triumphantly hoisted above the ancient Græco-Egyptian city of Alexandria, with its ruins, its harbour and shipping, its domed mosques, its Cleopatra's Needle, and its Pharos jutting into the sea. But a melancholy reverse was in store! In order to the safe possession of Alexandria, it was necessary to reduce Rosetta, a considerable town, with a low wall, narrow streets, and houses built of dirty red bricks, standing five miles from a branch of the Nile, in a beautiful country, where the date, the orange, the pomegranate, and all manner of fruit-trees proper to the climate, flourish luxuriantly. On the 27th, Wauchope and Meade were detached to the assault of this place, with the 31st and the corps of Chasseurs Britanniques. "A town like Rosetta," says General Stewart, "with high houses, flat roofed, and windows like loopholes, and with streets only a few feet wide, forms a better defence to a weak enemy than a walled town which brave troops might scale in the face of strong opposition. General Wauchope, in the firmness of his own mind, slighted these defences, and, forgetting that an imbecile enemy may become formidable if placed out of danger, he marched into the town at the head of the 31st regiment, directing his course to an open space, or market-place, in the centre of the town. The streets were totally deserted. Not a sound was to be heard, nor a person seen. When they had proceeded half-way to the market-place, in an instant every house was in a blaze, from the first floor to the roof, and showers of musketry were fired from every part, while the troops were unable to return a shot with any effect. There was not a man in sight, nor had the British anything to direct their fire but the smoke and flashes from the muzzles of their opponents' guns, pointed out of the loophole windows, and over the eaves and roofs of the houses. To remain in this situation, exposed to an invisible and sheltered enemy, would only have been a sacrifice of troops. They therefore retired, with the loss of the brave General Wauchope killed, General Meade wounded, and 300 soldiers and officers killed and wounded."

Disconcerted and mortified as General Fraser was at this unexpected reverse, he decided on making a second attack, for which, indeed, there was now more necessity than ever, for famine was threatening Alexandria more and more distinctly every day. The execution of this second attack was intrusted to Brigadier-general Stewart and Colonel Oswald, with the 35th, 78th, De Rolle's, a detachment of the Royal Artillery, and a body of seamen. This force marched out of Alexandria on the 6th April, and on the 7th, after some trifling skirmishes, took possession of the fort and heights of Abûmandûr, which command the town. Rosetta was next day summoned to surrender, but the Turks, having been reinforced by a great body of kilted Albanians, who had sailed down the Nile, returned a haughty refusal. The British then took up a position between the Nile and the gate of Alexandria—for they were too few to invest the whole town—erected batteries, and opened fire, but with little effect on the strong masses of buildings. "The Turks gave themselves no concern about the fate of the inhabitants, looking upon them with the same indifference as the Dey of Algiers did on his subjects when a British Admiral threatened to bombard and blow the town about his ears. 'At that rate,' he said, 'and to save them some money, I will undertake to do it myself for half the price.'"

Day after day the siege went on, but little impression was made on the town, and there was no appearance of the reinforcement of Mamelukes which General Stewart expected from Upper Egypt. The Turks and Albanians, on the other hand, increased in numbers and boldness, and made several successful attacks on the pickets and advanced posts between Lake Etko and El Hamet, a village up the Nile about six miles above Rosetta. One of the pickets of De Rolle's regiment was completely cut off, not a man escaping.

But El Hamet itself was soon to witness a darker tragedy.

Major Vogelsang of De Rolle's was stationed there with a detachment of his regiment, and so important was the post deemed, that, on the 20th, Lieutenant-colonel Macleod of the 78th was ordered to reinforce and take the command of the position. He had with him five companies of his own regiment, two of the 35th, and a small body of cavalry. When he arrived at El Hamet, Colonel Macleod divided his small force into three bodies, proportioning the artillery and dragoons between each. One party was stationed on the banks of the Nile, one in the centre, and the third on a dry canal with a broad embankment, which ran between the Nile and Lake Etko, a distance of about two miles. All was quiet on the 20th, but next morning a flotilla of about seventy djerms (large boats) was observed descending the Nile, while numerous detached bodies of Turkish cavalry began to assemble round the British posts. With the intention of concentrating his force, and, if unable to make any effectual opposition, of retreating to the camp before Rosetta, Colonel Macleod proceeded to the post on the right, which was occupied by a company of the 35th and the grenadiers of the 78th. But concentration of the little force was out of the question, for the enemy landed from the boats, and proceeded with great rapidity against the posts in the centre and on the left, while the post on the right was surrounded by the cavalry and a body of Albanian infantry, who attacked it with great fury at all points. Colonel Macleod formed his men into a square, which for a long time resisted every effort of the enemy, who formed a circle round the position, and fired in their usual confused manner, shooting so wildly that their lead passed over the heads of the British, and struck their own men and horses on the other side. But their numbers and bravery made up for their want of discipline. With loud shrill cries of "La la ha il Allah! Vras! Vras!" ("There is no God but God! Kill! Kill!") the cavalry charged up to the very points of the bayonets, and attempted to cut down our men in the front of the square, which, incessantly assailed on all sides by the sabres, pistols, yataghans, matchlocks, and long lances of the foe, was every minute thinning in numbers and lessening in size. But the survivors fought the disastrous and disheartening fight as bravely as if they had been hewing their way to victory. Their comrades were every moment falling around them, and they knew that their own fate could not be long delayed; still they closed in upon the vacancies, and fought with the desperation of despair. Completely surrounded as they were, they could not venture to charge to any front of the square, lest they should be assailed in the rear the moment they faced about. So numerous were the assailants, that the cavalry frequently crossed and jostled each other, and impeded their own movements, as they advanced on the square, or retired from its fire; but the boldness of their attacks, however irregular, and the dexterity with which they handled the sword, proved destructive to the little band of British.

In this desperate conflict many deeds of valour were performed. Sergeant John Macrae, of the 78th Highlanders, a young man of about two-and-twenty, but of great size and unusual strength of arm, hewed down seven men with his broadsword. After the sixth man fell, he dashed out at a Turk, whom he cut down, but as he was returning to the ranks, he was killed by a blow from behind, his head being nearly cut in two by a sabre stroke. The sergeant was one of eight Macraes who fell in this fatal fight.

At length Colonel Macleod and all the officers were killed, except Captain Mackay of the 78th, who was severely wounded, and of the men, only eleven of the 78th and an equally small number of the 35th were left standing. Captain Mackay, seeing that further resistance was useless, made a desperate push to join the centre. He and the few survivors, most of them wounded, charged furiously through the enemy, and several succeeded in making good their way, but others perished in the attempt. Captain Mackay himself had nearly reached the centre, when an Arab horseman struck at his neck, and with such force as must infallibly have severed his head from his body, but for the cape of his coat and a neckcloth, both of which were unusually thick. As it was, the sabre cut to the bone, and the captain fell flat to the ground, when he was taken up and carried to the post by Sergeant Waters, the only individual who escaped unhurt.

The annihilation of the right decided the fate of the centre and left posts, of which the commanding officers, seeing that further resistance was hopeless, and desirous of saving the lives of their men, hung out a white handkerchief as a signal of surrender.

And now an extraordinary scene occurred, in the struggling and scrambling of the enemy for prisoners, who, according to the custom of the Turks, became the private property of the person who took them. In this contest for prize-money, the British soldiers were pulled and hauled about with little ceremony, till the more active of the Turks had secured their prey, after which they were marched a little distance up the river, where every Turkish soldier received payment for his prisoners at the rate of seven dollars a head. Some of the horsemen, less intent upon prize-money than their companions, amused themselves by galloping about, each with the head of a British soldier stuck on the point of his lance. The morning after the battle, the ferocious Turks exhibited, in front of the place where the British soldiers were confined, upwards of a hundred stuffed scalps, arrayed in regular order; and when the captives arrived in Cairo, they were paraded through the streets for seven hours, exposed to the scoffs and insults of the populace.

This disastrous affair at El Hamet virtually closed the campaign. Despairing of succour, either from Britain or from the discontented beys whom he had ostensibly come to aid, General Fraser quitted Alexandria, and, after an exchange of prisoners, sailed for Sicily.

Some of the captives rose to high rank among the Turks. Among those taken and reserved for slavery was Thomas Keith, a private of the 78th. This young man in after years became governor of Medina, aga of Mamelukes, and one of the greatest leaders in Mohammed's war with the Wahabees, by whom he was slain in the battle of El Ross. A drummer boy, reserved for the same fate, attained high rank in Egypt, and lived there under the name of Osman.

The secret articles of the treaty of Tilsit by some means or other became known to the British Cabinet, which learned with apprehension that Portugal, Sweden, and Denmark were to be forced to close their harbours against all British vessels, and place their fleets at the disposal of France. Napoleon, it seemed, had not given up his favourite idea—the invasion of Britain. His plan was to get possession of all the fleets of Europe, and unite them on some central point, whence an irresistible army could be poured on the British shores. Therefore, when the march of French troops to Holstein indicated that a commencement was to be made with the Danish fleet, our cabinet took the alarm; and as the government of Copenhagen was known to be far from averse to the French alliance, prompt measures were necessary. Admiral Gambier was despatched to Copenhagen, with a fleet of 25 sail of the line and about 40 smaller vessels, carrying an army of 27,000 men, under General Lord Cathcart. On the 4th of August the force appeared before Copenhagen, and a summons was sent to the city. Its terms not being complied with, the British ships and batteries opened fire (September 2). Great damage was done; 2000 persons were slain in the streets or on the ramparts, and whole quarters were laid in ashes. The stubborn valour of the Danes gave way, and a treaty was signed (September 7), by which the Danish fleet of 18 sail of the line, 15 frigates, and upwards of 30 smaller vessels, was surrendered to Britain.

CHAPTER VI.—THE PENINSULAR WAR.

ROLIÇA TO CORUNNA.—1808-1809.

Roliça—Vimiero—Sir John Moore's March into Spain—The Retreat to Corunna—Battle of Corunna—Lord Cochrane in the Basque Roads.

WE have now reached a point when the interest of the European struggle, as far as Britain is concerned, centres in the Peninsular war. Napoleon's first designs in the Peninsula were on Portugal. A secret treaty with Spain enabled him to send his troops through Spanish territory. The march of Junot to Lisbon was heralded by an ominous line in the "Moniteur," which proclaimed that "the house of Braganza had ceased to reign in Europe." The Prince-regent fled across the Atlantic, to seek in other climes "that freedom of which Europe had become unworthy." An insane quarrel was meanwhile distracting the royal house of Spain. Napoleon saw the opportunity which he had long sought. Inveigling the royal family to Bayonne, he plied them with cajolery and threats, until he succeeded in extracting from them a complete transference to himself of the crown of Spain. He then removed his brother Joseph (June 6, 1808) from Naples to Madrid, where he was upheld by French bayonets, while the Spanish royal family was sent to Valençay, a seat of Talleyrand's, in the heart of France.

These arrangements did not, however, meet with the approval of the great body of the Spanish nation. They were alike distasteful to the peasantry, animated by religious enthusiasm, and to the citizens, fired by democratic ambition. The people flew to arms, and when worsted in the field maintained a terrible guerilla warfare. In their extremity they applied to our government for help. The application was received with enthusiasm by all classes and parties, and for the first time the war against Napoleon's ambition was carried on without a dissentient voice.

Sir Arthur Wellesley, the hero of Assaye, was selected for the command of the English forces destined for the Peninsula. Sailing from the Cove of Cork, 12th July, 1808, he called at Corunna to confer with the Junta of Galicia, and upon their advice proceeded southward to effect a landing in Portugal. The bay into which the Mondego flows was selected as the place of disembarkation (August 1). Sir Arthur then marched south, holding on by the coast for ship supplies, and keeping his troops in mass, to strike a blow as near Lisbon as possible, and bring the affairs of Portugal to a crisis. Including the Portuguese, his force amounted to 13,480 infantry, 470 cavalry, and 18 guns. The French general De Laborde, whom Junot had sent forward to check his progress, had under him 5500 infantry and 500 cavalry, with 5 field-pieces. With consummate skill De Laborde had chosen his ground, the heights of Roliça, whose steep rocks were rendered more difficult to climb by the tangling growth of myrtle and arbutus. At seven in the morning (August 17) the British army moved forward to the attack in three columns. The brunt of the contest fell on the centre, 9000 strong with 12 guns, commanded by Sir Arthur in person. The French position could only be approached by narrow paths winding through deep ravines, and our columns advanced with great difficulty. The skirmishers dashed into the rugged glens, and pressed forward with ringing cheers and an incessant roll of musketry, the French gallantly disputing every inch of ground. The right of the 29th arrived first at the top, exposed to a withering fire from the enemy, who were concealed by the shrubs and stones. The leading company was destroyed, and the dead and wounded blocked the mouth of the pass ; but the regiment halted only for a moment. Colonel Lake called on his men to follow him, waved his hat, and spurred on his charger. His men answered with cheers, and struggled on to the top, but before they could deploy, some French companies, which had been cut off on the right, broke through the column, and carried with them a major and fifty or sixty other prisoners. Thus pressed, the head of the regiment fell back, but at this moment the 9th issued from the pass, led by Colonel Stewart. The 29th had already lost some 300 men in their desperate attempts to reach the plateau, but on being joined by the 9th they again pushed forward with unabated ardour, and both regiments formed on the crown of the hill. Then came the final struggle of the day. Lake and Stewart both fell. The former was pierced by seven balls, and his sergeant-major, who stood over his body, received no less than thirteen wounds. The French charged again and again, with all their wonted bravery, but they failed to destroy the two British regiments before they could be succoured, and on the approach of the 5th and Ferguson's division to turn his right, De Laborde began to retire by alternate masses, protecting his retreat by bold charges of cavalry. The French loss was 600; ours was 70 killed, 335 wounded, and 74 missing. The firing ceased a little after four o'clock, and thus ended the first fight of the war, affording an earnest of the future successes of the British arms in the Peninsula.

In a day or two the victor of Roliça sank to be a mere general of division. A ship was off the Spanish coast with Sir Harry Burrard, who had been appointed to act as second in command to Sir Hew Dalrymple, and Sir John Moore was also on his way to the Peninsula. But before the *bâton* of command had actually passed from his hands, Sir Arthur Wellesley had the satisfaction of scoring a second, and more important, victory. The armies met at Vimiero, a village about thirty miles north of Lisbon (August 21). The British force numbered 18,000 men, with 18 guns, exclusive of Trant's Portuguese. The French, 14,000 strong (1300 being cavalry), were under the command of Junot himself, who had De Laborde, Brennier, Loison, Kellerman, Solignac, and Margaron, all men of tried military ability, for divisional leaders. Junot took the offensive. He formed two principal attacks, one under Brennier against the British left, and the other under De Laborde against the British centre.

The action commenced at ten o'clock. De Laborde's skirmishers came on with all the impetuosity of their nation; the British pickets were at once driven in, and De Laborde's lines were suddenly deployed in front of the brigades of Fane and Anstruther. But Brennier had got entangled in the ravine which protected the British left. Ackland's brigade, therefore,

G

which was moving along the heights to support Bowes, Nightingale, and Ferguson on the left, halted and opened a battery against De Laborde's right. Junot issued orders to Loison to support De Laborde's attack, and to Solignac to turn the ravine in which Brennier was entangled, and fall on the left extremity of the British line. Thus supported, De Laborde's people rushed up the hill, drove in the English skirmishers, and reached the summit of the plateau; but their ranks were torn by showers of musketry, round shot, and shrapnell. They staggered under the storm, but re-forming under a green hillock, again advanced to the attack. The gallant 50th, or Black Half Hundred, so called from the colour of its facings, poured in a volley at twenty yards and then rushed on with the bayonet, and the shattered ranks were forced over the edge of the plateau. Part of the 20th Light Dragoons charged the huddled mass and completed the rout. The French artillerymen cut their traces and fled. The minor attack on Anstruther's position was repulsed by the 52d and 97th. Kellerman reinforced the assailants with a column of grenadiers. These choice troops came on at a running pace, and beat back the advanced companies of the 43d, which were stationed in the churchyard on Fane's left. But Robe's artillery and the muskets of Bowes' and Ackland's brigades crushed and disordered their ranks. "Then," says Napier, "when the narrowness of the way and the sweep of the round shot was crushing and disordering the French ranks, the 43d, rallying in one mass, went furiously down upon the very head of the column, and with a short and fierce struggle drove it back in confusion. In this fight the British regiment suffered severely, and so close was the combat that Patrick, sergeant-armourer of the 43d, and a French soldier, were found dead, still grasping their muskets, with the bayonets driven through each body from breast to back!"

The French, having completely failed in their attack on the centre, now began to fall back along the whole front. Colonel Taylor of the 20th Light Dragoons pressed the pursuit with the handful of cavalry, but was in turn charged by Margaron with his whole brigade of horsemen. Taylor was shot through the heart, and half his squadron were cut to pieces. Kellerman then threw his reserved grenadiers into a pine wood, and with Margaron's cavalry covered the retreat of the beaten masses.

The three hours' struggle in the centre was almost terminated before the attack on the left was delivered. Solignac encountered Ferguson's brigade, which closed the left of the English position, but was repulsed with the loss of 6 guns. Ferguson left the 71st and 82d to guard these pieces, and pressed on in pursuit. Just at that moment Brennier issued from the ravine. The 71st and 82d had lain down on the grass to rest, no enemy being visible, and Brennier appeared so unexpectedly that he retook the guns. His success, however, was but momentary. The two regiments retired to a little eminence, where they re-formed, and, after pouring in a heavy fire of musketry, returned to the charge with a shout, overthrew their opponents, recovered the guns, and took Brennier himself prisoner. He was wounded, and would have been bayoneted but for Corporal John Mackay of the 71st, to whom in gratitude he offered his watch, but the Highlander would not accept it. Stewart, the piper of the grenadier company of the 71st, had his thigh broken by a musket ball, but he had no thoughts of quitting the field, and, sitting on his knapsack, continued to play a stirring pibroch. For this devotion to duty he received a handsome stand of pipes from the Highland Society of Scotland. The French right was utterly broken, and Ferguson would have cut off the greater part of Solignac's division, but for Sir Harry Burrard, who had arrived on the field shortly after the commencement of the action, and now assumed the chief command. Neither would he allow Sir Arthur Wellesley to press the pursuit, although, had he done so, Junot must have lost all his artillery and several thousand stragglers. As it was, the French lost 2000 killed or wounded, 400 prisoners, 13 guns, 23 ammunition-waggons, and upwards of 20,000 cartridges. The British loss was 135 killed, 534 wounded, and 51 missing.

The result of the battle was a convention, concluded at Cintra (Aug. 23), for the evacuation of Portugal, and between the 15th and 30th September the whole French army, to the number of 22,000, sailed from the Tagus, with all their artillery, arms, and baggage, which meant the whole of the booty they had amassed by the plunder of the country. The convention was received in Britain with a burst of indignation, and Sir Hew Dalrymple lost the command of Gibraltar.

Sir Hew Dalrymple and Sir Harry Burrard having gone to England to attend the inquiry, the command in the Peninsula devolved on Sir John Moore, who pushed in a north-easterly direction from Coimbra, and entered Spain. Five Spanish armies, he was told, were waiting to unite with his small force. At Mayorga he was joined by Sir David Baird, and his army amounted to 25,580 men; but alarming tidings reached him. Napoleon had crossed the Pyrenees in person, to drive into the sea "those leopards whose hideous presence was contaminating the Peninsula." The Spanish armies had been scattered like chaff, and Napoleon had entered Madrid in triumph (Dec. 4). A force of 100,000 French was moving in four great bodies to crush Moore at a single blow. The retreat was at once commenced. The bridge of Castrogonzalo over the swollen torrent of the Esla was destroyed, and the cavalry of the Imperial guard were routed at the fords of the river by the British dragoons. On the last day of the year (1808) the French columns were concentrated at Astorga, and Napoleon looked from the hills upon the files of the English disappearing in the distance. But news of hostile designs on the part of Austria called him away from the Peninsula, and he left Soult to press the retreat.

To reach our shipping at Corunna and abandon the country by sea, without the slaughter of a useless battle with a foe whose numbers were overwhelming, was Moore's object. And now began the masterly but disastrous retreat, which has few parallels in the annals of warfare. Closely pursued by the French cavalry, and destitute of every necessary, the army struggled for 250 miles through the snow-drifts of the Galician mountains, without the loss of a single standard or piece of cannon. Their sufferings were intense. While the rear-guard of cavalry kept the enemy in check, the jaded, famished, worn-out infantry pushed on, hopeless, heartless, and in rags, leaving terrible traces of their route by the wayside on the snow—dead or dying men, women, children, horses, and mules. "I looked round," says an officer, "when we had gained the highest point of these slippery precipices, and saw the rear of the army winding along the narrow road. I saw the way marked by the wretched people, who lay on all sides expiring from fatigue and the severity of the cold; their bodies reddened in spots the white surface of the ground." The disappointment and chagrin of the soldiers knew no bounds. They blamed the general for the tardiness of his former advance and the rapidity of his present retreat. They cursed the Spaniards, who, they had been told, were to be their fellow-soldiers in the field and their friends and brothers in quarters, and whose coldness and inhospitality had caused them much privation and suffering which might otherwise have been spared. The first ebullition of their rage naturally broke out against the unfortunate people, whom they unreasonably supposed to be the authors of their disappointment and disgrace. Their turbulence and depredations rose to a pitch hitherto unheard of in a British army. Worn out with fatigue, benumbed with cold, and frequently without food, they were driven to the madness of despair, and seemed utterly reckless of life. Discipline was gone; the word of command was lost in the cry of plunder and vengeance. Villages and houses blazed in all directions. Stores and cellars were burst open, and the madness of intoxication was added to the madness of despair. Men were murdered, women violated, houses plundered. It was a frightful scene of misery, intoxication, and disorder. Yet the men on all occasions displayed their native courage and intrepidity. "Whenever the enemy appeared," says General Stewart, "he was met with spirit, and never, in any instance, obtained the most trifling advantage. At Lugo, where General Moore offered battle, which Soult thought proper to decline, the greatest alacrity and animation were exhibited. The lame, the sick, or the fatigued, who were lagging along, or lying on the ground seemingly unable to move, no sooner heard the firing, or were led to believe that an attack was to be made, than their misery and weakness appeared instantly to vanish. At the slightest indication of a brush with the enemy, they sprang up with renewed animation, and seizing their arms, prepared to join their comrades." A private of the 71st, who has left an interesting account of his campaigning in the Peninsula, gives a very graphic picture of the retreat and its miseries, and the readiness of the starving soldiers to meet the enemy. "From Castro to Lugo," he says, "is about 48 miles, where we were promised two days' rest. Donald fell out again from sickness, and I from lameness and fatigue. When the French arrived we formed with the others as before, and they fell back. I heard them more than once say, as they turned from the points of our bayonets, that they would rather face a hundred fresh Germans than ten dying English."

After a forced night-march, the crowd of weary and spectral figures reached the heights above Corunna (Jan. 11, 1809), but not a ship was visible in the bay. The transports lay wind-bound at Vigo, 120 miles distant, and did not arrive until the 14th. For two days Soult suffered the embarkation to proceed without molestation, but on the 16th his columns were seen advancing to the attack, 20,000 strong. The British, now reduced to 14,500, were quickly arrayed to oppose him. The French occupied the range of hills which surrounds Corunna on the land side; De Laborde on the right, Merle in the centre, and Mermet, with a great battery, on the left. The cavalry formed to the left of the battery. The French position was strengthened by the villages of Palavia-abaxo and Portoza, and a great wood in the centre. Moore formed his men on a lower range of hills nearer Corunna. Baird's division occupied the right, and Hope's formed the centre and left. Paget's reserve was posted behind the centre at Airis; one battalion kept the French cavalry in check, and was connected with the main body by a line of skirmishers extended across the valley. Fraser's division held the heights immediately above the gates of Corunna, and was ready to succour any point. In front of Baird's position was the village of Elvina, which was held by the pickets of the 50th.

The battle began about two in the afternoon, by a heavy fire from the great French battery, and the lighter guns which Soult had distributed along the front of his position. The French infantry then advanced to the attack in three columns, throwing out clouds of skirmishers as they descended the grassy slopes. The British pickets were driven in pell-mell, and the village of Elvina was carried by the first French column, which then separated into two divisions, and assailed Baird's front and right. The second column attacked the centre, and the third made against the left. The British centre was raked by the heavy guns of the French battery, to which Moore's nine 6-pounders could make no effectual reply. Moore, therefore, ordered Paget to advance with the reserve, to turn the French left and menace the great battery. Fraser he ordered to support Paget, and then threw back the 4th regiment, which formed the right of Baird's division, to pour volleys into the flank of the French troops that were penetrating up the valley, while the 50th and the 42d met those breaking through Elvina.

The battle raged most fiercely at Elvina. The struggle was maintained in every house and garden, and the two British regiments suffered severely. Stewart and Moore, the ensigns of the 50th, were slain, but the colour-sergeants seized the colours and bore them through the combat. One of the majors, Stanhope, was severely wounded, and the other, Charles Napier (the future conqueror of Scinde), received five bayonet wounds, and was taken prisoner. "Well done, the 50th!" cried Moore; "Highlanders, remember Egypt!" and the two gallant regiments again rushed to the attack, and drove the French out to the slopes behind the village. The struggle was terrible; the dead and wounded lay in ghastly piles in the streets and gardens of Elvina. The guards were now ordered forward to fill the gap in the line caused by the advance of the 42d and the 50th. The 42d, thinking, as their ammunition was all spent, that the guards had come as a relief, began to fall back, and the enemy, being reinforced, renewed the fight beyond the village. At this crisis Moore galloped up to the 42d, and crying out, "My brave Highlanders, you have still your bayonets," sent them back to the attack. Moore was watching the result of the fight about Elvina when he was flung from his horse by a cannon-ball, which shattered his shoulder and fearfully mangled his breast; but notwithstanding the dreadful agony of the wound, he rose again in a sitting posture, and not till he saw the plumes of the 42d waving in Elvina would he suffer himself to be taken to the rear. Six soldiers—Highlanders and guardsmen—carried him into Corunna. His sword got entangled, and the hilt entered the wound, but he would not suffer it to be removed. "I had rather it should go out of the field with me," said the dying commander, with a soldier's pride. He often stopped his bearers that he might look on the field, and at last he had the satisfaction of learning that his troops were victorious along the whole line. "I hope the people of England will be satisfied," he said, just before life passed away; "I hope my country will do me justice;" and then, muttering something about his mother, and about Lady Esther Stanhope, whom he is said to have loved with great tenderness, the hero expired.

During the night the wounded men were collected by torchlight and all the troops were embarked. Our loss was 800; the French loss was estimated at 3000. One duty remained— the burial of the slain chief, who was interred by the officers of his staff in a hastily-dug grave in the citadel of Corunna. The fallen hero was buried "with his martial cloak around him," for there were no means to provide a coffin. The feeble light of a wintry morning was breaking over Corunna, and the

French guns were beginning to boom across the harbour, while the Rev. H. J. Symonds, the chaplain of the guards, read the funeral service. None of the usual military honours were paid, that the enemy might not know the great loss which the army had sustained, but when the French took possession of Corunna their guns paid his funeral honours, and the tricolour of France was hoisted half-mast high on the citadel. Soult, in the noble spirit of chivalry, raised a monument to his memory on the field of battle. Thus ended this disastrous but not altogether inglorious campaign, our first in the Spanish Peninsula.

The hopes of the nation, cast down by the disasters of the Corunna campaign, were again raised by a partial naval success in the Basque Roads. A squadron of 8 sail of the line and 2 frigates, under Admiral Villaumez, had stolen out of Brest, and formed a junction with another force of 3 ships and 5 frigates. They were immediately blockaded by Lord Gambier with 11 sail of the line; and as the strength of the French position, under the batteries of Isle d'Aix and Oleron, and surrounded by shoals, made a regular action hazardous, it was resolved to make the attack by fire-ships. The conduct of the attack was entrusted to Lord Cochrane, who was well acquainted with the French coast, and had proved himself equal to any deed of daring. The force prepared for the attempt consisted of 20 fire-ships, 3 explosion vessels, and a transport laden with congreve rockets. The explosion vessels were equipped under Lord Cochrane's immediate supervision, as it was on them he chiefly relied. He calculated that the novelty of these engines of attack would impress the French with the idea that every fire-ship was an explosion vessel, and that, in place of offering opposition, they would be driven ashore in their attempt to escape. Each explosion vessel contained 1500 barrels of powder, several hundred shells, and 3000 hand grenades, placed on a firm floor of logs, and pressed down into a solid mass by means of wedges and sand. The French ships were in double line, close to the Isle of Aix. Three frigates were about 700 yards in advance. About 110 yards in front of these frigates again was a strong boom moored across the channel. This boom was protected by the French ships of the line, consisting of one 120 gun-ship, two of 80 guns, seven of 74 guns, and one of 50. Their broadsides bore right upon it, while the anchorage was protected by the shore batteries, mounting upwards of 30 heavy guns, besides mortars.

At length the great day came (April 11, 1809), and the British proceeded to the attack with the comfortable reflection that if a red-hot shot reached them from the batteries of Aix—and they were not more than half a mile distant—nothing could prevent them being "hoist with their own petard," and blown into the air. It blew hard, with a high sea. The *Impérieuse, Aigle, Unicorn,* and *Pallas* frigates were anchored close to the edge of the Boyart shoal, for the purpose of receiving the crews of the fire-ships on their return, as well as to support the boats of the fleet assembled alongside the *Cæsar* to assist the fire-ships. Lord Cochrane himself embarked on board the largest explosion vessel, accompanied by Lieutenant Bissel and a volunteer crew of four men, and led the way to the attack. The night was dark, and the wind, though blowing hard, was fair, and he soon reached the estimated position of the advanced French ships. Judging his distance as well as he could, the crew entered the gig, while Lord Cochrane kindled the port fires; and then, descending into the boat, urged the men to pull for their lives. In about seven or eight minutes the explosion vessel blew up, "the effect," says Lord Cochrane in his autobiography, "constituting one of the grandest artificial spectacles imaginable. For a moment the sky was red with the lurid glare arising from the simultaneous ignition of 1500 barrels of powder. On this gigantic flash subsiding the air seemed alive with shells, grenades, rockets, and masses of timber, the wreck of the shattered vessel; whilst the water was strewn with spars, shaken out of the enormous boom, on which the vessel had brought up before she exploded. The sea was convulsed as by an earthquake, rising in a huge wave, on which our boat was lifted like a cork, and as suddenly dropped into a vast trough, out of which, as it closed upon us with the rush of a whirlpool, none expected to emerge." The strong boom, more than a mile in length, was completely shattered; and on his way back to the *Impérieuse* Lord Cochrane had the satisfaction of seeing two fire-ships pass over the spot where it had been moored. The French were panic-struck by the suddenness of the awful explosion, and in their alarm and confusion fired into each other. Every fire-ship that bore down on them they took for a dreaded explosion vessel; and their only thought being how to escape certain destruction, they allowed themselves to drift away broadside on the wind and tide.

At daylight (April 12) not a spar of the boom was visible, and thirteen of the French ships were aground. The entire fleet was helpless, with the exception of the *Foudroyant*, 80, and the *Cassard*, 74, which had brought up. The other ships, by the fall of the tide, were lying on their bilge, with their bottoms completely exposed to shot, and therefore beyond the possibility of resistance. Lord Cochrane signalled the state of affairs to the admiral again and again, but Lord Gambier refused to move, although the French fleet was in his power. His opinion that explosion vessels were "a horrible and anti-Christian mode of warfare" may have had something to do with his inaction; at any rate he would not move, and at one P.M. Lord Cochrane, full of indignation and disgust, and knowing that every hour was allowing the French to recover themselves, ordered the anchor of the *Impérieuse* to be hove atrip, and drifted stern foremost towards the enemy, with the object of compelling the admiral to send vessels to his assistance.

Proceeding thus for half an hour, exposed to every gun on the Isle of Aix, he suddenly made sail after the nearest of the enemy's vessels escaping. "In order," says Lord Cochrane, "to divert our attention from the vessels we were pursuing, these having thrown their guns overboard, the *Calcutta* (French line-of-battle ship) which was still aground, broadside on, began firing at us. Before proceeding further it became, therefore, necessary to attack her, and at 1.50 P.M. we shortened sail and returned the fire. At two the *Impérieuse* came to an anchor in five fathoms, and, veering to half a cable, kept fast the spring, firing upon the *Calcutta* with our broadside, and at the same time upon the *Aquilon* and *Ville de Varsovie* with our forecastle and bow guns, both these ships being aground, stern on, in an opposite direction. After engaging the *Calcutta* for some time, and simultaneously firing into the sterns of the two grounded line-of-battle ships, we had at length the satisfaction of observing several ships sent to our assistance—viz., *Emerald*, *Unicorn*, *Indefatigable*, *Valiant*, *Revenge*, *Pallas*, and *Aigle*. On seeing this, the captain and crew of the *Calcutta* abandoned their vessel, of which the boats of the *Impérieuse* took possession before the vessels sent to our assistance came down."

Before dusk the *Aquilon* and the *Ville de Varsovie* struck, and the crew of the *Tonnerre*, setting fire to her, made their escape in their boats. The *Cassard, Ocean, Regulus, Jemmappes*, and *Tourville* were all aground, and their crews deserting them, and might easily have been destroyed, but Lord Gambier ordered the advanced ships to be recalled. Notwithstanding this, Lord Cochrane continued the attack; but on the morning of the 13th he received a letter from the admiral, ordering his return in such peremptory terms that he could no longer refuse compliance. On this the French crews returned to their ships and warped them into the Charente.

Next day the *Impérieuse* sailed for England, with Lord Gambier's despatches. Lord Cochrane was the hero of the hour, and received a knighthood and the blue ribbon of the Bath. But evil days were in store for him. The Ministry determined to propose a vote of thanks to Lord Gambier. As member for Westminster, Lord Cochrane signified his intention to oppose the resolution from his place in the House of Commons. Lord Gambier, accordingly, demanded a court-martial. The Ministry espoused the cause of Lord Gambier, witnesses and log-books alike were tampered with, and the result was that Gambier was honourably acquitted on all the points at issue. This meant professional ruin to Lord Cochrane. He was never again employed in the British navy, and he became the victim of an official persecution which embittered his whole life and lasted almost to its close. The remainder of his professional activity was devoted to the cause of liberty, as admiral of the fleets of Chili, Brazil, and Greece. On the other side of the Channel two captains were condemned to terms of imprisonment, and Captain Lafon, for shamefully abandoning the *Calcutta* in the presence of the enemy, suffered death on board the admiral's ship.

Napoleon's opinion was that if Cochrane had been supported he would have taken every one of the French ships. The victory, however, partial as it was, led to the capture of the French West India Islands, which it had been the object of the Brest squadron to relieve. Martinique fell in February, and by the capture of St. Domingo, in July, the French flag was wholly excluded from the West Indian sea. This year also were captured the African settlement of Senegal, the Isle of Bourbon, in the Indian Ocean, and the Ionian Islands.

CHAPTER VII.—THE PENINSULAR WAR.

DELIVERANCE OF PORTUGAL.—1809-1811.

Passage of the Douro—Wellington's First March into Spain—Talavera—
The Walcheren Expedition—Busaco—Barosa—Fuentes d'Oñoro.

N the death of Sir John Moore, Sir Arthur Wellesley was reinstated in the Peninsular command. Since the battle of Corunna the French had overrun all the north of Portugal. Wellesley lost no time in moving north to Oporto, where Soult lay. Wellesley had 15,000 foot and 1600 horse; while Beresford, with 6000 foot and 1000 horse, marched towards the Upper Douro. The advanced posts of Wellesley's and Soult's armies met on the 11th May, and the French, rapidly retreating, crossed the Douro, and burned the bridge of boats. A deep swift river, more than 300 yards wide, and guarded by 10,000 veterans, might have proved an impassable obstacle, but for the negligence of Soult and the daring of Wellesley. By a lucky accident Colonel Waters discovered that a barber had come over in a skiff the previous night, and that this boat, hidden away among the bulrushes, had escaped the notice of the French. Waters, and the barber, and the Prior of Amarante, crossed in the skiff, and brought over three barges.

At ten in the forenoon (May 12, 1809) it was reported to Wellesley that one boat had reached the point of passage. "Well, let the men cross," was the laconic order, and in a quarter of an hour an officer and 25 men of the 3d Buffs were silently placed in the midst of the French army. This small detachment took possession of a large isolated building on the bank of the river called the Seminary, which was easily approached from the river, but was surrounded by a high wall on the land side, the only egress being by an iron gate on the Vallonga Road. The Seminary commanded all the country on the north bank, but was itself commanded by the Serra Rock on the south side, where Wellesley placed 18 guns in battery. A second boat crossed, and no sound was heard, but as the third boat was making its passage a tumultuous noise rang through Oporto, the drums beat to arms, and the French troops rushed out of the city, and threw out swarms of skirmishers against the Seminary. The guns on the Serra Rock, which completely swept the ground to the west of the Seminary, cut off the French in the town from the scene of the struggle, but the attack on the iron gate was so violent that Wellesley would have crossed in person but for his confidence in Hill. Murray, who had been sent with the German brigade, the 14th Dragoons, and two guns, three miles up the stream, with orders to seek for boats and pass there if possible, had not yet come down the right bank. The moment was critical, but towards one o'clock the waving of handkerchiefs from the windows of Oporto announced that the French had quitted the lower town. As soon as the guards were withdrawn from the quays, the citizens jumped into boats and rowed across, and in these the guards under Sherbrooke began to cross at one o'clock. At the same time Murray was seen advancing down the right bank of the river. The French at once broke and rushed in confusion along the Vallonga Road. Hill, who had now three battalions in the Seminary, advanced to the enclosure wall, and poured in a destructive fire on the retreating masses. Five guns came out of Oporto, and as the artillerymen were hastening to pass the line of Hill's fire, a volley from behind laid many of them low, and the rest dispersed and left their guns on the road. The fugitives were now plied by Hill's fire, Sherbrooke's fire, and the fire of the 18 guns on the Serra Rock; and had Murray done his duty, their rout would have been complete. The opportunity offered to him might, says Napier, "have tempted a blind man," but he suffered column after column to pass without firing a shot. None of his troops advanced, with the exception of two squadrons of dragoons under General Charles Stewart (afterwards Marquis of Londonderry) and Major Hervey, who rode over the rear-guard as it was pushing through a narrow road, unhorsed

De Laborde and wounded Foy. This finished the action. Our loss was only 20 killed and 95 wounded. The French lost 500 men and five guns on the field, and in Oporto they left 50 guns, a large quantity of ammunition, and all their sick, amounting to several hundreds. So complete was the surprise that Wellesley sat down to the dinner prepared for Soult. In his retreat Soult had to relinquish his artillery, ammunition, and baggage, and joined Ney at Lugo in a much worse plight than Moore six months before.

After a month's stay at Oporto, caused chiefly by the want of money, Wellesley marched for the Spanish frontier, with 22,000 men, including 3000 horse. On the 20th July he effected a junction at Oropesa with the Spanish General Cuesta, who had 32,000 foot, 6000 horse, and 46 guns. Vanegas, at the same time, moved from the north, with 26,000 men, towards Toledo, and King Joseph, alarmed for Madrid, called in all his detachments, and faced the enemy at Talavera de la Reyna. The town of Talavera stands on the right bank of the Tagus, embosomed in vineyards, trees, and enclosures. Between the town and the Alberche, a tributary of the Tagus, the ground is covered with olive and cork trees; and nearly parallel with the Tagus, at a distance of two miles, a chain of round steep hills bounds this woody plain. Beyond these hills, and separated from them by a deep and rugged valley half a mile wide, is the mountain range which divides the Alberche from the Tietar. The allies' line was disposed from Talavera to the heights on the west. Cuesta and his Spaniards occupied the right at Talavera. Their front was covered by a convent, mud walls, ditches, and felled trees, and their left rested on a mound, on which a large redoubt was constructed, and behind which a brigade of British cavalry was posted. Campbell's division touched Cuesta's left; then came Sherbrooke and the guards, supported by Mackenzie; then Cameron's brigade and the Germans; then, on the round hills, Donkin's, Hill's, and Tilson's divisions; and last of all, in the ravine, between the round hills and the mountains, the 23d Light Dragoons and the 1st German Hussars. That part of the position was afterwards strengthened by placing Bassecour's Spaniards on the mountains. The line was two miles in length, and the front was covered by the Partida rivulet. The whole force of the allies was 53,000 men with 100 guns, and of this total the British and Germans were only 19,000 strong with 30 guns. Little reliance could be placed on the Spaniards, who composed two-thirds of the force. Joseph had 50,000 troops (of whom 7000 were cavalry), all hardy veterans, with 80 guns.

At dawn (July 27, 1809) the brilliant lines of the French cavalry moved down through the plain between Talavera and the Alberche, and so suddenly that the British outposts were surprised, and Sir Arthur Wellesley himself narrowly escaped capture. Many of the men were killed without rising from the ground. The brigades were separated, and the young soldiers fired on each other, but the steadiness of the old troops, and notably the 45th and some companies of the 60th Rifles, enabled Sir Arthur to rally his men and check the French advance. It was even worse with the Spaniards. When the French horsemen rode up and commenced a pistol skirmish, the Spaniards discharged one volley of musketry, and then, panic-struck, 10,000 of the infantry and all the artillery broke and fled. Cuesta himself went off in his huge coach drawn by nine mules, and Sir Arthur could with much difficulty stay the advance of the French with some English squadrons and two Spanish battalions. The fugitives ran to Oropesa and spread the rumour that the allies were defeated, and the French in hot pursuit.

As the sun was sinking and the twilight deepening into gloom, Victor made an attack on the hill on the left of the British, which was the key of the position. Hill's troops had not yet taken post, and Donkin had enough to do to hold his position, but Hill brought up the 29th and 48th, and a battalion of detachments composed of Sir John Moore's stragglers. Volleys of musketry were poured in at twenty yards, and then a British shout and a rush with the bayonet, and Lapisse's broken troops were driven into the ravine below. In the darkness and confusion Hill was nearly taken prisoner. "While giving orders to the colonel of the 48th," says Napier, "he was shot at by some troops from the highest point; thinking they were stragglers from his own ranks firing at the enemy, he rode up to them in company with his brigade-major Fordyce, and in a moment found himself in the midst of the French. Fordyce was killed, and Hill's horse was wounded by a grenadier who roughly seized the bridle also, but the general, spurring hard, broke the man's hold, and galloping down met the 29th regiment, which he led up with such a fierce charge that the French could not sustain the shock."

In this day's fighting the French lost 1000 men and the British 800. The bivouac fires now blazed up, and the troops lay down on the ground; but the night was disturbed by constant alarms. When the rosy flush of dawn (July 28) was spreading over the heights, dark masses of the French were seen moving up the ravine to the left, which as yet Wellesley had neglected to occupy. The attack was preceded by a burst of artillery, which mowed down the English ranks by sections. Then came the rattle of musketry and the hand to hand struggle, and after a combat of forty minutes, the French were driven back with the loss of 1500 men. During the cannonade the heat was so great that orders were given to bury the dead on the heights. It was after this attack that Wellesley occupied the ravine with the cavalry and Bassecour's Spanish infantry. At the same time Albuquerque, discontented with Cuesta, came there with the Spanish horse.

Joseph now held a council of war with Jourdan and Victor, to determine his future proceedings. This gave the wearied armies a rest from nine till noon. The French cooked and ate their dinners, but the British slept, their only dinner consisting of a few ounces of wheat in the grain. The excessive heat led many of both armies to the banks of the Partida to assuage their thirst, and an interchange of flasks and courtesies took place between the men who had been engaged in mortal combat an hour before. Before one o'clock the roll of drums along the French line heralded the renewal of hostilities. While Milhaud's dragoons kept the Spaniards in check, the 4th corps of the French fell upon Campbell's division on the British right; but Campbell's men, aided by Mackenzie's division and two battalions of Spanish infantry, drove then back with terrible carnage, and captured ten guns. Campbell did not pursue, in order not to break the line, and the French rallied on their supports and made head for another attack; but, broken by a heavy artillery and musketry fire, and taken in flank by a regiment of Spanish horsemen, they retired in confusion, and victory was secured on the right.

In the meantime the French grenadiers, Villatte's division, two regiments of light cavalry, and Ruffin's division, were seen advancing upon the British left. Sir Arthur ordered Anson's brigade of cavalry to charge the head of these columns. The horsemen went off at a canter, but came upon a sudden hollow

H

formed by a watercourse, and the French, throwing themselves into squares, opened fire. Colonel Arentschild of the 1st German Hussars, saying in his broken English that he would not kill his "young mans," reined up on the brink; but the 23d Light Dragoons continued their course, and rolled down, men and horses, in a confused mass. The survivors scrambled to their feet, mounted their chargers, re-formed under Major Ponsonby— Colonel Seymour being severely wounded—passed through the midst of Villatte's columns, and fell with inexpressible fury on a brigade of French chasseurs in the rear. Victor had seen the advance of the dragoons, and sent his Polish Lancers and Westphalian Light Horse to the support of Villatte, and these fresh men coming up entirely broke the 23d. Only about half the regiment escaped to Bassecour's division from this glorious charge; 207 men and officers were left dead on the field. Villatte's men, however, were paralysed by the desperate valour of the charge, and by the sight of Albuquerque's horsemen in reserve, and made no further movement in advance.

While these attacks on the left and right were going on, Lapisse was making desperate efforts on the centre. The guards repulsed him, but in the excitement of success advanced too far and were driven back by the French reserves and cavalry. The Germans, too, were hard pressed, and fell into confusion. At this critical moment Sir Arthur ordered up the 48th. Wheeling into open columns of companies, that regiment let the disordered masses of the guards through, and then, resuming its formation in line, fell on the flank of the advancing French columns and checked their offensive movement. The guards and the Germans rallied, Cotton's cavalry came up at a trot, the artillery battered the wavering ranks, and loud cheers along the whole British line proclaimed the defeat of the enemy. The French covered their retrograde movement by skirmishers, and an augmented fire of artillery. The British, now reduced to less than 14,000 sabres and bayonets, were too much exhausted by hunger and toil to pursue. The Spaniards were incapable of any such movement. The last shots were exchanged about six o'clock. The British lost 6200 killed, wounded, and missing; the French 7200, and 150 men and 17 guns taken (including seven left in the woods); the Spaniards estimated their losses at 1200. The battle was scarcely over when the long grass and shrubs caught fire from the smouldering of some cartridge papers, and a large part of the field was swept by a sea of flame, in which many of the wounded perished.

Talavera won for Sir Arthur Wellesley a peerage, with the title of Baron Douro and Viscount Wellington. It was by far the most important battle which had yet been fought in the Peninsula. A French general and military critic says it "recovered the glory of the successors of Marlborough, which for a century had declined. It was felt that the English infantry could contend with the best in Europe." Napier says, "Hard honest fighting distinguished the battle of Talavera, and proved the exceeding gallantry of the French and English soldiers. The latter owed much to their leader's skill, and something to fortune; the French owed their commanders nothing; but 30,000 of their infantry vainly strove for three hours on the 28th to force 16,000 British soldiers, who were for the most part so recently drafted from the militia that many of them still bore the distinctions of that force on their accoutrements."

Wellington was preparing to follow up his victory by an advance on Madrid when he was informed that the combined forces of Soult, Mortier, and Ney, to the number of 34,000, had already reached Placentia in his rear. In danger of being crushed between converging masses, Wellington crossed to Deleitosa on the south of the Tagus. After a month's stay here, he was compelled, by the failure of the Spanish authorities to furnish him with supplies, to cross the mountains and fix his headquarters at Badajos. Meanwhile, the Spaniards made desperate efforts for the recovery of Madrid, but their armies were destroyed in succession, and early in December Wellington retired from the valley of the Guadiana, and quartered his troops on the Agueda, between Almeida and Ciudad Rodrigo, commencing the famous lines of Torres Vedras.

During this year Austria was again at war with Napoleon, and Britain agreed to make diversions in her favour in Holland and Italy. An Anglo-Sicilian force of 15,000 men was sent to the coast of Naples under Sir John Stuart, but failed in gaining any durable advantage. Not more successful and far more disastrous was the miserable Walcheren expedition. Yet its strength was on a scale which ought to have ensured success: 37 ships of the line, 23 frigates, 82 gunboats, 400 transports, and 40,000 troops formed the largest and most powerful armament which had ever put to sea in modern times. But generalship was wanting. The command was entrusted to the Earl of Chatham, elder brother of the late William Pitt, a respectable veteran totally devoid of energy. Instead of moving at once on Antwerp, the great object of the expedition, where Napoleon had a squadron of ten sail of the line, with an arsenal and dockyard on which he had spent millions, the British general wasted precious time at Flushing, which capitulated after a three days' bombardment, with its garrison of 6000 men (August 16, 1809). By the time Lord Chatham was ready to move forward Antwerp had been put in a state of defence, and 30,000 troops under Bernadotte and the King of Holland were prepared to do battle with the invaders. Further advance was considered impossible, and the troops were withdrawn into the unhealthy island of Walcheren, where the swamp-fever committed fearful ravages in their ranks. Before the army was sent home 7000 men had fallen victims to the pestilence, and of the survivors many had their constitutions broken for the remainder of their days. After the bloody battles of Echmuhl, Aspern, and Wagram, the peace of Vienna (October 14, 1809) put an end to the war between Austria and Napoleon.

The peace with Austria left Napoleon at leisure to attend to the affairs of the Peninsula, and 120,000 of the heroes of Wagram were sent across the Pyrenees. In the summer of 1810 the French forces in the Peninsula amounted to 366,000 men. Soult, with 60,000, was in Andalusia; Joseph had 24,000 men in Madrid; and 80,000 of the corps of Ney, Reynier, and Junot, were massed at Salamanca. The command of this last-named force was conferred on Massena, the ship-boy of Nice, who had gradually risen from the ranks to the dignity of a marshal's *bâton*, and the rank of Duke of Rivoli and Prince of Essling. So unvarying was his success that Napoleon called him "the spoiled child of victory" (*l'enfant gâté de la victoire*). His ferocity was the feature of his character which chiefly attracted the attention of his enemies, who called him "the Son of Rapine." Massena was ordered to invade Portugal. To oppose him Wellington had only 23,500 British troops and 30,000 Portuguese. Ciudid Rodrigo fell to the invaders (July 11, 1810), Wellington not daring to risk a battle in its defence; and after a smart skirmish with the

British rearguard under Crawford, at the bridge of the Coa, Almeida was invested. The explosion of the great powder magazine deprived the garrison of the means of defence, and (August 27) this stronghold also was yielded to the French.

Wellington now retreated down the valley of the Mondego, followed on the north bank by Massena. The roads were crowded with fugitives, whose wretched appearance on their arrival at Lisbon struck consternation into the capital, the soldiers themselves were becoming despondent, the Ministry at home daily expected the embarkation of the army for England; and to restore confidence to all parties, the Portuguese, the army, and the Ministry, Wellington departed from his plan of acting solely on the defensive, and prepared to make a stand on the Sierra Busaco. He had been joined by Hill, and his army now amounted to 50,000 men, but half of them were raw soldiers, and Massena had 72,000 veterans.

Wellington's line on the Sierra Busaco extended eight miles, from the Mondego on the right to impassable ravines on the left. Hill held the right. Leith, with the 5th division, and Picton, with the 3d division, held the centre. Spencer, with the 1st division, held the left, the highest point of the ridge, near a great convent of the Barefooted Carmelites. Cole was on the extreme left, covering a path leading to the flat country about Milheada. A regiment of heavy dragoons was posted in reserve on the summit of the sierra. Pack's Portuguese lay in front of Spencer, half way down the mountain, and on their left Crawford's Light Division, the Germans, and the 19th Portuguese occupied a spur jutting out nearly half a mile in front of, but lower than, the convent. Fifty pieces of cannon were planted on the most advantageous points, and the whole sierra was covered by a cloud of skirmishers. From the nature of the ground the divisions were separated by long and unassailable intervals.

Massena was under the impression that Wellington had not yet been joined by Hill. He was ignorant of the existence of the lines of Torres Vedras also, and thought he could force Wellington to retreat and embark. The attack was fixed for the morning of the 27th. "The weather," say the records of the 88th, the gallant Connaught Rangers, "was calm and fine, and the dark mountains rising on either side were covered by innumerable fires. The French were apparently all bustle and gaiety, and following their usual avocations with as much *sang-*

froid as if preparing for a review, not a battle. Along the whole British line the soldiers in stern silence examined their flints, cleaned their locks and barrels, and then stretched themselves on the ground to rest, each with his firelock in his grasp. In their rear, unsheltered by any covering but his cloak, lay their distinguished leader."

About an hour before daybreak Ney planted three columns of attack opposite the convent, on the British left, and Reynier two at Antonio da Cantara, opposite the British centre. Ney and Reynier were three miles apart; Junot was in reserve. The grey mist of early morning still shrouded the sierra when Reynier's columns sprang up to the attack, and dashed in among the pickets and skirmishers of the "fighting third." Six guns played on their ranks with grape, but they would not be denied. The right centre of the British division was forced back; the Portuguese were broken. The surging masses of the enemy gained the highest portion of the crest, just between the 3d and 5th divisions, and the leading battalions seized commanding positions on the rocks and proceeded to establish themselves, while the rear wheeled to the right to sweep the summit of the sierra. At this crisis Wellington ordered two guns to open with grape on their flank, a heavy fire of musketry tore their front, and Colonel Wallace with the 88th and a wing of the 45th charged so furiously, that after a twenty minutes' struggle the French were driven down the sides of the sierra. In like manner the French grenadiers, who had first gained the crest, were fiercely attacked by the 38th and the 9th, under Colonel Cameron, and sent after their comrades. This ended the battle on this part of the field, for Leith and Hill had closed up to Picton's right, and Reynier had neither reserves nor guns to restore the fight.

Colonel Wallace's address to the 88th before proceeding into action was a model of soldierly terseness and brevity. "Now, mind what I tell you! When you arrive at the spot I shall charge, and I have only to add that the rest must be done by yourselves. Press on them to the muzzle; I say, Connaught Rangers, press on to the rascals!" When it was all over, Wellington rode up to the 88th, and, taking the colonel by the hand, said, "Wallace, I never saw a more gallant charge than that just made by your regiment."

Ney's attack on the left met with as little success. The

ground was steeper than where Reynier attacked. It was yet dark when a straggling musketry fire was heard in the valley, and when day dawned three huge masses were seen to enter the woods below and throw forward a profusion of skirmishers. One of these, under Marchand, moved to turn the right of the light division; another, under Loison, made straight up the face of the sierra along the convent road; the third remained in reserve. Loison's front brigade, led by Simon, never faltered or relaxed its speed, though plied with a storm of artillery and musketry which searched its ranks from the first to the last section. The riflemen and the caçadores, who had been planted on the top as skirmishers, were obliged to fall back step by step. Ross's guns, placed in the embrasures of the rocks, were worked with incredible quickness, but their range was more and more contracted every round. At last the English skirmishers rushed over the edge of the sierra, breathless and begrimed with powder. The artillery drew back. The jubilant cries of the French were heard within a few yards of the summit. But Crawford was prepared. In the hollow, between the convent and the jutting spur of rock on which the light division was posted, the 43d and 52d were drawn up in line, concealed by the configuration of the ground; Crawford was standing alone on a rock watching the progress of the attack, and now at this critical moment he shouted to these two regiments to charge. "The next moment," says the historian of the war, "a horrid shout startled the French column, and 1800 British bayonets went sparkling over the brow of the hill. Yet so brave, so hardy were the leading French, that each man of the first section raised his musket, and two officers and ten soldiers fell before them. Not a Frenchman had missed his mark! They could do no more. The head of their column was violently thrown back upon the rear, both flanks were overlapped at the same moment by the English wings, three terrible discharges at five yards' distance shattered the wavering mass, and a long trail of broken arms and bleeding carcases marked the line of flight." Marchand's column, which ought to have been sent forward to the attack at the same time as Loison's, gained a pine wood half way up the mountain, but was dislodged by artillery. About two o'clock the firing ceased along the line, and parties from both armies were mixed together carrying off the wounded. The loss of the allies was 1300, that of the French 4500.

Wellington had hoped that this battle might stop Massena's advance, but Napoleon's orders for the invasion of Portugal were peremptory, and the French marshal defiled to the right and gained the great road from Oporto to Lisbon. As the French, with their superior numbers, could not be met in the open country, Wellington had no option but to fall back, and before the middle of October he had his whole force safely entrenched within the lines of Torres Vedras. These formidable defences formed an effectual bar to the further progress of Massena, who had not so much as heard of their existence. For more than a month he watched the impregnable barrier, in the vain hope of starving out the allies, who were supplied by sea, and then retired into winter-quarters at Santarem.

Major-general Graham (afterwards Lord Lynedoch), a lineal descendant of the warlike house of Montrose, and himself "a daring old man and of a ready temper for battle," commanded the British and Portuguese troops in Cadiz, then besieged by Marshal Victor. The absence of Soult, who had gone to co-operate with Massena, gave him hopes of compelling Victor to raise the siege. Graham landed at Algesiras, and marched up the coast, to take Victor in flank. But the enterprise was ruined by the misconduct of the Spanish General La Peña, to whom Graham, to preserve unanimity, ceded the command, though it was contrary to his instructions. La Peña had the army in so scattered a state that it was divided into several distinct bodies. Victor, who was keeping close in the woods of Chiclana, with 9000 men and 14 guns, had his eye on this state of matters. The Spaniards were in advance near the Almanza Creek ; Graham was struggling through a pine wood between Almanza and Barosa ; Major Brown, with the flank companies of the 9th and 82d, was with the baggage on Barosa, a low ridge, extending about half a mile from the coast ; a Spanish detachment was still far behind. Victor sent Villatte to keep the Spaniards in check and cover the works of the camp ; he ordered Laval to attack Graham while entangled in the wood ; while he himself led on Ruffin's brigade to attack the rearguard on the Barosa heights. Major Brown retreated in good order, and sent a message to Graham asking for instructions. "Fight!" was the laconic reply of the gallant Graham, who imagined that La Peña, with the corps of battle and the cavalry, was on the Barosa Hill. But when he cleared the wood and regained the plain, as Napier says, "he beheld Ruffin's brigade, flanked by the two grenadier battalions, near the summit on the one side, the Spanish rearguard and the baggage flying toward the sea on the other, the French cavalry following the fugitives in good order, Laval close upon his own left flank, and La Peña nowhere!" (March 6, 1811.)

As the British emerged from the wood, ten guns under Major Duncan opened a terrific fire on Laval's column, and Colonel Andrew Barnard, with the riflemen and some Portuguese, ran out to keep the enemy in play while the troops formed. So sudden was the attack that all distinctions of regiments and brigades were ignored, and the troops formed in two masses, with one of which General Dilkes hurried across the hollow to attack Ruffin, while Colonel Wheatley led the other against Laval. In the case of Wheatley and Laval the contest was quickly decided. The infantry on both sides pressed forward under a furious cannonade and pealing discharges of musketry, but when the masses drew near, the fierce charge of the 87th overthrew the first line of the French, dashed it violently against the second line, and sent both off the field in disorder. At the Barosa Hill the combat was for some time more doubtful. At the edge of the ascent, Dilkes' column was met with a shower of bullets from Ruffin's people, with whom Major Brown had hitherto been maintaining the fight, though half his detachment had fallen. Whole sections were mowed down by the murderous fire, but the British bore strongly onward, and forced the French from the hill, with the loss of three guns. The British were too exhausted to pursue, but Frederick Ponsonby's German hussars charged the French squadrons in their retreat, overthrew them, and captured two guns.

The whole affair was over in an hour and a half, but 1210 British and 2000 French lay on the field, and the French lost besides 400 prisoners, 6 guns, and an eagle, and had two of their generals, Ruffin and Rousseau, mortally wounded. The eagle, the first taken during the Peninsular war, was captured in the furious charge of the 87th, the Royal Irish Fusiliers—"Faugh-a-Ballaghs" ("Clear-the-Way"), as they delight to call themselves. It first attracted the attention of a young ensign, who called out to a sergeant, "Do you see that, Masterman?" and then rushed forward to seize it, but was shot in the attempt. Sergeant Masterman instantly revenged his death, ran his antagonist through the body, cut down the standard-bearer, and took the eagle. For this achievement the gallant Masterman was afterwards rewarded by a commission in the second battalion of his regiment. During the Peninsular war some general-officer observed to Wellington how unsteadily the 87th marched. "Yes, general," was Wellington's reply; "indeed, they do, but they fight like devils."

Four thousand British troops overthrew 9000 French, but the victory of Barosa was barren. La Peña had quietly surveyed the desperate struggle without sending any help to his allies. Graham remained some hours on the height, hoping he would follow up the victory; but although the Spanish general had 12,000 infantry and 800 cavalry, all fresh, and the French might have been cut to pieces, he would not move a man, a horse, or a gun. The French were able to renew the blockade of Cadiz, the whole object of the expedition was lost, and violent disputes on the subject arose in the Cortes. La Peña had the impudence to claim the credit of the victory, and Graham, disgusted with the Spaniards, refused the honours of the Cortes, resigned his command, and joined Wellington.

His troops having eaten up all the food in the country round Santarem, Massena broke up his encampment and commenced his retreat (March 2, 1811). It is spoken of as an admirable example of military ability, but his way up the valley of the Mondego was marked by blood and flame, and his conduct to the unhappy Portuguese was characterised by such barbarity as, in the words of Wellington, has been "seldom equalled, and never surpassed." Napier, himself an eyewitness, says, "Every horror making war hideous attended this dreadful retreat!—distress, conflagration, death, in all modes! from wounds, from fatigue, from water, from the flames, from starvation: on every side, unlimited ferocity!" Wellington followed close at Massena's heels, and combats occurred at Pombal, Redinha, and other places on the line of march, notably Sabugal (April 3), where Reynier was defeated with the loss of 1500 men to 200 British. Wellington called the combat of Sabugal "one of the most glorious actions the British troops were ever engaged in." On the 5th April Massena repassed the frontier and occupied Salamanca, having lost during the invasion and retreat, by want, sickness, and the sword, 30,000 men.

The frontier-fortress of Almeida was now invested by Wellington, and Massena, in obedience to the peremptory orders of Napoleon, advanced to its relief with 40,000 infantry, 5000 cavalry, and 36 guns. Wellington had but 32,000 infantry, 1200 cavalry, and 42 guns, and of these the Portuguese were almost useless through the shameful neglect of their Government. The Portuguese were starving: the infantry abandoned their colours and dropped from exhaustion by thousands, the cavalry was entirely ruined, and the artillerymen were so devoid of ammunition that in the ensuing battle they had to collect the enemy's cannon-balls. Wellington chose his ground on the level summit of a rocky plateau between the Duas Casas and the Turones, two rivulets near the Coa. The 5th division was posted on the left near Fort Conception, the 6th division in the centre opposite the village of Almeida, and the 1st and 3d divisions were massed on the right, among the hedgerows and vineyard walls behind Fuentes d'Oñoro, a village on the Duas Casas. Most of the houses were in the ravine, but a craggy eminence, crowned by a picturesque old chapel and some houses, gave a point for rallying. The British line was five miles long.

Massena came on in three divisions (May 3, 1811). The 8th and 2d corps, under Reynier, threatened Almeida and Fort Conception; and Loison, with Drouet's division, the 6th corps, and the cavalry, moved against Fuentes d'Oñoro. Loison, without waiting orders, at once attacked the village, which was held by five battalions from the 1st and 3d divisions, and with such fury that the British were driven out of the streets in the ravine, and had some difficulty in maintaining the high ground about the chapel; but the 21st, 71st, and 79th regiments came to the rescue, and charging with the bayonet, hurled the assailants back over the Duas Casas. During the night the French detachments were withdrawn, and the three succouring regiments were left in possession of the village. "We stood under arms," says a soldier of the 71st, "until three in the morning, when a staff-officer rode up to our colonel, and gave orders for our advance. Colonel Cadogan put himself at our head, saying, 'My lads, we have had no provisions for two days; there is plenty in the hollow in front, let us down and divide.' We advanced as quick as we could run, and met the light companies retreating as fast as they could. We continued to advance at double-quick time, our firelocks at the trail, our bonnets in our hands.

They called to us, 'Seventy-first, you will come back quicker than you advance.' We soon came in full view of the enemy, and the colonel cried, 'Here is food, my lads; cut away.' Thrice we waved our bonnets, thrice we cheered, brought our bayonets to the charge, and forced them back through the town. . . . During this day the loss in men was great. In our retreat back to the town, when we halted to check the enemy, who bore hard upon us in their attempts to break our line, often was I obliged to stand with a foot upon each side of a wounded man, who wrung my soul with prayers I could not answer, and pierced my heart with cries to be lifted out of the way of the cavalry. While my heart bled for them, I have shaken them rudely off. We kept up our fire till long after dark. About one o'clock in the morning each man got four ounces of bread, which had been collected from the haversacks of the Foot Guards. After the firing had ceased, we began to search through the town, and found plenty of flour, bacon, and sausages, on which we feasted heartily, and then lay down in our blankets, wearied to death."

On the 4th, Massena examined the line and made dispositions for the next day. An attack in front was impracticable, for the Duas Casas is a brawling rivulet, in an irregular rocky bed, and made the allies secure in that direction. He dared not turn the allies' left at Fort Conception, for Wellington would then have crossed the Duas Casas at Almeida and Fuentes d'Oñoro, and fallen on his flank. He decided to make his main attack on Fuentes d'Oñoro, while he turned the allies' right. The nature of the ground permitted of this arrangement. The rocky plateau ends at Fuentes d'Oñoro in a sudden ridge which runs between the two rivulets at right angles to both; beyond this the ravine gradually sinks into open ground, running as a wooded swamp in the direction of Poço Velho, and affording comparatively easy access to the lower steppe, rectangular in form, which lies between the two rivulets on the north and south, and the sudden ridge at Fuentes d'Oñoro and the hill behind Nava d'Aver on the west and east. Wellington divined this was Massena's plan, and to cover all the bridges to the beleaguered fortress, he extended his right to Nava d'Aver, posting Don Julian Sanchez and his irregulars on the hill beyond, and ordering Houston with the 7th division to take possession of Poço Velho, the swampy wood, and part of the plain towards

Nava d'Aver. The line of the allies was now about seven miles long.

It was broad daylight before the French were in motion (May 5, 1811), and all their movements were apparent. The 8th corps was withdrawn from Almeida, and attacked Houston's left in Poço Velho, while Drouet's division and the 6th corps took ground to their own left, but still keeping a division before Fuentes d'Oñoro, to menace that point. Houston's left was driven out of Poço Velho, and the 6th division was gaining ground in the wood, but the light division and the cavalry hurried up to his support, and enabled him to contest every inch of ground. The French cavalry under Montbrun, 4000 cuirassiers covered with the glories of Wagram, now crossed the Duas Casas, and formed in order of battle between the Poço Velho wood and the hill of Nava d'Aver. Julian Sanchez at once withdrew from the hill to the Turones, and after following him for about an hour, Montbrun wheeled round, turned Houston's right, and charged the British cavalry, of whom scarcely 1000 sabres were in the field, drove in the cavalry outguards at the first shock, "cut off," says Napier, "Ramsay's battery of horse artillery, and came sweeping in upon the reserves of cavalry and upon the 7th division. The leading French squadrons, approaching in a disorderly manner, were partially checked by fire, but a great commotion was observed in their main body; men and horses were seen to close with confusion and tumult towards one point, where a thick dust and loud cries, and the sparkling of blades, and flashing of pistols, indicated some extraordinary occurrence. Suddenly the multitude became violently agitated, an English shout pealed high and clear, the mass rent asunder, and Norman Ramsay burst forth sword in hand at the head of his battery; his horses, breathing fire, stretched like greyhounds along the plain, the guns bounded behind him like things of no weight, and the mounted gunners followed close, with heads bent low and pointed weapons, in desperate career." A charge of the 14th Light Dragoons somewhat checked the pursuit, General Charles Stewart (Lord Londonderry) taking Colonel Lamotte prisoner in a hand-to-hand combat; but as the main body of the cuirassiers was coming on strongly, the British cavalry retired behind the light division, which, with the 7th division, was thrown into squares. Not, however, before some were cut down; but the mass stood firm, and the Chasseurs

Britanniques, a Swiss regiment which had deserted to us, poured in such a fire from behind a loose stone wall that the bewildered cuirassiers recoiled, with many empty saddles.

Meanwhile the 6th corps was making progress in the Poço Velho wood, and as the British divisions were now separated and the right turned, defeat could only be averted by an immediate abandonment of the extended position. Wellington gave orders to move at right angles to his present position, on the sudden ridge which runs between the two rivulets, with the village of Fuentes d'Oñoro as pivot. It was a perilous movement, but executed with invincible steadiness. Crawford threw the light divisions into squares, and Montbrun found it too dangerous to meddle with him. The cuirassiers surrounded and sabred some of the Scots Guards under Colonel Hill, and made that officer and fourteen men prisoners; but they broke their teeth on the 42d Highlanders, under Lord Blantyre, and were sent back with many a riderless horse. "This crisis," says Napier, "passed without a disaster, yet there was not during the whole war a more perilous hour. For Houston's division was separated from the position by the Turones, and the vast plain was covered with commissariat animals and camp-followers, with servants, led horses, baggage, and country people, mixed with broken detachments and pickets returning from the woods, all in such confused concourse that the light division squares appeared but as specks; and close behind those surging masses were 5000 horsemen, trampling, bounding, shouting for the word to charge." Had Loison brought forward the 6th corps, while Drouet assailed the village, and the cavalry made a general charge, the mob would have been driven in upon the 1st division, and the battle lost; but these things did not happen, and the action on this side resolved itself into a cannonade.

But a fierce fight still raged in the village of Fuentes d'Oñoro. Drouet's light troops swarmed on the village with such fury as at once to carry the nearest houses. Colonel Cameron of the 79th fell mortally wounded by the bullet of a Frenchman who took aim at him from a doorway, and his clansmen were paralysed till Major Petre seized the flag, and called out, "There are your colours, my lads, follow me!" when the Highlanders threw themselves upon the enemy with a wild shout of rage and revenge. But they were greatly outnumbered; two companies were taken, and the remainder, and the 24th and

71st, were driven up the eminence to the churchyard, where a fierce hand-to-hand fight was carried on over the graves and tombstones. The combat surged to and fro, now on the banks of the stream, now on the rugged heights and around the chapel, but Wellington sent up reinforcements, and the village was cleared by a splendid charge of the 71st Highland Light Infantry, 79th Cameron Highlanders, and the 88th Connaught Rangers. The French retired a cannon shot from the stream, and the fighting ended about five o'clock. Both armies bivouacked on the ground they occupied at the end of the battle.

There is a story told in the "Eventful Life of a Soldier" about this last bayonet charge of the 71st, 79th, and 88th, which was much admired by all competent judges. "General Picton had had occasion to check the 88th for some plundering affair they had been guilty of, when he was so offended at their conduct, that, in addressing them, he told them they were the greatest blackguards in the army! But as he was always as ready to bestow praise as censure where it was due, when they were returning from this gallant and effective charge, he exclaimed, "Well done, the brave 88th!" Some of them, who had been stung by his former reproaches, cried out, "Are we the greatest blackguards in the army now?" Picton smiled, as he replied, "No, no; you are brave and gallant soldiers! This day has redeemed your character."

The allies lost 1200 killed and wounded, and 300 prisoners. The French loss was certainly as great, perhaps twice as great, but the British were more nearly defeated at Fuentes d'Oñoro than anywhere else in the Peninsula. The French indeed claimed the victory, because they won the passage of Poço Velho, turned our right flank, and forced the army to relinquish ground and change its front; but all the fruits of victory lay with the allies. Massena made no further attempt to relieve Almeida, and sent orders to the governor, General Brennier, to evacuate the fortress and rejoin the army. Brennier destroyed his guns and sprung his mines, and through the negligence of General Campbell, who had charge of the investment, effected his escape with the greater part of the garrison. The 36th pursued, killed several, and made 300 prisoners, but in their eagerness advanced too far, and themselves lost 40 men. With the evacuation of Almeida the soil of Portugal was finally cleared of the enemy.

CHAPTER VIII.—THE PENINSULAR WAR.

THE SALAMANCA CAMPAIGN.—1811-1812.

Albuera—Arroyo dos Molinos—Frigate Action off Lissa—Ciudad Rodrigo—Badajos—Almaraz—Wellington's Second March into Spain—Salamanca—Wellington enters Madrid—Retreat from Burgos.

THE battle of Fuentes d'Oñoro having secured the safety of Portugal, Wellington turned his attention to the two great frontier-fortresses of Badajos and Ciudad Rodrigo, the former of which had been surrendered to Soult by the treachery of the Spanish General Imaz in the early part of the year. Until these two defences were reduced it was hopeless to enter Spain. Wellington proposed to deal with Ciudad Rodrigo himself, and to Badajos he sent Beresford, who immediately invested the place; but the British were at this time little skilled in siege work, and small progress had been made when intelligence was received that Soult was advancing from Seville to the relief. Beresford was averse to battle, but allowed himself to be talked over by his officers, who had been in none of the recent engagements, and were athirst for glory. Had he been defeated, Wellington's army would have been recalled to Lisbon to save the capital from Soult, Portugal would once more have been prostrated, and the liberation of Spain deferred for an indefinite period.

Beresford took post (May 15, 1811) on the Albuera range, about seven miles from Badajos. His army numbered 30,000 infantry, 2500 cavalry, and 38 guns; but the Spaniards were 16,000, and the Portuguese 8000, and, unfortunately, the French held Spanish and Portuguese troops in contempt. The British, on whom the brunt of the battle fell, did not exceed 7000.

Soult had with him 19,000 veteran infantry, 4000 chosen cavalry, and 40 guns; and his troops, says Napier, were "all of one discipline, animated by one spirit, and amply compensated for their inferiority in number by their fine organisation and their leader's capacity, which was immeasurably greater than his adversary's."

The Albuera range is about four miles in extent, and rises in gentle undulations, practicable for cavalry and artillery. The river Albuera (with the Feria rivulet) flows along the eastern base, and on the west of the ridge there is a brook, the Aroya. The village of Albuera stands on the eastern side of the range, at the junction of the roads to Badajos and Seville, Talavera and Valverde. Near the village, the river is spanned by a stone bridge. A densely-wooded range occupies the space between the Feria and the Albuera.

Beresford drew up his battle with Blake's Spaniards on the right, William Stewart's and the 2d division in the centre, and the Portuguese on the left. The stone bridge was commanded by a battery, and the village of Albuera was held by Alten's German brigade.

But Beresford calculated only on an attack in front. Soult arrived in the evening, and saw that Beresford had neglected to occupy an isolated hill on the Spanish right, which trended back towards the Valverde Road, and looked into the rear of Beresford's line. If Soult could succeed in suddenly placing his masses there, he might roll up the allies on their centre, seize the Valverde Road, cut off the retreat, and finish the victory with his cavalry. Beresford had also neglected to occupy the wooded range between the Albuera and the Feria. Of this range Soult made able use. During the night he placed behind it the greater part of Girard's 5th corps, Latour-Maubourg's heavy cavalry, and Ruty's guns. A force of 15,000 men with 30 guns was thus concentrated within ten minutes' march of the allies' right wing, entirely unknown to Beresford. Godinot's brigade, with 10 guns and the light cavalry, was left to make a feint on the bridge and village, and Werlé's brigade was placed in reserve.

At nine in the morning (May 16, 1811) Godinot issued from the woods and attacked the bridge and the village, but Beresford's suspicions were aroused by observing that Werlé did not follow closely. Correctly judging that the main effort would be made on the right, he sent Colonel (after Viscount) Hardinge to desire Blake to form part of his first and all his second line on the broad part of the hill at right angles to the actual front. The Hibernian-Spaniard refused with great heat, maintaining that the real attack was at the village and bridge, and only yielded when the French were upon him in force; for Werlé had joined the 5th corps, and the light cavalry had joined Latour-Maubourg's dragoons. Ere the Spaniards could execute their perilous movement Ruty's guns opened on their disordered ranks, and drove them back in confusion with great slaughter. Soult thought the battle was won, and pushed forward his columns, but just then William Stewart —"Auld Grog Willie," as he was familiarly termed in the Scottish regiments, from his frequent orders for extra allowances of grog—brought up a brigade of the 2d division, under Colborne. Stewart, "whose boiling courage generally overlaid his jugment," would not wait to form in order of battle, but hurried the men up the hill in columns of companies, passed the Spanish right, and attempted to open a line by succession of battalions as they arrived; but the French fire was too destructive to be borne passively, and the foremost troops charged. At this time (about noon) a heavy rain was passing over the heights, and obscured the view; and as the foremost troops were charging, the French hussars and lancers swooped down upon them, captured six guns, and sabring to left and right, almost annihilated the 3d (Buffs), 48th, and 66th—the 31st alone, which was on the left, having time to form square. An exciting contest took place over the colours of the Buffs. Ensign Thomas was cut down and his flag was seized, but it was recovered in the struggle over his body. Ensign Walsh was severely wounded, but he tore the flag from the broken staff and thrust it into his breast, where it was found after the battle saturated with blood. During the tumult a lancer rode at Beresford, but the marshal, a man of great personal strength and as bold as a lion, pushed the lance aside and hurled him from the saddle, and his orderly despatched him. A gust of wind blew the mist and smoke aside, and revealed the state of matters on the heights to General Lumley in the plain. Lumley immediately sent four squadrons against the straggling lancers and cut a great many of them off. He also ordered Penne-Villemur's Spanish cavalry to charge the French horsemen in the plain: the Spaniards galloped forward until within a few yards of their foes, and then fled pell-mell.

The thick weather which ruined Colborne's brigade also prevented Soult from gaining a view of the whole field, and his heavy columns had been kept inactive when the decisive blow might have been struck. And now Beresford was trying to bring the Spaniards forward, but they would not advance. He seized an ensign by the breast and bore him and his colours to the front in his iron grasp, but as soon as the man was released he ran back to his countrymen, who remained immovable. But the 29th was advancing to the succour of Colborne's brigade, clearing their path of the flying Spaniards by musketry. Julius Hartman's British guns were fast coming into action—over the wounded, "deaf to their cries, and averting their gaze from the brave fellows thus laid prostrate in the dust," according to Londonderry. And Stewart, who had escaped the slaughter, brought up Houghton's brigade; and the battle was renewed.

The cannon belched grape at half range, the musketry pealed incessantly, often within pistol-shot, and the carnage on both sides was terrific. No British regiment had more than a third of its number standing. The 57th—the old "Die-Hards"—entered the action with a total of 570, and lost 430, including their colonel, Inglis, who cried to his men as they swept over him, "Well done, my lads, you'll die hard at any rate!" Worst of all, ammunition began to fail, the English fire slackened, and a French column was established in advance upon the right flank. Beresford wavered, and gave the necessary orders for a retreat; but the battle was saved by the happy inspiration of Colonel Hardinge, who, entirely on his own responsibility, urged Cole, who had just come up from Badajos, to advance with the 4th division, and Colonel Abercrombie to advance with the 3d brigade of the 2d division. Cole led on his fusiliers (7th and 23d), flanked by a battalion of the Lusitanian legion, mounted the hill, drove off the lancers who were riding furiously about the captured guns, recovered five of the guns and a colour, and dashed up to the right of Houghton's brigade as Abercrombie passed to the front on its left.

"Such a gallant line," says Napier, "issuing from the midst of the smoke, and rapidly separating itself from the confused and broken multitude, startled the enemy's masses, which were increasing and pressing onward as to an assured victory; they wavered, hesitated, and then vomiting forth a storm of fire, hastily endeavoured to enlarge their front, while a fearful discharge of grape from all their artillery whistled through the British ranks. Myers was killed, Cole and the three colonels, Ellis, Blakeney, and Hawkshawe, fell wounded, and the fusiliers, struck by the iron tempest, reeled and staggered like sinking ships; but suddenly and sternly recovering, they closed on their terrible enemies, and then was seen with what a strength and majesty the British soldier fights. In vain did Soult with voice and gesture animate his Frenchmen, in vain did the hardiest veterans break from the crowded columns and sacrifice their lives to gain time for the mass to open out on such a fair field; in vain did the mass itself bear up, and, fiercely striving, fire indiscriminately upon friends and foes, while the horsemen hovering on the flank endeavoured to charge the advancing line. Nothing could stop that astonishing infantry. No sudden burst of undisciplined valour, no nervous enthusiasm weakened the stability of their order, their flashing eyes were bent on the dark columns in their front, their measured tread shook the ground, their dreadful volleys swept away the head of every formation, their deafening shouts overpowered the dissonant cries that broke from all parts of the tumultuous crowd, as slowly and with a horrid carnage it was pushed by the incessant vigour of the attack to the farthest edge of the hill. In vain did the French reserves mix with the struggling multitude to sustain the fight, their efforts only increased the irremediable confusion, and the mighty mass, breaking like a loosened cliff, went headlong down the steep: the rain flowed after in streams discoloured with blood, and 1800 unwounded men, the remnant of 6000 unconquerable British soldiers, stood triumphant on the fatal hill."

The battle was over. All firing ceased before three o'clock. There was no pursuit. In four hours 7000 of the allies and 8000 of the French had been struck down. Blake churlishly refused Beresford's request for a detachment to assist in the removal of the wounded, who lay all night amidst the piles of dead, drenched by the torrents of rain which swept over the heights. The Feria was choked with the bodies of the wounded, who crawled down to the stream to quench their parching thirst. Well might Byron exclaim—

"O Albuera, fatal field of strife!"

The loss, in proportion to the numbers engaged, is unparalleled in modern war. Of 7000 British, 4400 were slain or disabled. But the moral results of the unconquerable firmness which produced this terrible carnage were, as things go in war, worth the purchase. On their own confession, the French, after fighting all Europe, felt they had at last met their match, and never afterwards joined battle with the British without a secret fear of the terrible charge of their infantry. As to the immediate results, Soult would not hazard a second attack to retrieve his failure, and on the day but one after retired to Seville. Beresford went to Lisbon to reorganise the Portuguese army, and the siege of Badajos was undertaken by Wellington in person. Little progress was made, however, when Marmont and Soult advanced with 64,000 men and 90 guns to raise the siege. Another attempt on Ciudad Rodrigo brought Dorsenne and Soult with 60,000 men into that quarter, and after the skirmishes of El Bodon and Aldea del Ponte, Wellington put his army into cantonments on the Coa.

When Beresford went to Portugal, the command in North Estramadura was conferred on General (afterwards Lord) Hill—"Daddy Hill," as he was called in his own division from his habitual kindness. Hill was ordered to drive Girard from Carceres, that the district might be open to Murillo for forage, and in the execution of this service an opportunity occurred of effecting a very neat and complete surprise. Girard was driven from Carceres, but the weather was wet and stormy, and no certain information could be obtained of his movements, till, as Hill was pursuing by a cross-road, in hopes to intercept his march, he heard that Girard had halted at Arroyo dos Molinos, leaving a rearguard at Albala, on the main road to Carceres. This showed that Girard knew nothing of Hill's route, and only looked to a pursuit from Carceres; so Hill resolved to surprise him, and made a forced march to Alcuesca, within a league of Arroyo dos Molinos. A soldier of the 71st, who accompanied his regiment on this occasion, says, "It was now nigh 10 o'clock. We were placed in the houses, but our wet and heavy accoutrements were on no account to be taken off. At 12 o'clock, we received our allowance of rum, and shortly after the sergeants tapped at the doors, calling not above their breath. We turned out, and at slow time continued our march. The whole night was one continued pour of rain. Weary and wet to the skin, we trudged on without exchanging a word, nothing breaking the silence of the night but the howling of the wolves. The tread of the men was drowned by the pattering of the rain."

At two in the morning (Oct. 28, 1811), the troops arrived within half-a-mile of Arroyo, and under cover of a low ridge formed three columns of attack, the infantry on the wings and the cavalry in the centre. The left column (50th, 71st, and 92d), under Lieutenant-colonel Stewart, marched straight upon the village; the right column, under Howard, moved upon the Truxillo Road; and Penne-Villemur's cavalry kept a due place between both. One brigade of the French had already marched out upon the Medellin Road, and the rest were preparing to depart. The horses of the rearguard were unbridled and tied to olive trees, and the infantry gathering on the Medellin Road outside the village. It was now dawning light, but a thick mist rolled down from the craggy Sierra Montanches. Amid the clatter of the elements, for a perfect tempest was raging, arose a terrific shout. Girard was in a house waiting for his horse; he thought it was a mere raid of Spaniards, for the British were not usually such early risers, but he was undeceived when he heard the bagpipes playing the appropriate air of "Hey, Johnny Cope!" and before he could form his infantry, the 71st and 92d Highlanders came charging down the street.

"The French rearguard of horsemen," says Napier, "fighting and struggling hard, were driven to the end of the village, while the infantry, hurriedly forming squares, endeavoured to 'cover the main body of the cavalry, which was gathered on the left. Then the 71st, lining the garden-walls, opened a galling fire on the nearest square; the 92d filed out upon the French right; the 50th regiment secured the prisoners in the village, and the rest of the column, headed by the Spanish cavalry, skirted the outside of the houses, and endeavoured to intercept the retreat. Soon the guns opened on the French squares, and the 13th Dragoons captured their artillery, while the 9th Dragoons and German Hussars charged and dispersed their cavalry. Girard, an intrepid officer, although wounded, still kept his infantry together, and continued his retreat by the Truxillo Road; but the right column of the allies was in possession of that line, their cavalry and artillery were close upon the French flank, and the left column was again coming up fast. In this desperate situation, his men falling by fifties, Girard would not surrender, but sought to escape in dispersion by scaling the almost inaccessible rocks of the sierra. His pursuers, not less obstinate, also divided. The Spaniards ascended the hills at an easier part beyond his left, the 39th regiment and Ashworth's Portuguese turned the mountain on the Truxillo Road, and the 28th and 34th, led by General Howard, followed the French step by step up the rocks, taking prisoners every moment, until the pursuers, heavily loaded, were unable to continue this trial of speed with men who had thrown away their arms and packs." Of 3000 French troops, the finest in Spain, who had slept in Arroyo dos Molinos that night, but 600 escaped. Including General Bron and the Prince of Aremberg, 1300 were taken; and Girard also lost all his artillery and baggage and a large sum of money. The loss of the allies was only a few men killed and wounded.

Among the stirring events of 1811, there occurred a frigate-action off Lissa, an island off the coast of Dalmatia, since rendered memorable by the defeat, in 1866, of an Italian fleet by Admiral Tegethoff. Commodore Dubardieu had sailed thither from Ancona, with five hundred troops, as a garrison for the island when they should conquer it, and fell in with a British squadron under Captain William Hoste (March 13, 1811). The hostile force, partly French and partly Venetian, numbered four large 40-gun frigates, and two carrying 32 guns, besides a 16-gun brig and four small vessels. The British squadron consisted of the *Amphion*, 32, Captain Hoste; *Active*, 32, Captain A. Gordon; *Volage*, 28, Captain Phipps Hornby; and *Cerberus*, 32, Captain Whitby. In all, the enemy's ships carried 300 guns and 2500 men, and the British 154 guns and 880 men.

In an official letter published in the "Moniteur," Commodore Dubardieu had expressed regret that he should on a former occasion have been "avoided" by Hoste; but he had not the slightest cause to complain on that score now at least, notwithstanding the great disparity between the forces. Hoste eagerly accepted battle, and bore down in compact line. Just before the two squadrons got within gun-shot he telegraphed, "REMEMBER NELSON!" and loud hurrahs rose from the four ships' companies. The action began at 9 A.M., the wind at north-west. Dubardieu formed his squadron in double line, and bore down to cut Hoste's squadron in two, but the British kept their line so close and compact as completely to fustrate the attempt. The French commodore, in the *Favorite*, now evinced a disposition to board the *Amphion* upon the quarter, and his men were all ready upon the forecastle; but when the ships were only a few yards apart, a brass $5\frac{1}{2}$-inch howitzer upon the *Amphion's* quarter-deck, loaded with 750 musket-balls, was discharged at the *Favorite's* larboard bow, and committed dreadful havoc among the crowd of boarders assembled on the forecastle. Among those who fell was Dubardieu himself, who was standing ready to lead on his men to the assault. Foiled in her endeavours to board the *Amphion*, or to cut the line astern of her, the *Favorite* stood on engaging the *Amphion*, with the intention of rounding her bows and placing the British squadron between two fires. Hoste allowed her to continue this attempt until 9.40 A.M., when the ships were within half-a-cable's length of the shore of Lissa; he then threw out the signal for his ships to wear together; the *Favorite* attempted to do the same, and got to leeward of the *Amphion*, but scarcely had she put her helm up when she struck on the rocks and bilged. This was precisely Hoste's object in standing so near the shore. In the afternoon, the *Favorite* was set on fire by her surviving crew, and blew up with a great explosion.

The *Flore* and *Bellona*—the latter Venetian—now took up a station on either quarter of the *Amphion*, and Hoste gradually bore up to close with the *Flore*, his heaviest and most annoying antagonist. At 11.15 A.M., he brought his larboard broadside to bear directly on the French ship's starboard bow, and opened so heavy a broadside, that in five minutes the *Flore* ceased firing and struck her colours. No sooner had he finished with this enemy than he turned his attention to the *Bellona*, which had been raking the *Amphion* astern with destructive effect. Wearing round on the starboard tack, and taking a position on the *Bellona's* weather bow, the *Amphion* poured in one or two broadsides, and compelled her to strike a few minutes before noon.

When, at 9.40 A.M., Captain Hoste threw out the signal to wear, the rudder of the *Cerberus* was choked with a shot, and the *Volage* got round before her. The little *Volage* now led, followed by the *Cerberus*, the *Active*, and the *Amphion*, then beginning to be engaged with the *Flore* and *Bellona*. Thinking to make an easy conquest, the *Danäe* took up a position abreast of her, but was soon taught to keep her distance by the *Volage's* carronades. The *Corona* and the *Carolina* attached themselves to the *Cerberus*, and in a short time that vessel, which wanted 90 men of her complement, was much shattered in her hull and nearly disabled in her rigging. The *Active* was in the meantime doing her best to come up to the assistance of her friends, and the moment she made her appearance the *Danäe*, *Carolina*, and *Corona* made all sail to the eastward; but after a smart chase, and a spirited action of three-quarters of an hour, the *Active* closed the *Corona*, and at 2.30 P.M. compelled her to haul down the Venetian flag. The other vessels were all by this time safe under the batteries of Lessina, as also was the *Flore*, which dishonourably made sail away after she had struck her flag.

In this brilliant action the loss of the British was 45 killed and 145 wounded. The loss of the French was never known, but it must have been severe. The *Favorite* and the *Corona* had each about 200 killed and wounded, and the *Bellona* 140. The captains present at Lissa, one of the most glorious actions to the British arms, each received a medal, and the first lieutenants were promoted to the rank of commander. "Fresh and unfaded," says Mr. James, "will be the laurels which Captain Hoste and his gallant companions gained at Lissa."

The year 1811 is also memorable for the conquest of Java (September 26), by a land force of 12,000 men, under Sir Samuel Achmuty, and a powerful fleet under Rear-admiral Stopford. The maritime war was thus closed by the extinction of the last remnant of the colonial empire of France, and Lord Minto, who accompanied the expedition, was able to announce in his despatches that "the French flag was nowhere to be seen flying, from Cape Comorin to Cape Horn!"

At this period (1811–12) the French force in the Peninsula amounted to 370,000 men, including 40,000 cavalry; and at least 140,000 men were disposable for active service against the British, after providing for garrisons and detachments. To cope with this enormous force Wellington had an army nominally 80,000 strong, but the reduced state of the Portuguese regiments, and the vast number of the British sick—many of whom had served in the ill-fated Walcheren expedition—left no more than 50,000 fit for actual service. Then Wellington was hampered by the incurable corruption and imbecility of every branch of the Portuguese administration, the total want of discipline and equipment of the Spanish troops, the pride and obstinacy of their generals, and the timidity and ignorance of the English Ministry at home. The French, on the other hand, had so completely exhausted the country that they were unable to keep together for any length of time in large bodies; guerilla bands cut off their communications and murdered their stragglers, while the bitter animosity that prevailed between King Joseph at Madrid and the marshals in the provinces, and the discord between the marshals themselves, prevented any unity of design or co-operation. And now, when Napoleon's power had reached its culminating point, and the hour was at hand for its decline and fall, the difficulties of the French in the Peninsula were on the increase; while Wellington commenced that brilliant series of operations which compelled the attention of the Portuguese, extorted the respect of the Spaniards, and secured the hearty co-operation of his own government: that series of operations which, though momentarily checked, burst forth into a full flood of victory, drove the French across the Pyrenees, and planted the British standards in triumph on the walls of Paris.

As soon as the French armies of Portugal and the North had dispersed into winter quarters, Wellington made arrangements for the reduction of Ciudad Rodrigo—the City of Roderick. Ciudad stands on the right bank of the Agueda. It was defended by a rampart, 30 feet high, and outside of this a second bulwark, called a fausse-braye, raised 12 feet above the level of the ground; by the old castle, which stood on an elevation in the south-west of the town, and commanded the bridge; by two ridges on the north of the town, the Great Teson and the Little Teson, the former with a redoubt in the centre; by the strongly-fortified convent of Santa Cruz between the Little Teson and the river; and the two convents of St. Francisco and St. Domingo, in the north-eastern suburbs, fortified for musketry. The garrison numbered 1900. Wellington had 35,000 men available for the siege, and 70 guns, but from the difficulty of transport only 38 could be brought to the trenches, and there would have been a lack of ammunition even for these if 8000 shot had not been found amidst the ruins of Almeida.

Hill remained in the south to keep Drouet in play, and exaggerated reports were circulated about the sickness prevalent in the British camp, in order to lull the watchfulness of Marmont. Wellington calculated that the place might be won in twenty-four days. On New-Year's Day, 1812, a trestle bridge was laid down on the Agueda 6 miles below Ciudad, and the materials for the siege were brought forward as fast as the native carters could be induced to drive their teams. On the 8th January the light division passed the Agueda at a ford three miles above the town, and took a position behind the Great Teson, from which it was intended to advance the trenches. During the night, after a furious onset, Colonel Colborne carried the redoubt on the Great Teson, and before daybreak the first parallel was sunk. On the 9th the 1st division moved into the trenches, a cordon of posts was established round the fortress to prevent any message for relief being sent to Marmont, and 1200 workmen commenced three counter-batteries for 11 guns each. On the 12th, under cover of a heavy fog, pits were dug in front of the trenches, and riflemen posted in them to pick off the French gunners. On the night of the 13th the Germans captured the Santa Cruz convent, and the arming of the batteries was completed. The enemy made a sally on the 14th, but did not do much damage, and at half-past four that afternoon the signal was given for 25 guns to open fire on the fausse-braye and rampart, while two pieces were directed against the convent of St. Francisco. The evening was remarkably clear and still. Napier describes the spectacle as at once "fearful and sublime. The enemy replied to the assailants' fire with more than 50 pieces; the bellowing of 80 large guns shook the ground far and wide; the smoke rested in heavy volumes about the battlements of the place, or curled in light wreaths about the numerous spires; the shells, hissing through the air, seemed fiery serpents leaping from the darkness; the walls crashed to the stroke of the bullet; and the distant mountains faintly returning the sound appeared to mourn over the falling city. And when night put an end to this turmoil, the quick clatter of musketry was heard like the pattering of hail after a peal of thunder, for the 40th regiment then carried the convent of St. Francisco by storm, and established itself in the suburb."

On the night of the 15th five more guns were mounted to batter a small breach at the turret. The cannonade continued during the 16th, 17th, and 18th; on the 19th both breaches were reported practicable. The assault was then ordered, and the battering-guns were turned against the artillery of the ramparts. The 3d and light divisions and Pack's Portuguese were told off into four columns:—(1) On the right attack, Colonel O'Toole, with a company of the 83d and the 2d Caçadores, to issue from some houses on the south side of the river, cross the bridge, and assail the outworks in front of the castle; the 50th and 94th, posted behind the convent of Santa Cruz, and having the 77th in reserve, to enter the ditch at the extremity of the counterscarp, escalade the fausse-braye, and scour it on their left as far as the great breach. (2) To the assault of the great breach, a storming party of the 3d division, supported by Mackinnon's brigade, and preceded by 180 men carrying hay-bags to throw into the ditch. (3) On the left attack, a storming party of the light division, supported by Vandeleur's and Andrew Barnard's brigades, and preceded by the 3d Caçadores with hay-bags, to make for the small breach; to send three companies to scour the fausse-braye to their right, and so connect the left and centre attacks; to their left to force a passage at the Salamanca gate. (4) For a false attack, Pack's Portuguese to make an escalade at the St. Jago gate at the opposite side of the town.

The town clock had struck seven, and the men were all at their posts. Lord Londonderry, himself a witness of the scene, tells us, "The evening was calm and tranquil, and the moon, in her first quarter, shed over the scene a feeble light, which, without disclosing the shape or form of particular objects, rendered their rude outline distinctly visible. There stood the fortress, a confused mass of masonry, with its open breaches like shadows cast upon the wall; whilst not a gun was fired from it, and all within was still and motionless, as if it were already a ruin, or its inhabitants buried in sleep. On our side, again, the trenches, crowded with armed men, among whom not so much as a whisper might be heard, presented no unapt resemblance to a thunder-cloud, or a volcano in that state of tremendous quiet which precedes its most violent eruption."

In an instant the scene was changed, and the slumbering volcano awoke. The attack commenced on the right, and was instantly taken up along the whole line. The men sprang from the trenches and made for the ditch, pelted by a tempest of grape from the ramparts. Ridge, Donkin, and Campbell, with the 5th, 77th, and 99th, scoured the fausse-braye, and pushed up to the great breach. The French exploded their combustibles and mine prematurely, but General Mackinnon and some others fell. The British pushed on and drove the French behind the retrenchment, but these rallied, aided by the musketry from the houses, and the fight was obstinate. Two guns that flanked the top of the breach raked the passage with grape, and filled it with piles of dead and dying. On the left the stormers of the light division would not wait for the hay-bags, but ran forward and cleared the 300 yards that lay between them and the edge of the glacis, jumped down the scarp, a depth of eleven feet, and rushed up the fausse-braye under a smashing discharge of grape and musketry. The fiery Crawford fell mortally wounded, but the forlorn hope and the stormers surged together into the breach and carried it. Then the supporting regiments came up in sections abreast, the 52d wheeled to the left, the 43d to the right, and by this attack, which lasted only ten minutes, the place was won. The 43d and the stormers took the defenders of the great breach in the rear, the 3d division burst through the retrenchment, and the French fled to the castle, where Lieutenant Gurwood received the governor's sword.

"Now," says Napier, "into the streets plunged the assailants from all quarters, for O'Toole's attack was also successful, and at the other side of the town Pack's Portuguese and the reserves, meeting no resistance, had entered. Throwing off the restraints of discipline the troops committed frightful excesses; the town was fired in three or four places, the soldiers menaced their officers, and shot each other; many were killed in the market-place, intoxication soon increased the tumult, and at last, the fury rising to absolute madness, a fire was wilfully lighted in the great magazine, by which the town would have been blown to atoms but for the energetic courage of some officers and a few soldiers who still preserved their senses."

Such was the siege of Ciudad Rodrigo, which lasted twelve days—only half the time calculated on by Wellington. The allies lost during the whole operations 324 killed and 1378 wounded, of whom 146 were killed and 560 wounded in the assault; of the French 300 were killed, and 1500 men and 80 officers were made prisoners. Unfortunately the slaughter did not end with the storm, for next day as the prisoners and their escort were marching out by the breach, an accidental explosion blew numbers of both into the air. Immense stores of ammunition were captured, with 150 guns, including Marmont's battering-train. The place was put in repair as soon as possible and handed over to the Spaniards, from whom Wellington received the title of Duke of Ciudad Rodrigo. The Portuguese made him Marquis of Torres Vedras, and the Home Government rewarded him with the title of Earl and an additional pension of £2000.

Wellington now turned his eyes to Badajos, which was much stronger than Ciudad. The garrison numbered 5000 men, French, Hessians, and Spaniards, and Phillipon, the governor, had done everything that art and labour could do to secure the fortress entrusted to his care. The place was defended by the Guadiana and the tributary Rivillas, by a castle at the confluence of these two waters, by strong works containing eight regular bastions and five gates, the works of San Christoval and a fortified bridge-head on the other side of the Guadiana, the work of the Pardaleras on the high ground to the south, the lunette of San Roque to the south-west of the castle beyond the Rivillas, and to the south-east of the lunette the enclosed and palisaded outwork of the Picurina. It was on this side it was determined to proceed: to attack the Picurina and breach the Trinidad and Santa Maria bastions, where Phillipon had not had time to complete the additional defences. If secrecy and speed were necessary at Ciudad, they were still more necessary at Badajos. More than one ruse was practised to deceive the enemy. Depôts were ostentatiously formed across the Douro, as if for a march to the north. The siege train was embarked at Lisbon ostensibly for Oporto, but when the vessels were at sea they altered their course and landed it at Setuval, whence it was conveyed by water and by carts to Elvas. By the beginning of March, 53 battering-guns and a large quantity of stones, gabions, and fascines were collected, and a pontoon bridge had been sent on from Lisbon.

Sir Thomas Picton took charge of the investment, with 15,000 men of the 3d, 4th, and light divisions, and Pack's Portuguese. The covering army, of 30,000 men, was divided into two corps, under Graham and Hill. On the night of the 17th March, when the sound of the pickaxes was drowned by a storm, ground was broken 160 yards from the Picurina; and next night two batteries were traced out. On the 19th, the garrison sallied out and made a raid on the engineer's park, but were repulsed with the loss of 300 men. Another sally was made the following night: the defenders gave the besiegers no rest; the equinoctial rains fell in torrents, saturating the ground and flooding the Guadiana; and for a few days the siege was in danger of being abandoned. But on the 24th, when the weather had cleared, the batteries were armed with ten 24-pounders, eleven 18-pounders, and seven 5½-inch howitzers. On the 25th the bombardment commenced; San Roque was silenced, and the Picurina seemed so much damaged that on that same night it was carried by storm by Kempt and the 3d division, but not without the loss of 54 killed and 265 wounded.

On the 6th April the third breach was made, and the assault was ordered for that evening. It was to be made by 18,000 men, on four points—(1) Picton with the 3d division to cross the Rivillas from the trenches, and escalade the castle; Major Wilson of the 48th to storm San Roque. (2) Colville with the 4th and Barnard with the light division, with reserves in the quarry, to storm the breaches. (3) Leith with the 5th division to make a feint on the Pardaleras, while he sent Walker and his brigade to make a real attack on the St. Vincent bastion at the other end of the town. (4) Power's Portuguese, on the right of the Guadiana, to make a feint on the fortified bridge-head.

The night was dry and foggy. Not a sound was heard but the croaking of the frogs in the ditches, and the deep voices of the French sentinels telling that all was well in Badajos. The assault was fixed for ten o'clock, but half an hour before that time a carcass—shell filled with inflammable matter—thrown from the castle discovered the ranks of the "fighting third," and Kempt at once led them forward. Passing the Rivillas in single file by a narrow bridge, under a withering fire, they ran up the hill, reached the foot of the castle, spread along the front, and reared their ladders. The defenders plied them with musketry from the flanks, hurled down stones, logs of wood, and blazing shells on their heads, bayoneted those who reached the top, and pushed the ladders from the walls. Amid the rattle of musketry, the shouts of the combatants, and the cries and groans of the maimed and wounded, the dreadful strife continued until all the ladders were overthrown, when the assailants retired under the ridge of a hill and re-formed. Again, in a few minutes, Ridge of the 5th sprang forward, and calling on his men to follow him, planted a ladder to the right of the former attack, where the wall was lower and an embrasure afforded some facility; a second ladder was planted by the grenadier officer Canch; the next moment Ridge and Canch were on the ramparts, their men swarmed up after them, and the garrison was driven through the gate into the town. New French troops came up, and there was a sharp action, ending in favour of the besiegers, but Ridge fell, "and no man died that night with more glory—yet many died, and there was much glory."

The castle was won, but who shall describe the tumult at the breaches? Napier says it was such "as if the very earth had been rent asunder, and its central fires bursting upwards uncontrolled. The two divisions had reached the glacis just as the firing at the castle commenced, and the flash of a single musket discharged from the covered way as a signal showed them that the French were ready: yet no stir was heard, and darkness covered the breaches. Some hay-packs were thrown, some ladders placed, and the forlorn hopes of the storming parties of the light division, 500 in all, descended into the ditch without opposition, but then a bright flame shooting upwards displayed all the terrors of the scene. The ramparts crowded with dark figures and glittering arms were on the one side, on the other the red columns of the British, deep and broad, were coming on like streams of burning lava; it was the touch of the magician's wand, for a crash of thunder followed, and with incredible violence the storming parties were dashed to pieces by the explosion of hundreds of shells and powder barrels.

"For an instant the light division stood on the brink of the ditch amazed at the terrific sight, but then with a shout that matched even the sound of the explosion the men flew down the ladders, or, disdaining their aid, leaped reckless of the depth into the gulf below—and at the same moment, amidst a blaze of musketry that dazzled the eyes, the 4th division came running in and descended with a like fury. There were only five ladders for the two columns, which were close together, and a deep cut made in the bottom of the ditch as far as the counterguard of the Trinidad was filled with water from the inundation; into that watery snare the head of the 4th division fell, and it is said above 100 of the fusiliers, the men of Albuera, were there smothered. Those who followed checked not, but, as if such a disaster had been expected, turned to the left and thus came upon the face of the unfinished ravelin which, being rough and broken, was mistaken for the breach and instantly covered with

K

men: yet a wide and deep chasm was still between them and the ramparts, from whence came a deadly fire wasting their ranks. Thus baffled they also commenced a rapid discharge of musketry, and disorder ensued. . . . Great was the confusion, for the ravelin was covered with men of both divisions, and while some continued to fire, others jumped down and ran towards the breach, many also passed between the ravelin and the counterguard of the Trinidad, the two divisions got mixed, the reserves, which should have remained at the quarries, also came pouring in until the ditch was quite filled, the rear still crowding forward, and all cheering vehemently. The enemy's shouts also were loud and terrible, and the bursting of shells and of grenades, the roaring of guns from the flanks, answered by the iron howitzers from the battery of the parallel, the heavy roll and horrid explosion of the powder barrels, the whizzing flight of the blazing splinters, the loud exhortations of the officers, and the continual clatter of the muskets, made a maddening din.

"Now a multitude bounded up the great breach as if driven by a whirlwind, but across the top glittered a range of sword-blades, sharp-pointed, keen-edged on both sides, and firmly fixed in ponderous beams chained together and set deep in the ruins; and for ten feet in front the ascent was covered with loose planks studded with sharp iron points, on which feet being set the planks moved, and the unhappy soldiers falling forward on the spikes rolled down upon the ranks behind. Then the Frenchmen, shouting at the success of their stratagem and leaping forward, plied their shot with terrible rapidity, for every man had several muskets, and each musket in addition to its ordinary charge contained a small cylinder of wood stuck full of wooden slugs, which scattered like hail when they were discharged. Once and again the assailants rushed up the breaches, but always the sword-blades, immovable and impassable, stopped their charge, and the hissing shells and thundering powder barrels exploded unceasingly. Hundreds of men had fallen, hundreds more were dropping, still the heroic officers called aloud for new trials, and sometimes followed by many, sometimes by a few, ascended the ruins; and so furious were the men that in one of these charges the rear strove to push the foremost on to the sword-blades, willing even to make a bridge of their writhing bodies, but the others frustrated the attempt by dropping down: and men fell so far from the shot, that it was hard to know who went down voluntarily, who were stricken, and many stooped unhurt that never rose again. Vain also would it have been to break through the sword-blades, for the trench and parapet behind the breach were finished, and the assailants, crowded into even a narrower space than the ditch was, would still have been separated from their enemies, and the slaughter would have continued." For two hours these vain attempts continued, and at last the assailants rested sullenly on their muskets, while the defenders on the ramparts took aim at them by the light of carcasses, and mockingly asked why they did not come into Badajos. At midnight, when 2000 brave men had fallen, Wellington sent an order to withdraw and re-form.

Similar bloody scenes were being enacted in the west of the town at the St. Vincent bastion, but fortunately some of the defenders had been called away to aid in recovering the castle, the ramparts were not fully manned, and a corner of the bastion was discovered where the scarp was only twenty feet high, and the embrasure without a gun. At this point three ladders were raised, and some of the men scrambled up with difficulty, the leading men being pushed by their comrades, and then drawing others up after them; and while half the 4th regiment entered the town, the rest scoured the ramparts towards the breach. The French were now conscious that all was lost, and when the attack in front was renewed the defenders at the breach broke. The brave Phillipon, though suffering from a wound, passed the bridge with a few hundred soldiers and entered San Christoval, but surrendered next morning upon summons to Lord Fitzroy Somerset, afterwards Lord Raglan, commander in the Crimea.

"Now," says Napier, "commenced that wild and desperate wickedness which tarnished the lustre of the soldier's heroism. All indeed were not alike, hundreds risked and many lost their lives in trying to stop the violence, but madness generally prevailed, and as the worst men were leaders here, all the dreadful passions of human nature were displayed. Shameless rapacity, brutal intemperance, savage lust, cruelty and murder, shrieks and piteous lamentations, groans, shouts, imprecations, the hissing of fires bursting from the houses, the crashing of doors and windows, and the reports of muskets used in violence, resounded for two days and nights in the streets of Badajos. On the third, when the city was sacked, when the soldiers were exhausted by their own excesses, the tumult rather subsided than was quelled: the wounded were then looked to, the dead disposed of, and the conquerors counted their gains and their losses." They had won a first-rate fortress, 179 guns and mortars, Soult's pontoon train, a vast quantity of military stores, and 3800 prisoners, 1300 having been killed or wounded during the siege. They had lost 72 officers and 963 men killed, and 306 officers and 3483 men wounded. More than 2000 fell at the breaches alone.

"Let it be considered," says the historian of the war, "that this frightful carnage took place in a space of less than 100 yards square; that the slain died not all suddenly nor by one manner of death—that some perished by steel, some by shot, some by water, that some were crushed and mangled by heavy weights, some trampled upon, some dashed to atoms by fiery explosions; that for hours this destruction was endured without shrinking and the town was won at last. Let these things be considered, and it must be admitted a British army bears with it an awful power. And false would it be to say the French were feeble men; the garrison stood and fought manfully and with good discipline, behaving worthily: shame there was none on any side. Yet who shall do justice to the bravery of the British soldiers! the noble emulation of the officers! Who shall measure out the glory of Ridge, of Macleod, of Nicholas, of O'Hare of the 95th, who perished on the breach at the head of the stormers, and with him nearly all the volunteers for that desperate service! Who shall describe the springing valour of that Portuguese grenadier who was killed the foremost man at the Santa Maria! or the martial fury of that desperate rifleman, who, in his resolution to win, thrust himself beneath the chained sword-blades, and then suffered the enemy to dash his head to pieces with the ends of their muskets! Who can sufficiently honour the intrepidity of Walker, of Shaw, and of Canch, or the hardiness of Ferguson of the 43d, who having in former assaults received two deep wounds was here, his former hurts still open, leading the stormers of his regiment, the third time a volunteer, the third time wounded! . . . No age, no nation ever sent forth braver troops to battle than those who stormed Badajos.

"When the extent of the night's havoc was made known to Lord Wellington, the firmness of his nature gave way for a moment, and the pride of conquest yielded to a passionate burst of grief for the loss of his gallant soldiers."

After repairing and victualling the two Spanish fortresses, Wellington prepared to assume the offensive in Spain. As a preliminary step it was desirable to cut the connection between Marmont and Soult by the boat-bridge at Almaraz. This, as the only passage the French had over the Tagus from Toledo to Portugal, was strongly fortified. On the south side of the river was a bridge-head, regularly entrenched and flanked, and commanded by Fort Napoleon, placed on a height in advance. On the north side the bridge was connected by a field work of two faces with Fort Ragusa. The works were armed with 18 guns and garrisoned with 1000 men, and the mountain road over the steep sierra was blocked at the pass of Mirabete by the old castle and other works.

The task of surprising this position was entrusted to Hill, who had with him the 50th, and the 71st and 92d Highlanders. Chowne had been sent to make a false attack on the castle of Mirabete, and the garrison of Fort Napoleon, crowded on the ramparts, were anxiously watching the pillars of white smoke rising on the sierra, and listening to the echoes of the artillery, when (May 19, 1812) a British shout struck their ear, and the 50th and a wing of the 71st came rushing down the hills. The French, however, were not altogether taken by surprise, and opened on the assailants a heavy fire of musketry and artillery, while the guns of Fort Ragusa on the opposite side of the river took them in flank. The assailants made a rush and gained a rising ground, only twenty yards from the ramparts, which covered them from the front fire, leaped into the ditch, spliced their ladders, swarmed up, climbed over the rampart, and fell on the enemy. The French fled towards the bridge-head, and would have crossed the bridge itself had not some of the boats been destroyed by stray shots from the forts, for the English artillerymen had turned the guns of Napoleon on Ragusa, and the two forts were now cannonading each other. Only a few escaped; many of the French leaped into the water and were drowned, and the rest were taken prisoners. To the amazement of the British a panic spread to the garrison of Fort Ragusa, the commander of which evacuated it and fled with his men to Naval-Moral, where he was brought to trial by court-martial, was sentenced to death, and shot at Talavera. Some grenadiers of the 92d Highlanders dashed aside their bonnets and muskets, plunged into the stream, and brought back several boats, by which the bridge was restored, and Fort Ragusa was also won. All the works at the bridge, with a great quantity of stores, thus fell into the hands of the conquerors, and were destroyed.

This preliminary operation accomplished, Wellington crossed the Agueda (June 13), and four days after reached Salamanca, Marmont retiring before him. The forts fell on the 26th; and then commenced an extraordinary series of manœuvres, marchings and countermarchings on the Tormes, in which at one time the two armies were in such close proximity that the officers saluted each other by lowering their swords, and French and British were daily in the habit of bathing in the same stream, until the practice was forbidden by a general order. In these manœuvres, "grand French military combinations," the "Moniteur" called them, "which command victory and decide the fate of empires," the advantage was all on the side of Marmont, who effected a junction with Bonnet from the Asturias, and reopened his communications with the army of the centre under King Joseph. On the night of the 21st July the two armies lay facing each other on the heights of San Christoval, near Salamanca, and Wellington, hearing that Marmont was about to be joined by General Chauvel with the cavalry from Caffarelli's Biscay army, and that Joseph was coming up by forced marches, resolved to begin his retreat the following day; but Marmont was aware that on the arrival of Joseph or Jourdan he would be superseded, and was ambitious of gaining a victory before they came up. Next day (July 22, 1812), therefore, Marmont sent some troops to seize the Arapeiles or Hermanitos, two heights on Wellington's right; and as this would have compelled Wellington to fight on disadvantageous ground, with his back to the Tormes, a detachment was sent to stop them; the French gained the height next to themselves, but were repulsed from the other. This rendered a new disposition of the allies necessary, and thinking to take advantage of it, Marmont sent Maucune with two divisions, 50 guns, and light cavalry, along his left, to menace the Ciudad Rodrigo road; but the movement was made so carelessly that a great chasm was created between the French left and centre. It was three o'clock, and Wellington had retired for some refreshment, but no sooner did he see the movement, than he cried, "At last I have them!"

Suddenly the dark mass of troops on the English Hermanito rushed violently down into the basin between the hills, amidst a storm of bullets, and the order of battle was immediately formed—(from the left) the 4th and 5th divisions, Bradford's Portuguese, and Le Marchant's heavy cavalry in the first line; the 6th and 7th divisions and Anson's light cavalry in the second line, which was prolonged by the Spaniards in the direction of the 3d division, which, reinforced by Arentschild's German hussars and D'Urban's Portuguese horsemen, closed the extreme right far behind at Aldea Tejada. On the highest ground behind all was a reserve composed of the light division, Pack's Portuguese, and Bock's and Alten's cavalry. When this disposition was completed, the 3d division and its attendant horsemen received orders to form in four columns, and, flanked on the left by 12 guns, to cross the enemy's line of march. The rest of the first line was to advance whenever the attack of the 3d division should be developed; and Pack's brigade was to assail the French Hermanito.

At five o'clock Pakenham with the 3d division fell on Maucune's first division under Thomières, who had just then reached the brow of a hill in the expectation of seeing the allies in full retreat. Two batteries of artillery took Thomières in flank, and Pakenham's columns, forming lines as they advanced, assailed him in front. The gunners of the French stood manfully to their guns, and their light troops poured in a cloud of musketry, under cover of which the main body strove to open a front of battle; but Pakenham's advance was irresistible, and the half-formed lines were dashed into fragments and driven in on the supporting lines. In half an hour the French had been reduced to a perilous state—Thomières was killed, and his division shattered; Bonnet had made an attack on the English Hermanito and been beaten back, severely wounded; the 4th and 5th divisions were steadily pushing back the French centre and right; and, to crown all, Marmont's right arm was shattered by a howitzer shell, and he was born in a litter from the field.

The command now devolved on Clausel, whose division reinforced Maucune's wasted ranks on the left, where the stifling clouds of dust and smoke, and the powerful rays of the sun beating full in their faces, rendered their position far from comfortable. "In this oppressed state," says Napier, "while Pakenham was pressing their left with a conquering violence, while the 5th division was wasting their ranks by fire, the interval between those divisions was suddenly filled with a whirling cloud of dust, which moved swiftly forward, carrying within it the trampling sound of a charging multitude; it passed the left of the 3d division in a chaotic mass, but then opening, Anson's light cavalry and Le Marchant's heavy horsemen were seen to break forth at full speed, and the next moment 1200 French cavalry were trampled down with a terrible clamour and disturbance. Bewildered and blinded, they cast away their arms and crowded through the intervals of the squadrons, stooping and crying out for quarter, while the dragoons, big men on big horses, rode onwards smiting with their long glittering swords in uncontrollable power, and the 3d division following at speed shouted as the French lines fell in succession before this dreadful charge." Le Marchant fell, but Cotton led the victorious horsemen against a second column. The French left was completely broken, and 2000 prisoners, 2 eagles, and 11 guns were taken. It was the work of forty minutes.

Meanwhile a terrible struggle was raging in the centre, where the 4th and 5th divisions were fiercely engaged with Bonnet's troops, who were driven back step by step, though not without causing terrible slaughter. But Pack's Portuguese failed in their attack on the French Hermanito, and the victorious French infantry pressed on the foremost battalion of the 4th division, and drove it back, breathless with previous fighting, till the two regiments in reserve opened fire.

Clausel made astonishing exertions. Ferey's division, with the light cavalry and Bonnet's dragoons, and Sarrut's and Brennier's divisions so long expected from the forest, were drawn up behind Bonnet's infantry, while Foy's division was untouched on the right. Having thus massed his troops for a safe retreat, Clausel made a last throw for victory, and assailing the 4th and 5th divisions in front and flank, fanned the flame of battle till it raged more fiercely than before. The men fell fast, and Anson's cavalry could not charge for the fire of the enemy's artillery. But Wellington sent forward Clinton with the 6th division, while Pakenham pressed on with the 3d. All was lost: the French gallantly bore up against the torrent, but had not the Spaniards, contrary to orders, evacuated the castle of Alba de Tormes, no retreat would have been left for them— their whole army would have been involved in destruction. As it was, their loss was terrible. Out of 44,000 men who had gone into action, they had 14,000 killed, wounded, and prisoners. The loss of the allies—out of 46,000—was 5200, of whom 3179 were British, 2013 Portuguese, and 8 Spaniards! "a fair index, probably, to the share each had taken in the battle." Wellington was rewarded with the dignity of Marquis and £100,000 to buy estates, and the Spanish Government conferred on him the insignia of the Golden Fleece.

Napoleon heard of Salamanca when in the heart of Russia, and felt that his hold on the Peninsula was shaken.

Next day (July 23) Wellington pressed the pursuit, and the rear of the French army was overtaken by Bock's Hanoverian dragoons, who broke three squares of infantry and took 1000 prisoners, with a loss to themselves of only 70 men. It was one of the most brilliant cavalry affairs of the war. The pursuit was continued to Valladolid, and finding that the French were totally disabled for the time, Wellington turned against the army of the centre under Joseph, and entered Madrid (August 12) amid the unbounded joy of the people. Joseph and his court fled to Aranjuez. Many fortresses which had been occupied by the French yielded, Andalusia and Estramadura were evacuated, and Hill advanced to cover Madrid on the south. Wellington again set out for the north, Clausel retreating before him, and laid siege to Burgos (Sept. 19), which contained all the stores and reserve artillery of Marmont's army.

The castle of Burgos was in ruins, but the strong thick walls of the ancient keep were equal to the best casemates, and the keep was strengthened by a hornwork, which had been erected on Mount St. Michael. A church had also been converted into a fort, and the whole was enclosed within three lines, so connected that each would defend the other. The garrison was under the orders of the gallant Du Breton, a soldier of consummate skill and courage. Owing to the great distance from Lisbon, Wellington's heavy artillery could not be brought forward in time. His siege-train was utterly insignificant—only three 18-pounders and five 24-pounders.

Possession of the hornwork was the necessary preliminary to an attack on the castle; and on the evening of the 19th, the light battalion, consisting of the light companies of the 24th, 42d, 58th, 60th, and 79th, drove in the outposts, and lodged themselves in the outworks. After it was dark, the light battalion assailed the gorge of the works, while the 42d made a direct attack in front, to draw off the fire of the garrison. The light companies, on arriving at the gorge, were received with a brisk fire of musketry through the openings of the palisades, causing severe loss; but they continued to press forward, and, without waiting for the application of the felling axes and ladders with which they were provided, the foremost in the attack actually climbed on each other's shoulders and leaped the palisades. In this way, and by means of the scaling ladders, the whole battalion was in a few minutes formed within the work, and a sergeant and twelve men of the 79th having been placed as a guard, at the gate leading to the castle, to prevent the escape of the fugitives, a charge was made on the garrison. But the French in Mount St. Michael numbered between 400 and 500 men, and, forming themselves into a solid mass, they rushed towards the gate, overpowered the small guard placed there, and effected their escape to the castle.

Four assaults achieved no permanent success. 2000 men were lost in these vain attempts, which occupied thirty-three days, and gave the French time to reassemble their forces. Clausel, now joined by the army of the north, was again at the head of 44,000 men; while Soult and Drouet had effected their junction with Joseph, and were marching on Madrid with 58,000 men. It was obviously necessary to retreat on the base of operations, and the retrograde movement commenced (Oct. 21). At the passage of the Carrion (Oct. 25) a severe combat took place, in which the French were defeated. The Douro crossed (Oct. 29), a junction with Hill was effected (Nov. 8), and Wellington took post on the old position of the Arapeiles, and offered battle to the French, who had also effected a junction and amounted to 95,000 men, including 12,000 cavalry, with 120 guns. Jourdan wished to fight, but Soult overruled him, and extending his left wing, compelled Wellington to prosecute his retreat, which ended at Ciudad Rodrigo (Nov. 18).

The British soldier shows nowhere less to advantage than in a retrograde movement. As it was in the retreat on Corunna, so it was in the retreat from Burgos. Peasants were murdered, houses plundered, wine vaults broken open. Men straggled from the colours by the dozen and never returned. In the cellars of Valdemoro, the French found 250 in a helpless state of intoxication. There is no doubt the hardships which the soldiers endured were great. During the last part of the retreat the march lay over a country of flooded clay. Every hour was filled with alarms that the French were upon them. Provisions were not to be had from the difficulty of transport. The private of the 71st, whom we have already quoted, tells an amusing story which shows how the habit of foraging had spread to all ranks. It was when the 1st brigade of the 3d division (50th, 71st, 92d) was retiring from Alba de Tormes. "There was a mill on the river-side near the bridge, wherein a number of our men were helping themselves to flour, while the others were fording. Our colonel (the Hon. Henry Cadogan) rode down and forced them out, throwing a handful of flour on each man as he passed out of the mill. When we were drawn up on the heights, he rode along the column looking for the millers, as we called them. At this moment a fowl put her head out of his coat pocket, and looked first to one side and then to another. We began to laugh; we could not restrain ourselves. He looked amazed and furious at us, then around. At length the major rode up to him and requested him to kill the fowl outright and put it into his pocket. The colonel in his turn laughed, called his servant, and the millers were no more looked after." The total loss of the allies during the retreat from Burgos (including Hill's retreat from Madrid) is estimated at 9000 men, besides a great quantity of baggage. The loss was none the less sad that much of it need never have occurred, as was shown by the condition of the light division and the foot guards, who preserved their discipline. But whenever the army went into winter quarters on the Coa, discipline was restored as if by magic, and the memory of hardship and suffering was lost in the pleasures of the bull-fight and the fandango.

It is true that Wellington was forced to retreat, but the march into Spain was not a failure. The national hostility to the French was fanned, the patriotism of the Cortes was revived, the guerrillas were reanimated, and again hung in swarms on the French lines. The French lost the Asturias, Estramadura, Andalusia, and Murcia, their arsenals and stores were destroyed, and their armies were confined to the exhausted north and centre. They could never hope to recover their sway. Napier says, "Whatever failures there were, and however imposing the height to which the English general's reputation has since attained, this campaign, including the sieges of Rodrigo, Badajos, the forts of Salamanca and of Burgos, the assault of Almaraz, and the fight of Salamanca, will probably be considered his finest illustration of the art of war. Waterloo may be called a more glorious exploit because of the great man who was there vanquished; Assaye may be deemed a more wonderful action,—one indeed to be compared with the victory which Lucullus gained over Tigranes; but Salamanca will always be referred to as the most skilful of Wellington's battles."

CHAPTER IX.—THE PENINSULAR WAR.

LIBERATION OF SPAIN.—1813.

Vitoria—Battles of the Pyrenees—Storming of San Sebastian.

WE now come to the last chapter in the history of the Peninsular War. The struggle was virtually over, and only waited the crowning victory. The winter of 1812–13 saw Wellington on something like an equality with the Imperial legions in point of numbers; for nearly half a million of the veterans of France had perished among the snows of Russia, and enormous drafts were required from the Peninsular armies for the Leipsic campaign, where Napoleon made his last great effort to prop his falling throne. From these reductions, and the wasting losses inflicted by the guerillas, the French troops in the Peninsula in the spring of 1813 did not amount to more than 197,000 who were with the eagles, while the allied armies were swelled to 200,000. Not more than half this great force, however, were British, Germans, or Portuguese, on whom reliance could really be placed, but even the Spaniards were rapidly improving in efficiency under Wellington's system. And what was of the utmost importance, Wellington had at last obtained from the Cortes the supreme command of all the forces engaged in the war, while the French had lost their only military head in the Peninsula in Marshal Soult, who, disgusted at the manner in which his plans had been treated, had demanded his recall from Napoleon, and was serving in Germany.

Active operations were begun about the middle of May. The advanced guard of the allies crossed the Esla (May 31, 1813) after a march of 200 miles in ten days. The castle of Burgos, where so many British lives were lost the year before, was blown up (June

14). The flank of the French was turned; they were compelled to abandon position after position, and fall back across the Ebro. Biscay was evacuated, with the exception of San Sebastian, Santona, and Bilbao; the ports were instantly filled with British vessels, and the British were able to change their base from Portugal to the northern coast. King Joseph, also, in dread of being severed from his friends in northern Spain, quitted Madrid in panic, and fell back across the Ebro.

The concentration of the French forces took place at Vitoria, a little town in the Basque Provinces, 190 miles north-north-east of Madrid, and 70 miles west of the great frontier fortress of Pampeluna. The position was a strong one, and capable of being well defended, but Joseph was no general, and he was to a large extent deprived of the advice and assistance of Marshal Jourdan, who was suffering so severely from fever that he could not mount a horse. In front of Vitoria, which stands on a gentle elevation, a plain, diversified by woods, corn-fields, ditches, vineyards, and hamlets, stretches down to the Zadora, a narrow stream within difficult banks, which keeps a westerly course along the plain for about three miles, and then sweeps round to the south, where it becomes entangled among the offshoots of the Morillo mountains, then rushes through a narrow gorge, called the Puebla Pass, between these mountains and the Puebla range. The cardinal defect of the position was that it contained only one line of retreat, namely, by the royal road from Madrid to Bayonne, which enters the plain at the Puebla Pass on the south-west, traverses it in a north-easterly direction, passes through Vitoria, and again touches the Zadora at Durana. For the impending battle Joseph had 70,000 combatants, and these were spread over a line of nearly eight miles, along the royal road, from Durana on the extreme right to the heights of Puebla on the extreme left. Reille held the right, Gazan the centre, and Maransin the left. D'Erlon's division formed a second line on the centre and left. Fifty guns were massed in front to command the bridges of Mendoza, Tres Puentes, Villodas, and Nanclares, by which the allies must cross to attack the position; but none of these bridges were broken, or covered with field-works to enable Joseph to sally forth upon the attacking army, nor was the Puebla entrenched, nor the heights above occupied in sufficient strength.

Wellington had 78,000 men, 18,000 of them Spaniards, and

arranged his battle in the following order :—On the left, Graham, with 20,000 men, composed of the 1st and 5th Anglo-Portuguese divisions, Bradford's and Pack's independent brigades, Longa's Spanish division, Anson's and Bock's cavalry, and 18 guns, to descend from the north by the Bilbao road, fall on Reille, and attempt the passage at Gamara Mayor and Ariaga, about three-quarters of a mile from Vitoria—by which it was hoped that the French would be completely turned, and cooped up between the Puebla range on the one side and the Zadora on the other; in the centre, Wellington himself, with 30,000 men, composed of the 3d, 4th, 7th, and light divisions, the heavy cavalry, D'Urban's Portuguese horsemen, and the great mass of the artillery, to march across the ridges leading down to the Zadora, and attack the bridges at Mendoza, Tres Puentes, Villodas, and Nanclares; on the right, Hill, with 20,000 men, consisting of Murillo's Spaniards, Silveira's Portuguese, and the 2d British division, with some cavalry and guns, to force a passage at the Puebla Pass, assail Maransin on the heights, and so turn and menace all the French left.

The day (June 21, 1813) dawned in thick mist and a drizzling rain, and the three columns of the allies broke from their encampments on the Bayas—separated from the Zadora by the Morillo range—and marched on the positions severally assigned them. At ten o'clock Hill seized the village of La Puebla, and sent Murillo to climb the steep sides of the range. No opposition was offered to the Spaniards until the foremost troops were near the summit, and then a sharp skirmishing commenced. Murillo was wounded, but his second brigade came up, and the French, aware of the importance of the position, sent a fresh regiment to reinforce Maransin. Colonel Cadogan, with the 71st Highlanders—their pipers playing the favourite regimental air of "Hey, Johnny Cope!"—and a battalion of light infantry, was sent to succour Murillo, and Gazan sent Villatte's division to reinforce Maransin. Hill sent fresh troops, and the struggle was obstinate and long doubtful, but the British secured the summit and gained ground along the side of the mountain, nor could all the efforts of the French dislodge them. In this fight the brave Cadogan, colonel of the 71st, fell mortally wounded. With the remainder of the troops Hill turned to his left, marched through the Puebla Pass, and at one o'clock carried the village of Subijana de Alava in front of

Gazan's line, thus connecting his own right with the troops on the mountain.

The 71st soldier already quoted gives an interesting account of the battle in this part of the field. "Forward," he says, "we moved up the hill. The French had possession of it, but we soon forced them back, and drew up the column on the height, sending out four companies to our left to skirmish. The remainder moved on to the opposite height. As we advanced, driving them before us, a French officer, a pretty fellow, was pricking and forcing his men to stand. They heeded him not— he was very harsh. 'Down with him,' cried one near me, and down he fell, pierced by more than one ball. Scarce were we upon the height, when a column dressed in great-coats, with white covers on their hats, gave us a volley which put us to the right-about at double-quick time, the French close behind, through the 'whins.' Before the four skirmishing companies got the word the French were on them. They likewise thought them Spaniards, until they got a volley which killed or wounded almost every one of them. We retired to the height, covered by the 50th, who gave the pursuing column a volley which checked their speed. We then moved up the remains of our shattered regiment to the height, where we kept shooting away till the bugle sounded to cease firing. We lay on the height for some time. Our thirst was excessive. There was no water on the height, save one small spring, which was rendered useless. One of the men called out in the heat of the action, that he would have a drink let the world go as it would. He stooped to drink; a ball pierced his head, and he fell with it in the well. Thirsty as we were we could not use the water."

Wellington had meanwhile crossed the Morillo range, and placed the 4th division in the rugged grounds and woods opposite the bridge of Nanclares, and the light division, similarly protected, opposite the bridge of Villodas. The day was now clear, and when Hill's battle began, the light division spread along the banks and exchanged fire with the enemy's skirmishers on the other side of the river. The 3d and 7th were delayed by the rough nature of the ground they had to traverse, and while waiting for them to come up, Wellington was told by a Spanish peasant that the bridge of Tres Puentes on the left of the light division was unguarded. The peasant, further, offered to guide the troops over it; Kempt's brigade was directed to the point, and crossing at the double, mounted a steep curving rise of ground, and halted close under the crest, behind the French advanced post, and within a few hundred yards of their line of battle. They were discovered by the French cavalry, and two round shots were fired by the enemy, one of which killed the poor peasant; but, extraordinary as it appears, no further movement was made, and Kempt was reinforced by the 15th Hussars, who galloped over the bridge in single file.

It was now one o'clock, and the sun was shining brightly in a cloudless sky. The musketry of Hill's troops was rattling among the houses of Subijana de Alava, and the distant booming of cannon and a curling smoke faintly seen on the upper reaches of the Zadora showed that Graham was at work on the left. Joseph, finding both his flanks in danger, withdrew the reserve from Gomecha, and ordered Gazan to retire by successive masses; but at that moment the 3d and 7th British divisions were seen moving rapidly towards the bridge of Mendoza. The French guns opened, a body of their cavalry came up, and their light troops commenced a vigorous musketry. Some British guns replied to the French cannon from the opposite bank, and the light troops and the gunners were attacked in flank by Andrew Barnard with the riflemen of Kempt's brigade, and so closely, that the English artillerymen thought his dark-coated troops were enemies, and for a short time played upon them equally with the French. This singular attack enabled the British divisions to cross by the bridge and the fords higher up; the French abandoned the ground in front of Villodas, Hill pressed the enemy harder, the smoke and sound of Graham's attack became more distinct, the French were dispirited and perplexed, and the banks of the Zadora presented a continuous line of fire.

Steadily the allies advanced. Colville and his brigade of the 3d division crossed by one of the fords and engaged the French in front of Margarita and Hermandad, exactly in the centre of their line. Almost at the same time Wellington noticed that the "Englishman's Hill" in front of Arinez was weakly held, and led Picton and his "fighting third," preceded by Andrew Barnard's riflemen, and followed by the remainder of Kempt's brigade and the hussars, in close columns of regiments at a running pace diagonally across the front of both armies towards that central point. Cole, too, advanced from the bridge of Nauclares, and the heavy cavalry galloped between Cole's right and

L

Hill's left, and completed the confusion of the French. But the French covered their retreat to the heights in front of Gomecha with a cloud of skirmishers and the fire of 50 pieces of artillery. They clung to Arinez with the courage of despair. Picton's troops, headed by Barnard's riflemen, plunged into the streets amidst a heavy fire, and in an instant three guns were captured; but more French troops came in, and the smoke, the dust, the clamour, the rattle of musketry, and the roar of the artillery, were deafening and bewildering; yet in the end the British troops issued forth victorious on the other side. Margarita and the battery posted in it were carried by Colonel Gibbs with the 52d. Hermandad was won by Colonel Gough with the 87th. The French troops near Subijana de Alava were turned, and, hard pressed on their front and left flank by Hill and the troops on the Puebla range, fell back in a disordered mass, striving to regain the great line of retreat to Vitoria. The whole basin of the Zadora was a scene of fierce battle: every valley, height, and woodland was sheeted with flame, every house was contested, every vineyard, wall, and hedgerow formed a temporary breastwork, yet the allies steadily gained ground, and took gun after gun in their victorious progress towards Vitoria.

"At six o'clock," says Napier, "the French reached the last defensible height one mile in front of Vitoria. Behind them was the plain in which the city stood, and beyond the city thousands of carriages and animals and non-combatants, men, women, and children, were crowding together in all the madness of terror; and as the English shot went booming overhead, the vast crowd started and swerved with a convulsive movement, while a dull and horrid sound of distress arose; but there was no hope, no stay for army or multitude; it was the wreck of a nation! Still the courage of the French soldier was unequalled. Reille, on whom everything now depended, maintained the upper Zadora; and the armies of the south and centre, drawing up on their last heights, between the villages of Ali and Armentia, made their muskets flash like lightning, while more than eighty pieces of artillery, massed together, pealed with such a horrid uproar that the hills laboured and shook and streamed with fire and smoke, amidst which the dark figures of the French gunners were seen bounding with frantic energy. This terrible cannonade and musketry kept the allies in check, and scarcely could the 3d division, which bore the brunt of this storm, maintain its advanced position. Again the battle became stationary, and the French endeavoured to draw off their infantry in succession from the right wing; but suddenly the 4th division rushing forward carried a hill on their left, and the heights were at once abandoned. Joseph, finding the royal road so completely blocked by carriages that the artillery could not pass, then indicated the road of Salvatierra as the line of retreat, and the army went off in a confused yet compact body on that side, leaving Vitoria on its left. The British infantry followed hard, and the light cavalry galloped through the town to intercept the new line of retreat, which was through a marsh; and the road also was choked with carriages and fugitive people, while on each side there were deep drains. Thus, all became disorder and mischief, the guns were left on the edge of the marsh, the artillerymen and drivers fled with the horses, and the vanquished infantry, breaking through the miserable multitude, went off by Metauco towards Salvatierra: the cavalry, however, still covered the retreat, and many of the generous horsemen were seen taking up children and women to carry off from the dreadful scene."

While the left and centre were thus being destroyed, Graham was carrying position after position on the extreme right of the French line. Reille made a most obstinate defence, and the bridges were several times taken and re-taken; but when the centre and left were defeated, the British cavalry galloped out of Vitoria on his rear, and it was all he could do to secure a retreat to Betonio. Here he rallied his men, but the triumphant allies closed in upon him from all sides, and he hurried along the road to Metauco, protecting his retreat by bold charges of cavalry. It was not till he had passed that village, and night had fallen for some hours, that the last shot was fired.

"Never," says Napier, "was an army more hardly used by its commander, for the soldiers were not more than half-beaten, and yet never was a victory more complete. The trophies were innumerable. The French carried off but two pieces of artillery from the battle. Jourdan's *bâton* of command, a stand of colours, 143 brass pieces, two-thirds of which had been used in the fight, all the parks and depôts from Madrid, Valladolid, and Burgos, carriages, ammunition, treasure, everything fell into the hands of the victors. The loss in men did not, however, exceed 6000, including some hundreds of prisoners. The loss of the allies was nearly as great, the gross numbers being 5176 killed, wounded, and missing. Of these, 1059 were Portuguese and 550 Spanish; hence the loss of the English was more than double that of the Portuguese and Spaniards together; and yet both fought well, and especially the Portuguese, but British troops are the soldiers of battle. The spoil was immense, and to such an extent was plunder carried, principally by the followers and non-combatants, for with some exceptions the fighting troops may be said to have marched upon gold and silver without stooping to pick it up, that of five millions and a-half of dollars indicated by the French accounts to be in the money-chests, a fiftieth part only came to the public." All the public and private plunder which the French had been collecting for five years fell into the hands of the victors: rich brocades, gold and silver plate; pictures from the royal galleries, cut from their frames for safe transit; jewels, female trinkets, theatrical decorations, furniture, wines; together with all the regimental records, the archives of Joseph's court, and much of Napoleon's cipher correspondence. French officers, and even generals, were reduced to the clothes on their backs, and many of them were barefooted. Joseph's own carriage was overtaken and stopped on the road to Pampeluna by Captain Wyndham with a squadron of the 10th Hussars, and he only saved himself by mounting a fleet horse and spurring for the fortress. It was in Joseph's carriage that Marshal Jourdan's *bâton* was found, along with the king's sword and papers and one of Correggio's pictures. Wellington sent it to the Prince Regent, who sent him in return the *bâton* of a field-marshal in the British army.

So ended the battle of Vitoria, the crowning victory of the Peninsular War. Alison remarks, that "the campaigns of Marlborough present no example of so remarkable a triumph; the campaigns of Cressy and Agincourt were fruitless in comparison." It resounded like a thunderclap through Spain. At one blow the French were swept like a whirlwind from the Peninsula, and Joseph's crown dropped from his head. Madrid was evacuated (June 27), and all the French authorities hurried across the Ebro. Suchet left Valencia. Clausel, with 14,000 men, reached France only by a circuitous route, and after having a great part of his artillery and baggage taken by Mina. Graham, with the British left, pressed the retreat of Foy, and after a severe conflict at Tolosa, drove him across the Bidassoa; while

Hill, with the centre, followed the main body of the beaten army, which retired up the Bastan valley into France, *sans* ammunition, *sans* baggage, and with only one gun. All that now remained to the French in the north-west of Spain were the strongholds of Santona, San Sebastian, and Pampeluna, the last of which was closely blockaded by Hill. Graham undertook the siege of San Sebastian, the "Gibraltar of the Biscay coast." Its main strength lies in its citadel, the castle of La Mota, which crowns the promontory, a rugged conical hill 400 feet high. The north front of this promontory is incessantly lashed by the waves of the stormy Atlantic, the river Urumea, fordable for two hours before and after low water, protects it on the east, the waters of the bay wash it on the west, and on the south or land front the approach is by a low sandy isthmus, at the narrowest part of which was placed a low circular redoubt, composed of casks. The garrison, 3000 strong, was commanded by the brave Emmanuel Rey, who took full advantage of his splendid position, and made every preparation for an obstinate defence. Graham's besieging force numbered about 10,000 men, but only 100 regular sappers and miners, who were assisted by some seaman under O'Reilly, from the *Surveillante* frigate. The first attempt, however, was unsuccessful, and as the besiegers' ammunition was nearly suspended, and fresh supplies had not yet arrived from England, it was necessary to suspend operations and turn the siege into a blockade.

On the first tidings of the battle of Vitoria, Napoleon put aside all family considerations, superseded Joseph in command of the army, and sent Soult to take the supreme command, under the title of Lieutenant of the Emperor. Soult arrived on the 13th July at Bayonne, which he fortified, and mustering the wrecks of the beaten armies under its walls, found he had still 70,500 infantry and 7000 cavalry. Suchet had 66,000 men in Catalonia and Valencia, but throughout the ensuing campaign he remained inactive and avoided co-operating with Soult. That great tactician formed a plan to overwhelm Wellington's right and relieve Pampeluna, and then, passing along the rear of the allies' line, crush their divisions in detail as they descended from the hills, unite with a corps advancing by the coast, and destroy the left wing at San Sebastian. On the 24th July, more than 66,000 men, with 66 guns, were in position to force the passes of Roncesvalles and Maya.

On the morning of the 25th July (1813), under cover of a thick fog, Clausel pushed forward 18,000 troops, and forced back Byng and Murillo, who held the heights of Altobiscar in the Roncesvalles with scarce 5000 bayonets. Reille endeavoured to turn the British right, but on the summit of the Lindouz encountered the advanced guard of General Ross, who called aloud to charge. Captain Tovey of the 20th ran forward with his company, crossed a slight wooded hollow, and dashed with the bayonet full against the front of the French. Brave men fell on both sides, but at length numbers prevailed, and Captain Tovey and his people were pushed back. But Ross gained his object; the remainder of his brigade had come up, and the pass was secured.

At Maya there were three passes to defend—Aretesque on the right, Lessessa in the centre, Maya on the left. The Aretesque was defended by Pringle's brigade (28th, 34th, 39th), and the Lessessa and Maya passes by Cameron's brigade (50th, 71st, 92d). The six British regiments furnished no more than 3000 bayonets, and William Stewart, who commanded here, so little expected an attack that he had gone to Elisondo, leaving orders for the soldiers to cook. On the morning of the 25th D'Erlon advanced with 20,000 men in two columns, Maransin's division on the right against the Maya Pass, and the divisions of D'Armagnac and Abbé on the left against the Aretesque Pass. After a fierce struggle the last two were lost, and the first was only held by a wing of the 71st. Stewart, therefore, who now arrived on the scene, withdrew the force to a rocky ridge in the rear; but this position was also forced, Stewart was wounded, the Portuguese guns were taken, the ammunition failed, the last crag was defended with stones, and the mountain was about to be entirely abandoned, when Barnes arrived with the 7th division, charged the French, and drove them back to the Maya Pass, with the loss of 1500 men and a general. The British lost four guns and 1400 men. "Never did soldiers fight better, seldom so well," says Napier; "the stern valour of the 92d would have graced Thermopylæ." This noble regiment was nearly annihilated, and so dreadful was the slaughter in its ranks, that "it is said the advancing enemy was actually stopped by the heaped masses of dead and dying."

Sergeant Robertson of the 92d gives a very interesting account of this disastrous fight. "It was customary," he says, "to send all the mules of the three regiments (50th, 71st, and

92d) to the rear to forage once in the three days, so that by this arrangement more or less of them were every day in this position. On the morning of the 25th July all the three regiments had large foraging parties out for wood, and it was the turn of the 92d to have their mules out on this day. I was with the party for wood, which we were taking from some empty sheepcots that were in a ravine in our front, and of which the French apparently wished to possess themselves. By the time we arrived, the officer on duty said he saw something like a column advancing, and seemingly forming to wait for the advance of other columns. Information was immediately conveyed to Colonel (Brigadier-general) Cameron, who was the senior officer on the spot, when he repaired to the beacon, attended by a great number of all ranks, to ascertain the cause of the alarm, when the colonel said it was only a drove of bullocks, and remarked that the officer (Captain Armstrong of the 71st) was a stupid fellow for mistaking them for the enemy. Upon this accusation the captain offered to forfeit his commission if it was not a column of the enemy; but the colonel being positive, none of the other officers would take upon them to contradict the commanding officer. I now went and got a spy-glass, and saw plainly that it was a column of infantry, and packed my knapsack and got everything ready either for the affray or the march, as it might turn out. The colonel had reached his own tent when the pickets of the other regiments commenced firing. He still persisted in his obstinacy, and would neither allow the alarm gun to be fired nor the beacon to be lighted. At length a strong column came up the ravine (the Maya Pass) that was immediately in our front, where we had been for wood in the morning. But it was now too late to retrieve matters. We were hotly engaged with five times our own number, but we managed to keep them in check until the light companies arrived, but not before we were almost surrounded, and obliged to abandon our camp, leaving all the tents, the whole of the baggage, and everything belonging to the officers of the regiment. My wife lost everything belonging to herself and the children, and I did not see her for seven days after the affair. During the action the men were calling out to the colonel what he thought of his cattle now; and when his horse was killed, and himself severely wounded, he was told it was nothing but a touch from one of the horns of the oxen." The regiment lost 400 in killed, wounded, and missing. Of 78 men that Sergeant Robertson had in the morning, in the evening there remained but eleven, and of that small number two were wounded in the legs and unable to march.

The successes of the French at Roncesvalles and Maya were partially neutralised by the delay of D'Erlon and Reille to join Soult, and the British fell back to Pampeluna, taking up a position on the rugged cliffs opposite Sorauren, four miles in front of the fortress. Two fierce battles were fought here (July 28, 30), in which the French were defeated, and Soult hastily retreated up the valleys of the Pyrenees, closely pursued by the allies. Step by step the French retreated, disputing every inch of the way, but so dispirited did they become by their repeated defeats that, at the combats of Echallar and Ivantelly (August 2), 6000 of the veterans who had assailed the terrible rocks above Sorauren were unable to sustain the shock of 1500 British soldiers! The French then evacuated Spanish territory, and resumed their former positions. Both armies required rest. During the last nine days of continual movement ten serious actions had been fought. Since they crossed the frontier the French had lost 15,000 men, including 4000 prisoners. The loss of the allies during the various battles of the Pyrenees was 7300.

Wellington now bent all his energies to renew the siege of San Sebastian under Graham. On the 5th August the guns were re-landed, and the works against the fortress resumed. A battering train arrived from England on the 19th, and another on the 23d, raising the number of guns to 117, but the authorities at home, with great negligence, had sent from England no more shot and shells than would suffice for one day's consumption! A sally was made on the 25th, and on the 26th fire was opened on the fortress from 57 pieces of cannon. The assault was entrusted to Robinson's brigade of the 5th division. It was formed in two columns, one to attack the old breach between the towers, and the other to storm the bastion of St. John and the end of the high curtain. The small breach on the extreme right was left for Bradford's Portuguese, who were on the sand hills across the Urumea.

The morning of the 31st August, 1813, broke in a heavy fog, which prevented the besiegers' batteries opening until eight o'clock; at nine the sea breeze rolled it away; and at eleven, after a heavy fire from the batteries, Robinson's brigade sprang from the trenches and advanced through the openings in the sea-wall to the assault of the breaches. While the head of the column was gathering on the strand, thirty yards from the salient angle of the horn-work, a sergeant and twelve men leaped forward to cut the sausage of the mine; the French were startled and fired the mine prematurely; the sergeant and all his followers were destroyed, and the high sea-wall fell on the front of the column, but only about forty men were buried in the ruins, and the rush of the column was hardly checked. The forlorn hope had already passed beyond the play of the mine, and now sped along the beach, but their gallant leader, Lieutenant Macguire of the 4th, fell dead at the foot of the great breach. The stormers went sweeping over his body, and reached the top of the breach, but found progress impossible from the large gulf behind it. Nevertheless, they remained doggedly on the lower part of the breach, though exposed to a storm of fire in flank and rear.

In the meantime the efforts to force the curtain were attended with great slaughter, and General Leith let loose the volunteers, —750 men of the 4th and light divisions, " men who could show other troops how to mount a breach "—who went at the breaches like a whirlwind. " The crowded masses," says Napier, " swarmed up the face of the ruins; but on reaching the crest line, they came down again like a falling wall: crowd after crowd were seen to mount, to totter, to sink; the French fire was unabated, the smoke floated away, and the crest of the breach bore no living man!"

General Graham, who had surveyed this frightful carnage from the right bank of the river, and saw the survivors huddled together at the foot of the breach, now turned 50 heavy guns upon the curtain over the heads of the men. For half an hour the iron tempest continued, and under cover of it a lodgment was effected in some ruined houses within the rampart on the right of the great breach. At this time the Portuguese and a detachment of the 24th, under Colonel Macbean, waded the Urumea, which was 200 yards wide. When they reached the middle of the stream, with the water up to their waists, the head of the column was struck by a dreadful discharge of grape. The havoc was fearful, but still the survivors closed and moved on. A second discharge tore the ranks from front to rear; still these brave men never faltered, and landing on the beach, the Portuguese rushed against the third breach, while Macbean's men reinforced the stormers of the great breach.

The fighting now commenced again at all the breaches, and once more the mass of stormers rushed up to the assault—once more unable to win. The tide was rising, the strength of the men was exhausted with five hours' mad fighting, and it seemed that the assault must fail; but at this crisis fortune interposed. The combustibles which the French had collected behind the traverses suddenly caught fire; a sheet of flame wrapped the whole of the curtain, a succession of loud explosions were heard, hundreds of the French grenadiers who had so bravely maintained their post were destroyed, and the remainder were blinded by the smoke and thrown into confusion. The British rushed in at the first traverse, and the French, bewildered and half stupefied, maintained a desperate conflict on the summit of the curtain; but the fury of the stormers was not to be stemmed, and the tide of battle went pouring into the town. The French rallied and maintained the combat at the barricades; but it was only for a short time; several hundreds of them were cut off and taken in the horn-work, and the remainder retreated to the Santa Teresa convent and the castle.

It was now five o'clock, and, just when the place was carried, a thunder-storm came down from the mountains and added to the terrors of the scene. "This storm," says Napier, "seemed to be a signal from hell for the perpetration of villany that would have ashamed the most ferocious barbarians of antiquity. At Rodrigo intoxication and plunder had been the principal object; at Badajos lust and murder were joined to rapine and drunkenness; but at San Sebastian, the direst, the most revolting cruelty was added to the catalogue of crimes,—one atrocity of which a girl of seventeen was the victim staggers the mind by its enormous, incredible, indescribable barbarity." The long endurance of the assault, the slaughter of their comrades, and the conduct of the inhabitants—many of whom, as at Badajos, took part with the enemy and fired upon them—had wrought the soldiers up to perfect madness. Throwing off all discipline, they broke open the burning houses; they rolled spirit casks into the streets, and emptied them on the spot, till vast numbers fell down motionless, and many lifeless; they cut down everything, plundered or burned everything in their way. The camp-followers crowded into the place, and in spite of all the efforts of the officers, many of whom were killed in trying to stem the torrent of disorder, the rage of the maddened soldiery could not be quelled till the flames left nothing standing but bare and blackened walls.

From these horrors it is refreshing to turn to the high sense of honour and heroism displayed by Sergeant Ball and six grenadiers of the 28th—the celebrated "Slashers." While the regiment was with the rest of the army in the Pyrenees, Colonel Cadell says, that "some of the officers requested Colonel Belson to send a party to Passages, near San Sebastian (where supplies of every description were brought from England for the army), to purchase tobacco for the men, and tea and sugar for the officers: $2000 were collected, and given in charge to Sergeant Ball and six grenadiers. The party arrived at Passages on the 30th, and learning that San Sebastian was to be stormed the next day, the sergeant addressed his men, telling them there was hardly an action in the Peninsula in which the 28th had not a share, and proposed to them to volunteer on the storming party for the credit of their regiment. To this the men joyfully assented, and the next question was, how to dispose safely of the money with which they had been entrusted. It was determined to place it in the hands of a commissary, taking his receipt for the amount, which document the sergeant again lodged in the hands of a third person. Having thus carefully provided for the property of their officers, those brave fellows volunteered for the desperate enterprise, and joined the ranks of their gallant comrades of Barosa Heights—the grenadiers of the 9th. It would be superfluous to say they did their duty, and most fortunately—indeed singularly—none of them were hurt. After the town was taken, the gallant sergeant collected his men, reclaimed the money, purchased the supplies, and returned to his regiment with a handsome testimonial of their conduct, addressed to Colonel Belson, from the general commanding the brigade."

The citadel still held out, but 60 guns and mortars were opened on its walls, and on the 9th September it surrendered. The brave Rey and the survivors of the garrison marched out of the fortress and laid down their arms on the glacis, "with the proud air of men who had nobly done their duty." Theirs was an achievement of which they might well be proud; for a third-rate fortress, defended by only 3000 men, had detained the allies for 63 days, and cost them 3800 men, 2500 of whom fell in the last assault. On the very day of the assault (31st August) Soult had endeavoured to relieve the fortress by attacking the heights of San Marcial. But Wellington was there, a host in himself, and at his bidding the Spaniards dashed down on their adversaries with loud shouts. The French recoiled from the unwonted fury of the attack, hesitated, wavered, and finally fled pell-mell. Many of them were driven into the Bidassoa, but the great mass of the fugitives betook themselves to the bridge; the pontoons gave way, and nearly all who were on them at the time were drowned. Soult lost 3600 men, and the allies 2600—1600 of them Spaniards, who for once bore the brunt of the attack.

CHAPTER X.

CAMPAIGN IN THE SOUTH OF FRANCE—1813-1814.

Passage of the Bidassoa—Passage of the Nivelle—Passage of the Nive—
Battles before Bayonne—St. Pierre—Orthes—Toulouse.

SOULT'S efforts to carry the war into Spain had failed, the gates of the Pyrenees were in the hands of the allies, and now the nation which had so often and so wantonly inflicted the horrors of war upon others was itself to feel the iron hand of the conqueror. Napoleon had scored the last of his great victories, disasters began to come thick upon him, nothing remained for him but to fight his way through Leipsic to the Rhine; and the allied sovereigns on the Elbe were anxious that Wellington should carry his conquering arms into France, and take the Napoleonic army in the rear. For many reasons, Wellington's own views pointed more to Catalonia, but his government ordered the invasion of France, and like a good soldier he prepared to obey.

"Soult's position north of the Bidassoa," says Alison, "was the base of a triangle of which Bayonne was the apex, and the great roads thence to Irun on the coast, and St. Jean Pied-de-Port in the interior, formed the sides. This space was filled with a mass of rugged mountains, on the last ridge of which, overlooking the Bidassoa, the French army was stationed; while all the hill-roads were commanded by works; and the summit of the Grand Rhune mountain, the highest part of the ridge, was crowned by a complete redoubt. The attack of Wellington was delayed by the tides and the swollen state of the Bidassoa, from rain, till the 7th September, when the pontoons were brought down under cover of a dark and stormy night; and at daybreak (Sept. 8, 1813) 24,000 men were directed against the Lower Bidassoa, and 20,000, chiefly Spaniards, against the Rhune and its ridges. The French were completely taken by surprise," the attack was successful, " the whole of the almost impregnable position which the French had been fortifying for a month past fell into the hands of the allies; and thus was Britain, the most persevering opponent of the Revolution, rewarded by being the first nation, since the rise of Napoleon, whose victorious standards were planted on the soil of France." The total loss of the French in the actions comprised in the "Passage of the Bidassoa" was 1400; the loss of the allies was 1600, of whom half were Spaniards.

Wellington had now to wait for the fall of Pampeluna, which, after enduring all the extremities of famine, surrendered at discretion (October 31), with its garrison of 3500 men: Santona, the only fortress in north-west Spain still held by the French, continued blockaded till the end of the war. Soult availed himself of the respite thus granted him to erect a triple line of defences, strong and solid, on the Nivelle, a little river which runs into the sea at St. Jean de Luz. Soult's force was again raised to 70,000 men, by the accession of 16,000 recruits, while Wellington weakened his army by sending home all the Spanish battalions, except Murillo's, for their plundering the inhabitants. The passage of the Nivelle was effected on the 9th and 10th November, and on the 11th Soult was driven from his second line of defence. He rallied his troops on the third line, about 8 miles in the rear; but continued disasters had weakened the spirit of his soldiers, and next day he fell back to the entrenched camp at Bayonne. In the three days' actions comprised in the battle of the "Nivelle," Soult lost 4300 men, 51 guns, and all the field magazines at St. Jean de Luz and Espalette. The loss of the allies was 2694.

Wellington would immediately have followed up his advantage, but incessant rains from the middle to the end of November turned the winter-torrents into rivers, and so destroyed the roads that the troopers' horses sank up to the knees in mud, and the artillery could not be moved at all. Among the officers, excursions and convivial parties were the order of the day, varied by visits to St. Jean de Luz, where Wellington had fixed his headquarters. St. Jean was at this time a scene of the greatest gaiety. There might be seen the officers of the guards and the scions of the British aristocracy dashing through the streets, bedizened with gold and silver. And there, too, might be seen the Great Captain himself, dressed in a plain blue surtout, a white cravat, and a round hat, lounging about and looking at the markets, as if he were merely a passing traveller, having nothing to do but amuse himself.

Soult's position in the entrenched camp at Bayonne, situated as it was at the confluence of the Adour and the Nive, and commanding the bridges over both these rivers, was very advantageous for forage, while the allies found a difficulty in obtaining supplies. Wellington, therefore, resolved to extend his cantonments by forcing the passage of the Nive, extending his line to the Adour, and driving Soult entirely back under the cannon of Bayonne. The attack was made on the morning of the 9th December. Hill, with the right, forded the river at Cambo; Beresford, with the centre, crossed by a pontoon bridge which he had laid down to an island in the Nive during the night; and Hope and Alten, with the left and Vandeleur's cavalry, drove in the advanced posts in front of the entrenched camp. The passage was forced, and the French left driven close to Bayonne, with a loss to each side of 800 men. But the allied army was thus cut in two by the stream of the Nive, an almost unfordable river, over which the only communication was maintained by Beresford's pontoon bridge, while Soult held the interior lines, and was able to throw the whole weight of his force on the one flank or the other at pleasure. On the morning of the 10th December, Soult threw 60,000 men on the allies' left wing, where there were only 30,000 men and 24 guns to resist his attack. The allies were taken a little by surprise, but the light division held the church and village of Arcangues against all the efforts of Clausel, and the extreme left at Barrouilhet repulsed the divisions of Reille. Soult would have renewed the attack, had not Wellington threatened Urdains with the 3d, 4th, 6th, and 7th divisions. This combat cost the French 2000, and the allies 1200 and 300 prisoners. Both armies bivouacked on the field of battle, and during the course of the night two German regiments, one of Nassau and one of Frankfort, acting on secret instructions from the Prince of Nassau, who had now abandoned Napoleon's falling cause, came over to the allies. They were received with drums beating and presented arms, and soon after were embarked to join their countrymen on the Rhine. Some skirmishing took place on the 12th, and each side lost 600 men.

Heavy rains fell during the night of the 12th, swelled the Nive, and broke the bridge of boats. Hill, with the right, was thus isolated on the right bank of the Nive, and Soult launched 35,000 men against his front, while 7000 more menaced his rear. Hill had but 14,000 men and 14 guns to resist this attack. The left (28th, 38th, and 39th) under General Pringle, occupied a wooded broken ridge, covering the pontoon bridge over the Nive, and separated from the centre by a stream and a chain of ponds in a deep, marshy valley. The centre, under General William Stewart, occupied a crescent-shaped height on both sides of the hamlet of St. Pierre, broken with rocks and close brushwood on the left, and on the right streaked with thick hedges, one of which, 100 yards in front of the line, was impassable; the 71st on the left, the 50th and the 92d on the right; Ashworth's Portuguese in advance; Ross and Tulloch with 12 guns massed in front and looking down the great road; Le Cor's Portuguese and 2 guns, half a mile to the rear, in reserve. The right, under General Byng, consisted of the 3d, 31st, 57th, and 66th. The 3d occupied a position in advance, but the other three regiments were covered by a mill-pond which nearly filled the valley. The nature of the ground and the state of the roads prevented the action of cavalry, and for the same reason Soult could not strike with large masses, but was forced to bring his troops into line in succession and fight in detail. This tended to counterbalance his immense superiority in numbers.

The 13th December broke in heavy mist, under cover of which Soult formed his order of battle. D'Erlon, having D'Armagnac's, Abbé's, and Daricau's infantry, Sparre's cavalry, and 22 guns, marched in front; he was followed by Foy and Maransin. At half-past eight, as the sun broke through the clouds, Soult pushed back the British pickets, and the noise of battle spread along the hillsides. When the French columns were about 2 miles from St. Pierre, D'Armagnac took the road to the left to attack Byng, and Daricau the road to the right against Pringle, while Abbé assailed St. Pierre. Abbé's attack was delivered with characteristic vigour; Ashworth's Portuguese were hard pressed on their left; and the French skirmishers won the wood on their right. Stewart, therefore, sent forward the 71st and two guns to their aid, and half the 50th to retake the wood. This secured the flanks of his position, but his centre was very much weakened. Abbé concentrated all his fire upon the centre, and, though torn by artillery in front, and galled by musketry on the flanks, pushed the attack with such vigour that he gained the top of the position, driving back Ashworth's Portuguese and the half of the 50th which remained in position. Colonel Peacocke of the 71st shamefully withdrew that regiment out of action, a proceeding for which he was afterwards deservedly compelled to quit the service.

At this crisis General Barnes brought forward the 92d from the village of St. Pierre. The French skirmishers fell back on each side, leaving two regiments in column to meet the Highlanders' charge, which was made with such vigour that the French mass wavered and gave way. But more French troops were brought forward, the French guns on the opposite heights redoubled their play, and a battery of horse artillery came galloping into the valley and opened fire at short range. Under this storm of shot and shell the 92d had to regain their position behind St. Pierre, and the Portuguese guns limbered up to retire. Barnes made them resume firing, but the artillerymen fell fast at their guns, most of the staff were hurt, Ashworth's line was crumbling away, and the French skirmishers were assailing the impassable hedge which protected the right of the Portuguese and the advanced part of the 50th. The ground in front was strewed with dead, and many wounded were crawling to the rear. Foy's and Maransin's divisions had now traversed the wretched roads, and were moving up to support Abbé; and Colonel Bunbury of the 3d had been guilty of the same crime as Colonel Peacocke, for which he suffered the same punishment.

The situation of the allies seemed desperate, and Hill had no resource but to throw his reserves into action. Galloping up, he sent back Colonel Peacocke to his post, then despatched one brigade of Le Cor's Portuguese to aid Byng, and led the other brigade (Da Costa's) to support the 71st. That gallant regiment, burning to efface the memory of its colonel's weakness, rushed to the attack with such fury that the French centre wavered. The 92d had now re-formed behind St. Pierre, and Colonel Cameron led it forth to the charge with pipes playing and colours flying as

M

if marching past at a review. Upon this the skirmishers, who had been falling back, advanced. "A small force," says Napier, "was the 92d, compared with the heavy mass in its front, and the French soldiers seemed willing enough to close with the bayonet; but an officer at their head suddenly turned his horse, waved his sword, and appeared to order a retreat, for they faced about and retired across the valley to their original position; in good order, however, and scarcely pursued by the allies, so exhausted were the victors."

The pontoon bridge over the Nive had by this time been repaired, and the 6th division, which had been marching since daybreak, now appeared on the heights behind, followed by the 3d, 4th, and part of the 7th divisions, with Wellington in person. But Hill had won his own battle, and "after a manner," says Napier, "that in less eventful times would have made him the hero of a nation." "It is agreed by French and English that the battle of St. Pierre was one of the most desperate of the whole war. Wellington said he had never seen a field so thickly strewn with dead; nor can the vigour of the combatants be well denied when 5000 were killed or wounded in three hours upon a space of one mile square." The British lost 1500 of this enormous total. And yet, though the ground was so bravely held, neither this nor any of the other "Battles before Bayonne," fought on the 10th–13th December, is commemorated on any of the regimental colours.

The results of the passage of the Nive and the battles before Bayonne were that Soult was confined within his entrenched camp, his communications were cut with St. Jean Pied de Port, his navigation of the Adour was menaced, and he could obtain supplies only by night. The allies, on the other hand, had now a fertile district for the cavalry to forage in, and drew abundant supplies for their men from the rich fields of Bearn and the harbour of St. Jean de Luz. But the country was one vast quagmire, and no further offensive movements could take place till the weather hardened the roads. Once more there was some leisure in the camp, and the officers spent their mornings in making excursions to the rear and to the front, where it was a common thing for French and English officers to meet midway, betwixt their respective sentries, to discuss the news of the day, the affairs of Europe, and a glass or two of cognac. There were certain deserted houses in the neighbourhood which were occupied day and night alternately by the French and English pickets, who drew caricatures of each other upon the walls, which were also covered over with sarcastic remarks and courteous retorts, forming the medium of a correspondence half-angry, half-humorous.

Great Britain was at this time (1814) making the most extraordinary efforts to secure the object for which she had been striving for so many years—the freedom of Europe from the aggression of France. The naval war was at an end, still she had in commission 99 ships of the line and 545 frigates and smaller vessels, manned by 140,000 seamen and marines; and her whole land and sea force in arms, including the yeomanry and local militia at home, 40,000 militia in Canada, and the Indian army, amounted to 1,053,000 men. The expenditure of 1814 reached the enormous total of £117,000,000!

Operations in the south of France were resumed on the 12th February, 1814. After some sharp fighting the investment of Bayonne was completed on the 26th, and Soult, driven from the shelter of its guns, took up a strong position on the heights of Orthes, behind the Gave du Pau. Soult had now only 40,000 soldiers, for Bayonne had been garrisoned from his ranks, and the necessities of Napoleon—struggling, after his retreat from the "Battle of Nations" at Leipsic, with Blucher and Schwartzenberg on the north-east of France—had made him withdraw 10,000 men from the army of the south. On the 27th February Wellington advanced to the attack with 37,000 men, all Anglo-Portuguese veterans, including 4000 cavalry and 48 guns. Beresford, with the left, was to turn the enemy's right, Picton to attack the centre, and Hill, with the right, to force the passage of the Orthes, and turn the enemy's left. The general movement commenced at nine in the morning. On the British left, Cole moved with Ross's British brigade and Vasconcello's Portuguese against the village of St. Boes, and after a fierce struggle gained it. But every effort to get out from the cottages and their enclosures to the open ground beyond was defeated by the heavy concentric fire of Reille's artillery. Five desperate attempts were made without success, and then Taupin's musketry also assailed the battered columns. After a struggle of three hours the Portuguese gave way in disorder, and the British brigade effected its retreat with difficulty. Picton had no better success in the centre, where his attack was roughly repulsed by Foy, and Soult is said to have slapped his thigh and cried, "At last I have him!"

His exultation, however, was short-lived. Wellington changed his plan of attack; he supported the 4th division at St. Boes with the 7th and Vivian's cavalry, he sent the 3d and 6th divisions upon Foy's flank, and launched Colonel Colborne and the 52d through the swamp and up the hill, to separate Taupin's division, disordered by its success against Beresford, from Foy and the centre. These simultaneous attacks were perfectly successful. Colborne made his march unperceived except by the skirmishers, and with a mighty shout and a rolling fire the soldiers of the 52d dashed forward between Foy and Taupin, beating down a French battalion in their course and throwing everything into disorder. General Bechaud was killed, Foy was dangerously wounded, and his soldiers got into confusion. The disorder spread to Reille's wing, who was forced to fall back and take a new position to restore his line of battle. This movement opened up the pass of St. Boes, and the 4th and 7th divisions, Vivian's cavalry, and two batteries of artillery, were immediately pushed through and spread out beyond. The 3d and 6th divisions were equally successful in the centre, where they won D'Armagnac's position, and established on a knoll a battery of guns, which ploughed through the French ranks. A squadron of chasseurs galloped down to take these guns, but got into a hollow and were nearly all destroyed. Hill having by this time forded the Gave, and cut off the retreat by the great road of Pau, Soult ordered a general retreat, which was made in good order, till the fugitives were so hard pressed by the dragoons of Sir Stapleton Cotton and Lord Edward Somerset that they threw away their arms and knapsacks, and the retreat became a rout. Many thousand prisoners might have been taken, but Wellington, wounded in the thigh by a musket ball, was unable to ride fast to superintend the pursuit. The loss of the allies in this battle was 2350 killed and wounded, and 53 prisoners. From the slackness of the pursuit Soult lost only 4000, but so many deserted the colours that a month afterwards the stragglers still amounted to 3000.

The last great struggle of the war took place at Toulouse, whither Soult retreated after the battle of Orthes. The place was capable of great defence, surrounded as it was with strong walls, the great canal of Languedoc, and fortified suburbs. On the east of the city was Mont Rave, a ridge of hills running parallel with the Garonne; the summit of this ridge was occupied by a fortified platform called the Calvinet, about two miles long, and strengthened with fieldworks. This formed the first line of defence, the canal with its fortified bridge formed the second, and the walls of the city the third. Soult had 40,000 men and 80 guns; Wellington 52,000 men, including 7000 cavalry, and 64 guns. Picton, with the 3d division, was to menace the Jumeux bridge-head and the Minimes convent, but not to attack; the Spaniards were to assail the Calvinet plateau; Beresford, with the 4th and 6th divisions, was to attack the St. Sypière summit—a continuation of Mont Rave, to the southeast, and divided from it by the Lavaur road; to distract the enemy, Hill was to menace the suburb of St. Cyprien on the west side of the river.

At seven in the morning (April 10, 1814) the allies proceeded to the attack. Freyre and his Spaniards, 9000 strong, advanced with great resolution at first, throwing forward their flanks to embrace the end of the Calvinet; but they were greeted with such a storm of fire that they fell back in disorder. Again they tried, and again they failed, leaving 1500 of their number on the field. Nor was this the only disaster, for Picton, with his usual impetuosity, instead of merely threatening the north front of the town, attacked it, and was repulsed with the loss of 400 men. Hill carried the outer line of the entrenchments of St. Cyprien, but he could make nothing of the strong inner line, and Soult was thus enabled to reinforce his battle on Mont Rave with 15,000 men under Taupin. These he placed on the St. Sypière summit, with orders to fall on Beresford, who was now winding up out of the marsh; but instead of attacking at once, Taupin took ground to the right, giving Beresford full time to wheel into line at the foot of the ridge. When at length Taupin did charge down the slope, his ranks were torn by rockets; the French were dismayed at the noise and terrible appearance of this strange missile, the British rushed forward with shouts, and the French fled back up the hill. Viall's horsemen came trotting down the Lavaur road and charged on the right flank of the pursuers, but the 79th, thrown into squares, repulsed them, and the British swept up the heights. Taupin was slain. A French regiment at the St. Sypière redoubt, on seeing its commanding officer slain by a soldier of the 61st, fled in a panic, the other fort on the Caraman road was abandoned, and the French were pursued down the other side of the ridge to the fortified suburbs of Sacarin and Cambon. The British, having thus obtained possession of St. Sypière, were enabled to attack the works on Mont Rave, against which the Spaniards had already made so fruitless an attempt. This task was entrusted to the Highland brigade of Pack and the Portuguese brigade of Douglas; and so vehement was the rush of the 42d and 79th, who ascended the heights from the Lavaur road under a wasting fire of cannon and musketry, that they instantly carried the Colombette and Calvinet redoubts. But the French, under Harispe in person, fought desperately, large reinforcements were brought up, the two redoubts were surrounded with a surging multitude, Calvinet was recovered by storm, the 42d was almost annihilated, the remnant fell back in disorder on the 79th, and that regiment also was forced to quit Colombette. Still the two Highland regiments, though reduced to a thin line of skirmishers, clung to the brow of the hill, and maintained what seemed a lost battle with frenzied courage; two French generals—Harispe and Baurot—were borne wounded off the field, and the arrival of the 11th and the 91st (Argyllshire) Highlanders turned the tide of battle. The French were at length driven down the hill to Toulouse, and the Spaniards, who had rallied for another attack, were moved up to take possession of the entrenchments on Mont Rave. Soult then withdrew all his troops behind the canal, which formed the second line of the defence, and the battle ended.

Mr. Malcolm of the 42d gives us some idea of the desperate nature of the struggle on Mont Rave. The men, he says, were mown down by sections. He saw six of the company to which he belonged fall together, as if swept away by the discharge of one gun, and the whole ground over which they rushed was covered with the dead. The enemy still possessed two fortified houses close by the redoubt, and kept up a galling and destructive fire. It was necessary to dislodge them. "Forward, double-quick!" and forward the 42d drove, in the face of apparent destruction. The field had been lately rough ploughed, and when a man fell he tripped the one behind. Thus the ranks were opening as the regiment approached the fortified houses, but in a minute every obstacle was surmounted. The French did not wait to cross bayonets, but fled as the 42d leaped over the trenches and mounds like a pack of noisy hounds in pursuit. Two officers and about sixty of inferior rank were all that now remained of the right wing of the regiment. The flag was hanging in tatters, and stained with the blood of those who had fallen over it. The standard, cut in two, had been successively placed in the hands of two officers, who fell during the advance. It was now borne by a sergeant, and amongst the handful of soldiers who still rallied round it, covered with mire, sweat, smoke, and blood, the front files of a French column that was advancing were pouring in destructive showers of musketry. To have disputed the post with such overwhelming numbers would have been madness. The order was given to retire. The Highlanders were now under two fires. Fortunately the distance to the supports did not exceed a hundred paces, and all ran as if they had been running a race, the balls whistling over and amongst them.

The victory remained with Wellington, and the greater share of the loss, as was only to be expected in the attack of such entrenchments. The French had five generals and 3000 men killed and wounded, and the allies four generals and 4659 men, 2000 of whom were Spaniards. The 42d and the 79th were very heavy sufferers. The 79th went into action with 494 officers and men, and only 263 came out unhurt; the 42d was not much stronger, and lost 423. Amid all this carnage it is pleasing to read an incident like the following, told by a soldier of the 71st, who took part in Hill's attack on the suburb of St. Cyprien:—"We were in extended order, firing and retiring. I had just risen to run behind my file, when a shot struck me in the groin, and took the breath from me. 'God receive my soul,' I said, and sat down resigned. The French were advancing fast. I laid my musket down and gasped for breath. I was sick, and put my canteen to my head, but could not taste the water; however, I washed my mouth, and grew less faint. I looked to my thigh, and seeing no blood, took resolution to put my hand to the part to feel the wound. My hand was unstained by blood; but the part was so painful I could not touch it. At this moment of helplessness the French came up. One of them made a charge at me, as I sat pale as death. In another moment I would have been transfixed, had not his next man forced the point past me. 'Do not touch the good Scot,' said he; and then addressing himself to me, added, 'Do you know me?' I had not yet recovered my breath to speak distinctly; I answered — 'No.' I then recognised him to be a soldier whose life I had saved from a Portuguese, who was going to kill him as he lay wounded on the ground. 'Yes, I know you,' I now said faintly. 'God bless you!' said the Frenchman, and taking a pancake from the crown of his hat, moved on with his company. I soon recovered so far as to walk, though with pain, and joined the regiment next advance."

On the 11th both armies remained on the same ground, but Soult, finding Wellington was taking measures to cut off his retreat, decamped during the night, leaving 1600 wounded to the humanity of the British. Next day Wellington entered the city, and was rapturously received by the inhabitants, most of whom had mounted the white cockade. That same afternoon the news arrived of the capture of Paris by the allies, the abdication of Napoleon, and the proclamation of Louis XVIII.; and on the 18th a convention was entered into between Wellington and Soult, for the conclusion of hostilities, and the evacuation of the fortresses still held by the French in Spain. Before it was arranged, however, the garrison of Bayonne made a desperate sally, in which, though they were repulsed with the loss of over 900 men, they put 830 of the allies *hors de combat*, killed General Hay, and took Sir John Hope prisoner. But hostilities now everywhere ceased. The British infantry embarked at Bordeaux, some for America and some for England. The cavalry marched in triumph across France, and embarked from Calais. Thus ended this long and arduous war, in which the army of Great Britain and her allies had given independence to two kingdoms (Spain and Portugal), and had fought and won nineteen pitched battles against the bravest soldiers and the most experienced generals of Europe.

CHAPTER XI.

THE AMERICAN WAR.—1812-1814.

The Shannon and the Chesapeake.

WHILE Wellington was preparing to fight the battle of Salamanca, war was declared by the United States against Great Britain. A considerable amount of ill-feeling had arisen between us and our cousins across the Atlantic. The Americans were very anxious to create a navy, and by offering a high rate of pay and other advantages, easily induced a great number of our seamen to forswear the Union Jack and enrol themselves under the Stars and Stripes. The British Government claimed the right of searching American vessels for deserters; the Americans resisted, and (June 18, 1812) President Madison declared war against Great Britain.

America had no navy of such a size as to enable her to send fleets to sea and fight battles like the Nile and Trafalgar, but she had a considerable number of useful vessels which she chose to call frigates, but for which our frigates could not possibly be any match. In point of fact, they were line-of-battle ships in disguise, 74-gun ships cut down and armed with 56 heavy guns. It was a masterpiece of Yankee "'cuteness." No British line-of-battle ship could gain the slightest honour by the capture of one of these vessels, simply because they were called frigates; while our *bona fide* frigates were so much inferior in size and weight of metal as to have no chance of success. The first of the sea-duels occurred (August 19) between the British 48-gun frigate *Guerrière* (French prize), bound to Halifax to refit, and the United States frigate *Constitution*. A sanguinary action ensued. The British did all that a crazy ship and damp powder enabled them to do, but in the end victory rested with the Americans. Nor was this any wonder when we consider that the *Constitution* had 56 24-pounders to oppose to the 48 18-pounders of the *Guerrière*, and a crew of 476 picked seamen and marksmen to do battle with 244 men and 19 boys; when we consider moreover that of these 476 seamen and marksmen a considerable proportion had been British seamen, trained under such masters of the art of naval warfare as Nelson, Duncan, Collingwood, and Cochrane. On the 18th October the British brig *Frolic* (18), when almost crippled aloft by the effects of a severe gale, surrendered to the United States corvette *Wasp* (18). A week later the British *Macedonian* (48) surrendered to the American *United States* (56). On the 31st December the British *Java* (38) surrendered to the American *Constitution*, the same which captured the *Guerrière*; and on the 24th February, 1813, the British brig *Peacock* (18) hauled down her colours, when on the point of sinking, to the American corvette *Hornet* (20).

Such a succession of defeats filled our people with dismay. Ignorant of the real facts of the case, and naturally thinking that the so-called American frigates were of nearly equal force to the British frigates which surrendered to them, they hastily concluded that our seamen had lost much of their ancient spirit. But this uneasy feeling was completely dispelled by the memorable duel between the *Shannon* and the *Chesapeake*, which proved that British prowess had not degenerated, and was as likely to be victorious as ever when the disparity of force was not such as to render success impossible.

Captain Philip Vere Broke, of His Britannic Majesty's frigate *Shannon*, was a thorough seaman, whose heart lay entirely in his profession. From the day on which he joined the ship, 14th September, 1806, Captain Broke set himself to put his frigate in proper fighting order. Every day the men were exercised at the guns, at broadsword, pike, and musket, and in the course of a year or two, by paternal care and excellent regulations, his ship's company became as pleasant to command as they were dangerous to meet. With such a ship and such a crew, in all respects fitted for battle, Captain Broke ardently longed for a meeting with an American frigate of equal force, to wipe off the discredit which had been brought on the British flag. No opportunity occurred until the summer of 1813, when the *Shannon* and the *Tenedos* sailed from Halifax for a cruise in Boston Bay. In the harbour they saw the *President* and the *Congress* nearly ready to sail, and resolved to bring them to action; but the foggy weather of the beginning of May, and a sudden favourable shift of the wind, enabled the *President* and the *Congress* to elude the vigilance of the British frigates and put to sea. There now remained in the harbour but the *Chesapeake*, which had slipped into Boston by the eastern channel, about the middle of April, after a cruise of 115 days. As two frigates were not required to attack one, and as the appearance of such a superiority would naturally prevent the *Chesapeake* from putting to sea, Captain Broke detached the *Tenedos*, with orders not to join him before the 14th June. He then wrote a letter of challenge to Captain Lawrence of the *Chesapeake*, beginning thus:—" As the *Chesapeake* appears now ready for sea, I request that you will meet the *Shannon* with her, ship to ship, to try the fortune of our respective flags." The body of the letter is occupied with a candid description of the *Shannon's* force, &c., and thus concludes:—" I entreat you, sir, not to imagine that I am urged by mere personal vanity to the wish of meeting the *Chesapeake*, or that I depend only upon your personal ambition for your acceding to this invitation. We have both nobler motives. You will feel it as a compliment if I say that the result of our meeting may be the most grateful service I can render to my country; and I doubt not that you, equally confident of success, will feel convinced that it is only by repeated triumphs in *even combats* that your little navy can now hope to console your country for the loss of the trade it can no longer protect. Favour me with a speedy reply. We are short of provisions and water, and cannot stay long here."

Captain Lawrence of the *Chesapeake* was as brave a man as any in the American navy, and, anxious to add fresh leaves to his laurels, was not backward in accepting the challenge. Soon after midday on the 1st June (1813), the *Chesapeake* was seen coming out of Boston harbour under a cloud of canvas. News of the approaching duel had spread through the city like wildfire, and the most extravagant anticipations of victory were indulged in. Nobody doubted that the Stars and Stripes would once more wave triumphant over a fallen foe, and balls and suppers were in preparation to greet the return of the American conquerors. The day was fine, the wind light and soft, and every eminence along the coast was covered with thousands of spectators, while the *Chesapeake* was followed by quite a flotilla of yachts and pleasure-boats, filled with patriotic Yankees, come out to see the "Britisher whipped."

When Captain Broke saw his antagonist coming, he stood out from the land under easy sail until 5.10 P.M., when he hauled up and lay to, the *Shannon's* head being to the southward and eastward, Boston lighthouse bearing west, distant about six leagues. The drums beat to quarters, and while the crew stood to their guns, the watch on deck filled the foretopsail, set the jib and spanker, and kept the mainsail shivering. Captain Broke then addressed his crew, according to the good old custom. He told them to remember that "the event of the day would decide the superiority of British seamen, when well trained, over those of other nations; and that the *Shannon* would that day show how short a time the Americans had to boast when opposed to equal force." At 5.25 P.M. the *Chesapeake* hauled up her foresail, and steered for the starboard and weather quarter of the *Shannon*. The Stars and Stripes were flying at the main, and at the fore was a large white flag inscribed with the motto, SAILORS' RIGHTS AND FREE TRADE, which, it was hoped, would paralyse the efforts and damp the energy of the *Shannon's* crew. At 5.40 P.M. the *Chesapeake* luffed up within fifty yards of the *Shannon's* starboard quarter, and the mainyard being squared, Captain Lawrence and his crew gave three cheers.

The captain of the *Shannon's* aftermost maindeck gun, No. 14, had been instructed to reserve his fire until his gun should bear upon the *Chesapeake's* second bow port, and at 5.50 P.M. the gun was fired as directed, and with wonderful accuracy of aim. In a second or two No. 13 was fired, then the *Chesapeake's* bow gun went off, then the remaining guns on the broadside of each ship as fast as they could be discharged, and the cannonade proceeded with great fury. At 5.56 P.M. the *Chesapeake*, having had her jib-sheet and foretopsail-tie shot away, and her helm—probably from the death of the men stationed at it—being unattended to, came sharp to the wind, and exposed her stern and quarter to the broadside of the *Shannon*. She then began to pay round. Captain Broke tried to keep off, to delay the boarding till his guns should have done a little more execution among the American crew, but at that moment the *Shannon's* jib-stay was shot away, and the consequence was, that at 6 P.M. the *Chesapeake* fell on board the *Shannon*, with her quarter pressing upon the British frigate's side, just before her starboard main-chains, while her quarter port hooked the fluke of the *Shannon's* anchor stowed over the cross-tree. Captain Broke immediately ran forward, and ordered the great guns to cease firing, the ships to be lashed together, and the boarders to be called. Mr. Stevens, the boatswain, a veteran who had served under Rodney, attended to the lashing of the ships, and while employed on this duty, outside the bulwark, had his left arm hacked off by American sabres, and was mortally wounded by musketry. The like fate befell Mr. Samuel, the midshipman commanding the forecastle. The two ships, however, were successfully lashed together, and at 6.2 P.M. Captain Broke and 20 of the forecastle men stepped from the *Shannon's* gangway rail on the muzzle of the *Chesapeake's* aftermost carronade, and thence over the bulwark upon her quarterdeck.

Not a soul was to be seen in that part of the ship. From twenty-five to thirty Americans made a slight resistance in the gangway, but these were speedily driven towards the forecastle, where a few endeavoured to get down the fore hatchway, but in their eagerness prevented one another. Some fled over the bows, some plunged into the sea, some reached the main deck through the bridle ports. The remainder laid down their arms and submitted. By this time the small party of boarders had been largely reinforced, and some of the British rushed forward, while others answered a destructive fire still kept up from the *Chesapeake's* main and mizzen tops. The mainyard was gallantly stormed by Midshipman William Smith and five topmen, who fearlessly passed along the *Shannon's* foreyard, which was braced up to the *Chesapeake's* mainyard, and destroyed the Americans stationed there, or drove them on deck. And all further annoyance from the *Chesapeake's* mizzentop was put an end to by Midshipman Cosnahan, who took his station on the *Shannon's* starboard yard-arm, and fired at the enemy as fast as his men on the top could load the muskets and hand them to him.

When the Americans upon the forecastle had submitted, Captain Broke sent the men, all but one sentry, aft, where the struggle was still going on. The Americans on the forecastle thought this an opportunity not to be lost, and resuming their arms, three of them made a dastardly attack on Captain Broke. With his sword he parried the middle assailant's pike, but instantly received from the man on the right a blow with the butt-end of a musket, which bared his skull and nearly stunned him. The third man cut at him with his broadsword, and was about to despatch him, when William Needham, the captain of the *Shannon's* 14th gun, opportunely stepped forward, and in turn cut him down. The other two Americans also paid with their lives the penalty of their treachery. Needham and Midshipman Smith helped Captain Broke on his legs, and seated him on a carronade slide, and Mr. Smith was tying a handkerchief round his head when Needham, pointing aft, cried, "There, sir, there goes up the old ensign over the Yankee colours." To Captain Broke the sight was better than surgery.

The changing of the *Chesapeake's* colours proved fatal to Lieutenant Watt and four or five fine fellows of the *Shannon*. Lieutenant Watt, who had been already wounded in the foot by a shot from the *Chesapeake's* top, hauled down the Yankee ensign with his own hand, and the halliards being tangled, he unfortunately bent the English flag below instead of above it. Observing the Stars and Stripes going up first, the men left in the *Shannon* concluded that the boarding had been unsuccessful, and fired at the *Chesapeake's* mizzen-mast. A grape shot took off the upper part of Lieutenant Watt's head, and four or five of the men who followed him fell at his side. The flags were soon properly hoisted, and the men of the *Shannon*, horrified at the mistake they had made, ceased their fire.

The crew of the *Chesapeake* being driven below into her hold, a sentinel of the Royal Marines was placed over the main hatchway. The Americans treacherously fired from the hold and killed him. On this, Lieutenant Falkner directed three or four muskets, that were ready, to be fired down. Captain Broke, from his seat on the carronade slide, told Lieutenant Falkner to summon the Americans in the hold to surrender, if they desired quarter. The lieutenant did so; the Americans replied, "We surrender," and all hostilities ceased.

When the colours were changed, it was fifteen minutes from the firing of the first gun, and four from the time of boarding. It was a fair trial of strength, and the British gained the day. The *Shannon's* 50 guns threw a broadside of 538 lbs., and her crew numbered 306 men and boys; the *Chesapeake's* 50 guns threw a broadside of 509 lbs., and her crew numbered over 400. The *Shannon* had 24 killed and 50 wounded, and the *Chesapeake* 47 killed and 99 wounded, among the latter the brave Captain Lawrence, who died three days after the action, and was buried by his conquerors with military honours. The crowd of pleasure-boats returned to Boston, every one ventilating a favourite theory to explain how it was that the *Chesapeake* was taken so unexpectedly; and the balls and suppers which were to have greeted the American conquerors were all countermanded. On the 5th the *Shannon* sailed into Halifax, in company with her prize, and was received with loud cheering by the townsmen, assembled in thousands to greet the victors. For his gallant exploit Captain Broke was rewarded with a baronetcy.

The land operations of the war were by no means important. About a month after the declaration of war, in the summer of 1812, the American General Hill invaded Canada, but was soon obliged to retire to Detroit, where he was forced to surrender (August 16) with his whole army to the British General Brock. Another attempt to push an army across the Niagara river was foiled at Queenston (Oct. 13), but the gallant Brock fell at the moment of victory. In 1813 the Americans renewed their attempts for the invasion of Canada, and collecting a flotilla on Lakes Ontario, Huron, and Erie, took the city of York, and gained a footing on the Canadian shore close to the Falls of Niagara; but both here and at Detroit, where their chief efforts were concentrated, they suffered disaster from a night attack. In the boat-fighting on the lakes the Americans had much the best of it, chiefly through the incompetence of General Sir George Prevost, who, says Yonge, "was only saved by death from being called to a severe account for his conduct before a court-martial." In 1814 a large number of Wellington's veterans were sent to America, under the command of General Ross, but the operations in which they were engaged were fitter for filibusters than the heroes of that glorious army which marched from Torres Vedras to Toulouse. The American militia was routed at Bladensburg (August 24), and the public buildings of Washington were given to the flames. An attack was projected on Baltimore, and the Americans were defeated five miles from the city, but the fall of General Ross caused the attempt to be abandoned. The Americans, however, had their revenge at New

Orleans, the Walcheren of the American War, where General Pakenham and a host of brave men and officers, the flower of the Peninsular army, perished in a vain attempt to pierce the American lines. Before this disaster to the British arms, a treaty of peace had been signed at Ghent (Dec. 24, 1814).

CHAPTER XII.

THE HUNDRED DAYS.—1815.

Quatre Bras—Waterloo:

THE Congress of Vienna, which had assembled to remodel the map of Europe, was still in the midst of its labours, when it was announced that Napoleon had secretly escaped from Elba. There had been acrimonious disputes about Saxony and Poland, but these were all hushed in the anxious desire of the Powers to concert some scheme to encounter their arch-enemy. Napoleon was declared a public outlaw, and England, Austria, Prussia, and Russia bound themselves not to lay down their arms until he was driven from the throne of France, and rendered for evermore incapable of disturbing the public peace of Europe. The Rhine soon bristled with the bayonets of Prussians and Austrians, under Blucher and Schwartzenberg. The Russians were coming up through Poland under Barclay de Tolly. The English, with their contingents of Dutch, Belgians, and Hanoverians, were in the Low Countries under Wellington. Spain and Portugal began to organise their battalions to cross the Pyrenees. Sweden and Denmark called out their forces. Even Switzerland abandoned her neutrality. 700,000 men were in arms, and all were moving upon Paris in converging lines. The curtain was about to rise on the last act of the drama of which Europe had so long been the theatre.

All that genius, all that activity could do to stem this torrent of hostility was done by Napoleon; and by the beginning of June (1815) he had 220,000 men ready to take the field. His first blow he resolved should be delivered at the British and Prussians, the nearest and the most resolute of his many adversaries. These defeated, it would be an easy matter to cope with the other masses that were slowly labouring up against the eastern parts of his dominions. His plan was to separate the Prussians from the British, and so attack each singly. It was the favourite tactic which he had so often and so victoriously employed in his wars in Italy and Germany, and he felt sanguine that it would not fail him now. He was vastly outnumbered,—223,000 allies, if they were combined, to about 125,000 French; but he had many advantages. His army was composed of veterans, all under his sole command, "speaking one tongue, holding one creed of military loyalty," inspired with the utmost confidence in their commander, their officers, and themselves, and the most inveterate hatred of their enemies. The Prussian soldiers were by no means of a high quality,—one-half of them being landwehr, and a large proportion of the regulars consisting merely of recruits: equal to the French in nothing but the most inveterate hatred of their enemies. Wellington's army was a motley crew, composed of Nassauers, Dutch, Belgians, Brunswickers, Hanoverians, and British. Not a third were British; the Nassauers, Dutch, and Belgians were thoroughly unreliable, and the British were chiefly second battalions, or old regiments filled with recruits. The flower of the old Peninsular heroes had been sent on senseless filibustering expeditions against America. Another great advantage Napoleon had was the necessary dispersal of the allied forces, produced partly by the divergence of their bases of supply—Wellington's being on the coast and Blucher's inland at Maestricht—and partly by the importance of protecting Brussels. For, had Napoleon succeeded, either by manœuvring or fighting, in occupying Brussels, the greater part of Belgium would unquestionably have declared in his favour, and such a success, gained at the outset, might have had the most important results on the issue of the campaign. Moreover, from the French frontier there converged four roads upon Brussels, and every one of these had to be guarded, while Napoleon could concentrate his army behind the triple line of fortresses on the frontier, and conceal the precise line of attack which he intended to take until the very moment.

Accompanied by his brother Jerome, Napoleon arrived in the camp on the 14th June, and his soldiers, already elated by his presence, were excited to the highest pitch of enthusiasm by the following "Order of the Day :"—

"Soldiers! this day is the anniversary of Marengo and of Friedland, which twice decided the destiny of Europe. Then, as after Austerlitz, as after Wagram, we were too generous! We believed in the protestations and in the oaths of princes whom we left on their thrones. Now, however, leagued together, they aim at the independence and the most sacred rights of France. They have commenced the most unjust of aggressions. Let us then march to meet them. Are they and we no longer the same men?

"Soldiers! At Jena, against these same Prussians, now so arrogant, you were one to three, and at Montmirail one to six!

"Let those among you who have been captives to the English describe the nature of their prison-ships and the frightful miseries you endured.

"The Saxons, the Belgians, the Hanoverians, the soldiers of the Confederation of the Rhine, lament that they are compelled to use their arms in the cause of princes, the enemies of justice and of the rights of all nations. They know that this coalition is insatiable! After having devoured 12,000,000 of Poles, 12,000,000 of Italians, 1,000,000 of Saxons, and 6,000,000 of Belgians, it now wishes to devour the states of the second rank in Germany.

"Madmen! One moment of prosperity has bewildered them. The oppression and the humiliation of the French people are beyond their power. If they enter France they will there find their grave.

"Soldiers! we have forced marches to make, battles to fight, dangers to encounter; but, with firmness, victory will be ours. The rights, the honour, and the happiness of the country will be recovered!

"To every Frenchman who has a heart, the moment is now arrived to conquer or to die."

Napoleon finally resolved to advance through Charleroi, by the main road leading through Frasnes, Quatre Bras, Waterloo, and the Forest of Soignies to Brussels. This route lay right through the centre of the cantonments of the allies. At three in the morning of the 15th June, he crossed the Sambre in three columns, attacking the Prussian outposts and driving them back on their supports. With his left wing he defeated Zeithen at

Thuin, while with his right centre he advanced in person to Fleurus, inflicting considerable loss on the Prussians, who fell back before him. When night fell, he had a powerful force before Ligny, the point which Blucher had fixed for the concentration of his forces, and that concentration was still incomplete. With his right wing and centre he intended to attack the Prussians next day, while he employed the left wing (which he placed under the command of Marshal Ney) to oppose any troops that Wellington might send to the aid of Blucher, and then to turn round and assail the Prussian right flank. Ney advanced to Frasnes, two miles from Quatre Bras, where he came in contact with the advanced guard of Wellington's army—a battalion of Nassauers and a light battery. After a few cannon-shots, this outpost fell back from Frasnes to Quatre Bras, which was held by the remainder of the brigade under Prince Bernard of Saxe-Weimar. Ney then came up to reconnoitre, but the wood of Bossu and the failing light prevented him from ascertaining the number of the troops in his front, and as his own men had been marching for seventeen hours he decided to postpone the attack. Wellington was informed of the French advance about three in the afternoon of the 15th, but it was midnight before he received such intelligence as made him decide his movements. That night the Duchess of Richmond gave a ball at Brussels,

> "And Belgium's capital had gathered then
> Her Beauty and her Chivalry;"

and Wellington was there, and showed himself very cheerful. Most of the British officers were there too, but one by one they hurried from the ball-room to make their last preparations for the terrible struggle. The ball was over, the rattle of the carriages taking home the guests gradually died away, and the streets of Brussels were steeped in silence. But suddenly in the morning air a bugle-call rang from the Place d'Armes, and its echoes were answered by a confused rolling of drums, rumbling of artillery, and neighing of chargers,—the bagpipes screaming the pibroch, never more appropriate, an invitation to the ravens and the wolves, "Come to me, and I will give you flesh." The sergeants and the corporals ran to the quarters of their respective parties to turn them out; and each man, receiving four days' allowance from the store, fell into rank. By 4 o'clock, the troops commenced their march, and many and heartrending were the partings, for the families of British soldiers of all ranks had come to Brussels.

Between two and three in the afternoon of the 16th, while Blucher and Napoleon were fighting their terrible battle at Ligny, about six miles south-east of Quatre Bras, on the road to Namur, Marshal Ney commenced his battle at Quatre Bras—the name given to the farm-buildings at the intersection of the roads to Brussels and Charleroi, Nivelles and Namur. On the allies' right, the position was covered by the wood of Bossu, in an angle between the Nivelles and Charleroi roads, and on their left by the farm-steadings of Gemioncourt and Piermont, between the Charleroi and Namur roads. When the battle began, the Prince of Orange, who commanded here for the allies, had only 6832 Dutch-Belgian infantry and 16 guns, to meet Ney's attack with 15,750 foot, 1865 light horse, 4 batteries of foot artillery, and one battery of horse artillery. Ney's force indeed was nominally more than 40,000, but more than half of it, the first corps under Count D'Erlon, was kept by contradictory orders marching and countermarching all day between Quatre Bras and Ligny, and rendered no service. During the battle, however, Ney was reinforced by the magnificent heavy cavalry of Kellerman, 5000 sabres, and by several battalions of artillery.

Within half an hour after the battle begun, the Belgian outposts were driven in, and Piermont and Gemioncourt carried. Ney then ranged the chief part of his artillery on the high ground of Gemioncourt, whence it continued to play with destructive effect till the close of the day. At the same time he sent forward his infantry to the wood of Bossu, and the Dutch-Belgians were hard pressed. But at this critical moment Wellington arrived from his interview with Blucher at Ligny; masses of troops in the scarlet uniform of England were seen moving up the main road, after a twenty miles march, from Brussels; and Van Merlen's Dutch-Belgian cavalry came up from Nivelles. The British troops were the 5th division, under Sir Thomas Picton, including Sir Dennis Pack's brigade (42d, 44th, 92d, and 95th), Sir James Kempt's brigade (28th, 32d, 79th, 1st Royal Scots), and four battalions of Best's Hanoverians. Wellington was now superior to his opponent in mere numbers, but the British and Germans, on whom alone reliance could be placed, were still but 8000, and the cavalry on the field was utterly worthless.

Picton's division was deployed along the Namur road, to prevent Ney from obtaining possession of the way to Ligny. The British were in front, the Hanoverians behind. Scarcely were they posted when dark masses of the enemy were seen advancing, the skirmishers in front stealing by the hedges on the roadsides, and gliding from one clump of trees to another. The Duke of Brunswick's advanced skirmishers fell back. Wellington ordered Picton to charge. "There's the enemy! you must beat them," said that saturnine warrior, and the line advanced. And then was seen what the Peninsular fields had so often witnessed: the French skirmishers fell back on the flanks of their supports, the masses broke into columns, the columns were overflanked, a murderous fire shattered their fronts and flanks, they reeled, they broke, they fled pell-mell, followed at the point of the bayonet.

Meanwhile, ill-fared it with the allies' battle on the right of the road by the wood of Bossu. The Brunswick infantry, sorely galled by the French cannonade, became restless. "Brunswick's fated chieftain," son of the duke who fell in the Jena campaign, walked about and tried to encourage them, and Wellington sent them four guns to keep up their spirits; but when the French skirmishers pressed forward the cavalry closed in, and the infantry, seized with panic, broke and fled. The Duke of Brunswick attempted to rally his people, but received a musket-shot, and was borne off the field mortally wounded. Wellington ordered the Brunswick hussars to advance to cover the retreat; these horsemen trotted up to the French lancers bravely enough, but seemed suddenly to change their mind, and wheeling about, galloped off to Quatre Bras. Their retreat brought the French cavalry down on the 42d and 44th. The 42d was in the middle of a field of tall rye, and was under the impression that the advancing tide of horsemen was altogether composed of their friends the Black Brunswickers, till a German orderly dragoon galloped up crying "Franchee! Franchee!" The Highlanders instantly formed a rallying square, but the formation was not nearly completed when on came the lancers, flushed with success. Few of the skirmishers of the regiment escaped death or wounds, but the main body stood firm, and a well-directed volley sent the lancers to the right about, leaving many of their comrades dead among the rye, or in the square into which they had penetrated. Two companies of the regiment were not, however, so fortunate. These, struck by the lancers before they could take their places to complete the square, were forced in upon the other companies, and almost cut to pieces. The colonel, Sir Robert Macara, was with them and shared their fate. A lance struck him in the face, entering his chin and piercing his brain. The 44th was so suddenly taken by the lancers, both in front and in rear, that there was no time to abandon the formation in line, and Colonel Hammerton called out to the rear-rank to face about, present, fire. The volley, delivered at the distance of twenty paces, was murderous. But some of the survivors advanced with great spirit to the bayonets, and one of them struck Ensign Christie severely in the face. That gallant officer, however, though suffering severely from the agony of his wound, preserved the colours by throwing himself on his face; and the lancer, who had torn off with his weapon a piece of the silk, was instantly shot. Discomfited in this quarter, these detachments of lancers bore away to their own right, with cries of "Down with the English!" "No Quarter!" but Kempt's squares resisted every attack. The main body of the French cavalry—cuirassiers—continued their career down the Charleroi road to Quatre Bras. Right in their way was a ditch, where the 92d (Gordon) Highlanders were lying hid. Wellington was at this time trying to rally the Brunswick hussars, and so swift was the advance of the cuirassiers that he was nearly taken prisoner. He owed his escape to his own promptness and presence of mind, in ordering a part of the 92d to lie close down in the ditch they were lining, while he leaped his horse over them and across the ditch. The instant he had cleared it, up rose the plumed bonnets of the Highlanders darkly in a line, and a stream of fire was poured upon men and horses, which emptied many saddles, and checked the onward career of the squadrons. The greater part of the cuirassiers then withdrew, but some rode on and entered a farmyard with only one gate: in this *cul-de-sac* they were cut off by a party of the 92d, and perished to a man.

Foiled in his first great attempt, Ney redoubled his efforts to execute his orders—to carry the position and move to strike against the Prussian right. The wood of Bossu was at length yielded by the Dutch-Belgians, and Kellerman was sent forward with his splendid body of horsemen to trample down the British infantry. But the squares stood fire—rocks perpetually lashed by the surging breakers, but never shaken. Not only so; the

28th and the 1st Royals actually advanced to charge the enemy's cavalry, and took the pressure off the 42d and 44th, who, being on the flank, were greatly exposed.

So the battle continued, the British squares continually exposed, either to the charges of Kellerman's cavalry, or, when the horsemen withdrew, to the fire of the French guns planted on the high ground above Gemioncourt. The squares were in danger of melting away, but at six o'clock General Alten arrived with the 3d division. One part of it—Major-general Sir C. Halkett's brigade (30th, 33d, 69th, and 73d)—was moved towards the right between the wood of Bossu and the Charleroi road; the other part—Kielmansegge's Hanoverians—to the left, to reinforce the regiments there. Again did Ney renew his efforts, and send his cavalry thundering down the slope, but still the horsemen could make no impression on the British squares. But one regiment, the 69th, by a confusion of orders was caught in line and rolled up, and a private cuirassier, named Lami, captured one of the colours, which its bearer, Clarke, received twenty-three wounds in defending. Clarke survived, though with the loss of an arm, and afterwards became an officer of the 42d. Riding through the 69th the cuirassiers continued their career, but the volleys of the 32d sent them back quicker than they advanced. Meanwhile the French infantry debouched from the wood of Bossu, and, regardless of the fire of Kuhlman's guns, advanced towards the ditch still lined by the 92d Highlanders. Major Macdonald observed their advance and called Wellington's attention to it. "Yes, major," replied the duke, looking through his glass, and speaking in his usual tranquil tone, "yes, there is a considerable body of them." Then turning to Colonel Cameron—"Colonel," he said, "you must charge." Sir E. Barnes, Adjutant-general of the army, took off his hat and cheered. "Ninety-second, he cried, "whom I have often led, a column of the enemy is now advancing upon us, and the honour of repulsing them is entirely given to you." The Highlanders, who had been standing in the ditch impatient for action, instantly rushed forward and routed the enemy. On they pressed victoriously, till a farm-house and a garden on the other side of the road afforded the retreating French some shelter. From the windows of the house and the walls of the garden they opened a destructive fire on the pursuing Highlanders, who, moreover, were exposed to a heavy fire of grape, which rapidly thinned their ranks; but, in spite of all this, the French were driven out at the point of the bayonet, and forced back to the wood. In this short but bloody conflict the 92d lost 200 men and their colonel, Sir John Cameron of Fassifern, one of the most distinguished of Wellington's officers.

Ney despatched to Napoleon the captured colour of the 69th as an earnest of victory—a victory that was not destined to be won. At half-past six the guards and two light battalions of Brunswickers came up, and the guards were ordered to advance and retake the wood of Bossu. The French infantry gave way before them, but when the guards attempted to debouch to the open beyond, they were struck by round shot and canister, their flank was disordered by a charge of cuirassiers, and they were compelled to fall back to a broad ditch on the edge of the wood, where they obtained some shelter. Encouraged by this momentary success, the French troops advanced to retake the wood, but were repulsed with great slaughter, and as night wore on, observing the efforts of the enemy become feebler and feebler, Wellington ordered the whole line to advance. With three cheers the British rushed forward, and the enemy were driven back from the wood of Bossu, Gemioncourt, Piermont, and all the points they had made themselves masters of in the first onset. The battle closed as the summer night set in. Victory rested with the allies, but their loss exceeded that of the French by 1000 men, the numbers standing at 5000 on the one side and 4000 on the other. Picton's regiments suffered most severely, and the day was undoubtedly due to the stubbornness of the resistance their rocky squares offered to the fiery torrents of the French cavalry.

The victors passed the night on the field of battle amid the trampled rye. No fires were lighted. Every man lay down in rear of his arms, and silence was enjoined on all. Few slept, however, for the stillness of the summer night was broken by the arrival of the troops from Brussels, the tramp of the infantry, the jingle of the cavalry, and the heavy dull sound of the tumbrels; sometimes, too, by false alarms, and cries of "Stand to your arms!" followed by a dropping fire. Around lay the dead and the wounded, for night had fallen before the latter could be removed.

Next morning (June 17th) Wellington was prepared to take

the offensive against the enemy, his whole army being by that time assembled. But at nine o'clock an officer reached him from Blucher—the messenger sent the night before had been shot on the way—and told him of the defeat of the Prussians at Ligny, and of Blucher's intention to concentrate at Wavre. A corresponding retrograde movement was clearly inevitable. Wellington promised to halt at Waterloo if Blucher would pledge himself to come to his assistance with a single corps of 25,000 men. The promise was readily given, and after allowing his men a sufficient time for refreshment and rest, Wellington retired to Waterloo, a march of eight miles. The retreat was pressed by Napoleon in person, who about noon moved laterally from Ligny and joined the forces of Ney; but so skilful were Wellington's dispositions that he carried off his force successfully, and with very little molestation. The day was very hot, with a sulphureous atmosphere and dense masses of thunder-clouds, and the discharge of a few heavy guns, fired to check the advance of some French horsemen, was immediately followed by a deafening peal of thunder and heavy rain, amid which the troops took up their position on the battlefield of Waterloo. During the hours of darkness the rain fell in torrents, and brilliant flashes of lightning illuminated the sky, spreading a terrific radiance along the brow of night. Peels of thunder, louder than the discharge of whole parks of artillery, stunned the ears of the soldiers, who lay on the wet rye, with no covering, no fuel, and no food but what they carried in their knapsacks. The cavalry soldiers spent the night standing by their horses, with the arm passed through the stirrup. But no one thought of his own privations. The least reflecting soldier on the field knew that the fate of Europe hung in the balance. And both sides were equally confident—the allies in the captain who had never known defeat, and the French in the "Sun of Austerlitz," which would sweep away the clouds which had for a time obscured their great leader, and blast all the laurels of the "General of Sepoys."

As the morning wore on the weather cleared up, and the men set about cleaning themselves, drying their muskets, and cooking breakfast. Wellington and his staff took up their station on the green height in rear of La Haye Sainte, whence the whole line could be scanned from right to left.

Creasy says an accurate idea of the field of Waterloo may be formed by picturing "a valley between two and three miles long, of various breadths at different points, but generally not exceeding half a mile. On each side of the valley there is a winding chain of low hills running somewhat parallel with each other. The declivity from each of these ranges of hills to the intervening valley is gentle but not uniform, the undulations of the ground being frequent and considerable. The English army was posted on the northern, and the French army occupied the southern ridge. The artillery of each side thundered at the other from their respective heights throughout the day, and the charges of horse and foot were made across the valley that has been described. The village of Mont St. Jean is situate a little behind the centre of the northern chain of hills, and the village of La Belle Alliance is close behind the centre of the southern ridge. The high road from Charleroi to Brussels (a broad paved causeway) runs through both these villages, and bisects, therefore, both the English and the French positions. The line of this road was the line of Napoleon's intended advance on Brussels. . . . The strength of the British position did not consist merely in the occupation of a ridge of high ground. A village and ravine, called Merk Braine, on the Duke of Wellington's extreme right, secured his flank from being turned on that side; and on his extreme left, two little villages, called La Haye and Papelotte, gave a similar, though a slighter, protection. Behind the whole British position is the extensive forest of Soignies. As no attempt was made by the French to turn either of the English flanks, and the battle was a day of straightforward fighting, it is chiefly important to ascertain what posts there were in front of the British line of hills, of which advantage could be taken either to repel or facilitate an attack; and it will be seen that there are two, and that each was of very great importance in the action. In front of the British right, that is to say, on the northern slope of the valley at its western end, there stood an old-fashioned Flemish farmhouse called Goumont, or Hougoumont, with out-buildings and a garden, and with a copse of beech trees of about two acres in extent round it. This was strongly garrisoned by the allied troops, and, while it was in their possession, it was difficult for the enemy to press on and force the British right wing. On the other hand, if the enemy could take it, it would be difficult for that wing to keep its ground on the heights, with a strong post held adversely to its immediate front, being one that would give much shelter to the enemy's marksmen, and great facilities for the sudden concentration of attacking columns. Almost immediately in front of the British centre, and not so far down the slope as Hougoumont, there was another farmhouse, of a smaller size, called La Haye Sainte (not to be confounded with the hamlet of La Haye at the extreme left of the British line), which was also held by the British troops, and the occupation of which was found to be of very serious consequence. With respect to the French position, the principal feature to be noticed is the village of Planchenoit, which lay a little in the rear of their right (*i.e.*, on the eastern side), and which proved to be of great importance in aiding them to check the advance of the Prussians."

On the night of the 17th Wellington had caused every brigade and corps to take up its station on the part of the ground which it was intended to hold in the coming battle. The army was drawn up in two lines, the first stationed near the crest of the ridge, the other ranged along the slope in the rear. The right and right centre, under Hill, occupied Hougoumont and the ground west of the Charleroi road. Hougoumont was held by Byng's brigade of guards; further back was the 2d division under Clinton—comprising Adams' brigade (52d, 71st, 95th), Du Plat's Germans, and Colonel Hugh Halkett's Hanoverians—with Mitchell's brigade (14th, 23d, 51st) on its right; then came the 3d division under Alten—comprising Sir Colin Halkett's brigade (30th, 33d, 69th, 73d), Kielmansegge's Hanoverians, and Ompteda's Germans. The left centre and left was held by the 5th division under Picton—comprising Kempt's brigade (28th, 32d, 79th, 95th), with Bylandt's Dutch-Belgians in front, and Lambert (4th, 27th, 40th, 81st) in reserve, Pack (1st, 42d, 44th, 92d), with Best's Hanoverians in front, and Veneke's Hanoverians on the left. Best's brigade was protected by a ditch on its flank, impassable to artillery. The extreme left—the farms of Papelotte and La Haye and the hamlet of Smohain—was held by Nassauers and Dutch-Belgians, under the Prince of Saxe-Weimar. The extreme right at Braine-Laleud and the Old Foriez farm was also held by Dutch-Belgians, but the other troops of this nationality were scattered in detached bodies to prevent their running away. The cavalry stood in the second line: Grant (2d, 7th, 15th Hussars), Dornberg (German and 23d Light Dragoons), and Arentschild (3d German Hussars, 13th

Light Dragoons) behind the right wing; then the Cumberland (Hanoverian) Hussars; Somerset's Household Brigade (1st and 2d Life Guards, the Blues, and the 1st Dragoon Guards) behind Alten; Ponsonby's Union Brigade (1st Royal Dragoons, Scots Greys, and Inniskillings) behind Picton; Vandeleur (11th, 12th, 16th Light Dragoons) and Vivian (1st, 10th, and 18th Hussars) behind Picton's left. The reserve consisted of Dollaert's Dutch-Belgian cavalry (by the Mont St. Jean farm), Lambert's British (behind Kempt), and Olfermann's Brunswickers. The artillery was posted along the whole front, wherever a gun could command the enemy.

Napoleon's army was ranged in 13 columns; the infantry in front, the cavalry behind, and the Imperial guards in reserve. His artillery was posted along the Belle Alliance ridge about three-quarters of a mile from the British guns. His force consisted of 48,950 infantry, 15,765 cavalry, and 7232 artillerymen, being a total of 71,947 men, with 246 guns. Wellington's force consisted of 49,608 infantry, 12,402 cavalry, and 5645 artillerymen, being a total of 67,655 men, with 156 guns. But of this total scarce 24,000 were British, a circumstance of very great importance, if Napoleon was correct in estimating that a French soldier would not be equal to more than one English soldier, but would not be afraid to meet two of any other nation. Besides, the Dutch-Belgians were known to be thoroughly disaffected to the cause of the allies.

The Sunday morning wore on till near noon, when a heavy gun was fired in the French centre as a signal, and immediately the quick rattle of musketry was heard on the French left, as Jerome put his column in motion against the position of Hougoumont, throwing out clouds of skirmishers. When the struggle commenced the position was held by the light companies of the guards. Those of the 1st regiment, under Colonel Lord Saltoun, held the orchard and wood; those of the Coldstream and 3d Guards, under Colonel Macdonell, held the buildings and garden. In the outer grounds were a battalion of Nassau troops, 100 men of the Luneberg battalion, and a company of Hanoverian field-riflemen. But as the day wore on and the struggle grew fiercer, the whole of Byng's brigade was required to man this hotly-contested point. On came the French and drove back the Nassauers and the riflemen, but Major Bull's howitzers spread dismay in their ranks, and the light companies of the guards cleared the wood. Napoleon ordered Reille's cannon to give fire, and Kellerman to push forward his horse-batteries. The guns now opened on both sides along the whole line, and the noise was deafening. Under cover of the fire of Reille's batteries, the French again pushed forward, gained the wood, and attacked the chateau, but the loopholed walls of the building presented an insurmountable obstacle. The defenders had the advantage of a double tier of loopholes and a banquette, and their fire was withering, but however often repulsed, the French advanced again and again to the attack, and many of them were so daring that they madly seized and sought to wrench away the muskets as they were levelled through the loops. Once the besiegers forced an entrance by the north gate. The guards fired a volley, then sprang forward to a hand-to-hand struggle. British bayonets prevailed; the intruders were overpowered, and the gate was closed. The great number of shot and shell discharged into the place set the buildings on fire, and the French renewed their efforts, but were foiled by the incessant volleys from within. The violence of the struggle at Hougoumont has seldom been equalled. It has been calculated that within half an hour 1500 men were killed in the orchard alone, a small plot of ground not exceeding four acres; and that altogether, in the attack of the position, the French lost 10,000 men killed and wounded.

Ney, meanwhile, had been massing troops for an attack on the British centre and left. The infantry, consisting of 18,000 men, divided into four columns, under Donzelat, Alix, Marcognet, and Durutte, was supported by a strong division of cavalry under Kellerman; and 74 guns were brought forward to a gentle undulation between the two principal heights, to play on the allied line at 700 yards. With loud shouts of "Vive l'Empereur!" the French infantry advanced across the valley: Donzelat moving along the Charleroi road, Alix and Marcognet on his right, and Durutte upon the British left at Papelotte. As they descended from the intervening eminence, the 74 guns posted there opened over their heads with a tempest of shot and shell, ploughing Mont St. Jean, and inflicting great loss on Picton's division, Bylandt's Dutch-Belgians, and Best's Hanoverians. Durutte's division attacked Papelotte and won it, but the Nassauers were reinforced and drove them out again. Part of Donzelat's division attacked La Haye Sainte. The divisions of Alix and Marcognet advanced against the allied line.

Bylandt's Dutch-Belgians took to their heels, and the French poured in a destructive fire on Picton's division, which had suffered so severely at Quatre Bras that the eight regiments could scarcely show 3000 bayonets. When the heads of the French columns approached to within 20 yards, the columns halted and began to deploy into line, but Picton seized the critical moment. "A volley, and then charge!" he shouted to Pack's brigade (1st, 42d, 44th, 92d). The head of Marcognet's column was swept away by the sheet of musketry, and then with a shout the wasted regiments rushed on with cold steel. Marcognet's men reeled back in confusion, and at this instant Ponsonby's heavy cavalry (the Union Brigade, as it was called, from its being made up of the 1st Royal Dragoons, the Scots Greys, and the Irish Inniskillings), forced their way through, or leaped over the hedge of La Haye Sainte, behind which they were posted, and galloped forward on the column, Picton's men opening their files to let them pass. "Scotland for ever!" shouted the Greys, while the pipers struck up, and many of the Highlanders, breaking from their ranks, caught hold of the Greys' stirrups to keep up with them in the charge. In a few minutes the French column was utterly broken, the slope was covered with dead, wounded, and fugitives, and masses threw away their belts and cried, "Quarter!" and "Prisoners." Upwards of 2000 passed to the rear. Onward through the wrecks of the French column galloped the Greys and the Inniskillings, dashed up the French slope, sabred the artillerymen of Ney's 74 advanced guns, cut the traces, and hamstrung the horses. At least 40 of these guns were rendered useless for the rest of the day. "These terrible Greys!" exclaimed Napoleon. On the right, the 1st Royal Dragoons fell upon the right of Alix's division. This body was pursuing the flight of Bylandt's Dutch-Belgians, and had not yet met any infantry. The Royals mowed it down with great carnage. In this splendid charge the heavies captured two eagles, one taken by Sergeant Ewart of the Greys, and the other by Captain Clarke of the Royals. But the heavies committed the fault of advancing too far, and while disordered with success were charged by a large body of French lancers, and driven back with severe loss, till Vandeleur's light horse came to their aid, and beat off the French lancers in turn.

The left of Alix's column and part of Donzelat's drove the Germans from the orchard of La Haye Sainte, and advanced under a terrible storm of artillery fire to the hedge on which Kempt's brigade (28th, 32d, 79th, 95th) rested. "Charge! charge! Hurrah!" shouted Picton, who fell pierced in the forehead by a musket ball, but the charge to which he gave the impetus was completely successful; the French were broken and reduced to a disorderly mass. But a battalion of Kielmansegge's Hanoverians, sent to reinforce the position at La Haye Sainte, were struck by Milhaud's cuirassiers and cut to pieces; and the horsemen, in the pride of success, advanced upon the successful infantry of Kempt's brigade. The British regiments threw themselves into squares, and the cuirassiers were sounding the charge when the household brigade (1st and 2d Life Guards, the Blues, and the 1st Dragoon Guards) rushed forward to the encounter. "In an instant," says Creasy, "the two adverse lines of strong swordsmen, on their strong steeds, dashed furiously together. A desperate and sanguinary hand-to-hand fight ensued, in which the physical superiority of the Anglo-Saxons, guided by equal skill and animated with equal valour, was made decisively manifest. Back went the chosen cavalry of France; and after them, in hot pursuit, spurred the English guards. They went forward as far and as fiercely as their comrades of the Union Brigade; and, like them, the household cavalry suffered severely before they regained the British position, after their magnificent charge and adventurous pursuit."

It was now about half-past three, and after a furious cannonade Napoleon determined to try what effect could be produced on the British centre and right by charges of his splendid cavalry. At the same time fresh troops were sent to assail La Haye Sainte and Hougoumont. Forty squadrons—21 of them clad in glittering cuirasses—took part in this attack, which afforded the most imposing display of the whole battle. Mr. Clinton, a recent writer, graphically describes it:—"The rounds of grape and canister, discharged point-blank, made lanes in their ranks; but the brilliant lines continued to advance, and with a loud shout galloped in upon the advanced batteries. Resistance was quite impossible, and the gunners abandoned their pieces. But they had received instructions, in view of such an advance, to unlimber the rear wheel of each gun, and roll the wheel into the nearest square; so that when the horsemen threw round the guns the ropes they carried for the purpose, they could not move them, and in the interval they were themselves subjected to the volleys from the infantry. The enemy's cannonade, to cover the advance of the cavalry, had been so furious that Wellington had withdrawn his infantry regiments as much as possible behind the reverse slope, where they formed squares and lay down on the ground to rest. As the French squadrons now swept forward, the infantry sprang to their feet, and the enemy to their surprise beheld the invincible squares drawn up to receive them. For a moment there was perfect silence, and the cavalry, seeing the firm front of the infantry, paused. Then, with shouts, they rushed forward, but instead of charging the squares in front, they swept round by their flank and rear, so as to envelop the infantry, from which sheets of flame burst forth as from a volcano. The French horsemen recoiled in disorder from the ranks into which they were trying to break even at the sword's point, the artillerymen ran out to their guns, and sent a tempest of grape into the retiring squadrons, which were now also assailed by an advance of the British cavalry, and driven down the slope till joined by their reserves. Again the French guns opened; they were served with wonderful accuracy; and the bombs and ricochet shots continued to drop into the squares, the men of which were again lying down." Attempt after attempt was made, but without avail. "'These children of Albion,' as Foy remarks, stood as if 'they had taken root in the ground.' Every attempt to break these heroic bands failed; the horsemen surged as vainly upon them as waves beating upon an ironbound coast. Not a square was broken; and the French squadrons, exhausted and diminished, returned to their own ground, again pressed in their retreat by the British dragoons." But in another part of the field Napoleon was more successful. Between six and seven o'clock two columns of infantry from Donzelat's division took possession of La Haye Sainte, and thus the means was organised for making another formidable attack on the centre of the allies.

If that attack was to be made it must be made at once. Ever since three o'clock Napoleon had seen troops hovering on his right. Under the impression that Blucher had retreated, not to Wavre, but more to the eastward on his communications, Napoleon had persuaded himself that these troops were his own people under Grouchy. But the truth could no longer be hidden. It was the 1st corps of the Prussian army under Bulow.

All day long the Prussians had been striving to reach the field of battle. Wavre is but six miles east of Waterloo, but several mistakes and untoward circumstances had occurred to delay the march, and the narrow lanes were so broken that progress was almost impossible. The guns sank ankle-deep in mud, and the horses were too weak to draw them. The men took the traces, but almost despaired. "Forwards!" cried Blucher—his men called him "Marshal Forwards"—"You must get on: I have pledged my word to Wellington, and you would not have me break it. Courage, my children!" And here the Prussians were at last, fiercely assailing Planchenoit. Napoleon sent the young guard to keep them in check, while with the middle and old guard, who had never failed him yet, he made one last desperate effort to change the fortune of the day.

What need to enter into detail about the charge of the Imperial guard? Under Ney, "the bravest of the brave," they advanced majestically down the slope of the French hills, and with loud shouts of "Vive l' Empereur!" entered the valley and ascended the British heights, directing their march between Hougoumont and La Haye Sainte against the British right centre. The troops here were Maitland's brigade of guards, with Adams' brigade (52d, 71st, 95th) on the right. The guards had been ordered to lie down in the ditch behind the road which traverses the length of the ridge, to avoid the destructive effect of the enemy's artillery; and when the first column of the Imperial guard reached the ridge of the hill, and saw no enemy, they raised loud and exultant cheers, and beat their drums merrily, believing the day was at last won. Nothing could be seen save a small band of mounted officers, but presently one of these was heard calling, as if to the ground before him, "Up, Guards, and at them!" As if by magic, up sprang the guards, in line four deep, advanced a few paces, and poured in a well-directed volley, and 300 of the Imperial guard bit the dust. The decimated column grew more and more disordered in its vain attempts to expand itself into a more efficient formation; its head was overlapped, its flanks and front were assailed by musketry, and grape and canister swept its ranks at a distance of only 50 paces. The column reeled. "Forward, Guards!" cried Wellington, and the order ran along the line. With three cheers and bayonets at the charge, our guards rushed down the hill upon their antagonists, but when within 20 yards of each other, these chosen warriors of France, who had never yet been vanquished, spread out into a rabble, wheeled, and fled down the hill, closely pursued by the victors. Maitland, however, prudently halted his men before reaching the foot of the slope, and led them back to their post, where, aided by the regiments of Adams' brigade, they repulsed the other columns of the Imperial guard. "All is lost!" cried the French troops, "the guard is repulsed!"

Wellington saw the decisive moment was come, and closing his telescope and galloping to the front, he waved his hat and gave the long-wished-for order, "Let the whole line advance." The movement is well described by Mr. Clinton:—" An exulting cheer rang along the whole ridge: even the wounded who could limp along sprang from the ground, seized their arms, and fell in with their regiments; trumpets and drums sent forth their exultant notes, the tattered banners proudly waved aloft, and the triumphant soldiers descended the slopes, now bathed in the softened rays of the sinking sun. Never did a battlefield present a scene more glorious than the slopes of Waterloo, when the majestic line of horse and foot and field artillery swept forward—but, alas! trampling their own wounded." Some regiments of the old guard endeavoured to stem the torrent, but they were swept away. "All is lost!" said Napoleon; "let us save ourselves!"

At the Maison du Roi, or Maison Rouge, Wellington met Blucher, and hearty congratulations were exchanged. Blucher readily agreed to press the pursuit, and from the hatred which the Prussians bore to their former oppressors it was pressed with vigour. Scarce 40,000 men and 27 guns passed the Sambre. The grand army was completely broken; the infantry threw away their arms and dispersed, and the cavalry and artillery sold their horses to procure the means of reaching their homes. The loss of the French in the battle and the pursuit amounted to 40,000, and 150 guns and 6000 prisoners remained in the hands of the allies. The loss of the allies was over 22,000. The British loss was 1417 killed, 4923 wounded, and 582 missing; making a total of 6922. The Prussian total was about 100 more. The events that followed Waterloo—the occupation of Paris, and of France itself, Napoleon's surrender of himself to Captain Maitland of the *Bellerophon*, and his lonely exile at St. Helena—are matters of history. The gigantic war which ended on the field of Waterloo cost this country £600,000,000.

The instances of individual prowess at Waterloo are too numerous to mention. Who can forget the heroism of Picton, the leader of the "fighting third," who had two of his ribs broken at Quatre Bras, but concealed the wound, lest he should be solicited to absent himself from Waterloo, and fell pierced through the brain? Of Shaw the Life Guardsman, who cut down nine of the enemy, but was so slashed himself that he bled to death? Of Sergeant Ewart of the Greys and Sergeant Clarke of the Royals, who each captured a French colour? Of Sergeant Weir of the Scots Greys, who, as pay-sergeant of his troop, might have excused himself from serving in action, but disdained to avail himself of the privilege, and when he fell, fighting gloriously, wrote his name on his forehead with his own blood, that his body might be found and recognised, and that it might not be supposed he had disappeared with the money belonging to his troop? Of Sergeant James Graham of the guards, who fought like a hero when the French gained a momentary entrance into the Chateau of Hougoumont, and then surprised his commanding officer, Colonel Macdonell, with asking permission to fall out for a moment? "By all means, Graham," said the colonel; "but I wonder you should ask leave now." "I would not, sir," said Graham, "only my brother is wounded, and he is in that out-building there, which has just caught fire." Saying this, he ran and removed his brother to a place of safety, and was back at his post and plying his musket again before his absence was noticed.

Every regiment that fought at Waterloo has its own tale of service, and its own share of glory. In his despatch Wellington makes mention of but four British regiments, the 28th, and the 42d, 79th, and 92d Highlanders, but every regiment was deserving of praise. The 79th went into action at Quatre Bras with a strength of 776 men, and out of this number only 298 remained alive and unwounded at the close of the battle of Waterloo. The loss of the 79th exceeded by one that of any other regiment in the army, except the 3d battalion of the 1st Foot Guards, which was almost annihilated in the defence of Hougoumont. The 30th and the 73d were so much cut up that before the close of the day their colours were sent to the rear. The accounts of the battle which some of the survivors have left are very interesting, and enable one to understand the terrible nature of the struggle better than any amount of general description.

The soldier of the 71st, whom we have quoted before, says:—
"The artillery had been tearing away since daybreak in different parts of the line. About twelve o'clock we received orders to fall in for attack. We then marched up to our position, where we lay on the face of a 'brae' covering a brigade of guns. We were so overcome by the fatigue of the two days' march, that scarce had we lain down when many of us fell asleep. I slept sound for some time, while the cannon-balls, plunging in amongst us, killed a great many. I was suddenly awakened. A ball struck the ground a little below me, turned me heels-over-head, broke my musket in pieces, and killed a lad at my side. I was stunned and confused, and knew not whether I was wounded or not. I felt a numbness in my arms for some time. We lay thus about an hour and a half under a dreadful fire, which cost us about 60 men, while we had never fired a shot. About two o'clock a squadron of lancers came down, hurrahing, to charge the brigade of guns. They knew not what was in the rear. General Barnes gave the word, 'Form square.' In a moment the whole brigade was on their feet, ready to receive the enemy. The general said, 'Seventy-first, I have often heard of your bravery; I hope it will not be worse to-day than it has been.' Down they came upon our square. We soon put them to the right about. Shortly after we received orders to move to the heights. Onward we marched and stood for a time in square; receiving cavalry every now and then. The noise and smoke were dreadful. At this time I could see but a very little way from me; but all around the wounded and slain were thick. We then moved on in column for a considerable way and formed line, gave three cheers, fired a few volleys, charged the enemy, and drove them back. At this time a squadron of cavalry rode furiously down upon our line. Scarce had we time to form. The square was only complete in front when they were upon our bayonets. Many of our men were out of place. There was a good deal of jostling for a minute or two, and a good deal of laughing. Our quartermaster lost his bonnet in riding into the square, got it up, put it on back foremost, and wore it thus all day. Not a moment had we to regard our dress. A French general lay dead in the square; he had a number of ornaments upon his breast. Our men fell to plucking them off, pushing

each other as they passed, and snatching at them. We stood in square for some time whilst the 13th Dragoons and some French dragoons were engaged. The 13th retiring to the rear of our column, we gave the French a volley, which put them to the right about; then the 13th at them again. They did this for some time, we cheering the 13th, and feeling every blow they received. When a Frenchman fell we shouted, when one of the 13th we groaned. We wished to join them, but were forced to stand in square."

Still more fiercely raged the battle in the right centre, where Halkett's brigade (30th, 33d, 69th, 73d) was posted. Major Macready, who served in the light company of the 30th, gives us a glimpse of it in his journal, which we take the liberty of abridging. During the earlier part of the day Macready and his light company were thrown forward as skirmishers in front of the brigade; but when the French cavalry commenced their long series of attacks on the British right centre, he and his companions were ordered back. "Before the commencement of this attack," says the major, "our company of the grenadiers of the 73d were skirmishing briskly on the low ground, covering our guns, and annoying those of the enemy. The line of *tirailleurs* opposed to us was not stronger than our own, but on a sudden they were reinforced by numerous bodies, and several guns began to play on us with canister. Our poor fellows dropped very fast, and Colonel Vigoureux, Rumley, and Pratt, were carried off badly wounded in about two minutes. I was now commander of our company. We stood under this hurricane of small shot till Halkett sent to order us in, and I brought away about a third of the light bobs; the rest were killed or wounded, and I really wonder how one of them escaped. As our bugler was killed, I shouted and made signals to move by the left, in order to avoid the fire of our guns, and to put as good a face upon the business as possible.

"When I reached Lloyd's abandoned guns, I stood near them for about a minute to contemplate the scene: it was grand beyond description. Hougoumont and its wood sent up a broad flame through the dark masses of smoke that overhung the field; beneath this cloud the French were indistinctly visible. Here a waving mass of long red feathers could be seen; there, gleams as from a sheet of steel showed that the cuirassiers were moving; 400 cannon were belching forth fire and death on every side; the roaring and shouting were indistinguishably commixed —together they gave an idea of a labouring volcano. Bodies of infantry and cavalry were pouring down on us, and it was time to leave contemplation, so I made towards our columns, which were standing up in square.

"In a few minutes after, the enemy's cavalry galloped up, and crowned the crest of our position. Our guns were abandoned, and they formed between the two brigades, about a hundred paces in our front. Their first charge was magnificent. As soon as they quickened their trot into a gallop, the cuirassiers bent their heads, so that the peaks of their helmets looked like vizors, and they seemed cased in armour from the plume to the saddle. Not a shot was fired till they were within thirty yards, when the word was given, and our men fired away at them. The effect was magical. Through the smoke we could see helmets falling, cavaliers starting from their seats with convulsive springs as they received our balls, horses plunging and rearing in the agonies of fright and pain, and crowds of the soldiery dismounted, part of the squadron in retreat, but the more daring remainder backing their horses to force them on our bayonets. Our fire soon disposed of these gentlemen. The main body reformed in our front, and rapidly and gallantly repeated their attacks. In fact, from this time (about four o'clock) till near six we had a constant repetition of those brave but unavailing charges. There was no difficulty in repulsing them. The best cavalry is contemptible to a steady and well supplied infantry regiment; even our men saw this, and began to pity the useless perseverance of their assailants, and, as they advanced, would growl out, 'Here come these fools again!'

"Though we constantly thrashed our steel-clad opponents, we found more troublesome customers in the round shot and grape, which all this time played on us with terrible effect, and fully avenged the cuirassiers. Often as the volleys created openings in our square would the cavalry dash in, but they were uniformly unsuccessful. A regiment on our right seemed sadly disconcerted, and at one moment was in considerable confusion. At the height of their unsteadiness we got the order to 'right face' to move to their assistance; some of the men mistook it for 'right about face,' and faced accordingly, when old Major M'Laine, 73d, called out, 'No, my boys, it's right face; you'll never hear the right about as long as a French bayonet is in front of you!' In a few moments he was mortally wounded.

"About six o'clock I perceived some artillery trotting up our hill, which I knew by their caps to belong to the Imperial guard. I had hardly mentioned this to a brother-officer when two guns unlimbered within seventy paces of us, and, by their first discharge of grape, blew some men into the centre of the square. They immediately reloaded, and kept up a constant and destructive fire. It was noble to see our fellows fill up the gaps after every discharge. I was much distressed at this moment; having ordered up three of my light bobs, they had hardly taken their station when two of them fell horribly lacerated. One of them looked up in my face and uttered a sort of reproachful groan, and I involuntarily exclaimed, 'I couldn't help it.' We would willingly have charged these guns, but had we deployed, the cavalry that flanked them would have made an example of us.

"The '*vivida vis animi*'—the glow which fires one upon entering into action—had ceased; it was now to be seen which side had most bottom, and would stand killing longest. The Duke visited us frequently at this momentous period; he was coolness personified. As he crossed the rear face of our square a shell fell among our grenadiers, and he checked his horse to see its effect. Some men were blown to pieces by the explosion, and he merely stirred the rein of his charger, apparently as little concerned at their fate as at his own danger. No leader ever possessed so fully the confidence of his soldiery; wherever he appeared a murmur of 'silence—stand to your front—here's the duke,' was heard through the columns, and then all was as steady as on a parade. His aides-de-camp, Colonels Canning and Gordon, fell near our square, and the former died within it. As he came near us, late in the evening, Halkett rode out to him and represented our weak state, begging his grace to afford us a little support. 'It's impossible, Halkett,' said he. And our general replied, 'If so, sir, you may depend on the brigade to a man.'"

CHAPTER XIII.

FROM WATERLOO TO SEBASTOPOL.—1816-1854.

Bombardment of Algiers—First Burmese War—Navarino—First Chinese War—Second Burmese War—The War in Syria—Kaffir War.

WITHIN a year after the conclusion of the Great War, we were involved in hostilities with the semi-civilised power that held sway on the African seaboard of the Mediterranean. For centuries the corsairs of Barbary had been the terror of all peaceful voyagers on that inland sea; but during the long war with France their insolence and their exactions, their piracies and their outrages, rose in accordance with the difficulties in which the Christian nations of Europe were placed, and at length became intolerable. The measure of their iniquity was filled by the massacre which took place at Bona, of the crews of 300 or 400 small vessels engaged in the coral fishery. It was Ascension Day, and the fishermen were on their way to hear mass, when they were barbarously assassinated by a band of 2000 Turkish, Moorish, and Levantine soldiers. The victims of the massacre were mostly Italians, but in the interests of humanity this country felt bound to interfere, and an expedition was prepared to act against the forts and shipping of Algiers. The command of the expedition was entrusted to Lord Exmouth, one of the most dashing of our admirals, who had literally fought his way up to a peerage. It consisted of the *Queen Charlotte*, 100 guns, carrying the admiral's flag; the *Impregnable*, 98, carrying the flag of Rear-admiral David Milne; the *Superb*, *Minden*, *Albion*, 74; the *Leander*, 50; the gun-frigates *Severn* and *Glasgow*, 40, and *Granicus* and *Hebrus*,

36; the gun-brig sloops *Heron* and *Mutine*, 18; the *Britomart, Cordelia*, and *Jasper*, 10; and the bomb-vessels *Beelzebub, Fury, Hecla*, and *Infernal:* in all, 19 vessels of war, with a naval transport, a sloop with ordnance stores, and a despatch vessel.

On the 28th July, 1816, the fleet weighed from Spithead with a fine northerly wind. At two in the afternoon of the 9th August, Lord Exmouth anchored with his fleet in Gibraltar Bay, where he found a small Dutch squadron that had arrived the night before. The Dutch squadron, which consisted of four 40-gun frigates, one 30-gun frigate, and an 18-gun corvette, was commanded by Vice-admiral Baron Van T. de Capellau; and this officer begged so hard to be allowed to assist in the task of bringing the Dey to his senses, that Lord Exmouth could scarcely decline the offer.

On the 14th the British and their Dutch allies weighed and stood in to the Mediterranean. On the 16th, when the fleet was within 200 miles of Algiers, the ship-sloop *Prometheus*, Captain Dashwood, joined company direct from the port. The *Prometheus* had been despatched to Algiers some time before to get away our consul, Mr. M'Donnell. Captain Dashwood had with difficulty succeeded in bringing off Mrs. M'Donnell and her daughter in midshipmen's clothing—the child cried in the gateway and was detained, but the Dey sent it off next day; but Mr. M'Donnell himself was put in irons, and confined in a small room on the groundfloor of his own house; and the surgeon of the *Prometheus*, three midshipmen, and the crews of two boats, consisting in all of 18 persons, were seized and confined as slaves in the usual dungeons. Captain Dashwood reported also that the Dey had brought from the interior 40,000 troops, who were busily employed in strengthening the defences, and that his ships were all in port, where there were 30 or 40 mortar-boats in a state of great readiness.

At daybreak on the 27th, the fleet gained the first glimpse of the pirate city of Algiers, which lies on the side of a hill gradually rising from the sea, and forming a sort of amphitheatre, terminating in a point at the summit. The flat-roofed houses, rising above each other in tiers, were all whitewashed, and from a distance gave the town a remarkably clean appearance. The town was walled, and for a small place the fortifications were of considerable strength, especially towards the sea, where there were two moles, one of them stretching north-east about 250 yards, and connecting the town with a lighthouse built on a rock. Strong batteries were planted at every available point, and 500 guns on the sea-face, manned by 4000 fierce and fanatical Moslems, were mounted for the defence of Algiers.

The morning of the 27th was beautifully serene, with a silvery haze that foretold the coming heat, and as the ships were nearly becalmed within five miles of the shore, Lord Exmouth took the opportunity of despatching Lieutenant Samuel Burgess, in one of the *Queen Charlotte's* boats, towed by the *Severn*, to demand of the Dey the following conditions:—1. The abolition for ever of Christian slavery. 2. The delivery of all slaves by noon to-morrow. 3. The delivery of all money received for the redemption of slaves since the commencement of the year; the immediate liberation of the British consul and the two boats' crews of the *Prometheus:* failing which, he threatened the entire destruction of the place by shot and shell. Lieutenant Burgess proceeded on his mission, and in the meantime a breeze sprang up from the sea, and the fleet stood into the bay, and lay-to about five miles from the city. One o'clock, two o'clock came, and still no answer from the Dey; so, hoisting a signal to that effect, Lieutenant Burgess rowed out to the *Severn*. The ships' crews had been piped to dinner, and at the officers' mess bumpers were being pledged to a successful attack, when the signal, "Are you ready?" flew up to the masthead of the *Queen Charlotte*. "Ready!" replied every ship in the fleet. "Bear up!" and the fleet bore up before a fine steady breeze from the sea, the admiral leading the way in the stately *Queen Charlotte*. At 2.35 p.m. the flagship anchored with springs about 50 yards from the mole-head, and lashed herself to the mainmast of an Algerine brig fast to the shore at the mouth of the mole.

"Till this moment," says Lord Exmouth, "not a gun had been fired, and I began to suspect a full compliance with the terms which had been so many hours in their hands. At this period of profound silence a shot was fired at us from the mole," and almost at the same instant two other shots were fired at the *Impregnable* and the *Superb*, as they were advancing to take up their stations. It was enough; with characteristic humanity, waving his hand as a signal to descend to the crowds of people assembled on the parapet of the mole-head to gaze on the great three-decker, Lord Exmouth gave the order to fire; and just as the Moors were in the act of leaping through the embrasures, the *Queen Charlotte* opened her starboard broadside, which was thrown with a tearing crash into the batteries abreast of her. The cheers of the *Queen Charlotte* were mingled with the yells and groans of the Algerines, and taken up by the *Leander*. This plucky little ship came to anchor on the larboard bow of the flagship, in such a position as to engage the enemy's gunboats and row-boats, which lay at the mouth of the harbour, each with a gay flag at its stern, fully manned, and the crews lying on their oars, prepared for an attack, and ready to board should an opportunity offer. The *Leander's* first broadside carried destruction into these groups of boats. "The smoke opened," says one of the officers, "and fragments of boats were seen floating, the crews swimming and scrambling—as many as escaped the shot—to the shore, and another broadside annihilated them." So precise and tremendous was the fire of the *Queen Charlotte*, that her third broadside levelled the south end of the mole to its foundations. She then sprang her broadside towards the batteries over the town gate leading to the mole. Gun after gun came tumbling down over the battlements; the last fell just as the artillerymen were in the act of discharging it. It was a sight which moved the indignation of an Algerine chief, who sought relief to his feelings by leaping on the ruined parapet, and shaking his drawn scimitar at the ship whose cannon had so quickly demolished a defence which he had deemed impregnable.

So the bombardment commenced, and each ship as she took up her station opened with her guns. The sloops also took up their places, and the bomb vessels began a destructive discharge at the distance of about 2000 yards from the enemy's works. The bomb vessels were admirably seconded by the battering flotilla, consisting of gun boats, mortar boats, launches with carronades, rocket boats, barges, and yawls, to the number of 55. The Algerines made a fierce reply, and the din of the cannonade became deafening. The fresh breeze, which had brought the fleet into the bay, was put down by the heavy firing, and the smoke was so dense that the gunners had frequently to wait until it cleared a little. But the Algerines blazed away incessantly, and many of their shots found a billet. After the first and second broadsides 65 men were carried into the cockpit of the *Leander* alone, and before the close of the day this little ship had 125 killed and wounded. The *Impregnable* also suffered severely, and before long had lost 150 men. The *Glasgow* was sent to draw off some of the fire that assailed her. About 4 p.m. the Algerine frigate moored across the mole was boarded, and set on fire. This gallant service was performed in ten minutes by the *Queen Charlotte's* barge, under the command of Lieutenant Richards, with the loss of only two men killed. At 4.15 p.m. the frigate drifted out a perfect sheet of flame, and the British flagship shifted her berth to let the burning vessel pass.

By 7 p.m. all the enemy's vessels within the harbour were in a blaze; the flames communicated to the arsenal and storehouses on the mole; and soon afterwards the shells from the bomb-vessels set the city on fire in several places. The sun had now set, and the scene was grand and terrible beyond all description. In the lurid light of the flames the frightened Algerines could be seen running in crowds towards the gate of the city on the land side, to escape the destruction which seemed inevitable. At 9 p.m. a loud explosion shook every wall in Algiers to its foundations. It was the ordnance-sloop, charged with 143 barrels of powder, which the British had run on shore, close under the semicircular battery to the north of the lighthouse. Every moment was now becoming more perilous to the British fleet. Loose fire and burning brands were flying about in every direction, the guns had become heated, the ammunition had fallen short. At 10 p.m. the *Queen Charlotte* cut her cables and springs, and stood out before a light air of wind, which, fortunately for the British, had just sprung up from the land. The other ships followed, picking their anchorage by the blaze of the burning ships, which illuminated the whole bay. As if to add to the awful grandeur of the scene, the elements began their war as soon as the ships and batteries had ended theirs, and for nearly three hours the lightning and thunder were incessant, and the rain poured down in torrents.

As soon as daylight came, Lord Exmouth gave orders to resume the bombardment; but it was not needed. On the morning of the 29th the captain of the port came off with Mr. M'Donnell, the British consul; and that same afternoon a treaty was struck by which the Dey delivered to the British flag upwards of 1200 Christian slaves; undertook to abolish Christian slavery in future; restored 382,500 dollars for slaves redeemed by Naples and Sicily; made peace with the King of the Netherlands; paid 30,000 dollars to the British consul for the destruction of his property, and made him a public apology for the detention of his person. Thanks were probably never offered up in the British fleet for a victory more honourable to our arms than the bombardment of Algiers. It cost us 141 seamen killed and 742 wounded, 118 tons of powder, and 500 tons of shot. The Dutch had their full share both in the danger and glory of the day.

In 1824 a quarrel broke out between our Indian Government and the Court of Ava about Shapuree, a little muddy isle in the province of Bengal, but close to the coast of Aracan. So ignorant were the semi-barbarous Burmese of the strength of Britain, that they collected a great force on our southern frontier, and placed it under the command of Maha Bandoola, a mighty chief, who projected a scheme for the conquest of Bengal, and carried with him a set of fetters in which Lord Amherst, the Governor-general of India, was to be carried captive to the Victorious Lord of the White Elephant and the Golden Foot. This, it seems, was the proudest title of the monarch who ruled at Ava.

Lord Amherst resolved to carry the war into the enemy's country, and send a force to attack Rangoon, in the very heart of the Burmese Empire. The expedition assembled at the Andaman Isles. The land force, about 6000 strong, was commanded by Major-general Sir Archibald Campbell, Bart., a veteran of the Peninsula. The troops were conveyed in 40 transports, accompanied by quite a flotilla of armed small craft, among which the *Liffey*, *Larne*, *Slaney*, and *Sophie*, brigs or schooners of 18 or 20 guns, bulked like tritons among minnows. The naval department was under the charge of Commodore Grant, and it is worth mentioning that the captain of the *Larne* was Marryat, the great sea novelist.

The expedition sailed on the 5th May, 1824, and on the 10th of the same month anchored within the bar of the Rangoon river. Next morning the troops were disembarked. For a time no opposition was offered, but at length the natives took heart of grace and opened on the shipping. The *Liffey* was ready. She was anchored close to the principal battery, her sails furled, and her men at quarters. Her first broadside was the signal for all the other vessels to open fire. When he saw the invaders approaching, the Rewoon, a subordinate officer who governed the town, had vaingloriously said, "They are my prisoners! Cut me some thousand spans of rope to bind then;" but now he became so frightened at the mere noise of the cannonade, that he mounted his horse and fled through the south-eastern gate of the city. His soldiers, gorgeous with their bell-shaped hats, their banners, and their umbrellas, followed his example; and the inhabitants—Burman, Peguer, Portuguese, Parsee, Mogul, and Chinese—stood not upon the order of their going, but went at once. The bamboo houses of Rangoon were quickly empty.

We have no intention of following the British in their heroic progress from Rangoon up the Irawaddi to Ava. The feat they undertook was nothing less than the subjugation of an empire by a few boats and a handful of men, who had to fight their way for 600 miles against climate, privations, and a numerous enemy. The Burmese had at least 60,000 men under arms, with many stockaded strongholds, ample munition of war and provisions, and a numerous population from which to draw recruits to supply casualties. If they could not overwhelm the British in the field, they could at least have fatigued them into a retreat; but they wanted common sense and a knowledge of military tactics. Army after army was sent to the front, and general after general set up the umbrella of authority; but Kemmendine and Donoopew, Mellone and Pagahm-Mew, witnessed their discomfiture; they were driven from position to position, and from stockade to stockade; and on the 24th February, 1826, Sir Archibald Campbell dictated to the Lord of the White Elephant and the Golden Foot the terms of peace under the walls of Ava. By this treaty His Majesty ceded the provinces of Aracan, Yeh, Tavoy, Mergui, and Tenasserim with all its islands; admitted a resident British minister with a guard within the walls of Ava; and paid £1,000,000 towards the expenses of the war.

The regiments engaged in this war were the 13th, 38th, 41st, 45th, 47th, 87th, and 89th.

For two years the Greeks maintained the unequal struggle for independence, with no other aid than what they received from Lord Byron, Lord Cochrane, and other Phil-Hellenists. At length, however, the atrocities of Ibrahim, the ablest of the Sultan's generals, drew down on the Turkish Government the indignation of all Christendom. England, France, and Russia demanded an immediate armistice, and to enforce the demand each power sent a squadron to Navarino, on the western side of the Morea, where the Turkish fleet lay. The British squadron was under the command of Sir Edward Codrington, one of Nelson's captains.

Codrington's orders were to keep the peace with his speaking-trumpet, if possible, but, in case of necessity, by cannon-shot. On the 25th September, 1827, he and Admiral de Rigny, the commander-in-chief of the French squadron, held a conference with Ibrahim, at which the latter agreed to suspend hostilities until he should communicate with the Sultan; but the faithless pasha soon showed that he had no intention of keeping his word. Thrice he endeavoured to send ships against the Greeks in the Gulf of Patras, but Codrington turned the squadrons back. Foiled in his perfidious attempt to effect a junction with the army at Patras, Ibrahim wreaked his vengeance on the Greeks of the Morea, who were now in a more unfortunate position than ever. Driven from the plains, they were forced to take refuge in the mountain caves, where they died of absolute starvation. Few had any better food than boiled grass. Clearly something must be done, and amid a choice of difficulties it was resolved to take a position with the allied fleet at Navarino, in order to renew negotiations with effect.

On the 20th October, 1827, the combined fleets stood into the harbour of Navarino, the British and French squadrons forming the weather or starboard column, and the Russians the lee line. The British ships were—the *Asia*, of 80 guns, bearing the flag of Vice-admiral Codrington; *Genoa* and *Albion*, 74; *Glasgow*, *Cambrian*, *Dartmouth*, and *Talbot*, frigates of 50, 48, 46, and 28 guns; the corvette *Rose*; the *Mosquito*, *Brisk*, and *Philomel*, gunbrigs; and a cutter. The French squadron comprised two 80's, a 78, a 60, a 48, and two corvettes. Rear-admiral de Rigny's flag was hoisted on board the *Sirène*, of 60 guns. The Russian squadron comprised one 80, three 76's, a 48, and three 46's. Rear-admiral Heiden's flag was hoisted on board the *Azoff*, of 80 guns. Codrington held the chief command of the combined forces.

The harbour of Navarino is about six miles in circumference, but the island of Sphacteria stretches across its mouth, affording an entrance of only 600 yards in breadth. This passage was commanded by two powerful batteries, one on either side, while a third battery commanded the harbour. Here the Turkish fleet lay moored, in a very skilful manner, according to the instructions of Monsieur Letellier, a French naval officer in the service of the Pasha of Egypt, Ibrahim's father. The ships were arranged in the form of a crescent, with springs on their cables, the larger ones presenting their broadsides towards the centre, and the smaller ones drawn up inside, filling up the intervals. At the entrance to the harbour lay six fire-ships. The Turkish fleet consisted of 3 ships of the line, 4 double frigates, 13 frigates, 30 corvettes, 28 brigs, 5 schooners, 6 fire-ships, and 41 transports —in all 130 sail.

At 2 P.M. the *Asia*, leading the line, passed the heavy battery unmolested, and steering up the harbour, anchored alongside a ship of the line bearing the flag of the Capitan Bey. The other ships took up their positions, the French to the right hand on entering the harbour, and the Russians to the left in the bight of the crescent. A boat was sent from the fort to request the allied fleet to put to sea again, but Codrington answered that he had not come to receive orders but to give them; and that if a shot were fired at the allied fleet, the Turkish fleet would be destroyed. Still, his orders were that no gun should be fired unless the Turks fired first, and everything in the allied fleet appeared to wear a peaceful aspect. The ships were anchored, the sails were furled, and the band of the *Asia*—which flew a large white flag at the mizzen—was ordered to be sent on deck. But the spark was about to fall. The boats of the *Dartmouth* were sent to request that the Turkish fire-ships would move a little farther from the allied fleet. The Turks, pretending to be apprehensive that force was meditated, fired and killed Lieutenant Fitzroy and several of the crew. The *Dartmouth* opened a defensive fire to cover her boats, and the *Sirène* joined in the affray. As yet, however, nothing had been used but musketry, but one of the Egyptian ships now fired a shot, the first round shot discharged, and struck the *Sirène*. This brought on a return, and the action soon became general.

It must have been a grand and fearful spectacle to see 150 ships of war in action in a narrow basin. Soon the scene was shrouded in smoke, through which ever and anon burst the flames of a burning vessel, or the awful flash of an explosion. The smoke was so thick that the guns of the *Asia* were pointed from the masthead of the Capitan Bey's ship. It was the only object

P

discernible, and occasionally the *Asia* had to cease firing to allow the smoke to clear away. The ship of Moharem Bey, the commander-in-chief of the Egyptian contingent, was on the other side of the *Asia*, and even nearer to her than the Capitan Bey's ship, but as she did not fire, neither did the *Asia* fire at her. "Indeed," says Admiral Codrington in his despatch, "Moharem Bey sent a message to say that he would not fire at all, and therefore no hostility took place between Moharem Bey's ship and the English admiral's ship for some time after the *Asia* had returned the fire of the Capitan Bey. In the meantime, however, the excellent pilot, Mr. Peter Mitchell, who went to interpret to Moharem Bey the Vice-admiral's desire to avoid bloodshed, was killed by his people in the boat alongside, whether with or without his orders is not known, but his ship soon afterwards fired into the *Asia*, and was consequently effectually destroyed by the *Asia's* fire, sharing the same fate as his brother admiral on the starboard side, and falling to leeward a mere wreck." Moharem's second ahead, burning to the water's edge, blew up at her anchors. The destruction of these three ships allowed the Turkish inner line to rake the *Asia*, which suffered severely. Her mizzenmast was shot away, several guns were disabled, and the men fell fast. The admiral himself was struck by a musket ball, which knocked the watch out of his pocket. Great, too, was the slaughter on board the *Genoa*, which was exposed to a heavy concentrated fire. Her gallant captain, Bathurst, was early wounded by a splinter, which struck off his hat and lacerated his face; a second shot carried off his coat tails; at length a grape shot entered his side and passed through his body. He lingered eleven hours in great suffering. The *Albion* was in like manner exposed to the fire of a cluster of ships, and suffered severely. One of the Turkish vessels, a 64, attempted to board, but the *Albion's* crew drove them back with great loss, and boarded in turn. The prize, however, being discovered to be on fire, was relinquished, and soon after blew up with a terrible explosion.

A very pleasant interchange of good offices took place between English, French, and Russians, who behaved to each other in all respects like good allies. Captain Hugon, of the French frigate *Armide*, in particular, won the applause of all. Perceiving one of our frigates maintaining an unequal combat with a cluster of Turks, Captain Hugon wormed his ship through their inner line, and took off the fire of one Moslem foe, which struck to him in ten minutes. On taking possession, he hoisted the Union Jack alongside of the French colours, as if to indicate that he had only completed the work which the British frigate had begun. A Russian ship took off another of the enemy, and the British ship soon gave a good account of the remainder. Later in the day the *Armide* herself got into trouble, and was gallantly assisted by the *Rose*. The *Sirène*, too, the French admiral's flagship, was saved by the *Dartmouth*.

The action ceased at six o'clock. The Turkish fleet was literally destroyed. " Out of a fleet of 81 men-of-war," wrote the admiral, " only one frigate and 15 smaller vessels are in a state ever to be again put to sea." The Turks themselves largely helped the work of destruction. When they saw the fight was going against them, they set fire to their vessels and escaped to the shore. In the dense smoke of the cannonading daylight had faded away unperceived, and the night was now illuminated by the glare of burning ships, which every now and then blew up with a fearful explosion. The destruction of the Turkish navy cost the allies 177 men killed and 480 wounded, divided nearly equally between the three nationalities. The loss of the Ottomans was estimated at 5000 or 6000. Honours were showered upon the conquerors.

Navarino secured the independence of Greece.

In 1840 we were at war in the Levant. The interminable Eastern question was once more to the front: this time in the shape of an attempt on the part of Egypt to throw off the authority of Turkey. Not only did Mehemet Ali, who began life as a tobacco seller and a soldier, claim independence for Egypt, but he demanded possession of Syria; and his son Ibrahim led an army into that country, defeated the Turkish troops in three pitched battles, over-ran Asia Minor, and threatened Constantinople itself. The Sultan tried to patch up matters by offering Mehemet Ali the hereditary vice-royalty of Egypt, subject only to an annual tribute, and the vice-government of Syria; but this was refused by the arrogant old pasha, who demanded Syria on the same terms as his own province. The position of affairs was so critical that England, Austria, Russia, and Prussia concluded a treaty by which they bound themselves to compel the Egyptian viceroy to accept the terms of his suzerain.

The treaty concluded, Admiral the Hon. Sir Robert Stopford,

commander of the British fleet in the Mediterranean, went to Alexandria to present it to Mehemet Ali. That potentate flatly refused to accede to the demands of the Allied Powers; so Admiral Stopford left the *Asia*, *Implacable*, and a corvette, to prevent the pasha's fleet from quitting Alexandria, and set sail for Beyrout. Here he was joined by a Turkish squadron of five ships, under Captain Baldwin Walker, of the British navy (holding the rank of Vice-admiral in the Turkish marine, with the title of Bey), and three Austrian frigates under Admiral Bandiera. As Mehemet Ali would not listen to reason, hostilities were at once decided upon.

Beyrout, D'Jebaila, Batroum, Caiffa, and Trye, fell in rapid succession, and then, at the suggestion of Commodore Sir Charles Napier, an attack was projected on Sidon. By sunrise on the 27th September, 1840, Napier was in sight of the dirty, ill-built, ruinous streets of the great emporium of the ancient world. He had with him two steamers and five other ships, and a number of marines, English, Austrian, and Turkish. The *Thunderer*, *Guerriera*, and the *Gul Sapede*, were anchored abreast of the town, the first with the Union Jack flying at her peak, the second with the Austrian Eagle, and the third with the Turkish Crescent and Star. The *Wasp* and *Stromboli* took up their positions more to the south to flank the town; and the *Gorgon*, *Cyclops*, and *Hydra* placed themselves alongside the great castle. Commodore Napier was on board the *Gorgon*, from which he sent the following letter to the Governor of Sidon:—"Sir,—In the name of the five united Powers—Turkey, Britain, Austria, Russia, and Prussia—I demand that you immediately declare for the Sultan, your master. Pardon for past offences will be granted, and the arrears of the troops will be paid by the Sultan." With this summons the governor refused to comply, and the attack commenced. After a cannonade of about an hour, a breach was made in the sea-wall of the chief port, and the Egyptians were driven from the hasty entrenchments they had thrown up on the shore to prevent a landing. The boats then pushed off from the ships, and after a short and sharp struggle, Sidon was captured,—no less than 2700 Egyptians laying down their arms to 900 British and Austrian marines and 500 Turkish soldiers. The British loss was only 4 killed and 33 wounded. After the landing there was an amusing race, under a heavy fire, between Mr. James Hunt, a midshipman of the *Stromboli*, and

Signor Dominica Chinca, a midshipman of the Austrian frigate *Guerriera*, for the honour of first planting their national ensigns on the walls of the town.

Other places on the coast of Syria were soon afterwards evacuated, and at length the flag of Mehemet Ali flew only over Acre, which has thrice yielded glory to the British arms. The combined squadrons arrived before Acre on the 2d of November, 1840, and consisted of the *Princess Charlotte*, flagship, of 104 guns; *Powerful*, Sir Charles Napier, 84; *Bellerophon*, Capt. J. Austin, 80; *Revenge*, Capt. Waldegrave, 78; *Thunderer*, Capt. Berkeley, 84; *Edinburgh*, Capt. W. Henderson, 74; *Benbow*, Capt. Houston Stewart, 74; *Pique*, Capt. Edward Boxer, 36; *Carysfort*, Capt. H. B. Martin, 16; *Talbot*, Captain Codrington, 28; *Wasp*, Capt. Maxwell, 16; *Hazard*, Capt. Elliot, 16; in all, 698 guns, independent of the *Vesuvius*, *Phœnix*, *Stromboli*, and *Gorgon*, steamers, for throwing shells; the Austrian frigates *Medea*, bearing the flag of Admiral Bandiera, and *Guerriera*, commanded by the Archduke Frederick Charles, a Turkish 74, bearing the flag of Admiral Walker, and a corvette. The strength of the Egyptian garrison in the fortress of Acre was estimated at 4500 bayonets, with 800 horsemen outside the town.

The *Powerful*, *Princess Charlotte*, *Thunderer*, *Bellerophon*, and *Pique*, took up their positions from south to north in a line parallel to the works, while the other ships anchored against the southern face of the works. The guns opened at 2.17 P.M., and shortly afterwards the steamers outside began to fire shells. The cannonade was tremendous; nothing could stand against it. About four o'clock, the grand magazine of Acre was blown up by a shell from one of the steamships. The magazine contained some thousands of barrels of gunpowder, and the explosion was heard far and wide over sea and land. The Egyptians were blown into the air or buried in the casemates. Two entire regiments, formed in position on the ramparts, were annihilated; every living creature within the area of 6000 yards ceased to exist. The cannonade was continued until sunset, and when the troops were landed next morning they found the place deserted. The effects of the fire were seen to have been astounding. The town was almost entirely pulverised, parapets had been torn up, guns hurled from their carriages, and in some instances split from breach to muzzle. The Egyptians had left their sick and wounded, but the Turks paid little attention to them, and many of the poor creatures were seen lying in all directions, dying for want of relief. The casualties in the fleet were singularly small, amounting to only 12 killed and 32 wounded in the British portion, 6 killed and 10 wounded in the Turkish and Austrian; and yet the Egyptian gunners had kept up so furious a fire, that the water outside the ships was lashed into foam by the storm of projectiles thrown into the sea.

The fall of Acre, a fortress mounting 147 guns—a place which it had taken Ibrahim ten months to reduce with an army of 40,000 men—was regarded as irremediable. Ibrahim evacuated Syria, and Mehemet Ali agreed to confine himself to Egypt, which was secured to him under certain conditions as a hereditary possession.

The siege of Acre is noteworthy as being the first occasion on which the advantages of steam in battle became conspicuously manifest. This was shown by the rapidity with which the steamers took up their position, the assistance they rendered to the other ships, and the destruction they caused by their shells. Steam-vessels were first introduced into the navy in 1816.

The year 1840 saw us involved in our first war with the Celestial Empire. The emperor was determined to put down the illicit trade in opium, which was smuggled from India in large quantities, but unfortunately he went to work in such a way as to call down on him the vengeance of the British Government. After negotiations had completely failed, chiefly because the Chinese mistook our conciliatory bearing for weakness, it became necessary to teach them a lesson. The army was under the command of Sir Hugh Gough, and the fleet under Sir William Parker. The island of Chusan was seized, the far-famed Bogue Forts on the Canton river were destroyed, and Canton itself lay at the mercy of the British forces. The Celestials now seemed willing to come to terms, and agreed to pay an indemnity of 6,000,000 dollars, and to cede the island of Hong Kong. But it quickly became apparent that this treaty was but a pretence to gain time, and operations were resumed. Amoy was taken, Chusan was re-taken, Chinghae was stormed, Ningpo submitted without firing a shot, and Chapoo was captured. Preparations were now made for a grand attack on Nankin, the ancient capital of the empire, situated about 200 miles up the great river Yangtse-Kiang. The forts at the mouth of the river surrendered on the 16th June, 1842. Shanghai fell into our hands on the 18th. The town of Chin-Kiang-Foo was stormed on the 21st of July. Hitherto the Chinese had made very little resistance, but at Chin-Kiang-Foo the Tartars fought with all the fury of fanatic soldiers, who, with good arms, good discipline, and good chiefs, would have proved themselves formidable adversaries.

The scenes the troops witnessed when they entered the town in the evening were terrible. "Here," says a French authority, "the unhappy wretches, in order to escape with their families from the fury of their conquerors, cut their throats with their own swords, after having immolated their wives and children. There, isolated combatants struggled heroically on the threshhold of their dwellings, preferring death to surrender. Farther on, a little group of Tartars were seen to precipitate themselves, with the rage of despair, on the British bayonets. In one single house there were found the corpses of fourteen women and children, and the English saw a Chinese employed in cutting the throat of his wife, and ready to throw her into a well, over the mouth of which he held her, and into which he had already precipitated his sons, whose lives as well as that of the mother were fortunately saved. The mandarin Hai-Ling, General-in-chief of the Imperial forces, also preferring death to dishonour, set fire to his habitation with his own hands, and perished under its flaming ruins—a heroic death in the eyes of the sovereign, who ordered a temple to be erected and great honours to be paid to the memory of this faithful servant."

The victory cost the English 37 men killed and 131 wounded, but the moral effect of it practically ended the war. No sooner did the forces appear before Nankin than commissioners arrived from Pekin, with power to grant all demands; and a treaty was signed on board the *Cornwallis* flagship (August 29, 1842), by which the Chinese Government agreed to cede Hong Kong, to open Canton and four other ports for the purposes of trade, and to pay 21,000,000 dollars — 6,000,000 for opium illegally seized, 3,000,000 for debts due to British subjects by Hong Kong merchants, and 12,000,000 as indemnity for the expenses of the war.

The 18th, 26th, 49th, 55th, and 98th regiments bear on their colours and appointments the word "China" and a dragon. The loss of life in this war was very great, not so much by the jingall-balls and long spears of the enemy—though these were by no means contemptible—as by the pernicious influence of the climate. As an example, the 26th Cameronians lost nearly all those who left Calcutta with the colours in 1840. They reached China 900 strong; 900 recruits were sent out to them from Scotland; and but 900 remained when the regiment marched into the Castle of Edinburgh in 1843.

As in Burmah, the seamen had their full share in the dangers and glories of the war, and red-coats and blue-jackets fought side by side.

The Burmese gradually forgot the lesson taught them by Sir Archibald Campbell, and their insolence grew to such a height, that it became unsafe for all classes of foreigners to remain in Rangoon. At length, in the year 1851, the British flag was openly insulted. H.M. brig *Serpent*, Commodore Lambert, when on her way up the Rangoon river, to seek redress for an outrage committed on the person and property of the commander of a trading vessel, was fired on from the shore. No apology or redress being made, Lord Dalhousie, the Governor-general of India, resolved on war.

The troops detailed for the expedition were the 18th Royal Irish, 35th, 51st, and 80th, with the regiments of native infantry, and the Madras artillery and sappers. The whole force numbered 4388 men, and was under the command of Major-general Godwin, who had taken an active part in the first Burmese war. The fleet, consisting of the Queen's ships *Fox*, *Serpent*, *Rattler*, *Hermes*, and *Salamander*, the Indian navy steamers *Feroze*, *Moozuffer*, *Zenobia*, *Medusa*, *Sesostris*, and *Berenice*, and some of the Bengal marine steamers, was under the command of Admiral Austin. On the 5th April (1851) the expedition arrived in front of Martaban, which was speedily stormed by a party of the 18th Royal Irish, with little loss. Rangoon was bombarded on the 11th. The troops were landed next day. The heat was so intense that two officers died of sunstroke. The Golden Pagoda, a Bhuddist temple within the fortified lines of the city, and surrounded by stockades and cannon, was stormed on the 14th. In the attack, the 80th, with four guns, formed the advance, preceded by skirmishers. Fire was opened from a 9-pound gun and a 24-pound howitzer, while the naval brigade were bringing up the heavy 8-inch howitzers. The troops stood with bayonets fixed, all in readiness for a rush to the front the moment a breach was effected. The Burmese made good play with their cannon and jingalls, and with musketry from some bushes in front. Officers and men were falling fast, and a little before noon, Captain Latter, the interpreter, proposed an attack on the entrance of the Pagoda, and asked permission to lead the stormers. The assaulting force was composed of a wing of the 80th, two companies of the 18th Royal Irish, and two of the 40th Bengal Infantry, the whole under the command of Captain Coote; Captain Latter leading on sword in hand. The troops had to cross a valley, 800 yards wide, sloping down from the hill on which stood the mighty bell-shaped temple. The hill was divided into three terraces, each defended by a mud and brick wall, the first fourteen feet in height, the second forty-four. The heaviest guns were on the upper terrace. Forward rushed our troops, broke open the eastern gate with an exulting cheer, and swarmed up the long flights of steps that lay in the centre of each terrace. A perfect shower of missiles rained on the stormers, and many rolled down the steps dead or dying, but nothing could stop their impetuous advance, and soon a ringing cheer, immediately echoed by the seamen of the squadron, announced that the upper terrace was won, and that the Burmese, in their gaily-gilt hats, were flying in all directions before the British bayonets. The governor was the first to set the example of flight, by rushing out at the western gate. The casualties in the army at Rangoon were 149—17 killed and 132 wounded. The casualties in the fleet were 17, including one of the *Fox's* men drowned, and one of the *Tenasserim's* blown away from an after-pivot gun. The capture of Rangoon was followed by the capture of Bassein, Pegu, and Prome, and the close of the war was officially announced on the 30th June 1852. The province of Pegu was, by proclamation, annexed to the British Empire.

While the war was being prosecuted in Burmah, hostilities broke out with the Kaffirs on the frontiers of the Cape of Good Hope. These savages plundered post after post, and committed such dreadful outrages and murders, that the farmers abandoned their lands, leaving the cattle to perish. Sir Harry Smith, the governor, took the field in person, but as, in his confidence in a long peace, he had represented to the home authorities that the military establishment at the Cape would admit of a considerable reduction, he had not a sufficient force to strike a decisive blow at the outset. The principal operations of the war were the assault of the Kaffir stronghold on the Amatola Mountains, the clearing of the Fish River bush, the attack on the Waterkloof, and the defeat of the Basutos under their chief Moshesh. The Basutos had 6000 well-armed horse under considerable organisation. The battle lasted from morning till night, when the Basutos gave way with terrible loss. Moshesh directly after submitted; so did Sandilli, Macomo, and many other chiefs. Peace was proclaimed on the 12th March, 1853. As Sir George Grey said, in complimenting the troops at the conclusion of the war: "The field of glory opened to them in a Hottentot rebellion and Kaffir war is possibly not so favourable and exciting as that which regular warfare with an open enemy in the field affords; yet the unremitting exertions called for in hunting well-armed yet skulking savages through the bush, and driving them from their innumerable strongholds, are perhaps more arduous than those required in regular warfare, and call more constantly for individual exertion and intelligence."

Among the regiments, or detachments of regiments, that took part in the Kaffir war were the 2d Queen's, 6th, 12th, 43d Light Infantry, 45th, 60th Rifles, 73d, 74th Highlanders, 91st Argyllshire Highlanders, and the 12th Royal Lancers.

CHAPTER XIV.

THE RUSSIAN WAR—1854-1856.

Odessa—Bomarsund—Kola—Petropaulovski—The Alma—Bombardment of Sebastopol—Balaclava—Inkerman—Expedition to Kertch—Taganrog—Sveaborg—The Malakoff and Redan—Russians evacuate Sebastopol—Kinburn.

IT is hardly necessary to say anything about the origin of the Crimean War—the quarrel between Russia and Turkey about the Holy Places at Jerusalem, the march of the Russian troops across the Pruth, and the occupation of Moldavia, which the Emperor Nicholas wished to hold as a material guarantee (July 2, 1853), the declaration of war by Turkey (October 5), the entrance into the Bosphorus of a British fleet a few weeks later, the fighting on the line of the Danube, the massacre of Sinope, where a Russian squadron destroyed some Turkish frigates and slew 2000 men (November 30), and the despatch of the united fleets of France and England into the Black Sea (January 4, 1854). Suffice it to say that war was declared against Russia by France and England on the 27th March, 1854.

The first operation of the war was the bombardment of Odessa. When war was declared the allied fleets were lying in Varna Bay. The British fleet consisted of 10 ships of the line, and a considerable number of steam frigates and steam sloops, under the command of Vice-admiral Dundas, who hoisted his flag on board the *Britannia*, of 130 guns. The French fleet consisted of 15 sail of the line and 21 smaller vessels, under the command of Admiral Hamelin, who hoisted his flag on board the *Ville de Paris*, of 120 guns. As soon as he was informed of the outbreak of hostilities, Admiral Dundas sent the *Furious*, a paddle steam-frigate of 16 guns, commanded by Captain Loring, to bring away our consul from Odessa. The *Furious* hove to with a flag of truce flying at her masthead, and sent in a boat, flying the same pacific ensign, to demand the consul as a British subject. The answer General Osten-Sacken (governor of Odessa) returned was a volley of cannon-shot. Luckily no damage was done, and the *Furious* steamed back to Varna and reported progress. Admiral Dundas immediately gave the order to weigh, and on the 17th April, 1854, he and Hamelin appeared off Odessa, with all their ships and steamers. On explanations being demanded, General Osten-Sacken declared that he fired upon the *Furious* because she was steaming up the bay, heedless of the customary signals, for the sole purpose of examining it. This was considered unsatisfactory, and the allied admirals summoned the governor to make reparation for his offence against the laws of war, by the surrender of all the shipping in the port, threatening vengeance if no answer were returned by sunset on the following day. No answer was returned, and the bombardment of Odessa commenced.

Odessa, a town of fully 100,000 inhabitants, occupies a line of cliff facing the north-east, with an inward curve, giving the bay a radius of three miles. The buildings rise tier upon tier like the seats of an amphitheatre. The town is fortified in the modern style, and on the eastern side has a citadel which commands the port. At the other extremity of the cliffs is the Imperial mole, which then contained a wedged mass of Russian ships of every size and sort. A gigantic staircase leads from the centre of the town downward to the beach. Stretching out from below the cliffs at the south-east end of the town is the quarantine mole, a fortified pier capped by a lighthouse, within which lay ships of all nations.

The force told off for the bombardment consisted of the war-steamers *Tiger*, of 16 guns, Captain Giffard; *Retribution*, 28, Captain the Hon. T. R. Drummond; *Samson*, 6, Captain Jones; *Terrible*, 22, Captain M'Cleverty; the *Furious*; and four French steamers, the *Mogador*, *Vauban*, *Descartes*, and *Caton*. A detachment of rocket-boats, under Commodore Dixon, had orders to proceed in advance; our *Sanspareil*, 70, Captain Sidney Davis, and *Highflyer*, 21, Captain Moore, to act as a reserve; and the *Arethusa*, 50, Captain Mends, to assist. The whole force was under the command of Captain Jones of the *Samson*, whose orders were "to go as far as possible in-shore, so as to rake and destroy the Imperial mole; but to avoid firing upon any part of the town, or upon the shipping in the quarantine mole."

At 6.40 A.M. on the morning of the 22d April, the steamers stood in, the *Samson* leading the way, and began that witches' dance which was so favourite a manœuvre during the Russian war. The steamers were kept under weigh, steaming round in a circle of half-a-mile in diameter, each discharging her enormous guns when within a proper distance from the shore. The Russians replied with red-hot shot, and in less than an hour the French steamer *Vauban* bore away to the main body of the fleet to seaward, on fire in several places. But the flames were soon got under, and the *Vauban* resumed her place in the fiery circle that was pouring death and destruction on Odessa.

Both the moles displayed a formidable array of embrasures for cannon, and the Russian gunners blazed away very briskly. The southern side of the quarantine mole was particularly troublesome, so the *Arethusa* was sent to divert the fire of the guns in that quarter. The frigate, one of the last of the true wooden walls of old England, sailed into the bay in beautiful style, delivered her fire, filled, tacked, and fired again, just as she would have done in the days of Nelson. The breeze freshened, and, though under fire, the crew went aloft and reefed her topsails. Her performances were witnessed by all the admiring seamen of the fleet, who gave her three lusty cheers when, in obedience to the signal of the admiral, she came out of action.

The gunboats kept waltzing away, never touching or getting into scrapes, and seldom being hit. The Russian gunners grew disheartened, and gradually their fire became slower, though still persistent and regular. Suddenly, a Russian battery came galloping down to the beach, unlimbered, wheeled round, and opened fire on the rocket-boats, which were within musket-shot of the shore. Quite a shower of balls fell around the boats, ploughing up the water in white spouts, and dashing the oars to pieces; but, fortunately, no one was struck. Before the guns could be reloaded, every gunboat and rocket-boat was brought to bear on the intruders, who scampered off as fast as the horses could gallop.

By two in the afternoon a building of wood in the rear of the Tongue battery caught fire and blew up. A few moments afterwards and the shipping in the Imperial mole was sheeted in flames, chiefly by the cannonade of the *Terrible*, which went closer in shore than her comrades, and fired red-hot shot from her 10-inch guns. By and by the great magazine of Odessa blew up with a dreadful explosion, at which the fleet gave three cheers, the French commencing.

At five the admiral made the signal of recall, and the gun-boats steamed back to the anchorage, whence the crews of the line-of-battle ships had been eager spectators of the bombardment. The *Terrible*, whose paddle-boxes were considerably knocked about, was received with all the honours as she passed through the fleet, nor were cheers wanting for the plucky little *Samson*. Our loss was only 13 killed and wounded. The ships in the Imperial mole continued to burn for 48 hours, when they were entirely consumed. The dockyard, magazine, barracks, and a vast amount of Russian property, chiefly belonging to the government, shared the same fate.

On the 11th March, 1854, at Spithead, the Queen reviewed the Baltic fleet, the most powerful fleet ever assembled in one sea. It consisted of 19 line-of-battle ships, 11 frigates and corvettes, and 13 smaller vessels, carrying 2393 guns, and 32,114 seamen and marines. Most of the line-of-battle ships and heavy frigates were auxiliary screws, the smaller vessels being chiefly paddle steamers. This powerful armament was placed under the command of Sir Charles Napier—"Fighting Charley," as people loved to call him. Napier hoisted his flag on board the *Duke of Wellington*, of 131 guns, a ship which, alone, was almost equal in power to a whole fleet of the days of Nelson. In June the British admiral was joined by a French squadron, under Vice-admiral Parseval-Deschénes. The allied armaments now amounted to 54 sail, a force with which the Russian fleet of 30 sail could not pretend to cope. With such a superb fleet everybody expected that something was to be done; Sveaborg, Helsingfors, and Cronstadt might be captured, and St. Petersburg would then find itself defenceless.

The combined fleets did not do all this, but they did much. A strict blockade was established in the Gulf of Finland. Admiral Plumridge scoured the Gulf of Bothnia, and captured

46 merchantmen and a quantity of naval stores. And hearing that a Russian squadron of 7 ships of the line and a frigate was shut up at Helsingfors, Sir Charles Napier made sail in that direction, to prevent a junction of the Russian fleet, and thus completely defeated the enemy's plan of naval operations. Cronstadt was reported by the officers sent forward to reconnoitre to be impregnable, so the allied admirals turned their attention to Bomarsund, which the Czar Nicholas had erected to overawe Sweden and Denmark. When the allied fleet appeared before Bomarsund, in 1854, the works were rapidly advancing to a state of strength that would soon have made it another Sebastopol. The defences consisted of works mounting upwards of 160 guns, and garrisoned by 2500 men. But the masonry, artillery, and garrison very inadequately represent the strength of the place, which was largely due to its situation. The fortress stood nearly in the centre of the Aland Archipelago, in a fine sheltered roadstead called Lumpar Bay, communicating with the sea to the northward by Bomarsund, a narrow strait between the islands of Bomar on the west and Presto on the east. "The fortress itself," says the "History of the Baltic Campaign," "formed the segment of a circle, having a chord of about a quarter of a mile in length, and presenting to the roadstead a casemated battery of 120 guns in two tiers. The system of defence was made complete by a series of works commencing on the heights behind, and continued across the water by a chain of small islands to the island of Presto." The fortress was generally termed the Half Moon Battery. The other three forts were martello towers. That to the north on the Bomar side was called Fort Nottich, that to the south Fort Tzee, and that on the Presto side Fort Presto.

The passage leading to Lumpar Bay was so narrow and intricate that the Russians considered it perfectly impassable, and had entirely neglected to fortify or obstruct it; but Captain T. B. Sullivan, of the *Lightning* surveying ship, buoyed it out, and so judiciously, that our line of battle ships steamed up and down, and our frigates rattled back and forward at full power, without an accident of consequence. The first attack took place at 5 A.M. on the 21st June, when a small squadron, consisting of the *Hecla, Valorous,* and *Odin,* paddle steamers, under Captain Hall, went in and opened a cannonade. The Russians were saluted with 96 pound shot, 100 pound shells, and congreve rockets. They endeavoured to reply with both artillery and rifle fire, but their missiles generally fell short of the shipping. Within an hour the barracks and other buildings were in flames. At ten the Half Moon Battery was on fire, at which our people gave three cheers; another moment and a mighty bomb from the *Valorous* fell through the roof and exploded. "Well done, *Valorous!*" signalled Captain Hall, and "Well done, *Valorous!*" shouted every man of the squadron. At one the firing ceased, and the ships steamed back to their stations in the fleet, with one man on board the *Hecla*, and two on board the *Odin*, wounded.

During the cannonade a young midshipman of the *Hecla*, named Lucas, gave an example of great coolness and courage. A bomb with a burning fuse fell on deck; he lifted it up and flung it overboard, and it fell hissing into the sea. The place was again bombarded on the 26th and 27th, and the operations then subsided into a blockade. During the blockade a singular act of cool daring was performed by Lieutenant Bythesea of the *Arrogant*. Learning that some despatches of importance were expected from St. Petersburg, Lieutenant Bythesea landed with one seaman—William Johnstone, stoker—and lay concealed in the wood. On the third day he saw a Russian officer and four men landing the mail bags; he attacked them, two of them fled, but the mail bags were secured, and the other three were dragged off to the boat as prisoners. Both Lieutenant Bythesea and William Johnstone received the Victoria Cross.

The third and grand assault was delivered after the arrival of the troops—10,000 French under Marshal Baraguay d'Hilliers, and 1000 British under Colonel Jones. On the morning of the 8th August the Russians commenced firing from a mud battery, with 5 guns, which they had erected under Fort Tzee, close to the water. At daybreak the *Amphion* (British) and the *Phlegethon* (French) steamed in to engage this battery, and got within musket-shot, in a position where they took the enemy in flank, while not a single gun could bear on the ships. "The scene of havoc," says an eyewitness, "was complete: blaze after blaze from the ships, answered by corresponding flashes and thundering reports as the shells burst on the devoted battery. The enemy had very judiciously bolted as soon as he found himself outflanked, and the fire of the frigates was expended on the unoffending mud, till at length the admiral gave by signal

permission to land, and in a moment four boats were dashing
for the shore. The *Amphion* won the race, and the bowman
leapt ashore with the blue ensign, neither knowing nor caring
how many 'Rooshians' might be skulking behind the ruins.
However, the place was empty, and after spiking the guns,
which were already overturned and disabled, they returned to
their ships, and this smart little affair ended. The most creditable part of the business was that the ships were skilfully piloted
into a berth close to the shore, from which they performed the
service entrusted to them effectually in half an hour, without the
slightest loss or damage."

The *Bulldog* (British) and the *Stromboli* (French) were meanwhile shelling Fort Tzee, and the troops were in all the bustle
of landing. All the morning the shore was crowded with boats
and barges. The Russians looked grimly on through their
embrasures, and from time to time one of their guns roared
out a sullen defiance. By Sunday the 13th the French
had got their guns into position, and at daybreak began
hammering at Fort Tzee at 400 yards. Their metal was too
light, and no real damage was done. At midnight, however,
they sent up a storming party, and only one man was found
faithful to his post—the veteran commandant, who mounted
guard at the embrasure, and received the storming party
at the point of the sword. A thrust from a Frenchman's
bayonet sent him to the earth, and the place was taken. The
garrison had decamped, with the exception of some 30 men and
the medico, who were found drunk and helpless amid the ruins
of the fort.

Tuesday the 15th saw our breeching guns, consisting of three
32-pounders and four howitzers, in position on a sandbag
battery, within 750 yards of Fort Nottich. The engineers,
blue-jackets, and marines worked with a will, and before long
avalanches of stones and rubbish came tumbling down from the
tower. Soon after breakfast the *Amphion* opened on the Half
Moon, and the ships began to creep leisurely in to her support.
The *Asmodée*, *Phlegethon*, and two other Frenchmen, and on our
part the dashing little *Hecla*, *Valorous*, *Sphinx*, *Arrogant*, and
Bulldog, moved in to take part in the fray. The Russians fired
hot shot, cold shot, hollow shot, solid shot; but the ships did
not catch fire—as it was prophesied they would—or go to the
bottom, nor did shells burst on board and send the whole crew

Q

in fragments to the skies. While the cannonade was going on, Fort Tzee, which had been on fire since Monday afternoon, blew up with a thundering crash, and sent a jet of pitchy smoke and lurid flame high into the air. At one P.M. Fort Nottich hung out the white flag.

At 5 P.M. the signal appeared to cease action, and the ships engaged with the Half Moon left off firing; but the cannonade was resumed next morning. The noise was so great that the men were deaf for two days after, and at midday the *drapeau blanc* appeared on the Half Moon, in token of surrender. Fort Presto, which had been exposed to the cross fire of Captain Ramsay's guns (of the *Hogue*), and of the *Leopard*, *Hecla*, and the French steamer *Cocyte*, could hold out no longer now, and the capture of Bomarsund was complete. The prisoners were marched out of the fort, and collected under a strong guard of English marines and French infantry. Early in September the forts were blown up. The loss of the allies at Bomarsund was 53 killed and 86 wounded. The Russians were supposed to have lost about 600 in killed alone. It may be remarked, however, that throughout the war the actual loss of the enemy could never be ascertained.

In July a small squadron, consisting of the *Eurydice*, 26 guns, *Miranda*, 15, and *Brisk*, 14, was sent into the White Sea, to destroy the shipping and forts on the coast of Russian Lapland. Archangel was found impracticable, owing to a bank of sand; but on his return from reconnoitring, Captain E. Lyons of the *Miranda*—son of Admiral Sir Edmund Lyons,—aided by the *Brisk*, engaged and destroyed some Russian batteries on the island of Slovetskoi. A month later he penetrated to Kola, the capital of Russian Lapland, silenced the Russian guns, destroyed the government stores and buildings, and brought off the enemy's ordnance.

The allied forces were less successful at Petropaulovski, on the Pacific. Admiral Price shot himself in a fit of insanity, and his successor, Sir F. Nicolson, first delayed, and then engaged at such a distance as to effect little more than a great expenditure of ammunition. The small batteries were soon silenced by the heavy frigates, but when the land-force disembarked, a regiment of Russian sharpshooters sprang out of the brushwood, and opened a deadly discharge of musketry within only a few yards' range. Many were killed (26), many wounded, and many taken prisoners. No effort was made to retrieve the defeat, and the commanders of the combined squadrons retired to San Francisco. And yet the fortifications of Petropaulovski were so weak, that the Russian Government ordered them to be destroyed.

Meanwhile, it was resolved to invade the Crimea, and our troops were embarked at Varna—where they had been decimated by cholera—and landed at Old Fort, about 18 miles south of Eupatoria. The invading force consisted of 26,000 British, under Lord Raglan, 30,000 French, under Marshal St. Arnaud, and some 7000 Turks; making in all 63,000 men and 128 guns. The disembarkation occupied four days, and on the 19th September, 1854, the march southward to Sebastopol commenced. That night the allies bivouacked on the banks of the Bulganak, six miles from their landing place. At four next morning, the eventful 20th, the soldiers rose silently and got under arms. A reconnaissance made by the generals revealed the Russians strongly entrenched on the heights above the Alma, on either side of the road leading to Sebastopol. A five hours' march would bring the two armies face to face.

The position of the Russians was one of the strongest ever occupied by an army. They held the picturesque ridge of rocks rising on the south side of the Alma. At the mouth of the river the ridge terminated in a bold cliff, which overhung the waters of the Black Sea. About two miles up the ridge the hills broke away from the river, making an amphitheatre about a mile wide, and then returned to the stream again, but less abruptly. The great road to Sebastopol crossed the river by a wooden bridge, and ran through this amphitheatre, which was ribbed by a lower range of hills running across it. On these hills were posted the causeway batteries. Still farther up than the amphitheatre, the ground rose gradually to a height, terminating in a peak, called the Kourgané Hill. This was the key of the Russian position, and about half-way down the slope, Prince Menschikoff, the commander of the Russian forces, had constructed a great redoubt, on which about a dozen heavy cannon and howitzers were mounted, and a smaller redoubt a little higher up and to the right. Deep trenches had been dug all along the slope of the rocky ridge, and in the ravines many of the turpentine trees had been felled to form abattis to check the advance of our troops. The Russians, 39,000 strong and 106 guns, were massed behind the ridge, but the broken ground sloping to the river was occupied by swarms of riflemen, in ambush among the green vineyards and the thick leafy plantations. The Alma, which ran along the whole Russian front, was fordable in most places, but the banks on the Russian side were so steep that artillery could be got across only at certain points. On the allies' side of the river the ground sloped gently down to the stream, and was covered by gardens and orchards. Opposite the amphitheatre through which ran the post-road to Sebastopol, and on the allies' side, was the Tartar village of Bourliouk. The right of the allies' rested on the sea, where lay a fleet of steamers, ready to throw shot and shell on the Russian position.

Various delays prevented the commencement of the attack until 11 A.M. The allied army was in the following order, the French being on the right :—General Bosquet on the extreme right and about 1500 yards in advance. On Bosquet's left, General Canrobert, then Prince Napoleon, with General Forey in his rear in reserve. Then came the English. On Prince Napoleon's left was the 2d division, under Sir de Lacy Evans (30th, 41st, 47th, 49th, 55th, 95th). On the left of the 2d division was the light division, under Sir George Brown (7th, 19th, 23d, 33d, 77th, 88th, with the 2d battalion of the Rifle brigade). In the rear of the 2d division was the 3d division, under Sir Richard England (1st, 4th, 28th, 38th, 44th, 50th). In the rear of the light division was the 1st division, under the Duke of Cambridge (Grenadiers, Scots Fusiliers, and Coldstream Guards, and the 42d, 79th, and 93d Highlanders). Sir G. Cathcart, with the 4th division (20th, 21st, 57th, 63d, with the 1st battalion of the Rifle brigade) was in reserve on the left flank. The English cavalry (4th and 5th Dragoon Guards, 1st, 2d, 4th, 6th, 8th, 13th, and 17th Dragoons, and 11th Hussars), under the Earl of Lucan, was considerably farther to the left, also protecting the exposed flank and rear.

Bosquet undertook to turn the Russians' left flank. When it was supposed he was well on his way, Canrobert and Prince Napoleon were ordered to advance with their divisions, which they did, under a heavy fire; but Canrobert found it impracticable to drag up his artillery, and was obliged to send it round by the way Bosquet had taken. This operation could not but take a long time, and following the rule which forbids French generals to engage their infantry in open ground without the support of artillery, he lay on the side of the height he was assailing, as well out of the range of the Russian guns as he could, until his artillery should be brought round to him. Prince Napoleon's division hung back in the valley, and was not forward enough to have shelter from the hillside. To make matters worse, St. Arnaud pushed forward the reserves under General Forey; and huddled up as they were in a comparatively small space of ground, every ball from the Russian guns which fell among the French did great execution. It was not till late in the day that Canrobert's artillery was got round, and the French attack on the Russian left proved a comparative failure.

It was now about half-past one. Lord Raglan gave the order to advance; and the whole of the foremost British line (the 2d and light divisions), numbering about 10,000 men, rose from the ground, dressed their ranks, and marched grandly down the slope. In front of Evans's line was the village of Bourliouk, which the Russians had set on fire. This obstacle compelled the 41st and 49th to diverge to the right and cross the Alma by a deep and perilous ford, under a galling fire from the Russian riflemen, who lay in ambush on the opposite bank. The other regiments of the division, under Major-general Pennefather, crossed on the left of the blazing village. The whole division was soon engaged in a close and murderous strife. The men had to work their way forward under a perfect shower of cannon-shot, shells, and rifle bullets. Still the brave fellows struggled forward, sheltering themselves, when the Russian balls fell thickly, behind such little cover as the ground afforded, and when there came a lull, springing forward again to find shelter more in advance. But so long as the Causeway Batteries swept the ground, Evans could do little more than sustain an obstinate and bloody strife. Pennefather's brigade (30th, 47th, 55th) lost more than one-fourth of its strength.

While Evans was thus painfully struggling, Sir George Brown, with the light division, was rapidly advancing to storm the Great Redoubt on the Kourgané Hill. The 77th and 88th, under General Buller, crossed the stream on the extreme left, and stood prepared to resist any attempt that the Russian cavalry, standing idly on the extreme Russian right, might make to turn the flank of the attack. The other four regiments (7th, 19th, 23d, 33d, together with the 95th, which had been separated from the 2d division by the burning of Bourliouk) moved down the slope, cleared the vineyards and gardens of the Russian skirmishers, and waded rapidly across the river. The opposite bank was in some places from eight to fifteen feet high, and the men scrambled up in knots. On either side of the Great Redoubt, the Kazan column of Russian infantry marched down the slope, to throw our men back into the channel of the river, before they had time to form; but the Left Kazan was warmly engaged by the 7th Fusiliers under Colonel Yea, and the Right Kazan by part of the 19th and 23d, and in due time were overthrown. Between the two bodies of troops thus engaged on either flank with the Russian infantry, the remainder of the division (33d, 95th, and the greater part of the 19th and 23d) moved up to the assault of the Great Redoubt, under General Codrington. The regiments were not in line, but clubbed together and broken into clusters.

The Russian sharpshooters moved aside, and the gunners of the Great Redoubt opened on the storming party, with round shot, canister, and grape. The slope which led up from the top of the bank to the parapet of the Great Redoubt was only 300 yards, and quite smooth. Kinglake thus describes the attack :—
"First one gun, then another, then more. From east to west the parapet grew white, and because of the bank of new smoke, no gun could any longer be seen by our men, except at the moment when it was pouring its blaze through the cloud; but on what one may call a glacis, at 300 yards from the mouths of the guns, the thunder, the lightning, and the bolt are not far apart. It was at an early moment after emerging from the bed of the stream that the slaughter of our people began. Indeed some of them, when struck down, had so nearly reached the top of the bank that they fell back dead and dying into the channel of the river. Death loves a crowd, and many fell; but all who were not struck down continued to move forward. In some places, the closer portions of the advancing throng were eight or ten deep; and the round shot, tearing cruelly through and through, mowed down so many of our devoted soldiery that several times by sheer havoc the clusters for a moment were thinned . . .

"And now, whilst the assailing force was rent from front to rear with grape and canister poured down from the heavy guns above, another and a not less deadly arm was brought to bear against it; for the enemy marched a body of infantry into the rear of the breastwork; and the helmeted soldiers, kneeling behind the parapet at the intervals between the embrasures, watched, ready with their muskets on the earthwork, till they thought our people were near enough, and then fired into the crowd. Moreover, the troops on either flank of the redoubt began to fire obliquely into the assailing mass . . .

"The assailants were nearing the breastwork, when, after a lull of a few moments, its ordnance all thundered at once, or at least so nearly at the same moment that the pathway of their blast was a broad one; and there were many who fell; but the onset of our soldiery was becoming a rush. Codrington, riding in front of the men, gaily cheered them on; and all who were not struck down by shot pressed on towards the long bank of smoke which lay dimly enfolding the redoubt.

"But already—though none of the soldiery engaged then knew who wrought the spell—a hard stress had been put upon the enemy. For a while, indeed, the white bank of smoke, lit through here and there with the slender flashes of musketry, stood fast in the front of the parapet, and still all but shrouded the helmets and glittering bayonets within; but it grew more thin; it began to rise; and, rising, it disclosed a grave change in the counsels of the Russian generals. Some Englishmen—or many, perhaps, at the same moment—looking keen through the smoke, saw teams of artillery-horses moving, and there was a sound of ordnance wheels. Our panting soldiery broke from their silence. 'By all that is holy! he is limbering up!' 'He is carrying off his guns!' 'Stole away! Stole away!' The glacis of the Great Redoubt had come to sound more joyous than the covert's side in England.

"The embrasures were empty, and in rear of the work, long artillery-teams—eight-horse and ten-horse teams—were rapidly dragging off the guns.

"Then a small child-like youth ran forward before the throng, carrying a colour. This was young Anstruther. He carried the Queen's colour of the Royal Welsh (23d). Fresh from the games of English school-life, he ran fast; for, heading all who strove to keep up with him, he gained the redoubt, and dug the butt-end of the flagstaff into the parapet; and then for a moment he stood, holding it tight, and taking breath. Then he was shot dead; but his small hands, still clasping the flagstaff, drew it down along with him, and the crimson silk lay covering the boy with its folds. His successor in charge of the colour, namely, centre sergeant Luke O'Connor, was brought down nearly at that moment by a shot which struck his breast; but William Evans, a swift-footed soldier, ran forward, and had caught up the fallen standard, when O'Connor (finding strength enough to be able to rise) made haste to assert his right, and then proudly upholding the colour, he laid claim to the Great Redoubt on behalf of the Royal Welsh. The colour floating high in the air, and seen by our people far and near, kindled in them a raging love for the ground where it stood. Breathless men found speech. General Codrington, still in the front, uncovered, saluting the crisis, waved his cap as a sign to his people, and then, riding straight at one of the embrasures, leapt his grey Arab into the breastwork. There were some eager and swift-footed soldiers who sprang the parapet nearly at the same moment . . .

"The enemy's still lingering skirmishers began to fall back, and descended—some of them slowly—into the dip where their battalions were massed. The bulk of our soldiery were up, and they flooded in over the parapet, hurrahing, jumping over, hurrahing—a joyful English crowd."

But the Russians could not tamely submit to see their great work held by the handful of men who followed Codrington. The Vladimir column advanced to retake the Great Redoubt at the point of the bayonet, and our men being unsupported—for the 1st division had not yet crossed the river—had no alternative but to retreat. But the retreat, though without order, was not hurried. Our soldiers took care to ply the enemy well with fire, and they picked up and carried with them those of our wounded officers and men whom they found lying on the slope. Ill fared it then with the allies all along the line, but Lord Raglan had ordered up two guns to a knoll on the Russian side of the river; with these he took the Causeway Batteries in flank, causing them to be withdrawn up the hill, and drove the Russian reserves from the field. It was this diversion which had caused the Russians to desert the Great Redoubt. With the exception of five pieces of ordnance still remaining in the Lesser Redoubt, the enemy had now no guns remaining in battery. The remainder of the battle was a sheer fight of infantry.

Codrington's men were just retreating from the Great Redoubt, when the 1st division cleared the vineyards and crossed the river to their support, in a line nearly a mile and a half long and two deep. The regiments composing the division stood in the following order from right to left:—Grenadier Guards, Scots Fusilier Guards, Coldstream Guards, 42d Royal Highlanders, 93d Sutherland Highlanders, 79th Cameron Highlanders. The Scots Fusiliers, impelled by a message from Codrington for support, had hurried forward before the other regiments of the division, and, coming in contact with the retreating unwieldy crowd of the stormers, their formation was destroyed. Thus an unfortunate gap was left in the division, but its advance was nevertheless most imposing.

Their strength augmented by some of the 95th and a company of the Scots Fusiliers, the Grenadiers advanced up the slope, after suffering some loss from the Left Vladimir column, which now marched down the slope, with bayonets at the charge. The Russians were nearly on the Grenadiers' flank, when Colonel Hood ordered the left subdivision of the left company to wheel back, so as almost to face the front of the enemy's column. This manœuvre brought the Left Vladimir to a halt, and the half company poured in volley after volley of well-directed fire. Already the great unwieldy mass showed signs of wavering, when Colonel Hood gave the order to the main body of the Grenadiers to bend forward the right shoulder; a movement which enabled them to deliver a destructive fire from the whole of their line. Against such a deadly fire of bullets the Left Vladimir could not stand, and the Russian officers were seen frantically moving about, seizing the men by the throat, and threatening them with their swords. The Grenadiers were warming to their work, and they cheered. "The line will advance firing," shouted Colonel Hood. The Grenadiers advanced, pouring their destructive hail into the wavering column, which bulged and heaved, then broke and fled. The Coldstreams, meanwhile, poured a smart and crushing fire into the Right Vladimir, which was so galled that eventually it retired from the field, and the victorious guards took possession of the Great Redoubt.

The Highland brigade was advancing in échelon. Its leader, Sir Colin Campbell, rode on before, to view the ground and the dispositions of the enemy. He saw that the ground behind the Great Redoubt had a considerable dip, and that the dip was bridged over by a bending rib which connected the inner and the outer crest—"bridged over in such a way that a column on his left front might march to the spot where he stood without having first to descend to the lower ground." He saw that the Right Vladimir column, on its defeat by the Coldstream Guards, descended into the dip, and when it came abreast of the Right Kazan column on the other side, faced about. He saw two battalions of the Sousdal corps advancing along the "bending rib" or natural bridge over the dip ; the other two battalions of the Sousdal were on the extreme right, though Campbell could not then see them. And he saw, standing on the higher slopes of the Kourgané Hill, the four Ouglitz battalions, impending over the scene of the coming fight. The odds were three regiments to twelve—three in line, and twelve massed in five columns.

"The time," says Kinglake, "that it took Sir Colin Campbell to learn the ground before him, and to read the enemy's mind, proved almost enough for enabling his superb 42d to reach him. In the last part of their advance the men of the battalion had had to come over ground both broken and steep, but they traversed it with a speed which observers admired from afar. In the land where those Scots were bred there are shadows of sailing clouds skimming straight up the mountain's side, and their paths are rugged and steep, yet their course is smooth, easy, and swift. Smoothly, easily, swiftly, the Black Watch seemed to glide up the hill. A few instants before, and their tartans ranged dark in the valley—now, their plumes were on the crest. . . . Although at that moment the 42d was alone, and was confronted by the two columns (the Right Kazan and Right Vladimir) on the farther side of the hollow, yet Campbell, having a steadfast faith in Colonel Cameron and in the regiment he commanded, resolved to go straight on, and at once, with his forward movement. He allowed the battalion to descend alone into the hollow, marching straight against the two columns. Moreover, he suffered it to undertake a manœuvre which (except with troops of great steadiness and highly instructed) can hardly be tried with safety against regiments still unshaken. The Black Watch advanced firing."

But while this fight was going on between the 42d and the two Russian columns in its front, the Left Sousdal marched along the "bending rib," with the view of taking the regiment in flank.

Campbell was about to bend his line, and prepare for the Left Sousdal a front of five companies, when, looking behind, he saw the 93d springing up to the outer crest. The 42d then resumed its forward movement, and the 93d dealt with the Left Sousdal. "The two lines marched straight on. The three columns shook. They were not yet subdued. They were stubborn; but every moment the two advancing battalions grew nearer and nearer, and although—dimly masking the scant numbers of the Highlanders—there was still the white curtain of smoke which always rolled on before them, yet, fitfully, and from moment to moment, the signs of them could be traced on the right hand and on the left in a long, shadowy line, and their coming was ceaseless. But, moreover, the Highlanders being men of great stature, and in strange garb, their plumes being tall, and the view of them being broken and distorted by the wreaths of smoke, and there being, too, an ominous silence in their ranks, there were men among the Russians who began to conceive a vague terror—the terror of things unearthly; and some, they say, imagined that they were charged by horsemen, strange, silent, monstrous, bestriding giant chargers. The columns were falling into that plight—we have twice before seen it this day—that its officers were moving hither and thither, with their drawn swords, were commanding, were imploring, were threatening, nay, were even laying hands on their soldiery, and striving to hold them fast in their places. This struggle is the last stage but one in the agony of a body of good infantry massed in close column. Unless help should come from elsewhere, the three columns would have to give way." Help came. From the high ground on the left the Right Sousdal moved down, straight at the flank of the 93d. But at that moment the 79th came bounding forward, and poured into the flank of the Russian column such a fire that it could not live. It broke, and began to fall back in great confusion. Almost at the same moment the columns opposed to the 42d and the 93d were overthrown; the Russians were in full retreat, and the ground was thronged with the enemy's disordered masses. The cheers of the three Highland regiments, now once more reunited, proclaimed their victory.

The battle was won. The cavalry pressed the pursuit, but not far. The army bivouacked on the ground it had gained. The British loss was 2002—362 killed, 1621 wounded, and 19 missing. The French returned their loss at 1339—which is believed to have been a gross over-statement; and the Russians at 5709—which is believed to have been as gross an under-statement. Three of their generals, 700 prisoners, and 750 of their wounded, remained in our hands—that "grey acre" of Russian wounded which Dr. Thomson of the 44th, with noble humanity, volunteered to remain with on the field, a flag of truce being his only and frail dependence from the fury of the Cossacks. It seems that even thus early the Russians showed that treachery and barbarity which was afterwards so conspicuous at Inkerman. "You have heard," says a medical officer, "of the melancholy deaths of Captain and Lieutenant Eddington of the 95th. Captain Eddington fell first, with a ball in his chest, and was left for a few moments on the hillside while the regiment, which had been thrown into disorder, fell back to re-form; and the whole troops witnessed his brutal murder. A Russian rifleman knelt down beside him, and while pretending to raise his canteen to the wounded man's lips, deliberately blew his brains out! A shout of rage and hatred burst from the whole regiment, and at the same moment they again charged up the hill, Lieutenant Eddington many yards in advance, crying for men to follow him, and apparently mad with grief and excitement. He fell beneath a perfect storm of grape-shot and rifle-balls. His breast was absolutely riddled. The same grave holds them both."

The battle of Alma was fought on the 20th September (1854), and on the morning of the 23d the allied army resumed its march southward, all full of hope that their efforts would soon be crowned by the capture of Sebastopol. As it was considered impossible to invest the town on the north face, a flank movement was performed on the little seaport of Balaclava, so as to secure a new base of operations, and make the attack on the south side. Balaclava was taken possession of on the 26th, and presently the harbour was all bustle and stir. The siege-train was landed from the fleet, 2000 seamen lending their aid in dragging the heavy ordnance over the hilly ground between Balaclava and Sebastopol. Trenches and batteries were immediately commenced, strong working parties being detached from each regiment for this dangerous service. The British now occupied the right of the allied line, and had 66 guns and mortars in position; the French, on the left, had in position 53 guns and mortars. Meanwhile, the Russians were not idle; under the directions of the celebrated engineer Todleben, they strengthened the Malakoff, threw up the Redan and other batteries, and rendered the city well-nigh impregnable. To prevent the entrance of the allied fleets, the desperate resolution was taken of sinking six large line-of-battle ships at the mouth of the harbour.

The bombardment was fixed for the 17th October—the fleets to assist. At 6.30 A.M., the morning being fine and clear, the land batteries suddenly opened along the whole line. The Russians replied, and the earth seemed to vibrate and shake beneath the roar of the gigantic ordnance. Dense volumes of smoke hid Sebastopol. About half-past ten a skilfully-directed Russian shell fell into one of the French magazines, dismounting several guns, and destroying 50 artillerymen. Another explosion, and the French guns were silenced for the day. But the British guns still kept up their fire, and about noon the fleets went in, and ranged themselves in an imposing semicircle before the harbour's mouth; the French on the south, against the Quarantine Fort, the Turks in the centre, and the English on the north, against Fort Constantine and Fort Alexander. Inside the great outer line, Sir Edmund Lyons led his own ship, the *Agamemnon*, 91, followed by the *Leander*, 50, *Sanspareil*, 70, and *Albion*, 91. The sailing ships were towed to their positions by steamers lashed alongside. About two o'clock the *Agamemnon*, piloted by the little steamer *Circassian*, brought up in five fathoms of water, about 250 yards inside the main line, and opened fire on Fort Constantine. A lucky shell blew up the powder magazine in the fort, but the Russian gunners soon got the range, and handled the ships so roughly with red-hot shot, that the *Albion*, *Sanspareil*, and *London* were obliged to haul off. The two latter returned, but as the *Albion* was apparently unable to do so, Sir Edmund Lyons signalled to the outer ships to close up, and the *Rodney, Queen, Bellerophon*, and *Arethusa* bore down to his support. Not, however, to change the fortune of the day. The *Queen* was set on fire by a shell; the *Arethusa* was completely crippled; the *Retribution* had her mainmast shot away; the *Firebrand* had scarcely a whole spar left; the *Triton* was dreadfully mauled aloft; the *Rodney* grounded on a reef, whence she was towed off, amid a heavy fire, by Commander Kynaston of the *Spitfire*, who was wounded during his gallant exertions. About dusk the *Agamemnon* quitted her berth, and the other ships followed her motions. The naval attack on Sebastopol was admitted to be a complete failure. The Russian forts were not materially damaged, and in addition to the havoc caused among our ships, we had 44 men killed and 264 wounded, and the French nearly as many. On shore, however, our batteries almost destroyed the Redan, and had an assault been ordered that night, Sebastopol would in all probability have fallen. In the land attack our loss was 144; that of the French, including the 50 men blown up in the first explosion, 96; that of the Russians, 1100, including the brave Admiral Kermiloff killed, and Admiral Nachimoff, of Sinope celebrity, wounded. The number of projectiles thrown by the English from their land batteries was reckoned at 4700, by the French at 4000, and by the Russians at 20,000.

The British being on the right, the duty of defending the allied position devolved on them. The two weak points were Balaclava and Inkerman, at the two ends of the Sapouné Range, which bounds the Chersonese upland on the east.

At seven in the morning of the 25th October, news came to headquarters that the Russian General Liprandi, with a large body of cavalry, infantry, and artillery (25,000 men and 78 guns), had suddenly appeared at Balaclava, and was taking the Turkish redoubts, which had been hastily thrown up to defend the position. The British 1st and 4th divisions immediately got under arms, and began their march to the scene of action; and General Bosquet—who occupied the Sapouné ridge with two French divisions—was ordered with 200 Chasseurs d'Afrique and a force of artillery to their assistance. Meanwhile, the 93d Highlanders, with 30 or 40 men of the guards and about 100 invalids, were drawn up to defend the approach to Balaclava, a battalion of Turks on each flank. Above and behind, on the heights, stood the royal marines. To the left of the 93d were the heavy and light cavalry, drawn up in front of their encampment. The scene which followed will, on the whole, be best described in the words of Dr. Russell :—

"The heavy brigade in advance is drawn up in two lines. The first line consists of the Scots Greys and of their old companions in glory, the Inniskillings; the second, of the 4th Royal Irish, of the 5th Dragoon Guards, and of the 1st Royal Dragoons. The light cavalry brigade is on their left, in two lines also. The silence is oppressive; between the cannon bursts one can hear the champing of bits and the clink of sabres in the valley below. The Russians on their left drew breath for a moment, and then in one grand line dashed at the Highlanders. The ground flies beneath their horses; gathering speed at every stride, they dash on towards that thin red streak topped with a line of steel. The Turks fire a volley at 800 yards, and run. As the Russians come within 600 yards, down goes that line of steel in front, and out rings a rolling volley of Minié musketry. The distance is too great; the Russians are not checked, but still sweep onwards through the smoke, with the whole force of horse and man, here and there knocked over by the shot of our batteries above. With breathless suspense every one awaits the bursting of the wave upon the line of Gaelic rock; but ere they come within 150 yards, another deadly volley flashes from the levelled rifle, and carries death and terror into the Russians. They wheel about, open files right and left, and fly back faster than they came. 'Bravo, Highlanders! Well done!' shout the excited spectators; but events thicken. The Highlanders and their splendid front are soon forgotten, men scarcely have a moment to think of this fact, that the 93d never altered their formation to receive that tide of horsemen. 'No,' said Sir Colin Campbell, 'I did not think it worth while to form them even four deep!' The ordinary British line, two deep, was quite sufficient to repel the attack of these Muscovite cavaliers.

"Our eyes were, however, turned in a moment on our own cavalry. We saw Brigadier-general Scarlett ride along in front of his own massive squadrons. The Russians—evidently *corps d'élite*—their light and blue jackets embroidered with silver lace, were advancing on their left at an easy gallop, towards the brow of the hill. A forest of lances glistened in their rear, and several squadrons of grey-coated dragoons moved up quickly to support them as they reached the summit. The instant they came in sight, the trumpets of our cavalry gave out the warning blast which told us all that in another moment we should see the shock of battle beneath our very eyes. Lord Raglan, all his staff and escort, and groups of officers, the Zouaves, French generals and officers, and bodies of French infantry on the height, were spectators of the scene as though they were looking on the stage from the boxes of a theatre. Nearly every one dismounted and sat down, and not a word was said. The Russians advanced down the hill at a slow canter, which they changed to a trot, and at last nearly halted. Their first line was at least double the length of ours—it was three times as deep. Behind them was a similar line, equally strong and compact. They evidently despised their insignificant-looking enemy, but their time was come. The trumpets rang out again through the valley, and the Greys and Inniskillingers went right at the centre of the Russian cavalry. The space between them was only a few hundred yards; it was scarce enough to let the horses 'gather way,' nor had the men quite space sufficient for the full play of their sword arms. The Russian line brings forward each wing as our cavalry advances, and threatens to annihilate them as they pass on. Turning a little to their left, so as to meet the Russian right, the Greys rush on with a cheer that thrills to every heart —the wild shout of the Inniskillingers pierced through the dark masses of the Russians. The shock was but for a moment. There was a clash of steel and a light play of sword-blades in the air, and then the Greys and the red-coats disappear in the midst of the shaken and quivering columns. In another moment we see them emerging and dashing on, with diminished numbers and in broken order, against the second line, which is advancing against them as fast as it can to retrieve the fortune of the charge. It was a terrible moment. 'God help them! they are lost,' was the exclamation of more than one man, and the thought of many. With unabated fire the noble hearts dashed at their enemy. It was a fight of heroes. The first line of Russians, which had been smashed utterly by our charge, and had fled off at one flank and towards the centre, were coming back to swallow up our handful of men. By sheer steel and sheer courage the Inniskillingers and Scots were winning their desperate way right through the enemy's squadrons, and already grey horses and red-coats had appeared right at the rear of the second mass, when, with irresistible force, like one bolt from a bow, the 1st Royals, the 4th Dragoon Guards, and the 5th Dragoon Guards, rushed at the remnants of the first line of the enemy, went through it as though it were made of pasteboard, and dashing on the second body of Russians, as they were still disordered by the terrible assault of the Greys and their companions, put them to utter rout. The Russian horse in less than five minutes after it met our dragoons was flying with all its speed before a force certainly not half its strength." A few shots were fired against the retreating Russians by the troop of horse artillery which accompanied the light brigade, and by two of Barker's guns, under Sir Colin Campbell. Sixty or seventy of our heavies were killed or wounded; the Russian loss was estimated at 500.

And then came the glorious but disastrous charge of the Light Brigade. Lord Raglan, perceiving the enemy endeavouring to carry off the English guns taken in the Turkish redoubts, ordered the cavalry to advance rapidly to the front to prevent them from doing so. The order was misunderstood. Lord Lucan supposed "the guns" referred to were those in front of the Russian line at the head of the North Valley. Behind these guns was the defeated Russian cavalry, drawn up in six solid divisions; and behind the cavalry were six battalions of Russian infantry. Besides the force at the head of the valley, the Russians had a force of all arms on the Fedioukine Heights on the one side, and infantry and artillery on the Causeway Heights on the other. There was

> "Cannon to right of them,
> Cannon to left of them,
> Cannon in front of them."

Lord Lucan rode forward to Lord Cardigan, who was in his saddle in front of the 13th Light Dragoons, and told him the terms of the order. "Certainly, sir," said Lord Cardigan, "but allow me to point out to you that the Russians have a battery in the valley in our front, and batteries and riflemen on our flanks." Shrugging his shoulders, Lord Lucan replied, "There is no choice but to obey." Without further question or parley, Lord Cardigan tacitly signified his respectful submission to orders, and, turning quietly to his squadrons, he gave the word, "The brigade will advance." Then, followed immediately by his horsemen, he moved forward at a trot, making straight down the valley towards the battery, which crossed the valley at a distance of about a mile and a quarter. The front line of the brigade consisted of the 13th Light Dragoons and the 17th Lancers; behind the 17th Lancers were the 11th Hussars; behind the 11th Hussars were the 4th Light Dragoons, and to their right were the 8th Hussars. The whole brigade numbered only 673 horsemen.

"A more fearful spectacle," says Dr. Russell, himself an eyewitness of this famous charge, "was never witnessed than by those who, without the power to aid, beheld their heroic countrymen rushing to the arms of death. At the distance of 1200 yards, the whole line of the enemy belched forth from 30 iron mouths a flood of smoke and flame, through which hissed the deadly balls. Their flight was marked by instant gaps in our ranks, by dead men and horses, by steeds flying wounded or riderless across the plain. The first line is broken, it is joined by the second; they never halt or check their speed an instant; with diminished ranks, thinned by those 30 guns, which the Russians had laid with the most deadly accuracy, with a halo of flashing steel above their heads, and with a cheer which was many a noble fellow's death-cry, they flew into the smoke of the batteries, but ere they were lost from view the plain was strewed with their bodies and with the carcases of horses. They were exposed to an oblique fire from the batteries on the hills on both sides, as well as to a direct fire of musketry. Through the clouds of smoke we could see their sabres flashing as they rode up to the guns and dashed between them, cutting down the gunners as they stood. We saw them riding through the guns, as I have said; to our delight we saw them returning, after breaking through a column of Russian infantry, and scattering them like chaff, when the flank fire of the battery on the hill swept them down, scattered and broken as they were. Wounded and dismounted troopers flying towards us told the sad tale—demi-gods could not have done what we failed to do. At the very moment when they were about to retreat, an enormous mass of lancers was hurled on their flank. Colonel Shewell, of the 8th Hussars, saw the danger, and rode his few men straight at them, cutting his way through with fearful loss. The other regiments turned and engaged in a desperate encounter. With courage almost too great for credence, they were breaking their way through the columns which enveloped them, when there took place an act of atrocity without parallel in the modern warfare of civilised nations. The Russian gunners, when the storm of cavalry passed, returned to their guns. They saw their own cavalry mingled with the troopers who had just ridden over them, and to the eternal disgrace of the Russian name, the miscreants poured a murderous volley of grape and canister on the mass of struggling men and horses, mingling friend and foe in one common ruin. It was as much as our heavy cavalry brigade could do to cover the retreat of the miserable remnants of that band of heroes, as they returned to the place they had so lately quitted in all the pride of life. At 11.35 A.M. not a British soldier except the dead and dying was left in front of those bloody Muscovite guns." The charge lasted but twenty minutes, and the brigade, which had gone into action 673 strong, came out reduced to a mounted strength of 195. As many as 475 horses were killed and 42 disabled. Of the riders, 169 were slain or missing and 218 wounded. Only 10 men of the 13th came out unhurt.

Meanwhile, the 14th Chasseurs d'Afrique rode round the western base of the Fedioukine Heights, and charged the Russians posted there, rolling them up; and as Sir George Cathcart was approaching with the 4th division, the Russians abandoned the attempt to carry off the guns. The whole Highland brigade was now ordered down for the defence of Balaclava, and a large force of marines and seamen was landed from the fleet.

Britain will remember with pride the heroism of her soldiers at Balaclava: the ready "Ay, ay!" of the Highlanders when Sir Colin Campbell told them there was no retreat, they must die where they stood; the bravery of troop-sergeant Norris of the 1st Royals, who, separated by mischance from his regiment, and beset by four Russian horsemen, rose in his stirrups, dealt one of them a blow which killed him on the spot, and put the others to flight; the heroism of Lieutenant Phillips, in the disastrous "Death Ride," who, seeing private Brown disabled in both hands, protected him with his revolver till the recall was sounded; the miraculous escape of Captain Morris of the 17th Lancers, who ran a Russian officer through the body, but, unable to withdraw his sword, was beset by a swarm of Cossacks, wounded many times, and taken prisoner, yet ran into the thickest of the smoke, and escaped them, was again in danger of being dispatched by a Cossack, again ran into the thickest of the smoke, caught a horse, which was shot under him just as he was getting out of fire, crawled up the valley, and lay down exhausted beside the dead body of his friend Captain Nolan.

Next day, October 26th, 5000 Russians, with skirmishers and artillery, made an attack on that part of the British force which was posted above the ruins of Inkerman, but were defeated and chased down the ridge towards the edge of the bay. This was the prelude to the great battle of Inkerman, fought on the same ground on the 5th November. The disposition of the British was as follows:—On the extreme right, the 2d division, supported by the guards; on the left of the guards, but separated from them by a ravine, the light division; still farther to the left, the 4th and 3d divisions. Mount Inkerman was simply the north-eastern angle of the Chersonese. "This part of the heights," says Kinglake, "has, so to speak, been almost chipped off from the rest of the table-land by the deep Careenage Ravine; and it is only by an isthmus or neck of high land that the triangular quoin thus formed remains joined to the bulk of the Chersonese." Moreover, the ascent here was not so steep as at other parts of the Sapouné ridge, and everything seemed to favour what the Russians were meditating—a sortie in force from Sebastopol. Soimonoff, issuing from the Karabel Faubourg, and Pauloff, coming up from the bridge at the mouth of the Tchernaya, were to ascend the northern steeps of Mount Inkerman. With the 40,000 men thus collected, Dannenberg—who commanded in chief—was to sweep that part of the Chersonese, overwhelming the 2d division. Meanwhile, Timovieff, with 5000 men of the garrison, was to make a powerful sortie against the French left, so as to prevent Canrobert from withdrawing his forces to the real seat of attack on Mount Inkerman; while Prince Gortschakoff, with 22,000 men, was to march southward through the plain to the east of the Chersonese and menace Bosquet, so as to prevent him from sending help to Pennefather. Pennefather overwhelmed, Dannenberg would march south over the uplands, and, joined by Gortschakoff, entrench his victorious troops on the conquered ground. Thus, the assault which the French intended to make on the flagstaff bastion would be prevented; nay, the allies might be compelled to raise the siege.

On the morning of that ever-memorable Sunday, the 5th November, the bells of the besieged rang a tocsin, and at 3 A.M. the troops composing the sortie stole out of Sebastopol. Favoured by the mist, they surprised our pickets, who suddenly found themselves almost surrounded; but the pickets resisted bravely, and effected a retreat to the Sandbag Battery, which on this day was destined to be the scene of one of the most obstinate and sanguinary struggles ever recorded in the annals of war. The noise of the firing immediately roused our camp, and the 2d division, guards, the light division, and other troops, hurried up to the scene of the contest. The Russians, under Soimonoff and Pauloff, numbered 40,000 men, and few were the British soldiers who could be opposed to them.

Soimonoff immediately (at 5.45 A.M.) planted his batteries on Shell Hill, right in front of the camp of the 2d division, against whose tents he opened fire. Leaving sixteen battalions to guard the guns, he advanced with 15,000 men to the attack of General Pennefather,—at this time in command of the 2d division, Sir de Lacy Evans being on board ship, sick,—who had barely 3000 bayonets. For a few minutes he had the ascendant; advancing up the Mikriakoff glen on his right, he seized three English guns which had been moved forward along the Mikriakoff spur without infantry supports, and stood within a stone's throw of Pennefather's tents. But the mist, which had thus far favoured the Russians, now favoured the British, by taking from the many "their power of rightly wielding big numbers, and from the few their sense of weakness." Pennefather was reinforced by 660 men of the light division, and a series of encounters ensued which can scarcely be credited. Colonel Egerton, with only four companies of the 77th, overthrew the Tomsk regiment, 1500 strong; the 3d and 4th Catherinburg battalions retreated before a few men of the 47th and 88th, and the three guns were recaptured; five columns were overthrown at Home Ridge (just before the camp of the 2d division) by a fire of caseshot from three guns of Captain Turner's battery, and pursued by a crowd of pickets; Captain Bellairs and 183 men of the 49th overthrew the Kolivansk column; four Borodino battalions were routed at the Barrier, or main picket wall, by Colonel Maulverer and 200 men of the 30th, with sheer cold steel; and finally, General Adams advanced with the 41st, 500 strong, to the Sandbag Battery, and routed 4000 men of the Tarontine regiment, driving them down the declivities, and pouring into their disordered ranks a destructive fire. "Thus," says Kinglake, "though having already brought up nearly 25,000 infantry and 38 guns (of which 22 were 12-pounders), the enemy received a cruel discomfiture from forces which comprised altogether only 3600 foot, with 18 pieces of field artillery." This phase of the battle ended at 7.30 A.M.

General Dannenberg now assumed the command, and, with 19,000 fresh troops and 97 additional guns, assailed the English front at Home Ridge, under Pennefather, and their right at the Sandbag Battery. This Sandbag Battery was a sad cause of confusion to the British. It was the parapet of a dismantled earthwork, thrown up some weeks before, for the purpose of silencing a Russian gun placed in battery on the Inkerman ruins opposite, and from which, having achieved its purpose, the two 18-pounders which constituted its armament had been withdrawn; but our soldiers believed it must be part of the English defences, and held to it with a tenacity which had the most baneful results. For the English line of defence was thus separated into two unconnected masses, with a dangerous gap between them, of which the enemy failed not to take advantage. In front, Pennefather was still able to hold his ground and hurl back every attack, but at the Sandbag Battery, 700 yards to the right, the fortunes of the fight were more checkered. Soon after General Adams had cleared the post with the 41st, he was joined by Captain Bellairs with his three companies of the 49th, so that he had altogether a force of 700 men. But his enemies were 10,000 strong. Up, up, and round the battery they surged in howling throngs, and the little handful of British was forced. General Adams himself was struck in the ank'e and mortally wounded. At this crisis Captain Hamley brought up three guns, and plied some of the Russian columns with round-shot and case, and the Duke of Cambridge and General Bentinck arrived with the Grenadier and Scots Fusilier Guards, 700 strong. The guards were afterwards reinforced by a wing of the 95th, a wing of the 1st Rifle battalion, and a wing of the 20th, and sore and incessant was the fight at the Sandbag Battery. As often as the Russians were driven back, they formed under the acclivities, and again advanced, only to be again driven back. But under this incessant strain the British were in danger of spending all their cartridges, and the Russians advanced through the Gap to surround them and cut them off. At length arose a cry of "Charge!" and the Russians were driven headlong down the slopes, the British tearing after them and breaking their array. General Cathcart, with 400 men of the 4th division, joined the troops at the Sandbag Battery in their victorious charge down the slope, and fell pierced through the heart by a Russian bullet. Only about 150 men remained with the Duke of Cambridge round the colours of the Grenadier Guards, and these were nearly surrounded and had to fight their way home through a mass of 2000 Russians who came pouring through the Gap. Two French regiments arrived and retook the Sandbag Battery. It was half-past eight.

General Dannenberg now concentrated all his efforts on a

grand attack on Home Ridge, and Pennefather had but few troops to cope with him. Down came the Russian column, cased in a cloud of skirmishers, down and almost over Home Ridge; but Colonel Daubeny arrested its course by an audacious flank charge with only 30 men of the 55th, and Pennefather met it in front with the French 7th Léger, a few fragments of English regiments, and 60 Zouaves. The Russians retreated, pursued by the victorious allies. Another Russian column was overthrown by the 63d and the right wing of the 21st Fusiliers, and these troops then disposed themselves at the Barrier, which they held for the remainder of the day. It was a quarter-past nine.

But the allies had no troops in hand to press their advantage, and the Russians soon rallied; Lord Raglan, however, had ordered up two 18-pounders from the siege park, and these now arrived and were planted on Home Ridge. Every shot told, carrying havoc into the Russian batteries on Shell Hill. Moreover, General Bosquet arrived with 3000 French troops. It was ten o'clock.

Bosquet, however, fell into the same mistake as our own troops in the earlier part of the day, and diverged to his right in the direction of the Sandbag Battery. Some Russian columns proceeding through the Gap nearly surrounded him, and it was with the utmost difficulty he managed to retreat, with the loss of one gun. But, on being reinforced, Bosquet again advanced, and drove the Russians, not only out of the Sandbag Battery but out of the field of battle. Canrobert now came up in person, and Lord Raglan tried to induce him to press his advantage home, but failed, and the share of the French troops in the battle of Inkerman came to an end. It was eleven o'clock.

Although despairing of again taking the offensive himself, Dannenberg held on to his position on Shell Hill, suffering dreadfully from the two 18-pounders, in the hope that Prince Gortschakoff, who had 22,000 men in the Tchernaya Valley, would still be able to make a diversion in his favour. But Gortschakoff had withdrawn his men to Tchorgoun, and after enduring two hours' of martyrdom, Dannenberg resolved to retreat, his resolve being quickened by a daring charge which Lieutenant Acton made on one of his batteries, with a handful of the 77th. The retreat began at one o'clock. It was not pressed, and by eight o'clock in the evening the remains of the Russian army were safe in Sebastopol.

The Russians had a force of nearly 72,000 men operating in the open field on the day of Inkerman; but 5000 of these were engaged in a sortie which Timovieff made on the French lines, 22,000 were inactive with Gortschakoff, and 4000 were guarding the road. The force that fought on Mount Inkerman, where the battle was really decided, was 40,210 men with 135 guns. From first to last the British had only 7464 infantry, 200 cavalry, 36 pieces of artillery, and two 18-pounders. The French, during a part of the battle, had 8219 infantry, 700 cavalry, and 24 guns. The official return of the Russian loss was 11,959 in killed, wounded, and prisoners, and nearly all these fell on Mount Inkerman. The French stated their loss at 1800, but only 175 of these were killed. The British loss was 2573, of whom 635 were killed. In proportion to their numbers the British were very heavy sufferers. In their long and protracted struggle at the Sandbag Battery, the guards—1331 strong on the day of Inkerman—lost nearly half their numbers in the space of an hour; and in the 21st North British Fusiliers, the 20th, of Minden fame, and the 57th, the famous old "Die-Hards," the proportion was still greater. Inkerman brought sorrow to many a British hearth, but as Lord Raglan said, writing to the Duke of Newcastle, "It was a glorious day for the British arms."

Such is an outline of the great battle of Inkerman; but how would it be possible for us to fill up the picture? It would be necessary to describe the movements not only of each particular regiment, but also of each fraction of a regiment, of every knot of men, in many cases of individual men. Take the following example of how men fought at Inkerman. The guards were in the Sandbag Battery, and their ammunition was nearly exhausted, so it had to come to cold steel. The Russians were pressing on; one of them, a little in advance of the rest, had begun to get over the parapet of the right flank of the battery, but Captain Burnaby of the 3d company of the Grenadiers, raising his sword, laid him dead, and then cried, "We must charge!" Followed by Private James Bancroft and five or six other men of his company, he leapt down outside the parapet. Let Kinglake continue the story. "Bancroft, following his captain, was immediately attacked by several assailants, of whom he killed one by a bayonet-thrust in the chest; but the next instant he was so grievously wounded by a Russian bayonet tearing through his jaw and the cage of his teeth, as to be made to stagger back a few paces before he recommenced his exploits.

"Captain Burnaby had but just cleared the parapet when he found himself met by a Russian officer of great stature, who was heading the attack at this spot, and vehemently calling forward his men. Upon seeing Burnaby, the Russian officer sprang at him sword in hand, but Burnaby parried; and before his assailant could again raise the arm, brought him down with a cut so delivered on the side of the head, that the tall leader fell, and died at once with a groan. Then, still followed by five or six of his men, and getting quit of his next two assailants with nothing worse than a shot through the bearskin, Captain Burnaby made a dart at the thick of the troops confronting him. Surprised, and for the moment confounded, the mass of the Russians fell back several paces in avoidance of this sudden lunge; but they presently rallied, and a number of people swarmed forward in bevies undertaking to clear the front. On the other hand, Burnaby's original following of six or seven was by this time a little increased. Before long, he had with him more men belonging to his own company; and, whilst also Sir Charles Russell, with his valiant man, Anthony Palmer, approached this part of the ledgeway, there came besides from the left Captain Kinloch and Captain Robert Lindsay of the Scots Fusiliers, with a few more men of the guards. All these springing forward, opposed themselves singly or in knots to the thickening flakes of the Russian infantry thrown out in front of the columns; and hence it resulted that on the narrow belt of ground then dividing our English line from the enemy's aggregate masses, many separate personal combats were sustained by private soldiers of the guards.

"Before hearing of these, one should guard one's self against unjust conclusions by acknowledging that the two opposed armies were not made up of such elements that they could afford means of fair comparison between the individual Russian and the individual Englishman: for the first had been one in a gang of weeping peasantry seized, shaven, and torn from their homes by ruthless power; the other, a sturdy recruit, choosing freely the profession of arms, and now realising, perhaps, on the ledgeway, the favourite dreams of his boyhood. And there is yet another reason which helps to show why it was that our people in their man-to-man struggles got the better one after another of antagonists as strong as themselves. The Russian, like other foot soldiers, had been trained to use his weapon in the way appropriate to aggregate action; and, remaining under the sway of long barrack-yard lessons, he tried to maintain personal conflicts by lowering his weapon and bringing it 'down to the charge;' whilst the guardsman, on the contrary, had been trained by our 'bayonet drill' to make his weapon serve for close conflict, by raising it first high and far back over his right shoulder, and then making the thrust which, by arms acting thus at advantage, could be delivered with great power.

"Three Russians acting together attacked Edward Hill, but Hill's life was saved by Isaac Archer, who ran his bayonet through one of the assailants. Richard Wilkins, when shot through the bearskin by one of two Russians attacking him at the same time, sent a rifle-ball into the breast of the man who had thus barely missed him, drove off the other assailant with the point of the bayonet, and then reloaded so quickly as to be able to shoot the man running. Private Wilson, attacked by two Russians, and trying to run one of them through, chanced to stumble and fall; but Joseph Troy coming up bayoneted one of Wilson's foes, and Isaac Archer killed the other. William Overson, attacked by two Russians, killed one of them, and, it seems, drove the other away. Sergeant Minor, confronted by five or six Russians, ran one of them through the side; and another of them (who had that moment driven his steel through Minor's greatcoat) being pierced in the neck and killed by a bayonet thrust from George Bates, the two English made good their ascendant, and were not, it seems, further molested by the rest of Minor's assailants. Our people had learnt, or were learning, that the safest and best way of fighting was to deliver their thrust at the face or the neck, because it often proved difficult to drive a bayonet through the Russian greatcoat; and in piercing this tough, woollen armour, a man should so use his strength as to transfix the trunk of his adversary, and drive the blade home to its socket, this very success, it was likely, would make him, for the moment, defenceless; because he might find — as did Hilton Sayer when he thus killed his man—that it was a hard task to withdraw the imbedded steel. Men speak to an instance of two foes slaying each other, for a grenadier named Sellars was run through, they declare, by a bayonet, at the moment when he with his bayonet ran through that very assailant; so that one and the other alike fell back with a groan; and, the body of each proving tenacious of his antagonist's steel, it resulted that the two men in dying made a ghastly exchange of firelocks. Private Pullen so fought as to win the admiration of his captain for exceeding bravery; and indeed the man's coolness in danger left him time and inclination to indulge his cynical humour, for whilst still in the turmoil of the fight, though at a moment when the presence of close bodily struggles was a little relaxed, he affected to become fastidiously disdainful of the Russians herded close in his front, declaring he would shoot nothing less than a general, and sarcastically adjusting the sight of his firelock to a range of 300 yards.

"As for Bancroft, he had not been quelled; for although, as we saw, he staggered back a few paces when grievously wounded by a second assailant, he still kept his eye on the man, and presently shot him dead. His third assailant he killed by running him through. A fourth and fifth assailant then set upon Bancroft at the same moment; and, one of them bayoneting him in the right side, he fell; but the next moment he was again on his feet and driving his bayonet through one of the two last assailants. The Russian thus pierced fell to the ground, but without being killed or subdued; and by clutching, it seems at Bancroft's legs, he strove to hamper him in his hand-to-hand struggle with the other assailant. Bancroft—fighting for his life with one upstanding antagonist, and clutched at the same time round the legs by the one who had fallen—could only repress the fierce energy of the man on the ground by stunning him with kicks on the head. Curiously—and one welcomes the sentiment, even if it be wrongly applied—the sight of kicks given to a man on the ground brought out, in the midst of the combat, an Englishman's love of 'fair play;' for though Bancroft was but one defending his life against two, Sergeant Alger called out to him from a spot some way off, and forbade him to 'kick the man that was down.' It is believed certain that by fire, by steel, and by the sole of his boot, Bancroft killed altogether five men.

"Fighting thus—one or two of them singly, the rest in very

small knots—a few men of the guards proved able at length to break up the opposing clusters of the Russian soldiery and drive them down from the ledgeway upon the heads of the columns below."

It would be vain to attempt to describe the many gallant deeds performed by our soldiers at Inkerman, the numberless instances of their heroism in rescuing their wounded officers and comrades, or in saving their own lives when wounded themselves and exposed to the murderous attacks of the infuriated Russian soldiery. A volume might be filled with such instances, and yet the story of Inkerman would only be half told. Very many received the Victoria Cross; very many, equally deserving, did not bring forward their claims; and many more did not live to receive the honour.

Victory as it was, Inkerman was a very serious matter for Lord Raglan. The hospitals were full, cholera was still in the camp, no recruits were coming, and the Russians were perpetually troublesome. The storm of the 14th November, which tossed tents about like feathers, and wrecked the *Prince*, laden with stores, seemed to add the last bitter drop to the cup. Sick, weary, cold, crouching in the muddy trenches, or staggering under loads of beef and biscuit or ammunition over the six miles between Balaclava and the camp, our men passed the winter. Gradually, the truth leaked out that the heroes who had escaped Russian lead and steel at the Alma, Balaclava, and Inkerman, were perishing through the sheer mismanagement of those who had charge of the supplies and the transport. A howl of indignation arose all over Britain. A select committee was appointed to inquire into the condition of the army before Sebastopol. Better still, committees were formed to relieve the necessities of the soldiers, and supply them with warm clothing, good bedding, and wholesome provisions. A railway was constructed from Balaclava to the camp, and a submarine cable was laid from Bulgaria to the Crimea. Reinforcements were sent out, horse, foot, and artillery; and Florence Nightingale and a noble band of women went out to tend the sick and wounded.

The events of the next few months may be noticed very summarily. Sardinia joined the Anglo-French alliance (January 26, 1855). Omar Pasha and his Turks defeated the Russians at Eupatoria (February 15 and 18). The Emperor Nicholas died (March 2), but his son Alexander still carried on the war. Sebastopol was bombarded for the second time (April 9). Canrobert resigned (May 16), and the command of the French army devolved on Pelissier. More active operations began at once. An expedition sailed for Kertch. Possession of the sea of Azof afforded the Russians great facilities for the transport of troops and stores for the relief of Sebastopol, and practically shortened the distance between the besieged town and the interior of Russia by many hundred miles. It was resolved to put an end to this. An expedition was planned, numbering about 60 war-ships, under Admirals Lyons and Bruat, with a combined force of 17,000 English (the Highland brigade), French, and Turks, under Sir George Brown and General D'Autemarre. The expedition was entirely successful, and was attended with little difficulty or danger. The troops landed at Kertch on the 24th May, and as they advanced the Russians retired, blowing up their forts one by one. The work of destruction then commenced, and vast quantities of ammunition and stores fell a prey to the allies. Yenikalé was also abandoned, and small garrisons were thrown into both places. The shoals and bays were swept by a number of little active war-steamers, while the main body of the fleet went up to the very head of the sea, and on the 3d June bombarded the port of Taganrog. The quantity of Russian (government) property destroyed in this expedition was immense. About the middle of June the expedition returned to Kamiesch and Balaclava. On the 6th of that month the third bombardment of Sebastopol took place, and resulted in the capture of the Mamelon, the Quarries, and the *Ouvrages Blancs*. The fourth followed on the 17th. Next day an unsuccessful assault was made on the Malakoff and Redan, and all parties suffered severe loss. The British had 252 killed and 1207 wounded. On the 28th of the same month the gallant and gentle Lord Raglan succumbed to cholera, and the command devolved on the chief of the staff, General Simpson.

While so busy in the Crimea, we were not idle in the Baltic. The fleet sailed from England on the 4th April, 1855, and on the 10th May anchored at the Island of Nargon, in the Gulf of Finland. It was under the command of Admiral Dundas, who reconnoitred Cronstadt, and, like Napier, deemed it impregnable.

But something must be done; the summer was wearing apace, people at home were grumbling, and the seamen were getting disgusted at the long-continued inactivity. At length, on the 6th August, orders were given for Sveaborg. The British fleet consisted of 17 men-of-war, 15 gunboats, and 16 mortar vessels; the French of 2 men-of-war, 6 gunboats, and 5 mortar vessels.

Sveaborg, the Gibraltar of the Baltic, stands about a mile in advance of Helsingfors, the capital of Russian Finland, on a group of islands almost entirely covered by fortifications, barracks, magazines, and prisons. The channels between the islands—which extend over a convex line of some 5 miles—were protected by ships of the line, sunken vessels, and torpedoes. The whole place is supposed to have been armed with 810 pieces of cannon. The appearance it presented from the sea is thus described by an eye-witness: "No lofty cliffs, no perpendicular granite forts were here to offer a fair mark, and crumble down under the concentrated fire of heavy ships, no tier upon tier of guns in casemates, but a string of low, rocky islands, separated by narrow channels which the eye could scarcely distinguish, and presenting at some distance the appearance of one long shore of broken and shelving ground rising gradually, but irregularly, to the height of some 30 or 40 feet. Along this coast we saw continuous lines of sloping earth-batteries, showing nothing for a mark but the very muzzles of the guns; farther back, where the ground rose, little stone forts of seven or eight guns nestled in every nook, and here and there naked guns mounted *en barbette* upon every suitable slope of rock. Then among the buildings every now and then a window could be seen bearing a most suspicious likeness to an embrasure, and, on a closer examination, guns were seen projecting where, at first sight, nothing but a garret window showed."

On the morning of Thursday the 9th August, 1855, the ships took up their stations. In front, at a distance of 3600 yards from the face of the works, were the gunboats, all steam, each armed with two of the heaviest guns in the service. Immediately behind the gunboats, ranged in line, were the mortar-boats, sailing vessels, which carried one 13-inch mortar each. Behind the mortar-boats, again, were the line-of-battle ships and the frigates and corvettes, ready to support the gun and mortar boats, and put the finishing stroke to any success they might achieve. The store-ships, hospital ships, despatch vessels, tenders, and the whole generation of unarmed craft that swelled up the fleet, kept a little farther out at sea. At 6.45 A.M. a signal from the flagship ordered—" Gun and mortar vessels open with fire and shell." The yards of the frigates and the line-of-battle ships were manned by the seamen, while crowds of persons — many of them ladies dressed in the height of fashion—stood upon the batteries of Sveaborg, gazing eagerly upon the mighty fleet before them.

At 7.30 A.M. the first shell went hissing on its fiery errand, and the bombardment began. Report after report went roaring over the water as the long line of mortars opened fire. A blaze of fire girdled the earth and granite walls of Sveaborg as the Russians promptly replied; but their round shot fell short, and splashed harmless in the sea, while their shells all burst high up in the heavens, except some few that burst near the muzzles of the guns. So it went on, the gun-boats bristling against Sveaborg like a swarm of angry wasps. The mortar-boats remained stationary, but the gunboats ran in, shot their missiles, and retired, steaming round. In this way, three, four, six, or a greater number of gunboats, formed a circle, all steaming round and round, and giving the enemy a salute as their guns bore upon him. It was like a witches' dance, and rendered it impossible for the Russian gunners to keep a precise range. The sailors on the yards were never weary looking at it. Seldom was a gunboat hit, and then only slightly. While the gunboats thus circled in front, the mortar-boats kept blazing away behind, the vessels perceptibly flinching from the recoil. Each shell weighed more than 200 lbs., and made a report that was piercing and painful. The crews of the mortar-boats defended themselves against it by fortifying their ears with cotton, and wearing woollen flaps on either side of their caps; but notwithstanding all their precautions, many of them were partially deaf for days afterwards.

Suddenly, when the bombardment had continued for about three hours, a lurid pillar of flame and smoke leaped up into the air, and, bursting abroad, cast a shower of huge black fragments far and wide. A shell had found the large magazine in the centre of the principal island. Far over sea and land went the report, and our seamen, crowded in the tops, the cross-trees, and out upon the yards, cheered vociferously. At noon another explosion took place, fires broke out on every side, and crash followed crash. The Russian gunners began to lose heart; they could not get the range of those pestilent badgers, pelters, weasels, pinchers, biters, snappers, which tormented them, and their fire slackened for some hours. All through the afternoon the attacking force kept up a rolling fire, while the defenders replied at long and lazy intervals.

Grand as was the spectacle during the day, at night it approached the sublime. Soon after dark a squadron of cutters and launches from the ships, each fitted with a rocket tube, went in and let off their fireworks. "It was a splendid sight," says the eye-witness just quoted, "to see the curved flight of the rockets, five or six sometimes under way together, chasing and crossing each other as they flew. The rockets are some of 12, others of 24 lbs. weight, and contain a small shell, which explodes when the rocket reaches its destination, and flames and *disjecta membra* of smashed properties could sometimes be seen as they fell among the buildings of the enemy. All this time little bright stars might be seen, careering in bold curvilinear orbits over our heads. These were shells from the mortar-boats and the French battery, which never rested day or night."

All Thursday and Friday the bombardment continued, but on Saturday morning the small craft were withdrawn, and the operations ended. The guns of the allies hurled 1000 tons of balls and shells into an area of three square miles, and destroyed several hundred acres of buildings — barracks, and magazines filled with stores — belonging to the Russian Government. The loss of life was never known; the Russians declared they had only one man killed, and it is certain that on board the allied fleet no one was killed, and only a few were wounded. If Admiral Dundas intended no more than to make a demonstration to satisfy the public, and to do the enemy as much harm as could be done without loss or damage to himself, his success was complete.

The siege of Sebastopol was now drawing to a close. In the hope of forcing the allies to raise the siege, Prince Gortschakoff made an attack in force on the French position at Traktir Bridge on the Tchernaya (August 16), but was repulsed with great loss. This battle gave the Sardinians, under Della Marmora, an opportunity of meeting the soldiers of the Czar. The sixth and last bombardment began at dawn on the 5th September, and continued almost without intermission, till the 8th, when the signal was given for the assault. "At five minutes before twelve o'clock," says Dr. Russell, "the French, like a swarm of bees, issued from their trenches close to the doomed Malakoff, scrambled up its face, and were through its embrasures in the twinkling of an eye. They crossed the seven mètres of ground which separated them from the enemy at a few bounds; they drifted lightly and quickly as autumn leaves before the wind, battalion after battalion, into the embrasures; and in a minute or two after the head of their column issued from the ditch, the tricolour was floating over the Korniloff bastion. The musketry was very feeble at first—indeed, our allies took the Russians by surprise; but they soon recovered themselves, and from twelve o'clock till past seven in the evening, the French had to meet and repulse the repeated attempts of the enemy to regain the work, when, weary of the slaughter of his men, who lay in thousands over the exterior of the works, and despairing of success, the Muscovite general withdrew his exhausted legions. As soon as the tricolour was observed waving, through the smoke and dust, over the parapet of the Malakoff, four rockets were sent up from Chapman's battery, as a signal for our assault upon the Redan."

In this we were not so successful. Instead of sending up the Highlanders or the marines, both of whom volunteered and were refused, General Simpson entrusted the matter to his raw recruits, men who had spent their few days in camp in listening to long stories about what a dreadful place the Redan was, all undermined and stuffed full of powder. When the assault was made, there were not above 150 Russians in the place, and the storming party ran along the open space and were over the crest of the parapet with no great loss, but unfortunately, instead of following their officers and rushing on with the charged bayonet, they commenced independent file-firing. The moment of victory passed away; the Russian supports came up in vast numbers, drove the remnant of the 500 stormers over the parapet, recovered the guns, turned them on the British supports, who were standing irresolute between the trenches and the fort, and mowed them down in scores. The slaughter was dreadful: 29 officers killed and 125 wounded, with 356 non-commissioned officers and men killed and 1762 wounded. It was a great misfortune, independently of the loss of life, for if the Redan had been taken simultaneously with the Malakoff, the Russian army must have capitulated or been destroyed.

The Highlanders were brought up to the front to storm the place next morning, but that night Corporal John Ross of the engineers, humanely going out to look after some wounded comrades, observed the absence of the Russian outpost, crept cautiously forward, climbed the slope, and entered the Redan. The post was vacant, and returning to the trenches he reported that the Russians had fled. It was true. Without blare of bugle or tuck of drum they had filed over to the north side by the bridge of boats. Their retreat was followed by the explosion of forts, the burning of barracks, palaces, theatres, arsenals, stores, and the scuttling of all the ships in the harbour.

Sebastopol had fallen, and the war was virtually over, but all winter the armies lay inactive, facing each other beside the ruins for which they had so long contended. The allied fleets resolved to operate against all the sea-coast places in the Crimea still held by the Russians. They began with Kinburn, a fortress occupying a sandy spit of land at the mouth of the Dnieper, opposite to Oszakoff. Kinburn was a strong casemated fort, armed with 70 heavy guns, and supported by two well-made earthworks, each armed with ten guns. The troops were landed on the 15th, and on the 17th October, at nine in the morning, the attack was commenced. The three French floating batteries — the precursors of the present race of ironclads—were in line about 600 yards from the fort, and engaged the casemates. The mortar vessels anchored at a distance of 2800 yards. The gunboats attacked the earthworks. The Russians, exposed to a continuous shower of iron, replied sullenly at intervals. About eleven a fire broke out in their barracks. The flames spread from one end of the fort to the other. The heat and smoke drove the enemy from their guns, and explosions of ammunition were from time to time heard above all the din of the bombardment. At a quarter-past eleven the Russian ensign was shot away, and was not rehoisted.

At this crisis the ships of the line, headed by the *Royal Albert*, the stately flagship of the commander-in-chief, attacked the forts on the southern side from a distance of 1200 yards, while the steam frigates, led by Sir Houston Stewart and

Admiral Pellion, the seconds in command, attacked the northern face. It was a splendid sight to see the allies advancing in line under steam, and still more splendid to see the three-deckers veering round to deliver their fire, their jibs set to bring their guns to bear. The cannonade was deafening, and the fire in the Russian barracks, fed by constant bombs and rockets, grew terrible in its proportions.

Bravely did the Russians defend their post, but their guns were silenced one by one, and at length a man waved a white flag from the ramparts. As by magic the firing ceased, boats pulled to the shore, and Major-general Kokonovitch delivered his sword to Sir Houston Stewart and General Bazaine. Our loss was only two seamen wounded. The Russians had 43 killed, 114 wounded, and 1200 prisoners. A vast quantity of warlike stores, provisions, and guns, was the prize of the conquerors. Oszakoff was blown up by the Russians themselves, and the purposes of the expedition were completed by Sir Houston Stewart, who sailed up the Bog, and silenced a battery on its banks.

It was intended to operate against Simpheropol and other places, but the setting in of winter caused all further proceedings to be deferred to the spring. In the meanwhile Austria used her influence to induce Russia to accept terms of peace, and, after long negotiations, the treaty was signed at Paris, on the 30th March, 1856, amid the thunder of cannon and the rejoicings of all.

On a review of the Russian war, it will be found that what was positively effected by our navy was scarcely commensurate with its great reputation. This was largely due to the fact that the Russian fleet persistently declined an encounter on the open sea—which in itself was homage sufficient to our invincibility on our own element. Still, when looked at more closely, the services of the navy will be seen to have been not unimportant. Though our ships did not dare to attack Cronstadt, and, for obvious reasons, failed before Sebastopol, they captured Bomarsund and Kinburn, and battered Odessa and Sveaborg. Finally, the Baltic and Black Seas, which before the war were little more than Russian lakes, were swept clear of the Russian flag; and one Russian fleet dared not venture from behind stone fortresses in the shallow waters of Cronstadt, while another Russian fleet was sunk in the harbour of Sebastopol.

The conduct of the naval brigade on shore showed that the seamen of the fleet were still animated by all their ancient dash and daring. To take one example among many: on the 26th October, a conspicuous act of gallantry was performed by Mr. N. Hewitt, a young man, acting mate of the *Beagle*. It was on that day that the Russians made a sortie on the division of Sir de Lacy Evans. Mr. Hewitt was in charge of a Lancaster gun in that part of the field, and when the enemy were within 300 yards of the battery, he received an order to spike the gun and retreat. But Mr. Hewitt would not believe, or affected not to believe, that the order came from Captain Lushington, and with the aid of his blue-jackets and some soldiers, he slewed the gun round, blew away the parapet, and opened so effective a fire on the advancing column of Russians, that they gave way and retreated. Mr. Hewitt was promoted to a lieutenancy, and received the Victoria Cross.

CHAPTER XV.

PERSIA—CHINA—1856-1858.

Bushire—Khooshab—Mahommerah and Ahwaz—Fatshan Creek—Canton—
The Peiho Forts.

BEFORE the Russian War was over, Britain was embroiled with Persia, which endeavoured to infringe the Convention of 1853, by which Herat, a city and state on the borders of Khorassan and Afghanistan, so situated as to command the approaches to India through the Hindoo Koosh, was declared independent. A squadron, under Admiral Leeke, appeared before Bushire on the 7th December, 1856, and on the 10th the place fell before a cannonade. Then came Sir James Outram, with Stalker and Havelock. The decisive battle of the campaign took place at Khooshab, on the 8th February, 1857. The Persians attempted a midnight surprise, but failed, and when day broke their army was seen drawn up in line, with cavalry on both flanks, their right resting on the village of Khooshab, and their left on a hamlet with a round fortalice. In front of their centre were two rising mounds, where they posted their guns. Their right front and flank were protected by deep nullahs, lined with skirmishers. Their numbers were judged at 6000 foot and 2000 horse. The British army was drawn up in two general lines; the front line consisting of the 78th Highlanders, 26th Native Infantry, 2d Light Infantry, and 4th Bombay Rifles; the second line, of the 64th, 20th Native Infantry, and the Belooch battalion. The Persian artillery was soon silenced by ours, which advanced to close action, and the Persian cavalry was swept from the field by a brilliant charge of the 3d Bombay Light Cavalry, accompanied by

Blake's Horse Artillery. The British infantry, meanwhile, was advancing rapidly to the attack, but just as they were getting into action, the Persian infantry lost heart, broke, and fled, leaving 700 dead on the field, and casting away everything to accelerate their flight. Only three Persian battalions on the right made any stand. The British loss was only 19 killed and 64 wounded.

Two officers gained the Victoria Cross at Khooshab, Lieutenants Moore and Malcolmson of the 3d Bombay Light Cavalry. Lieutenant Moore was first in among the enemy. His horse sprang into the centre of their square, but instantly fell dead, crushing the rider, and breaking his sword. The Persians pressed around Moore, who endeavoured to force a way through the throng with his broken weapon; they would have bayoneted him, had not Lieutenant Malcolmson ridden up to his assistance, cut down the boldest of his assailants, and, giving him a stirrup, carried him out of the throng.

The capture of Mahommerah and Ahwaz taught Persia the folly of continuing the contest, and on the 2d May, 1857, a treaty was signed at Bagdad, by which the Shah agreed to evacuate Herat.

We were at this time at war with China also—our second war with the Celestial Empire. The Chinese forgot the lesson they received in 1842, and commenced a series of aggressive acts on British subjects. Their insolence culminated in the seizure of the *Arrow*, a lorcha or small native ship flying the British flag, which was boarded in the Canton river by the Chinese police, who, in search of a pirate, arrested the crew. Sir John Bowring, the English minister at Hong-Kong, demanded an apology, which Commissioner Yeh of Canton did not see fit to give. The British navy was therefore called upon to act, and Sir Michael Seymour, the admiral commanding-in-chief, sailed up the Bocca Tigris, destroyed several war-junks, captured the Bogue forts, mounting 200 guns, and on the 12th January, 1857, took possession of the suburbs of Canton, and put a stop to all native trade on the river. Commissioner Yeh now began to offer rewards for the heads of the barbarians, but this did not prevent the "barbarians" from attacking the Chinese fleet—80 war-junks, powerfully armed and manned by 6000 picked braves, and judiciously drawn up across the Fatshan creek. The attack was made on the 1st June by Admiral Seymour in person, assisted by Commodores Elliot and Keppel, with 11 gun-boats and 50 or 60 ships' boats. The Chinese fought bravely, and nearly all the boats in Commodore Keppel's squadron were lost or disabled; but when the British got to close quarters, the Chinese thought only of making their escape, and, pouring in a broadside of grape, which generally went over the heads of the boarders, leaped overboard on the other side, and swam towards the shore. Of the whole fleet only three or four junks escaped destruction.

During the first burst of the Indian Mutiny operations languished, but reinforcements gradually arrived from England, and the free admission of British subjects to Canton being refused, the fleet bombarded the town on the 28th December. Next day the troops advanced to the attack. These consisted of marines, artillery, engineers, the 59th and the 38th Madras Native Infantry, under General Van Straubenzee, the British naval brigade, 1829 strong (formed in three divisions under Captains Sir R. M'Clure, Key, and Stewart), under Admiral Seymour, and the French naval brigade, 950 strong, under Admiral de Grenouilly. As the troops advanced to the attack, the ships ceased firing, and the Chinese on the walls opened with their matchlocks. "Some minutes before the time," says Mr. Wingrove Cooke, "the French advanced, and the English could not be kept back. They had crossed the ditch, and were clustered under the walls before the scaling ladders could be brought up. A young Frenchman had taken off his shoes and gaiters, and was trying to work himself up to the southern angle of the bastion, aided by Major Luard (of the 59th), who was propping him up with the muzzle of the Frenchman's own firelock, when a ladder was placed, and Luard, leaping on it, stood first upon the wall. He was followed by a Frenchman, the bandmaster of the 59th, and Colonel Hope Graham (also of the 59th). At the same time, Stuart, of the engineers, was balancing in air on a breaking ladder at the north side of the bastion; but though he sprang to another, two or three Frenchmen got up before him. Here, also, Corporal Perkins and Daniel Donovan, volunteer sappers, pushing on with the French, were among the first over the wall. Meantime the Chinese had been tumbling down all sorts of missiles; but when the allies were once upon the walls, the great body of them retired. They poured down into the city, and fired from the streets; they dodged behind the buildings on the ramparts, and thence took aim with their cumbrous matchlocks. A few single encounters occurred, and Major Luard's revolver disposed of one lingerer; but the allies generally fired right and left, and pushed on to the right, so as to sweep the wall towards the hill. Helter-skelter they went, driving the Tartars close into the town and before them along the wall, until, some hundred yards in front, they came upon Captain Fellowes and his blue-jackets, who were just accomplishing another escalade."

Anxious to prevent the destruction of life, the allied chiefs would not allow the troops to descend into the streets, but the Chinese still continuing obstinate, this measure had at length to be adopted (January 5, 1858). Commissioner Yeh, a very fat man, with black teeth and a short pigtail, was taken by Captain Cooper Key, as he was trying to escape in a porter's dress, and sent to Calcutta. A portion of the fleet, accompanied by a French squadron, now sailed to the Peiho, and (May 20) the forts at the mouth of the river were taken with little loss. From thence the gunboats, having on board Lord Elgin and Baron Gros, the plenipotentiaries of England and France, sailed up to Tientsin, where (June 26) a treaty was signed opening to our trade five new ports, and allowing British subjects with passports to visit any part of the interior.

CHAPTER XVI.

THE CONQUEST OF INDIA—1600-1857.

ON the last day of 1600, a charter was granted by Queen Elizabeth to a number of London merchants, under the title of "The Governor and Company of Merchants of London trading to the East Indies." Ships were sent out to Java and Sumatra, and returned laden with calicoes, silks, indigo, and spices. In a few years it was determined to make settlements in Hindostan itself, and, about 1612, permission was obtained from the native princes to establish factories at Surat, Ahmedabad, Cambay, and Gogo. The number of these factories was gradually augmented; Madras dates from 1640, Calcutta from 1645, and Bombay, which came to England with the Portuguese Queen of Charles II., from 1665.

In 1662, Charles II. granted the East India Company permission "to make war and peace on the native princes"—a privilege which was not suffered to lie idle, especially after the death of the famous Aurungzebe (1707), when the great Mogul Empire rapidly fell to pieces. The French were at this time our rivals in India, and long and severe was the struggle between the two European nations, but the genius and fortune of Clive at length gained the ascendancy. In his memorable capture and defence of Arcot (1751), he broke the spell of French invincibility, and laid the foundation of British supremacy in the East; and by the battle of Plassey (23d June, 1757), in which, with 3100 troops, of whom only 800 were British, he defeated the vast army, 70,000 strong, of Surajah Dowlah—the same who the year before cast 146 Englishmen into the Black Hole of Calcutta —he made the Company masters of Bengal, as well as Behar and

Orissa. The Company was confirmed in these possessions by the Mogul Emperor, Shah Alum, who after the battle of Buxar (1764) sought the protection of the British.

Warren Hastings (1773–85) was the first Governor-general of India appointed under the Regulating Act. Enraged at not receiving help from the British against the Mahrattas, and instigated by the French, Hyder Ali, the powerful Mussulman Sultan of Mysore, invaded the Carnatic with 100,000 men. While trying to join Sir Hector Munro at Conjeveram, Colonel Baillie was attacked by the whole Mysore army, and defeated, chiefly through the blowing-up of the powder-waggons. This disaster was followed by the fall of Arcot (November 3, 1780). Sir Eyre Coote, being sent to undertake the management of the war, defeated Hyder at Porto Novo, and besieged the Marquis de Bussy in Cuddalore (1781). Five naval actions were fought (1782–83) between the French and English fleets under Suffrein and Hughes; and Mangalore was defended (1784) by Colonel Campbell ("with a valour seldom equalled and never surpassed") against all the troops of Tippoo, whose father, Hyder, had died in 1782. Peace was made between England and France, and Tippoo found it necessary to follow the example.

The Marquis Cornwallis (1786–93) succeeded Warren Hastings. Another war broke out with Mysore, Tippoo having invaded Travancore, then under British protection. Cornwallis took the field himself, captured Bangalore, and dictated the terms of peace under the walls of Seringapatam (1793), compelling Tippoo to cede half his dominions.

The administration of Sir John Shore (1793–98) was not marked by any memorable event.

The Marquis Wellesley (1798–1805) soon found himself compelled to declare war against Tippoo, who was intriguing both with the French and with the native princes. He determined to strike a decisive blow. Seringapatam was besieged. The assault took place on the 4th May, 1799. On went Sir David Baird with the stormers of the 12th, 33d, 73d, and 74th, and in seven minutes the British flag floated on the breach. Tippoo was shot through the head by a soldier who sought to rob him of his jewelled sword-belt, and thus fell the great Mahommedan kingdom of Mysore.

The Mahrattas were now the most powerful native people in India, and our next war was with them. General Lake marched with a portion of the Bengal army towards Delhi; while General Wellesley—the future Duke of Wellington—crossed the Godavery in the south. Wellesley met the Mahrattas under Scindia at the village of Assaye, in the north-west corner of the Deccan (September 21, 1803), and with the 74th and 78th Highlanders, and five battalions of Sepoys, routed the immense hordes opposed to him. The blow was followed up at Argaum (November 29). General Lake was equally successful in the north. Storming the strong fortress of Allyghur (August 29th), he advanced and routed the Mahrattas at Delhi (September 11th), and finally broke the power of Scindia at Leswaree (November 1st), while General Fraser, with the 76th and other troops, routed Holkar at Deeg (November 13th), taking 87 cannon, all of the finest European fabric. The Mahratta war added considerably to the territory of the Company.

With the exception of the siege of Bhurtpore (1805), nothing of much importance occurred until the administration of the Marquis of Hastings (1813–23), who waged war with the Ghoorkas, Pindarees, and Mahrattas. The Ghoorkas were subdued at Mukwanpore by General Ochterlony (1816) with the 24th, 66th, and 87th; the Pindarees—a race of mounted freebooters, who roamed the country in large bands of from two to three thousand—were cut off in detail (1817); the Mahrattas were defeated at Nagpore (1817), Madeidpore, and Corregaum (1818); and, finally, Sir John Malcolm captured Aseerghur (1819), "the Gibraltar of the East," which, from its position, commands the great passes of the Deccan into Hindostan.

Earl Amherst's administration was marked by the first Burmese war, and the capture of Bhurtpore (1826), in Northern Bengal, by Lord Combermere. The loss of the besiegers was 565, and of the defenders, the warlike Jauts, more than 4000. The British regiments at Bhurtpore were the 14th, 59th, and 16th Lancers.

There was peace in India until the disastrous Afghan war (1839–42), entered into by Lord Auckland, who espoused the cause of Shah Soojah, because Dost Mohammed was believed to be under Russian influence. An army of 19,350 men, under Sir John Keane, marched northward through the passes on the western bank of the Indus, took possession of Candahar (May 4, 1839), stormed Ghuznee (July 23), and entered Cabul (August 7). The surrender of Dost Mohammed seemed to complete the conquest of the country; but the Dost's son, Akbar, was actively at work in secret. At the beginning of winter, when help was impossible from India, the outbreak took place at Cabul (November 2, 1841), where the inhabitants rose and murdered Sir Alexander Burnes, the political agent, his brother, and Lieutenant Broadfoot. Sir William Macnaghten was treacherously shot dead (December 23) by the Dost's son Akbar, by whom he had been invited to a conference. Then (January 6, 1842) began the fatal retreat. Out of a host of 16,000, or, including women and children, 26,000, with the exception of 70 who were made prisoners, only one man (Dr. Brydon) escaped to carry the dismal tidings to General Sale, who still held Jellalabad, as Nott did Candahar. All the rest perished of cold, or by the bullets of the long jezails of the Afghans. At length came the spring, and the Army of Retribution, under General Pollock, who forced the Khyber Pass, joined Sale at Jellalabad, and entered Cabul (September 15, 1842), where Pollock was joined by Nott from Candahar. Akbar delivered up his captives; and after burning the grand bazaar at Cabul, where Sir William Macnaghten's head had been exposed, and inflicting other punishments on the Afghans, the British returned to India. Shah Soojah having met his death, Dost Mohammed again mounted the throne after all. The British regiments engaged at Cabul were the 3d Light Dragoons, 9th, 13th, 31st, 40th, and 41st. The 13th, in particular, gained immortal renown by the heroic defence of Jellalabad, from October to April, against all the hosts of Akbar.

The Earl of Ellenborough (1842-44) was now Governor-general. It was he who sent the Army of Retribution to Cabul. Other two wars occurred during his short administration—the Conquest of Scinde and the Gwalior Campaign. The Ameers of Scinde fancied, from the disasters in Afghanistan, that the British power was on the wane; and Sir Charles Napier was ordered to take the field. He met the enemy at Meeanee, (February 17, 1843) near Hyderabad, 36,000 strong, all Beloochee mercenaries, fierce and warlike. Napier's little army numbered but 2600 fit for duty, yet he did not hesitate to attack them, and after a long and obstinate contest completely routed them, with the loss of 6000. Another victory at Dubba (March 24th), also near Hyderabad, finished the war, and Scinde was annexed to the Company's empire. The 22d were the heroes of this war; they bear "Meeanee," "Hyderabad," and "Scinde" on their colours. Gwalior was at this time rent by factions, insurrections, plots, conspiracies, and assassinations; and in the interest of tranquillity the British interfered. The enemy were found drawn up (December 29, 1843) at the village of Maharajpore—18,000 infantry and cavalry, and 100 guns. The British and Sepoys, under Sir Hugh Gough, were 14,000 strong and 40 guns. The Mahrattas fought with their usual bravery, but after losing their guns, and more than 4000 of their numbers, they dispersed and fled. Neither was the British loss light: 106 killed and 684 wounded. Another, though smaller, victory was won the same day at Punniar by General Grey, and the war was at an end. The 39th, "*Primus in Indis*"—which fought at Plassey nearly a century before—and the 40th, bear "Maharajpore" on their colours.

Lord Ellenborough was recalled by the East India directors, who thought his policy too warlike, and Sir Henry Hardinge (1844-48) was sent out to take his place; but scarcely had the new governor-general commenced his duties when he was called on to do battle with the Sikhs of the Punjaub. Not only were the Sikhs the bravest people in India, but they were highly disciplined, and possessed of a military organisation directed and controlled by French officers. Thinking more of Cabul than of Scinde or Gwalior, and indulging themselves with the idea of the conquest of British India, the Sikhs crossed the Sutlej. The war was short and sharp. Sir Hugh Gough repulsed the invaders at Moodkee (December 18, 1845), and stormed the rectangular camp at Ferozeshah (December 22). Then came a pause, which the Sikhs misinterpreted. Crossing the Sutlej they threatened Loodiana, but at Aliwal (January 28, 1846) they were met by Sir Harry Smith, who defeated them with great loss. The crowning battle of the war was fought at Sobraon (February 10, 1846) on the Sutlej, where the Sikhs had strongly entrenched themselves. The battle began at 6 A.M. After a three hours cannonade, the infantry (10th, 53d, 80th, and four regiments of Sepoys) advanced in line, leaped the ditch, swarmed up the walls, and jumping down engaged the Sikhs in their own camp, where for two hours the battle ebbed and flowed with the fortune of the combatants. However often they were checked, the British returned to the charge, and in the end discipline prevailed. The camp was won, and the

Sikhs crowded the narrow bridge which led over to their reserve camp on the other side of the Sutlej. Many were drowned, many were struck down by the British shot, and in the battle or the retreat more than a third of the Sikh army perished. A few days later the British took possession of Lahore. In the four battles the British had 1351 killed and 4885 wounded. The 3d, 9th and 16th Light Dragoons, 9th, 10th, 29th, 31st, 50th, 53d, 62d, and 80th, were the British regiments engaged in the first Sikh war.

The Marquis of Dalhousie (1848–55) succeeded Sir Henry Hardinge. A second Sikh war broke out in 1848. Lord Gough allowed himself to be drawn into a battle at Chillianwalla (January 13, 1849) when late in the evening; the 22d, rushing breathlessly on the guns, were almost annihilated, and the 14th Light Dragoons, thrown into disorder by a voice shouting 'Threes about!' fled, panic-struck, before a body of bhang-maddened Ghorchurras. In the end, however, the Sikhs retreated, and the British remained masters of the field. Our loss was terribly severe: 757 killed, and 1512 wounded. The surrender of Moultan (January 21) released General Whish, who reinforced Lord Gough. The enemy, 60,000 strong, including 1500 Afghan horse, and 59 guns, were met at Goojerat (February 21). Lord Gough halted his infantry out of range, and sent forward his artillery. The terrific fire of the British guns compelled the enemy to fall back. The infantry were then deployed and ordered to advance, the heavy guns and field batteries keeping pace with them, and unlimbering at successive points. The enemy were completely defeated, and their camp and baggage and 53 guns were captured. Then, at the proper moment, the cavalry was launched forward in pursuit. It was a total rout. The Sikhs dispersed over the country, and threw away their arms and accoutrements, in the hope that they might be taken for peasants or camp followers. The Afghans were pursued to Peshawur. By a proclamation, dated March 30, 1849, the Punjaub was annexed to the British Empire in India. The Marquis of Dalhousie pursued a vigorous policy of annexation, and added no less than four kingdoms to the empire—the Punjaub, Pegu, Nagpore, and Oude.

CHAPTER XVII.

THE INDIAN MUTINY—1857-1859.

Siege of Delhi—Massacre of Cawnpore—Defence of Lucknow—Relief of Lucknow by Sir Henry Havelock—Rescue of Lucknow by Sir Colin Campbell—Siege of Lucknow—Bareilly—Victorious march of Sir Hugh Rose—Capture of Jhansi and Gwalior.

THE Mutiny of the Sepoys burst upon the English in India like a thunderbolt. Everything seemed to be in the most perfect state of repose. The Marquis of Dalhousie, on resigning the reins of power to Viscount Canning, in 1856, penned a glowing picture of the country, describing its prosperity and peace. But it was only the treacherous calm before the storm. While the English in India were taking steps to render homage to Clive, "the Daring in War," on the hundredth anniversary of the battle of Plassey, the Mahommedans and some of the Hindus were preparing to celebrate the anniversary in a different fashion. A prophecy was current among them, said to have been made by a Punjaub fakir, or mendicant devotee, seven hundred years before, to the effect that after various dynasties of Mahommedans had held sway, the Christians should rule India for one hundred years; that the Christians would then be expelled, and the true believers resume their former position. Whether they were moved by this prophecy, or by the wholesale annexations of the Marquis of Dalhousie; whether they were inspired by the religious zeal which the proclamation of the Shah-in-Shah, the head of the faithful in the East, appealing to them to exterminate the Feringhees, was so well calculated to produce, or were merely stung by the snubs which General Anson, the commander-in-chief, levelled at caste; whether they were moved by a patriotic dislike of the foreigner, or were actuated by no higher motive than the lust of power, and a desire to tax and oppress their countrymen at their own pleasure, the ringleaders found an apt instrument in the religious prejudices of the Hindu and Mahommedan soldiery in the East India Company's service, and the introduction of the so-called greased cartridges for the new Enfield rifle, which was put into the hands of the Sepoys without a word of explanation or precaution. Now, this was a very serious matter for the Sepoys. In the East the fat of pigs and cows is regarded in a very peculiar light. The pig is as much held in abhorrence by the Mahommedans, as the cow is venerated by the Hindus; to touch the former with the lips is defilement to the one, and to touch the latter is sacrilege to the other. The religious feelings are different, but the results are the same. It was not difficult to persuade the Sepoys that the introduction of the so-called greased cartridges was part of a long-cherished design of the hated Feringhees to threaten purity of caste, to break down all religious distinctions, and convert them forcibly to Christianity. Such things had been done in India before, and why not again?

Intelligent observers among the English in India were, however, not altogether easy in their minds. The transmission of the chupatty, or flat cake, from station to station and from hand to hand, boded no good. During the early days of 1857 murmurs were heard at Dumdum, a great artillery arsenal six miles from Calcutta. Matters came to a crisis at Berhampore, where the 19th Native Infantry refused to make use of the cartridges served out to them, though the same which they had been long accustomed to use. Expostulation was of no avail, and at a general parade of the garrison (February 25), Colonel Mitchell so arranged matters that the refractory regiment found itself completely commanded by the loaded guns of a battery, supported by a battalion of Europeans. Ordered to ground arms, they were marched as disarmed prisoners to Berhampore, where (April 3) they were disbanded and turned adrift to spread their grievances through the upper provinces. Nearer and nearer the catastrophe was approaching. At Barrackpore, a private of the 34th Native Infantry, stationed there, named Mangul Pandy, inflamed with bhang and religious zeal, loaded his musket and drew his sword, and staggered about in front of the lines, uttering seditious cries (March 29). Lieutenant Baugh, adjutant, and Sergeant-major Hewson attempted to seize and disarm the fanatic, who in the struggle wounded them both, while the quarter-guard looked passively on. Mangul Pandy and the native officer of the guard were hanged next day, and that wing of the regiment was at once disbanded. The Oude Irregular Infantry were the next to mutiny, but Sir Henry Lawrence turned a battery of guns upon them, and they fled in disorder. Events were now fast ripening. At Meerut 90 sowars (*i.e.*, horsemen) of the 3d Light Cavalry were ordered out for carbine-practice with the new cartridges, and 85 who refused to use them were tried by court-martial, and sentenced to ten years' imprisonment. The sentence was read aloud at the general parade on Saturday, the 9th May, and then they were marched off to gaol. Next day (Sunday, May 10), while the Europeans were at church, the 11th and 20th regiments of Native Infantry rose tumultuously in their cantonments. The European officers rushed from church, seized their weapons, and hurried to the parade-ground, in the hope of pacifying them. While haranguing the 20th regiment, Colonel Finnis was shot through the back and cut to pieces. It was the signal for the outpouring of blood. Thirty other European officers were butchered, and their houses and bungalows given to the flames. The gaols were broken open, and the 85 sowars of the 3d Light Cavalry, with a great crowd of miscreants and felons of every description, were released. Through the supineness of the commandant at Meerut, a brave but aged veteran, the British troops were not called out till most of the mutineers had made good their escape.

The mutineers went to Delhi, which now became the focus of the revolt. The aged pensioner there, the last Great Mogul and heir of the house of Timour, assumed the title of Emperor of India. The British were all brutally murdered. Unfortunately, though there was no British force in the place, Delhi was the principal depôt for military stores in India. The mutineers assailed the magazine. It was guarded by only nine Englishmen —Lieutenants Willoughby, Forrest, and Raynor, Conductors Buckley, Shaw, and Scully, Sub-conductor Crowe, and Sergeants Edward and Stewart. These brave men defended the place for some time—nine against thousands. When further defence was hopeless, Lieutenant Willoughby gave the order to fire the magazine. This was done by Conductor Scully, who lighted the trains in the most careful and methodical manner. The explosion took place immediately, hurling hundreds of the enemy into the air, or burying them in the ruins. Strange to say, most of the little band of defenders escaped alive, though much stunned, blackened, scorched, and burned. Willoughby and three others were afterwards murdered in a village on the road to Meerut. The brave Scully, who was much hurt, was killed by a sowar while trying to escape. Lieutenants Forrest and Raynor and Conductor Buckley reached Meerut in safety.

Fortunately it is not our task to follow the progress of the mutiny, and describe the dreadful scenes that were enacted at every British station. Erelong the North-West Provinces were in a flame of insurrection. Lucknow, Agra, Cawnpore, and many other places, were either seized by the rebels, or so beset by them that no British commander was able to assist his brother officers. But the prompt energy of Sir John Lawrence saved the Punjaub, and the Sepoys were disarmed at Lahore, Peshawur, and Mooltan. Not only so, but he made the greatest efforts to collect a force for the recovery of Delhi, the heart and soul of the rebellion. A small army, under Sir Henry Barnard, was assembled at Alleepore, a day's march from the Imperial City. Besides artillery and sappers and miners, it contained the whole, or portions, of the 9th Lancers, 6th Dragoon Guards, 60th Rifles, 75th, 1st and 2d Bengal Fusiliers (European), and a battalion of Goorkhas, the warlike race of Nepaul. But in all it amounted to scarce 3000 men. On the morning of the 8th June this force proceeded from Alleepore to Delhi. A three miles' march brought the British upon a body of mutineers, 3000 strong, intrenched in a good position, with 12 pieces of cannon. The British artillery was unable to cope with the heavier guns of the enemy, who, thanks to British training, were able to use them with great precision. There was only one thing to be done. "Charge, and carry those guns!" shouted Sir Henry Barnard. Forward rushed the 75th, under a storm of musketry, and drove the Sepoys in rout and terror to their next position. By 9 A.M. the Army of Retribution was in possession of the parade-ground and the cantonments, on the plateau two miles from Delhi. The British advanced position was a large strong brick house on the top of a high hill overlooking the city. Near this house three batteries were constructed, and played on Delhi day and night. The mutineers had also three batteries, which played night and day on the British camp.

Fighting before Delhi was almost of daily occurrence. The mutineers generally sallied out in the afternoon, with a couple of guns, some cavalry, and a strong force of infantry, and skirmished up over the rocky entangled ground towards the large brick house on Hindoo Rao's hill. They were invariably repulsed, but not without the loss of many brave men who could ill be spared. But reinforcements arrived under Brigadier Nicholson, raising the besieging force to 9700 men, 4600 of whom were British.

On the 4th September the long-expected siege-train arrived in camp; and, what was of almost equal consequence, the command passed into the hands of General Archdale Wilson, of the Bengal Artillery, who was seconded by several able officers, among whom was Colonel Baird Smith, of the Bengal Engineers, who had been called, early in July, to the defence by Sir H. Barnard. Colonel Baird Smith turned his attention to the sanitary condition of the camp, to the strengthening of the position, and the carrying out of the plan which he had matured and talked over with friends before he had any thought of being called to such an onerous place. Colonel Baird Smith had been wounded early in his career in the foot, and was a prey to those scourges of the camp, scurvy and dysentery; but he neither would nor could give himself the rest he needed, his tact and firmness being considered by his brothers-in-arms essential to secure resolute action.

Forty heavy guns, mortars, and howitzers opened on Delhi; nine 24-pounders battered the towers and curtain of the Cashmere gate; and on the 13th two breaches were reported practicable for escalade near the Cashmere and Water bastions.

The assault took place next morning (September 14, 1857). In his general order, General Wilson told the troops he need hardly remind them of "the cruel murder committed on their officers and comrades, their wives and children, to move them in the deadly struggle. No quarter should be given to the mutineers! At the same time, for the sake of humanity and the honour of the country they belong to, he called upon them to spare all women and children that may come in their way." The stormers were divided into five columns of about a thousand men each. The first, composed of detachments of the 75th, 1st Fusiliers, and 2d Punjaub Infantry, under Brigadier Nicholson, to storm the breach near the Cashmere bastion. The second, composed of Her Majesty's 4th and 8th, and the 2d Fusiliers, under Brigadier Jones, to carry the breach in the Water bastion. The third, composed of the 52d Oxford Light Infantry, the Kumaon battalion, and the 1st Punjaub Infantry, to blow open and enter by the Cashmere gate. The fourth, composed principally of Ghoorkas, the Guides, and the Cashmere contingent, under Major Reid, to enter by the Lahore gate. The fifth, consisting chiefly of native troops, formed the reserve.

At one o'clock in the morning the men turned out in silence, the batteries keeping up an incessant fire on the city, and noiselessly moved down to the trenches. There they lay down, awaiting the signal, which was to be given at daybreak, by the blowing in of the Cashmere gate. The party selected for this hazardous operation were Lieutenants Home and Salkeld, with Sergeants Smith and Carmichael, and Corporal Burgess of the Royal Sappers and Miners, Bugler Hawthorne of the 52d, to sound the advance, and a number of native sappers, covered by the fire of the 60th Rifles. By some mistake it was daylight before the party reached the spot. Lieutenant Home rushed through the outer barrier gate, and across the broken drawbridge, followed by four men, each carrying a bag of powder. Having arranged his bags, under a heavy fire directed through the open wicket, he jumped into the ditch. The firing party then followed, with four more bags of powder and a lighted port-fire. Lieutenant Salkeld, while endeavouring to fire the train, was shot through an arm and leg. He sank, but handed the port-fire to Sergeant Carmichael, who fell dead in the attempt to apply it. Corporal Burgess seized the fatal port-fire: he too fell mortally wounded, but not before he had successfully fired the train. The mighty gate was burst into fragments; Bugler Hawthorne sounded the advance, and with a cheer the 52d burst through the gateway and secured the barrier. Of all the explosion party only Sergeant Smith and Bugler Hawthorne lived to be rewarded with the Victoria Cross.

But Delhi was not won without a severe struggle, for the rebels knew they fought with halters round their necks. At the Cashmere breach the fight was long and fierce. The ladders were thrown down, and some of the stormers fell to rise no more. Others, less injured, tried again, and the groans of the wounded and the feeble cries of the dying were overpowered by the shouts and shrieks of the combatants. The first to mount the breach was Lieutenant Fitzgerald of the 75th; he fell dead on the spot. But others followed; the enemy gave way, the British were in at last, and the old colours were hoisted over the broken wall. The first and second columns now dashed along the circuit of the walls, but on nearing the Lahore gate they were stopped by a narrow street, barricaded, and swept by some pieces of artillery. The brave Brigadier Nicholson fell mortally wounded, with Major Jacob and Lieutenant Speke. By nightfall, however, the British were in possession of all the northern front of Delhi. Progress was made day by day. At dawn on the 16th the magazine was stormed by Colonel Deacon and the 61st, and so completely were the enemy taken by surprise that the artillerymen dropped their port-fires and ran, though the breach was commanded by six pieces crammed with grape. Next morning the bank was captured, and General Wilson was able to turn his guns on the palace. By the 21st, after seven days of continuous fighting, the place was swept of the enemy; as the rising sun gilded the domes and minarets of the city, the guns on the battlements thundered forth a royal salute, and in the palace of the Great Mogul, Wilson and his officers drained a goblet to the health of Her Majesty as Empress of India. The storming of Delhi cost us 1145 in killed, wounded, and missing. The king and his infamous sons, the chief instigators of the atrocities, had fled to Hoomayon's tomb, but were discovered by Captain Hodson of the Guides. In respect for his hoary hairs and his ninety years, Hodson spared the king, who was sent as a prisoner for life to Tongu in Pegu; but the sons he pistoled, and hung their naked bodies by the neck in the mayor's court, in presence of the people.

Most of the mutineers who escaped from Delhi fled to Lucknow, which was now the great centre of the rebellion. But, meanwhile, we must turn to Cawnpore, the scene of the blackest treachery and most revolting cruelty that ever disgraced human nature. Sir Hugh Wheeler was in command here, with some 300 English troops, and the 1st, 53d, and 56th Bengal Native

Infantry, and the 2d Native Cavalry. Besides the combatants, there were in the cantonments upwards of 700 European civilians—merchants, railway officials, shopkeepers, and women and children. At two o'clock on the morning of the 5th June, the native cavalry rose in a body, gave a great shout, mounted their horses, set fire to the bungalow of their quartermaster-sergeant, took possession of 36 elephants in the commissariat cattle-yard, and marched off to join the mutineers. The three infantry regiments followed. Burning bungalows were now seen in all directions, and an alarm-gun was fired to call the English population of the city into the safety of the entrenchment. This was a sort of stronghold which Wheeler had wisely constructed, so as not to be totally unprepared in the event of the mutiny spreading to the native troops under his command. It stood on the grand military parade, measuring about 200 yards in each direction, and enclosing two barrack hospitals and some other buildings. Its boundary was formed by a trench and a breastwork of earth, intended to be armed and defended in case of need.

Early next morning four regiments of mutineers were seen advancing to besiege the entrenchment. They had with them a battery of six guns, and about ten in the morning opened fire. Instantly, the bugle sounded within the entrenchment, and every man, from the highest officer to the lowest clerk or drummer, flew to arms, and took up the position assigned to him. For three weeks the little handful of Englishmen heroically defended themselves against the bloodthirsty horde, but famine began to press them sore. The treacherous Nana Sahib, a name which will be held in everlasting infamy, opened negotiations through a Mrs. Greenway, whom he had in his hands, and in an evil hour Wheeler consented to surrender, on promise of a safe-conduct to Allahabad. Besides a savage desire for vengeance on all who bore the British name, Nana Sahib's object was to obtain possession of three or four lacs of rupees which he knew to be in the entrenchments.

On the morning of the 27th June, the survivors marched down to the landing-place on the Ganges, to go down the river to Allahabad, but before the embarkation was completed, they were startled by the report of a masked battery of three guns. The dreadful truth now became evident; the false-hearted Nana had given orders for the slaughter of the hapless Europeans. Volley after volley of musketry was poured upon the unfortu-

nates, who were shot dead by the score. Those who tried to
swim away were picked off. A few boats rowed hastily across
the river, but there a body of rebels intercepted all escape. The
ruffians on both banks waded into the water, and seizing the
boats within reach sabred all those in them yet remaining alive.
The women, many of whom were wounded, were reserved for a
worse fate. Of the men only four succeeded in escaping to tell
the dreadful tale. The massacre completed, Nana Sahib caused
it to be proclaimed, by beat of tom-tom, throughout Cawnpore
and the surrounding district, that he had entirely conquered the
British, and that the period of their reign in India was completed.

Wheeler's critical position had been well known at Calcutta,
and the utmost exertions were made to relieve him. On the 7th
July—too late, alas!—Brigadier-general Sir Henry Havelock
set out for Allahabad with a small movable column of about
2000 men. It was a long march of 130 miles between Allahabad and Cawnpore, and the worst season of the year; the heat
was intense, and the monsoon having set in the rain fell in torrents, rendering the country one great morass. But Havelock's
little band was of the right heroic stuff, and pressed on in the face
of all difficulties to the relief of their unfortunate countrymen—
for as yet they were ignorant of their fate. They had their first
brush with the enemy at Futtehpore (July 12), a town about
midway in the line of march. Thinking they had only the advanced guard, under Major Renaud, to deal with, the Sepoys,
3500 strong and 12 guns, boldly maintained their position, a
very strong one, and one which might easily have been defended
against a force thrice as large as Havelock's. Their army was
posted in front of the city, where were many enclosures of great
strength, with high walls, villages, hillocks, and mango groves.
Havelock placed his eight guns in and near the main road (from
Allahabad to Cawnpore), protected by 100 riflemen of the 64th.
The infantry came up at deploying distance, while the small
body of cavalry—mounted volunteers—moved forward on the
flanks. The action was soon decided. The Enfield rifle had
only recently been issued to part of the army, and the rebels
knew little of the length and accuracy of its aim. When the
riflemen advanced and set to work, the Sepoys shrank back in
amazement. And when Captain Maude, dashing over the road
and through the swamps with his artillery, poured in his fire,

they could stand it no longer, and three guns were abandoned at once. Havelock steadily advanced; the Madras Fusiliers and the 78th Highlanders on the right, the 64th in the centre, and the 84th and Ferozepore regiment of Sikhs on the left. In their advance the soldiers had to wade up to the knees in mud and water, for the rains had covered the fields on either side of the road to the depth of a couple of feet. As the British pressed forward, the enemy's guns were captured one by one, and the rebels, driven from the hillocks, villages, enclosures, and mango groves, retreated through the streets of the town to a mile beyond, where they were put to final flight.

By this victory Havelock became master of Futtehpore, and parked 12 captive guns. The list of casualties was perhaps the lightest that ever accompanied such success. Not a single British soldier was hurt in the action, and of the native troops only 6 were killed and 3 wounded. But 12 British soldiers were struck down by the tropical sun, and never rose again. "To what is this astonishing effect to be attributed?" said Havelock in his general order of the following day. "To the fire of the British artillery, exceeding in rapidity and precision all the brigadier-general has witnessed in his not short career; to the power of the Enfield rifle in British hands; to British pluck—that good quality which has survived the revolution of the hour; and to the blessing of Almighty God on a most righteous cause—the cause of justice, humanity, truth, and the good government of India."

On the 14th July Havelock again pushed forward. Next day he dislodged a strong party of rebels from the village of Aong, four miles from Pandoo Nuddee. The bridge over this place was strongly defended, but the rebels were quickly driven off, and the passage secured.

When Nana Sahib heard that Havelock had defeated his troops at Pandoo Nuddee, and cleared the road to Cawnpore, he ordered the massacre of all the English women and children in his power; and between four in the afternoon and nine next morning, 206 persons, mostly women and children of gentle birth, were barbarously butchered, and their bodies thrown into a dry well, situated behind the building in which they had been confined.

Ignorant of this brutal massacre, Havelock pushed swiftly forward from Pandoo Nuddee, and at an early hour next morning (July 16) came in sight of the forces of Nana Sahib, who had taken up a position at the village of Aherwa, where the road to the cantonment branches off from the Grand Trunk Road to Cawnpore city. The position which the Nana occupied was very strong. His troops had cut up both roads and rendered them impassable, and his entrenchments were armed with seven heavy guns. Havelock, seeing that his men would be shot down in great numbers before the entrenchments could be carried by a direct attack in front, resolved on a flank movement on the enemy's left. After giving his exhausted troops two or three hours' rest in a mango grove, until the fierce heat of the sun should be somewhat abated, he gave the word to advance. The Madras Fusiliers led, followed by two guns; then came the 78th Highlanders, followed by the central battery of six guns; the 64th and 84th had two guns more in the rear; and the regiment of Ferozepore Sikhs closed the column. The flank movement was screened for a considerable distance by clumps of mango, but when the Nana at length discovered it, he sent forward a large body of horse, slewed round his guns, and opened fire with shot and shell. Havelock, however, quietly continued his advance until the enemy's left was completely turned. He then ordered his little column to form in line, and while the British guns opened fire upon the rebel batteries, the infantry advanced in direct échelon of regiments, covered by a wing of the Fusiliers as skirmishers.

Then came a series of operations in which were strikingly displayed the superb qualities of the British infantry. Villages were attacked and captured one after another by mere fragments of regiments. Excluding the native troops, the Madras Fusiliers were only about 350 strong, the 78th scarcely 300, the 64th not much more than 400, and the 85th about 150. The 64th, 84th, and Sikhs pushed forward on the left, and gallantly captured two guns planted at the village of Aherwa. On the right were three guns, strongly posted behind a lofty hamlet, well entrenched. Havelock directed the 78th to advance, "and never," he says, "have I witnessed conduct more admirable. They were led by Colonel Hamilton, and followed him with surpassing steadiness and gallantry under a heavy fire. As they approached the village they cheered, and charged with the bayonet, the pipers sounding the pibroch. Need I add that the enemy fled, the village was taken, and the guns captured." Havelock himself followed close behind when this charge was made, and after the 78th were halted in rear of the village, rode up to them and exclaimed, "Well done, 78th, you shall be my own regiment! Another charge like that will win the day!" After taking breath a few moments, the regiment pushed on at the double to another village across the road, and sent the enemy flying pell-mell. "I never saw anything so fine," wrote an eye-witness; "they went on with sloped arms, like a wall, till within a hundred yards, and not a shot was fired. At the word 'Charge!' they broke like a pack of eager hounds, and the village was taken in an instant."

The enemy were now completely driven from their original position, and in full retreat towards Cawnpore; but Nana Sahib made a last desperate effort to retrieve the fortunes of the day, by opening fire from a reserve 24-pounder which he had planted on the cantonment road, in such a position as to cause Havelock's people considerable loss. Under cover of the fire of this piece the rebel infantry once more rallied, while two large bodies of their horsemen rode forward over the plain and threatened the British infantry, which was again drawn up in line, front changed to rear. Captain Maude endeavoured to bring forward the guns to reply, but the artillery cattle were so tired they could not drag them onward to the desired position. The men were suffering, not only from the fire of the gun, but from the Sepoy musketry; the sun was setting, darkness was at hand, and there was not a moment to be lost. "That gun must be taken by the bayonet," cried Havelock, riding up; "no firing, 64th and 78th, and remember that I am with you." The enemy sent in round-shot, and, at 300 yards, grape; but Havelock cheered on the men, who rushed along the road, and never slackened their pace until they reached the gun and captured it. The honour of taking this gun was more especially due to the men of the 64th, whose position in the line placed them directly in front of it.

This last charge was irresistible; the enemy, losing all heart, emptied their muskets at random, and gave way in total rout. Their flight was accelerated by four of the British guns, which had by this time been got up the road. In their retreat the Sepoys blew up the magazine at Cawnpore, and then went on to Bithoor, where their leader, the arch-fiend Nana Sahib, had his palace.

Next day (July 17) the British entered Cawnpore. Imagine their grief, their indignation, and their rage, when they learned the hideous revelations of the slaughter-room and the well, when they came upon the mangled bodies of upwards of 200 women and children as yet scarcely cold. One letter says, "The house was alongside the Cawnpore hotel, where the Nana lived. I never was more horrified. I am not exaggerating when I tell you that the soles of my boots were more than covered with the blood of these poor wretched creatures. Portions of their dresses, collars, children's socks, and ladies' round hats lay about, saturated with blood; and in the sword-cuts on the wooden pillars in the room, long dark hair was sticking, carried by the edge of the weapon, and there hung in tresses—a most painful sight. I picked up a mutilated Prayer-book; it appeared to have been open at page 36 of the Litany, where I have little doubt these poor creatures sought and found consolation in that beautiful supplication; it is there sprinkled with blood." Another letter: "It is an actual and literal fact that the floor of the inner room was several inches deep in blood all over; it came over men's shoes as they stepped. Tresses of women's hair, children's shoes, and articles of female wear, broad hats and bonnets, books, and such like things, lay scattered all about the rooms. There were marks of bullets and sword-cuts on the wall—not high up, as if men had fought—but low down, and about the corners where the poor crouching creatures had been cut to pieces." Some of the officers, by carefully examining the walls, found scraps of writing in pencil or scratched in the plaster, such as, "Think of us," "Avenge us," "Oh, oh! my child, my child." Officers and men did think of the poor victims, and the thought nerved their arms in many a bloody charge, and gave their countenances a look of grim satisfaction when they saw mutineers blown by fifties from the mouths of the guns.

But it was no time to mourn over the past. Brigadier Inglis and his handful of British, with many women and children, were besieged in the Residency at Lucknow by the bloodthirsty horde of mutineers who held the city, and the fate of the defenders of Cawnpore might be theirs at any moment. As early as April there had been burning of bungalows and cartridge troubles in the cantonment of Lucknow. On the 3d May, as we have seen, the 3d Oude Infantry was broken into fragments. Sir Henry Lawrence, the chief authority, both military and civil, in Oude, took prompt measures to protect his fellow-countrymen from the storm which he saw was brewing. In particular, he fortified the English quarter of Lucknow, or the Residency as it was called, from that being the principal building in the centre; he brought up all the women and children and the sick into this part of the town, and stored it with six months' provision for a thousand persons, and plenty of ammunition. On the last two days of May he had the vexation to see most of the other native troops under his command march off to join their countrymen in mutiny, and during the month of June was informed that the mutineers, after reducing nearly all the districts of Oude, were approaching Lucknow as a hostile army. On the last day of June, hearing that 6000 of the rebels were encamped eight miles distant on the Fyzabad Road, Lawrence marched out with 700 men and 11 guns to give them battle. Misled, either by accident or design, by informants on the road, he fell into an ambush of the enemy at Chinhut. Nothing daunted, he manfully struggled against superior numbers, and confidently looked forward to victory; but at the critical moment the Oude artillerymen proved traitors, overturned their six guns into the ditches, cut the traces of their horses, and went over to the enemy. This defection rendered a retreat imperative; the retreat soon became a rout, and officers and men fell rapidly, to rise no more. A sad day that for the English in Lucknow, all of whom, soldiers and civilians, men, women, and children, now found themselves hotly besieged in their own quarters by tens of thousands of deadly foes thirsting for their blood. On the second day of the siege the gallant Lawrence was mortally wounded by a shell, and the command devolved on Brigadier Inglis.

"There does not stand recorded in the annals of war," wrote Viscount Canning, Governor-general of India, "an achievement more truly heroic than the defence of the Residency of Lucknow." For the long period of eighty-seven days, the English, both soldiers and civilians, endured hardships which only the dread of their wives and children meeting the fate of those of Cawnpore could have nerved them to undergo. It was no impregnable fort which sheltered them, but simply a few houses in a large garden, with a low wall on one side and an earthen parapet on the other; and these houses were in the middle of a large city, of which the buildings completely commanded them. Such was the Residency. Not an open spot of it but was liable to be swept by the musketry of the enemy, shot in security from the loopholes of the neighbouring houses; not a building but was exposed to their heavy guns, posted within fifty yards of the entrenchment. Nor were the mutineers despicable assailants, for they had learnt the art of war in all its branches from the English themselves. They advanced no less than twenty mines against the outposts, and if but one of these had completely succeeded, Lucknow would have been a second Cawnpore. All ranks and all classes, civilians, officers, and soldiers, bore an equally noble part in the defence. All descended into the mine, all handled the shovel for the interment of putrid bullocks—all, accoutred with musket and bayonet, relieved each other on sentry, without regard to distinctions of rank. Day and night all were on duty, either repelling real attacks, or standing prepared because of the false alarms which the enemy were constantly raising to harass the small and exhausted force. Sleep was only to be had by snatches. Fatigue, want of all proper sustenance, cholera, and small-pox, claimed their victims as well as the shot of the enemy; and as the force diminished, the difficulty of defending all the posts necessarily increased. Amongst the women and children the mortality was frightfully great; and by the end of the siege there were only 24 English gunners to work 30 guns! The 32d and 48th greatly distinguished themselves in the defence of Lucknow.

Havelock knew the desperate condition of Lucknow, and burned to rescue its defenders. But, first, it was necessary to chastise Nana Sahib, who had collected his routed forces, and was preparing to make a stand to defend his palace at Bithoor. The enemy were defeated with the loss of 16 guns, the powder magazine was blown up, and the Nana's palace at Bithoor reduced to ashes. Then, leaving Brigadier-general Neill, who had arrived from Allahabad with 227 men, in command at Cawnpore, with his small band of about 1500 Havelock commenced his heroic march to relieve Lucknow. As expedition was of the first importance, all baggage was left behind, and though it was the season of the monsoon, and the whole country was one vast morass, the army took the field without tents or covering of any kind, their only chance of shelter being the deserted and ruined hamlets on the road.

Five days were spent in the passage of the Ganges, which at Cawnpore varies from 500 to 2000 yards in width, with a rapid current, and it was the 25th July before Havelock found himself in Oude, and fairly on the road to Lucknow. On the 29th, he encountered the mutineers at Oonao and at Busserut Gunge, the latter a walled town with wet ditches. In the two battles, he was successful in capturing 19 guns; but, notwithstanding these brilliant victories, he reluctantly found himself compelled to make a retrograde movement towards Cawnpore. Besides officers and men killed and wounded in battle, numbers had been struck down by the sun; while others, through exposure to swamps and marshes, had been seized with cholera, diarrhœa, and dysentery. In short, Havelock was losing at the rate of 50 men a day, and his force was further weakened by the necessity of taking all the sick and wounded with him, as he could leave no men behind to keep open the communications with Cawnpore. He fell back to Mungulwar. While he was lying entrenched there, General Neill sent over a dozen men, and with this small reinforcement Havelock once more took the field. He met the enemy at their old position of Busserut Gunge, and drove them from the town with severe loss; but his force being again diminished by sickness and the sword, he was once more compelled to fall back. This time, he resolved to retire to Cawnpore, now threatened on all sides by the Dinapore mutineers, the Gwalior contingent, and Nana Sahib at Bithoor. The rebels, however, had no intention of permitting him to repass the Ganges quietly, and again assembled at Busserut Gunge. A third battle was fought near this place (August 12). The action was decided by a charge of the 78th, who rushed upon the enemy's redoubt and captured two out of three of the horse batteries with which it was armed. Lieutenant Crowe, of the 78th, the first man to climb into the redoubt, received the Victoria Cross. By evening the next day, the whole of Havelock's little army had crossed the Ganges from the Oude bank to the Cawnpore bank, by a bridge of boats and a boat equipage, which had been prepared by the greatest exertions. Nana Sahib had taken advantage of Havelock's absence in Oude to re-collect a motley assemblage of troops near Bithoor, for the purpose of re-establishing his power in that region, and again attacking Cawnpore. Accordingly, after giving his troops a couple of days' rest, Havelock marched out with about 1300 men, almost all that Neill and he could spare between them, and came upon the enemy, 4000 strong, and completely routed them (August 16). During the next month Havelock and his small force rested at Cawnpore, while reinforcements arrived from Calcutta. In their wonderful campaign of thirty-seven days, Havelock's little army had fought ten battles—in each case against an enemy vastly superior in numbers; and now, reduced by shot, shell, sabres, bullets, heat, fatigue, and disease, its fighting power was almost extinguished.

On the 16th September, Sir James Outram arrived at Cawnpore with reinforcements, consisting of the 5th Northumberland Fusiliers, the 90th Perthshire Light Infantry, detachments of the 64th, 78th, and 84th, and an artillery company,—yet only 1500 men in all. Sir James had been appointed to the military command of the Cawnpore and Dinapore divisions, and as such might have claimed the command of the expedition, but with a magnanimity worthy of "the Bayard of India," as Sir Charles Napier called him, he resolved not to rob Havelock of the glory of relieving Lucknow, and rode on his staff as a simple volunteer.

Havelock's army now mustered 2500 men of all arms, and was divided into two brigades. The first consisted of the 1st Madras Fusiliers, 5th Northumberland Fusiliers, 64th, 84th, Maude's bullock battery, and the Volunteer Cavalry, about 150 strong. The second brigade consisted of the 78th, 90th, Ferozepore Sikhs, Olphert's horse battery, and a body of Irregular Cavalry. At length everything was ready for another attempt to relieve Lucknow, where the garrison was still successfully holding out, though in the utmost straits; and the British army crossed the bridge of boats and once more took the field (Sept. 21). Driving the enemy from Mungulwar, where they had been busily fortifying their position for some weeks, the army pushed forward in column of route over the well-known scene of its former struggles at Busserut Gunge; forced the village of Bunnee, on the Sye; and about two in the afternoon of the 23d came in sight of the Alum Bagh, a country palace situated in a large walled park to the south-east of the city of Lucknow, and about four miles from the Residency. The rebels were strongly posted, their left occupying the enclosure of the Alum Bagh, and their right and centre some low hills. The British had to advance along the trunk road between morasses, and suffered much from the enemy's guns; but these once passed, the troops deployed into line to the right and left, and, charging through a sheet of water, quickly added another to their list of victories. The men passed the night on the ground they had won, and as they had been marching for three days under a perfect deluge of rain, irregularly fed and badly housed in villages, Havelock gave them one whole day's rest on the 24th.

At length came the 25th September, the eventful day when the beleagured garrison of Lucknow were to see the faces of those for whose arrival they had so long anxiously wished and fervently prayed. Havelock got his troops under arms early in the morning, resolved that before night he should clear the three or four miles between him and the Residency at all costs. Sir James Outram commanded the first brigade, which led, with all the artillery. The second brigade, under Havelock, followed in support. A canal skirts the south-east side of Lucknow, and a bridge crosses the canal at Char Bagh. Here the enemy had determined to make a stand and dispute the entrance to the city. The bridge was defended by 6 guns in position, while a numerous force of rebel Sepoys occupied the gardens and enclosures of the villages, from which they poured a destructive fire on the advancing troops. Nearly every man of Captain Maude's two guns was killed or wounded, and volunteers had to be called for from the infantry to replace the artillerymen. Lieutenant Arnold and 19 men of the Madras Fusiliers boldly charged the bridge— a discharge of grape swept most of them down: but before the enemy could reload, the main body of the regiment advanced with a cheer, rushed on the guns, and bayoneted the gunners. From the Char Bagh bridge, the Cawnpore road runs in an almost straight line to the Residency, and the distance is less than two miles; but the rebels had cut up the road and crossed it by palisades, so that Havelock made a *détour* by a narrow roundabout road, which for some distance skirts the left bank of the canal. The column marched with little molestation until it came opposite the Kaiser Bagh (King's Palace), where two guns and a body of mutineers were placed, and here the fire was so tremendous that, in Havelock's words, "nothing could live under it."

The 78th Highlanders had been left at Char Bagh, to hold the position until the whole column, with the ammunition and stores, had passed; and as the lane through which the army marched was very narrow, and the heavy guns cut it up very much in their passage, rendering it a work of great difficulty to get the long line of commissariat carts and cattle along, the 78th were in a few hours separated from the main body by a long distance. No sooner did the enemy perceive that the Highlanders were isolated than they returned in swarms to attack them, and, bringing two guns down to within 500 yards of the position, opened a destructive fire of shot and shell. This became so intolerable that the Highlanders charged both guns at the point of the bayonet, spiked the one and threw the other into the canal. At length the main body of the army had passed over the Char Bagh bridge, bag and baggage, and the duties of the 78th in that position being over, they quitted it and proceeded along the narrow lane taken by the column on the left bank of the canal; thus forming the rearguard of the army. The mutineers immediately seized the bridge, and planting upon it a gun, enfiladed the narrow lane along which the Highlanders were marching, while their infantry lined the right bank of the canal, and under cover of a wall poured in a galling musketry fire. The regiment suffered much loss, but after about a mile and a half the road diverged from the banks of the canal and led up by Major Banks's house. A little beyond this four streets meet, and the question arose what road to take, to the right or to the left? The main body of the army was completely out of sight, but it was evident that the road to the left led straight up to the Residency. This road, therefore, the 78th took, with the volunteer cavalry and a company of the 90th, who had been sent back by Havelock to their assistance, on a report that they were hard pressed. They ran the gauntlet of a whole street of fine houses, loopholed and occupied by the rebels, until they got to the gate of the Kaiser Bagh, where they came in reverse upon the battery that was firing upon the main body of the army, who had taken the roundabout road to the right. After spiking the guns, they again pushed on under the walls of the palace, and about four in the afternoon joined the main body of the army near the entrance to the Furrah Buksk, where they got a short rest.

The Residency was now only half a mile distant, and it was here the rebel Sepoys were collected in greatest force. The Highlanders and Sikhs were ordered to take the lead. "They pushed on with a desperate gallantry," says Havelock, "led by Sir James Outram and myself and staff, through streets of flat-roofed, loopholed houses, from which a perpetual fire was kept up; and overcoming every obstacle, established themselves within the enclosure of the Residency. To form an idea of the obstacles overcome, reference must be made to the events that are known to have occurred at Buenos Ayres and Saragossa."

The deliverers were received with unbounded joy. "We ran up to them, officers and men without distinction, and shook them by the hands—how cordially, who can describe?" "Our new friends," says Mr. Rees, "were hungry and thirsty, but sat down to a repast that was spread for them unsparingly. But one great grief, one great sorrow damped the universal joy—the death of one of their bravest and most beloved leaders, General Neill. Yet even this loss was momentarily forgotten, and the evening found us dancing to the sound of the Highlanders' pibroch. The remembrance of that happy evening will never be effaced from my memory. Of course, I could not sleep that night. It was three o'clock when I retired to bed."

"Never," says a lady, "shall I forget the moment to the latest day I live. It was almost overpowering. We had no idea they were so near, and were breathing air in the portico as usual at that hour, speculating when they might be in—not expecting they could reach us for several days longer; when suddenly, just at dark, we heard a very sharp fire of musketry close by, and then a tremendous cheering. An instant after, the sound of the bagpipes, then soldiers running up the road, our compound and verandah filled with our deliverers, and all of us shaking hands frantically, and exchanging fervent 'God bless you's!' with the gallant men and officers of the 78th Highlanders. Sir James Outram and staff were the next to come in, and the state of joyful confusion and excitement was beyond all description. The big, rough-bearded soldiers were seizing the little children out of our arms, kissing them with tears rolling down their cheeks, and thanking God they had come in time to save them from the fate of those at Cawnpore."

Lucknow was relieved, but the united forces were too few to attempt to retreat, with 1500 sick, women, and children, to Cawnpore. Distracted by the double duty of protectors and combatants, the little army would have been found too weak for either. Indeed, so far from being able to escape to Cawnpore, fifty or sixty miles distant, the British cooped up in the Residency could hold no communication with the detachment under Major M'Intyre which held the Alum Bagh—could neither send aid to it, nor receive aid from it. There was nothing for it, then, but to continue to hold the position till Sir Colin Campbell, the commander-in-chief of the forces in India, should be able to advance with a new army.

After remodelling the whole military machinery of the empire, Sir Colin Campbell started from Calcutta on the 28th October, and arrived at Cawnpore after a week's journey, in which he narrowly escaped capture by the rebels. Remaining at Cawnpore no longer than was necessary to organise his various military arrangements, he crossed the Ganges, and on the 9th November joined Hope Grant's column at Buntara, six miles short of the Alum Bagh. Here he waited three days for reinforcements, and on the 12th advanced to the Alum Bagh, where he left the 75th in garrison, and formed the former garrison—400 men of the 7th, 64th, and 78th—into a battalion of detachments. His whole force now numbered something over 4000, including the 8th, 53d, 93d, 700 men of the 23d and 82d, 400 men of the 7th, 64th, and 78th, the 2d and 4th Punjaub Cavalry, the 9th Lancers, detachments of the 1st, 2d, and 5th Punjaub Cavalry, a detachment of Hodson's Horse, sappers and miners, artillery, the naval brigade, engineers, and military train—in all, 700 cavalry, 3400 infantry, and a considerable strength in the artillery arm. The naval brigade, under Captain Peel of the *Shannon*, was about 500 strong, and at least 100 of the men were sailors of the merchant service, who, on learning that there was "something" going on up at Lucknow, had agreed to join the brigade with great willingness.

As Sir Colin Campbell's object was not to strengthen the beleaguered garrison of Lucknow, but to clear a path by which it might safely retire, he did not advance by the direct Cawnpore road, and set about cutting his way through the heart of the city, as Havelock and Outram did two months before. The plan of approach he proposed to himself was, to make a flank march on the right, and, taking the city on the eastern side, batter down the enemy's defences step by step until he reached the Residency. A clear passage would thus be opened between the heart of the city and the river Goomtee, by which the beleaguered garrison might retire in comparative safety. This plan was the more feasible, as there was a large open space at this end of the city, containing many mosques, palaces, and other large buildings, and but few of those deep narrow lanes, the capture of which would have required a larger force than he had at his command. His tactics were therefore to consist in a series of partial sieges, each directed against some particular building, and each capture to form a base of operations for attacks on other buildings farther in advance. The principal buildings to be encountered on the route were the Dil Khoosha (Heart's Delight) palace and park, the Martinière College (Martin's college for half-caste children)—both on the east side of the canal, and therefore in the suburbs—the Secunder Bagh (Alexander's Garden), the Shah Nujeef (a domed mosque with a garden), the palace mess-house, the Matee Mohul (Pearl Palace), and the Kaiser Bagh (King's Palace).

At nine in the morning (November 14) the flank march commenced. The 4th Punjaub Rifles moved on in skirmishing order, supported by the 93d, while the naval brigade kept up a heavy fire from the great guns on the left. The enemy replied with spirit, but they were driven, first from the Dil Khoosha, and then from the Martinière College, across the canal, and the troops bivouacked on the ground they had won.

Next morning (November 15) the troops were under arms by six o'clock. All the baggage was left at the Dil Khoosha, and each soldier's haversack was filled with provisions for three days. The men were formed in quarter-distance column in a part of the canal where the bed was dry, and commenced their advance about nine o'clock, the line of march lying close along the western bank of the Goomtee. For a mile and a half or two miles no opposition was met with: not until the skirmishers of the 53d came upon a strong body of the enemy, posted in the loopholed buildings and garden enclosures of a cluster of houses near the Secunder Bagh. The enemy were quickly driven from this post, and some guns were brought up to batter a breach in the south-west angle of the Secunder Bagh—a palace with a high-walled enclosure of stone masonry, about 120 yards square, and held by the enemy in great force. The assault was delivered by the 4th Punjaub Rifles and the 93d (Sutherland) Highlanders, supported by a part of the 53d and the battalion composed of detachments of the 7th, 64th, and 78th. "Never," said Sir Colin Campbell in his despatch, "was there a bolder feat of arms." On went Sikh and Highlander side by side in a glorious and exciting rush. The breach was so narrow that only one man could enter at a time, but a few, having forced their way in, kept the mutineers at bay, until they were joined by a considerable number of their comrades, when they boldly advanced into the open square. In a short time a company of the 93d, which had been sent to clear a serai on the left, advanced to the main gate and blew it open, killing a number of the enemy in two large recesses on either side; then, pressing their way in, they rushed to the support of their comrades who had entered by the breach. The men of the 53d, too, forced an entrance through a window away on the right of the building. All assembled in the square, and now commenced a terrible struggle. The mutineers, knowing there was no escape for them, fought with the courage born of despair; the British, roused to fury by memories of Cawnpore, dashed furiously on, giving no quarter. For hours the terrible work continued, and by three in the afternoon the square of the Secunder Bagh was littered with the dead bodies of 2000 Sepoys, almost all bearing the deep gash of the Sikh tulwar, or the small but not less deadly bayonet wound. During the desperate struggle within, Captain Stewart of the 93d, with two companies of that regiment and a few men of the 53d, dashed forward, seized two of the enemy's guns which were raking the road, and immediately after effected a lodgment in the European barracks, thus securing the position on the left. For this achievement Captain Stewart was elected by the officers of the regiment for the Victoria Cross.

Captain Peel's naval siege train, with a field battery and some mortars, had meanwhile gone forward to batter the Shah Nujeef. A heavy cannonade was maintained for three hours, but with no visible effect, the Sepoys all the while keeping up a destructive fire of musketry. As it would soon be dark, fiery Sir Colin began to get impatient, and riding up to the 93d (his favourite regiment), then resting after its fatigues—"I had no intention," he said, "of employing you again to-day, but the Shah Nujeef must be taken; the artillery cannot drive the enemy out, so you must with the bayonet." The order was given to advance, Sir Colin accompanying the regiment himself. The artillery redoubled its fire, and under cover of the iron storm the 93d went forward to the nearest angle of the building, exposed to a galling musketry fire. A single glance showed that the wall was quite uninjured by the artillery; it was twenty feet high, there was no breach, and there were no scaling ladders. A party of the regiment pushed round the angle to the front gate, but found it perfectly unassailable. Determined to effect an entrance somehow or other, Captain Peel dragged forward two of his big guns, and opened fire on the masonry protecting the gate, at the distance of only a few yards. "Captain Peel," says Sir Colin Campbell, "led up his heavy guns with extraordinary gallantry to within a few yards of the building, to batter the massive stone walls. The withering fire of the Highlanders effectually covered the naval brigade from great loss; but it was an action almost unexampled in war. Captain Peel behaved very much as if he had been laying the *Shannon* alongside an enemy's frigate." But it would not do; the heavy shot made no impression, and as evening was fast closing in, the guns were withdrawn, and the wounded collected. Unwilling to give up the attempt without one effort more, Brigadier Adrian Hope took 50 men of the 93d, and crept cautiously through the brushwood, where a sergeant of the regiment named Paton discovered a spot so injured that he thought an entrance might be effected. The rent was just large enough for one man to be pushed through at a time, and after several of the officers and men had scrambled up and stood on the inside of the wall, the sappers were sent for to enlarge the opening. More men followed, and the small party then made a dash for the main gate, and threw it open to the rest of the regiment, who entered just in time to see the enemy in their white dresses gliding through the garden and disappearing in the darkness of the night. For his valuable services on this day Sergeant Paton received the Victoria Cross.

Havelock on his side had not been idle; and next day (November 17) the 53d and 90th captured the mess-house, hospital, and Matee Mohul, and communication with the Residency was opened. The British were now in possession of the whole river side of Lucknow, and a path was cleared by which the garrison might retire.

The women and children, the sick and wounded, were all removed, Sir Colin covering his real intentions by bombarding the Kaiser Bagh. On the night of the 22d, while the enemy hourly expected the assault, he withdrew the garrison and all the Europeans through his chain of out-pickets. "The retreat," says the commander-in-chief, "was admirably executed, and was a perfect lesson in such combinations. Each exterior line came gradually retiring through its supports, till at length nothing remained but the last line of infantry with the guns, with which I remained myself, to crush the enemy, had he dared to follow up the pickets. The only line of retreat lay through a long and tortuous lane, and all these precautions were absolutely necessary to insure the safety of the force." The joy of the garrison at their deliverance was clouded by the death of the great and good Sir Henry Havelock, who died at the Dil Khoosha camp (November 25) of dysentery, brought on by overfatigue and the severe privations of the campaign.

Sir Colin Campbell fully intended to afford the troops a few days' rest at the Alum Bagh; but on the 27th he heard very heavy firing in the direction of Cawnpore, and no news having reached him from that place for several days, he feared some disaster, and felt it necessary to push forward as quickly as possible. Leaving Outram in command of part of the forces at the Alum Bagh, to keep the enemy in check, and hold the place as a base for future operations, he hurried on with his enormous train of 2000 women, children, sick, and wounded to Cawnpore, whence he sent it forward under a sufficient escort to Allahabad.

When the cause of the heavy firing was ascertained, it afforded Sir Colin Campbell little satisfaction. General Windham, who had been left to maintain Cawnpore, had suffered himself to be surprised by the mutineers of the Gwalior contingent. After their victory the Sepoys took possession of the town, from which it was necessary to dislodge them. Their position was one of great strength. Their left was posted on some wooded high grounds, thickly intersected with nullahs and ruined bungalows, between the city and the river; their centre occupied the city itself, and lined the narrow barricaded streets and houses and bazaars overhanging the Ganges Canal; while their right stretched away into the plain. Their number was estimated at 25,000 men and 40 guns. The battle was fought on the 16th December. Campbell saw that the wall of the town really divided the enemy into two parts, and that if the right were vigorously assailed it would be defeated without assistance being able to come to it from the centre and left. General Windham, therefore, held the entrenchment beside the bridge of boats over the Ganges, and cannonaded the enemy's left, so as to draw their attention to that side, and lead them to accumulate their troops there. After a few hours of this cannonade, Brigadier Greathed advanced with his brigade (2d Punjaub Infantry, 8th, and 64th), and engaged in a sharp musketry battle across the canal, to keep the enemy's centre in play; while Brigadier Walpole (with the 2d and 3d battalions of the Rifle brigade and a wing of the 38th) crossed the canal just above the town, and, skirting the wall, effectually prevented all communication between the right and the centre and left. These arrangements completed, Brigadiers Hope Grant and Inglis (with the 23d, 32d, 42d, 53d, 82d, 93d, and Sikhs) assailed the enemy's right, while the cavalry and horse artillery crossed the canal about a mile farther up than the extreme right of the rebels, and turned their flank. Captain Peel and his naval brigade assisted in the direct attack of Grant's and Inglis's brigades in front, and received the highest praise for the energy with which they pushed forward their guns. "I must here draw," says the commander-in-chief in his despatch, "attention to the manner in which the heavy 24-pounder guns were impelled and managed by Captain Peel and his gallant sailors. Through the extraordinary energy and goodwill with which the latter have worked, their guns have been constantly in advance throughout our late operations, from the relief of Lucknow till now—as if they were light field-pieces. The service rendered by them has been incalculable. On this occasion there was beheld the sight of 24-pounder guns advancing with the first line of skirmishers."

The rout of the enemy was complete. The cavalry and horse artillery, followed by the 42d, 53d, and Sikhs, pursued them along the road to Calpee for fourteen miles, cutting them up terribly. The slaughter became so great that the mutineers, despairing of effecting their retreat by the road, or in anything like order, threw away their arms and accoutrements, and, dispersing over the country, took to the jungle. As soon as the rout of the Gwalior contingent commenced on the right, Nana Sahib's men in the town were pushed vigorously. In this part of the field the fortune of the day was decided by General Mansfield, with some guns, the Rifles, and the main body of the 93d, securing possession of the Subader's Tank in rear of the enemy's left. By sunset the Nana's men were completely routed, and during the night they retreated northward by the Bithoor road, leaving all their guns, fifteen in number, and a vast quantity of ammunition, provisions, and camp equipage.

Campbell now directed all his energies to the siege of Lucknow. By the beginning of March, 1858, he was again at the Alum

Bagh, with 1500 artillery, 1700 engineers, 4000 cavalry, and 18,000 infantry—a force of 25,000 men, and 36 guns; and during the course of the siege he was joined by the Ghoorka army under Maharajah Jung Bahadoor, numbering about 9000 men, and 24 guns. On a reconnaissance of the enemy's position, he found that the new lines of defence, constructed since the rescue in November, were both vast and well planned. Treating the Kaiser Bagh as a sort of citadel, the mutineers had raised three lines of defence between it and the besieging army. Almost every house and enclosure was loopholed and fortified, strong counterguards were constructed in front of gateways, and isolated bastions, stockades, and traverses were placed across the principal streets. It was computed that there were between 30,000 and 50,000 Sepoys in the city, 50,000 volunteers and armed retainers of the turbulent chieftains of Oude, and 100 guns. The city itself contained an ordinary population of 300,000, and all went about more or less armed with matchlock, pistol, gun, tulwar, and shield. Sir Colin's reconnaissance convinced him that no immediate attack could safely be made upon the enemy's position by infantry, without a great sacrifice of life, and as he was well supplied with artillery, he resolved to make a good use of that arm before sending his foot soldiers forward.

The Dil Khoosha palace was first seized. Sir James Outram was then directed to cross with a portion of the army to the left bank of the Goomtee, and drive the enemy before him, till he was enabled to enfilade the works on the canal —the first line of the enemy's defences (March 9, 1858). After a few hours Sir Colin, being informed by telegraph of Outram's success, ordered the naval brigade to open with four guns on the Martinière College. As soon as breaches were practicable, the 42d, 93d, and 4th Punjaub Rifles, with the 38th and 53d in support, were ordered forward to the assault—the 42d Royal Highlanders to lead the attack, and nothing but the bayonet to be used. Silently, at first, the 42d advanced, four companies in skirmishing order and the other five in line. At 200 yards they gave a wild cheer and rushed on at the double to the favourite tune of "The Campbells are Coming." The Sepoys did not wait to cross bayonets, but leaped from the trenches and ran towards the city, closely pursued by the 42d, and at a greater distance by the rest of the stormers, who pushed on and took possession of the whole of the enemy's first line of defences. So ended the operations of the 9th.

At sunrise next morning a few heavy guns were opened against Banks's bungalow, and, after the artillery had done its work, several companies of the 42d advanced and took possession of the house and adjacent gardens, with little opposition. The capture of this place enabled the commander-in-chief to proceed against the enemy's second line of defence, of which the Begum Kotee (Begum's Palace), strongly fortified and garrisoned by the Sepoys, was the key. Brigadier Napier—now Lord Napier of Magdala—the chief engineer, brought up his batteries. Two 68-pound naval guns commenced breaching, while the whole building was subjected to a destructive shower of shell from 16 mortars and cohorns placed in Banks's bungalow. All the night of the 10th, and all next morning, the guns roared and the iron storm rattled on the devoted Begum Kotee. Between three and four in the afternoon of the 11th, two breaches were reported practicable, and the 93d Highlanders, the 4th Punjaub Rifles, and 1000 Ghoorkas, were ordered forward to the assault, the 93d to lead the attack. The storming of the Begum Kotee was, Sir Colin Campbell said, " the sternest struggle which occurred during the siege." The place was held by a large portion of eight picked Sepoy regiments, numbering in all about 5000 men, who had sworn to die in defence of this position, the key to all the fortifications of Lucknow. Nothing had been left undone to obstruct the passage of the stormers through the buildings. Not a room, not a door, not a gallery, but was fortified and barricaded; not a window, loophole, or crevice but was occupied by the enemy. But steadily, if slowly, the stormers continued to advance, in small parties of twos and threes, and at length all emerged into the first square of the palace, where the great body of the enemy stood drawn up prepared for battle. Then occurred one of those dreadful fights at close quarters, of which we have already seen an example. No quarter was asked or given. As darkness was closing in, about seven o'clock, all resistance ceased, the enemy retreating to the Kaiser Bagh. More than 1000 of their dead bodies were buried next day, and as the wounded were probably twice or thrice as many more, few of them could have escaped unhurt. The desperate nature of the struggle may be inferred from one example: Lieutenant and Adjutant M'Bean of the 93d encountered eleven Sepoys in succession, and after a hand to hand struggle killed them all; a feat which was rewarded with the Victoria Cross. Dr. Russell visited the place next morning and says, "I saw one of the fanatics, a fine old Sepoy, with a grizzled moustache, lying dead in the court, a sword-cut across his temple, a bayonet thrust through his neck, his thigh broken by a bullet, and his stomach slashed open, in a desperate attempt to escape. There had been five or six of these fellows together, and they had either been surprised and unable to escape, or had shut themselves up in desperation in a small room, one of many looking out on the court. At first, attempts were made to start them by throwing in live shell. A bag of gunpowder was more successful, and out they charged, and with the exception of one man were shot and bayoneted on the spot. The man who got away did so by a desperate leap through a window amid a shower of bullets and many bayonet thrusts."

The Emaumbarra (or private mosque of Gazee-u-deen-Hyder), a magnificent building between the Begum Kotee and the Kaiser Bagh, was assaulted by sap and bombardment, and taken by Brigadier Franks on the 14th. Not only so, but Major Brasyer's Sikhs, pressing forward in pursuit of the enemy, entered the Kaiser Bagh along with them; and the third or inner line of defence was thus turned without a single gun being fired from it. Before the night closed in, the mess-house, the Tara Kotee, the Matee Mohul, and the Chutter Munzil, were all occupied by the British troops. Moosa Bagh was captured by Sir James Outram and Sir Hope Grant on the 19th, and by the 21st the rebels had been everywhere put down, and Lucknow was once more under British rule.

Lucknow was captured, but unfortunately the heart of the rebellion was not crushed. Fleeing from Oude, the rebels overran the equally mutinous province of Rohilcund. At Bareilly in that province were some of the best known rebel leaders —Khan Bahadoor Khan, Nana Sahib, and two shabzadas or princes of the royal family of Delhi. It became painfully evident that a summer campaign would be necessary, and the army before Lucknow was broken up into three divisions—the Azimgurh field force, under Sir Edward Lugard, the Lucknow field force, under Sir Hope Grant, and the Rohilcund field force, under Brigadier-General Walpole. Sir Colin Campbell joined the Rohilcund field force, and marched against Bareilly, now the focus of the rebellion. On approaching the town (May 5, 1858) his videttes detected a body of rebel cavalry, and Sir Colin immediately formed his army in order of battle. To the fire of our field guns the enemy replied from a battery set up at the entrance to the town, but they made little or no attempt to fortify or defend the nullah that crosses the high road, or the bridge that spans the nullah, and soon fell back to occupy the topes, or clumps of trees, and the ruined houses of the cantonments. As every tope and house had to be shelled in succession, the advance was necessarily slow.

About ten o'clock, the 4th Punjaub Rifles were sent forward to occupy the old cavalry lines, and the 42d and the 79th Highlanders were ordered to their support. Mr. Russell, who was with the army, describes what followed:—"As soon as the Sikhs got into the houses, they were exposed to a heavy fire from a large body of matchlockmen concealed around them. They either retired of their own accord, or were ordered to do so; at all events, they fell back with rapidity and disorder upon the advancing Highlanders. And now occurred a most extraordinary scene. Among the matchlockmen, who, to the number of 700 or 800, were lying behind the walls of the houses, was a body of Ghazees or Mussulman fanatics, who, like the Roman Decii, devote their lives with solemn oaths to their country or their faith. Uttering loud cries of 'Bismillah, Allah, deen, deen!' these fanatics, sword in hand, with small circular bucklers on the left arm, and green cummerbungs, rushed out after the Sikhs and dashed at the left wing of the Highlanders. With bodies bent and heads low, waving their tulwars with a circular motion in the air, they came on with astonishing rapidity. At first they were mistaken for Sikhs, whose passage had already somewhat disordered our ranks. Fortunately, Sir Colin Campbell was close up with the 42d; his keen quick eye detected the case at once. 'Steady, men, steady, close up the ranks. Bayonet them as they come on.' It was just in time, for these madmen, furious with bhang, were already among us, and a body of them sweeping around the left of the right wing, got into the rear of the regiment. The struggle was sanguinary but short. Three of them dashed so suddenly at Colonel Cameron that they pulled him off his horse before he could defend himself. His sword fell out of its sheath, and he would have been hacked to pieces in another moment but for the gallant promptitude of Colour-sergeant Gardiner, who, stepping out of the ranks, drove his bayonet through two of them in the twinkling of an eye. The third was shot by one of the 42d. Brigadier Walpole had a similar escape; he was seized by two or three of the Ghazees, who sought to pull him off his horse, while others cut at him with their tulwars. He received two cuts on the hand, but he was delivered from the enemy by the quick bayonets of the 42d. In a few moments the dead bodies of 133 of the Ghazees, and some 18 or 20 wounded men of ours, were all the tokens left of the struggle."

The result of the day's fighting was that the British entered Bareilly on the 7th March, but the main body of the enemy had made their escape the evening before. After the fall of Bareilly the Rohilcund field force was broken up, and placed under the command of various officers, to scour the country. The strongholds were quickly captured or evacuated at the approach of the victorious British arms, but the great body of the rebels invariably contrived to make their escape. In this desultory kind of warfare—this stamping out of the fire—the troops suffered comparatively little loss from the rebels, but they had a more deadly enemy to contend with in the climate. The summer of 1858 was an exceptionally hot one even for India—the hottest within the memory of man since 1833—and the British suffered severely in their "continuous and unexampled marching" after an enemy who was always reported to be near, was frequently in sight, but could seldom be caught. At the battle of Bareilly, ten men were sun-struck and fell dead in the ranks, and nine others, officers and men, had to be carried from the field, utterly exhausted with the heat. It was pitiable to see the poor fellows lying in the dhoolies breathing their last. The veins of the arm were opened, and leeches applied to the temples, but, notwithstanding every care, the greater number of cases proved fatal, and even of those who recovered, there were few who were fit for active service again, except after a long interval of rest.

The veteran Sir Colin Campbell seemed to be the man of all the army least incommoded by the extraordinary heat. "The natives, when any of them sought for and obtained an interview with him, were a good deal surprised to see the commander of the mighty British army in shirt sleeves and a pith hat; but the keen eye and the cool manner of the old soldier told that he had all his wits about him, and was none the worse for the absence of glitter and personal adornment."

All during the summer there was much suffering from sunstroke, diarrhœa, and fever. Sometimes there was a little hard fighting—as when 40 men of the 42d were cut off in a dense jungle from the remainder of the force, and, assisted by only 40 men of the Kumaon levies, raw recruits, who could with difficulty be held to their posts, kept 2000 rebels of all arms at bay from sunrise to sunset, the old soldiers cheering on the others after all the officers had fallen. Two companies of the regiment arrived at the scene of action about five o'clock in the afternoon, and the rebels were defeated with great slaughter, and two of their guns captured.

The Central India field force, organised at Bombay and Madras, and commanded by Major-generals Sir Hugh Rose, K.C.B., Whitlock, and Roberts, performed distinguished service during the mutiny. It prevented the spread of the mutiny south of the Gangetic provinces, afforded support to our staunch allies the Mahratta chieftains Scindia, Holkar, and others, and cleared Central India and Rajpootana of Sepoy mutineers, rebel rajahs, and scoundrel budmashes. The greatest interest attaches to the operations of Sir Hugh Rose, whose victorious campaign equals in brilliancy that of Havelock. Starting from Sehore (January 12, 1858), seizing town after town and fort after fort, relieving the British garrison at Saugor, and defeating the enemy in the field wherever he could find him, Sir Hugh pressed on to Jhansi, the principal town of Bundelcund.

Like Cawnpore, Jhansi had become a name hateful to British ears. Early in June the year before, all the British residents there, upwards of 50 in number, men women, and children, were mercilessly slaughtered by a crowd of mutinous Sepoys, irregular sowars, disaffected police, and fanatic Mussulmen, and not one left to tell the tale. The massacre at Jhansi was not attended by those revolting accompaniments which added so indescribably to the horrors of Cawnpore, but it had one dark feature which even that was without—it was committed at the instigation of a woman, the Ranee or chieftainess of Jhansi. This Ranee was a remarkable woman. Under the impression, right or wrong, that she had been unjustly treated by the East India Company, she espoused the cause of the mutiny, and was certainly one of the most able leaders the rebels had—abler than the Moulvie of Fyzabad or the Begum of Oude, and beyond all comparison better and braver than Nana Sahib or Tanteea Topee. Personally she was a perfect Amazon. She rode like a man, bore arms like a man, and fought like a man, leading her troops herself, and exhorting them to contend to the last against the hated Feringhees; and, but for her unbounded licentiousness and cruelty, bore a stamp of heroism which would have commanded respect.

Sir Hugh Rose arrived before Jhansi on the 21st March, 1858, and immediately commenced to besiege the town and fort, occupied by some eleven or twelve thousand rebel Bundelas and mutinied Sepoys. Tanteea Topee marched to the relief of his brother rebels shut up in the beleaguered city, but Sir Hugh defeated and pursued him, slew 1500 of his men, and took all his guns and ammunition (April 1). After this victory Jhansi was taken by breach and escalade (April 2), and 3000 of its defenders slain; but the Ranee had evacuated the place during the night, with such of her troops as were able to break through the cordon which Rose had endeavoured to draw round the city.

After the fall of Jhansi, the main body of the Bundelcund rebels assembled at Calpee, on the road to Cawnpore, and Rose set out to attack them. The Ranee and Tanteea Topee endeavoured to dispute his passage at a place towards Kooneh, but Rose drove them from their entrenchment, entered the town, cut them up severely, pursued them to a considerable distance, and captured eight guns. The heat was intense, and many men fell dead in the ranks from sunstroke.

The affair at Kooneh was followed by a great battle at Calpee. The enemy were 15,000 strong, but a grand bayonet charge put them completely to the rout, the 71st and 86th working terrible execution among the dense masses opposed to them. This victory was a great blow to the rebels, for there were three cannon foundries at Calpee, with all the requisites for a wheel and carriage manufactory; and there fell into the hands of the British, with guns, 24 standards of the mutinied regiments, and a great quantity of ammunition and ordnance stores.

After securing Calpee, and sending out flying columns in pursuit of the enemy, Sir Hugh Rose considered that his exhausted troops might take rest. On the 1st June he issued a glowing address, beginning:—"Soldiers! you have marched more than a thousand miles, and taken more than a hundred guns. You have forced your way through mountain passes and intricate jungles, and over rivers. You have captured the strongest forts, and beaten the enemy, no matter what the odds, wherever you met him." But his labours were not yet ended. On the very day this address was issued, the rebels defeated at Calpee engaged in battle with Maharajah Scindia, our firm ally. Scindia being deserted by a large body of his own troops, the day went against him, and the rebels entered Gwalior, the strongest and most important fortress in Central India. Scindia appealed to the British for assistance, and Sir Hugh Rose again took the field. Defeating the rebels in the encampment at Gwalior, by a series of well-planned manœuvres he captured both the town and the fort (June 19), the latter situated on a high isolated hill peculiar to the plains of India.

The Ranee of Jhansi fell in fighting beside Scindia's capital. In trying to make her escape over a canal she was cut down by a hussar; she still endeavoured to get over, when a bullet struck her on the breast, and she fell to rise no more. Tantcea Topee escaped from Gwalior, taking with him all Scindia's crowns, jewels, and treasures, to the value of £3,000,000 sterling. He managed to elude the British forces for many months, but was at last captured through the treachery of Maun Singh, and hanged at Sippree (April 18, 1859). The rebel leaders were thus cut off one by one, and the mutiny was gradually stamped out. By the beginning of 1859 India was again at peace.

The Mutiny led to the passing of an important Act of Parliament (Sept. 1858), transferring the government of India from the Company to the Queen, who, by another Act, recently passed, has been proclaimed Empress of India.

Sir Colin Campbell was raised to the peerage as Lord Clyde. "Too late!" said the war-worn veteran; "there is nobody alive to whom I care to tell the news."

CHAPTER XVIII.

CHINA, NEW ZEALAND, BHOTAN—1859-1866.

Capture of the Taku Forts—The Anglo-French troops enter Pekin—Destruction of the Chinese Emperor's Summer Palace.

THE second war with China was closed, as we have seen, by the treaty of Tientsin; but it soon became apparent that the Chinese Government had no intention of acting in good faith. While Mr. Bruce, the British envoy, was about to ascend the Peiho for the purpose of having the treaty of Tientsin ratified, he was fired on at the mouth of the river. This could not be borne, and Admiral Hope, who had succeeded Sir Michael Seymour as commander-in-chief in Chinese waters, resolved to storm the offending Taku forts. The attack was made (June 25, 1859) by a division of gunboats, consisting of the *Starling, Janus, Plover,* (flying the admiral's flag), *Cormorant, Lee, Kestrel,* and *Banterer,* with the *Forester, Nimrod,* and *Haughty* in reserve. At 2 P.M. the *Opossum* commenced operations by pulling up the iron stakes that lay between her and the boom. The gunboats then advanced, and the Chinese unmasked their batteries. From the first it was evident the gunboats were completely overmatched. In the *Plover* Lieutenant Rason was killed, the admiral was wounded, and of the crew of 40 men but nine remained unhurt. Admiral Hope shifted his flag to the *Opossum,* which was disabled and rendered unmanageable. Nothing daunted, though he had received a second wound, the admiral shifted his flag to the *Cormorant,* and, lying on the deck, issued his orders with his usual coolness, until he was compelled to resign the command to Captain Shadwell. The *Kestrel* was sunk; the *Lee* and *Haughty* were disabled; but the *Opossum* and the *Plover*, reinforced with fresh crews, returned into action, and after four hours' cannonading, only five of the enemy's guns replied.

It was now determined to land and storm the forts, and 500 men pushed on shore, under Captains Shadwell and Vansittart, and Colonel Lemon of the marines, supported by Commanders Heath and Commerell, and Major Fisher of the engineers. While the men were struggling through the mud left by the receding tide, the enemy opened a heavy fire of great guns and musketry. Vansittart was struck in the neck, and had his leg taken off by a cannon-ball; Shadwell's foot was smashed by a jingall-ball; and Lemon fell severely wounded. Still, the survivors pressed on, and passed the first ditch, which was nearly empty, but the second ditch, close under the walls, was full of water, and there remained but 200 men alive and unwounded. A retreat was inevitable. In this disastrous affair—in which a party of French seamen, under Captain Tricault, took part—we had 80 men killed and 350 wounded, many of them mortally; the *Cormorant*, *Lee*, and *Plover* were lost, and the *Haughty*, *Kestrel*, and *Starling* were only got afloat with difficulty.

The repulse at the Taku forts was not suffered to remain long unretrieved. An Anglo-French expedition was sent out to Hong-Kong—10,000 British, under Sir Hope Grant, of Indian fame, and 5000 French, under General Montauban. The British troops employed on the expedition were—(Cavalry Brigade) 1st Dragoon Guards, Probyn's Sikh Cavalry, Fane's Cavalry, and Milward's Battery; (1st Division of Infantry, 1st Brigade) 1st Royal Scots, 31st, Loodianah Infantry; (2d Brigade) 2d or Queen's, 60th Rifles, 15th Punjaub Infantry, Barry's and Desborough's batteries, and Engineers; (2d Division of Infantry, 3d Brigade) 3d or Buffs, 44th, 8th Punjaub Infantry; (4th Brigade) 67th, 99th, 19th Punjaub Infantry, Mowbray's and Gavin's batteries, and Graham's Engineers; (Reserve) Guns of Position, the Madras Sappers, the Mountain Guns, and Rotton's Battery.

On the 1st August (1860) the expedition, consisting of 66 sail, commenced disembarking on the bare mud of Pehtang, 12 miles north of the Peiho. The first brush with the enemy took place on the 12th at Sinho, where a body of 7000 Tartar horsemen, armed with bows and arrows, spears, and a proportion of matchlocks, attempted to arrest the invaders. In vain; the Armstrong guns—now employed for the first time—tore through their ranks, and laid many of them low. Our loss was but two Sikhs killed and a dozen wounded.

Advancing next day, the 13th, along the causeway which bridged the muddy flat, the allies attacked Tangku. The fortifications of this place consisted of a semicircular, crenellated mud wall, three miles long, and terminating at both ends on the banks of the river. 200 of the Rifles, under Major Rigaud, advanced in skirmishing order, to support the Armstrong batteries and the 9-pounders. After the guns came the Royal Scots and 31st, then the 60th Rifles and 15th Punjaubees. Some Chinese batteries and junks that annoyed the column of attack were silenced by a small party of blue-jackets from the *Chesapeake*, who crossed the river in a boat, routed the Tartars, spiked the guns, and left the junks in a blaze. The Chinese in front opened fire, at 800 yards, from their wall pieces and heavy guns, but these were soon silenced by the superior artillery of the allies, and Sir John Michell ordered forward the infantry, who poured into the works across a little dam. "The Rifles," says an eye-witness, "were first in, and bowled over the Tartars as they scampered with precipitancy from the wall across the open into the village; while rockets, whizzing fiercely through the air over their heads, in graceful curves, spread dismay among their retiring numbers and accelerated their speed. The fugitives escaped along a causeway to a village farther down the river, whence they crossed, by means of a floating bridge, to the village of Taku."

The way was now clear for the assault of the Taku forts. The upper north fort, the key to the whole, was stormed on the 21st. The British force told off for the assault was 2500 men, composed of the 44th, 67th, marines, and engineers, under Brigadier Reeves; the French force, about 1000 men, under General Collineau. We had 16 guns and 3 mortars in action, the French 4 guns; and at daybreak all these opened fire at about 800 yards from the doomed fort. The Chinese replied briskly, among their guns being 2 English 32-pounders, taken from the gunboats sunk the year before. Suddenly, about 6 A.M., when the fire waxed hotter and hotter, a tall black pillar shot up from the midst of the fort, and rising to a great height, burst, with a loud, booming sound, into a vast shower of wood and earth. A magazine had blown up, and half an hour afterwards a similar catastrophe occurred in the lower north fort.

On this, says Sir Hope Grant in his despatch, "the field-guns were all advanced to within 500 yards of the forts, and redoubled their efforts. The fire of the forts having almost entirely ceased, a breach was commenced near the gate, and a portion of the storming party was advanced to within 30 yards to open a musketry fire; the French infantry were on the right, the British on the left. The fire of our artillery being thus partially compelled to slacken, the enemy emerged from their cover, and opened a heavy fire of musketry on our troops. The French, under General Collineau, immediately pushed on to the salient next the river, crossed the wet ditches in the most gallant style, and established themselves on the berm, from which they endeavoured to escalade the walls; this, however, they were unable to effect, from the vigorous resistance of the Chinese. The efforts of the sappers to lay down the pontoon-bridge were unavailing; no less than fifteen of the men carrying it being knocked over in one instant, and one of the pontoons destroyed. At this juncture Sir Robert Napier caused the two howitzers of Captain Gavin's battery to be brought up within 50 yards of the gate, in order more speedily to create a breach; and a space sufficient to admit *one* man had just been made, when our storming party, now joined by the headquarter wing of the 67th, under Colonel Knox, which had partly crossed by the French bridge, and partly swam over, forced their way in by single file in the most gallant manner. Lieutenant Rogers, of the 44th regiment, and Lieutenant Burslem, of the 67th, were the first to enter, when they assisted in the regimental colours of the 67th, carried by Ensign Chaplin, who first planted them on the breach, assisted by Private Lane, of the 67th, and subsequently on the cavalier, which he was the first to mount. At the same moment, the French effected their entrance, and the garrison was driven back step by step, and hurled pell-mell through the embrasures on the opposite side. Here the same obstacles which had impeded our advance obstructed their retreat; in addition to two wet ditches and belts of pointed bamboo stakes, there was a third wet ditch and bank. The storming parties opened a destructive fire on them from the cavalier, and this was enhanced by the canister fire of Captain Gavin's guns, which had been moved to the left of the fort for this purpose. The ground outside the fort was literally strewn with the enemy's dead and wounded. Three of the Chinese were impaled on the stakes." Our loss in this capture was 17 killed and 183 wounded. The French casualties were 130. The lower north fort yielded without firing a single gun, the southern forts also hauled down their flags of defiance, and before night of the 21st August the capture of the Taku forts was complete.

The 3d Buffs were left to garrison the Taku forts, and the rest of the army received orders to march for Tientsin, which was entered on the 6th September. Foiled in arms, the Chinese had resort to treachery. San-Kolinsin, the Chinese Commander-in-chief, was determined that not one of the "Hats" should return alive. He pretended to negotiate in order to beguile the allies till they were quietly encamped, and he could fall upon them unawares and massacre them all. Fortunately, he sprung his mine too soon, and the only "Hats" that fell into his hand were a small party which had gone forward to arrange about the camping ground for the army, that day (September 18) on the march to Chang-Chai-wan. Those who fell into the enemy's hands were Mr. Parkes, interpreter; Lieutenant Anderson, Fane's Horse; Mr. De Norman, one of Mr. Bruce's attachés; Mr. Bowlby, "Times" correspondent; Mr. Loch, private secretary to the Earl of Elgin; Major Brabazon; one dragoon; and 18 Sikh sowars. Colonel Walker and his party escaped by clinging to their horses' necks and spurring their chargers through the Tartar ranks, which gave way before them; and though a fire was opened on them, only one man was wounded. The arrival in the camp of Colonel Walker and his people was the signal for instant attack. The battle lasted two hours, and the Tartars, unable to stand the fire of the Armstrong guns, broke and fled. In their retreat they were much cut up by Fane's Horse on the right, and by the Royal Dragoon Guards and Probyn's Horse on the left.

The Tartars suffered another severe defeat on the 21st, and the allies then advanced towards Pekin. The Chinese endeavoured to check their march by their usual crooked diplomacy, but the Emperor was informed that unless the prisoners were restored, and one of the gates of the Imperial City placed in the hands of the allies, Pekin would be stormed. On the 6th October the allies took possession of the Emperor's Summer Palace, situated without the city, in a park ten miles in diameter. The Chinese still endeavoured to avert the humiliation of surrendering one of the gates of Pekin, but Sir Hope Grant was not to be trifled with. If, he said, his terms were not complied with by noon on the 12th day of October, he would storm the city. The breaching guns were ready, troops were paraded to storm the breach when practicable, and Sir Hope Grant stood beside the guns, watch in hand. It was almost twelve, and the word "fire!" was hovering on his lips, when Colonel Stephenson came galloping up to say that the An-ting gate had been surrendered. The 67th and the 8th Punjaubees were immediately sent forward to take possession of it; and the strange spectacle was seen of a great city, strongly fortified, with a population of two millions, and a stationary garrison of 100,000 men, surrendering to 10,000 European troops.

The prisoners—those who survived of them—were restored by degrees. Their sufferings had been dreadful. Thrown down on their face, and their feet and hands tied together behind, they were left three days in the sunshine without food or water, subjected to the grossest indignities and the most brutal treatment. At the end of the third day a little food was given them, lest they should die too soon. Twelve succumbed to this treatment: Mr. De Norman, Lieutenant Anderson, Private John Phipps of the Dragoon Guards, Mr. Bowlby, and 8 Sikhs. Major Brabazon and the Abbé de Luc were decapitated; their headless bodies were afterwards found floating about in the canal. "The survivors of each party," said Sir Hope Grant, "tell the same sad tale of how they remained with their hands tightly bound with cords until mortification ensued, and they died. The whole party would have shared the same fate, had not their cords been cut on the ninth day, or thereabouts." It was well for the Chinese that the murder of the prisoners did not come to light until after Sir Hope Grant had given his word that Pekin should be spared if the An-ting gate were surrendered. However, the Summer Palace, the scene of the atrocities, was ordered to be looted and given to the flames, and the Chinese Government was fined £100,000 for the benefit of the murdered men's relatives.

"Even before the order had gone forth, French officers," says an eye-witness, "had taken the liberty to *arracher* everything they took a fancy to; gold watches and small valuables being thrust with amazing velocity into the capacious side-pockets of their voluminous red pantaloons. Though General Montauban asserted that nothing was to be touched till Sir Hope Grant arrived, yet the looting went on. One French officer found a string of gorgeous pearls, each being the size of a marble, which he afterward foolishly sold at Hong Kong for £3000. Others had pencil-cases set with pure diamonds; others, watches and vases, thickly studded with pearls." When the place was thrown open, it presented a terrible scene of destruction. Some, armed with clubs, smashed to atoms what they were unable to carry away; others took "cock" shots at the magnificent mirrors and chandeliers; all rushed about in search of valuables. The French were particularly adroit at this kind of work, and many of them amassed small fortunes, in watches, jewels, jade ornaments, silks and furs, bronzes, gold and silver statuettes, and state robes. The sale of plunder in the camp lasted three days. "Fancy," says Swinhoe, "the sale of an emperor's effects beneath the walls of the capital of his empire, and this by a people whom he despised as weak barbarians, and talked of driving into the sea. The proceeds of the sale amounted to 32,000 dollars, and the amount of treasure secured was estimated at over 61,000, making a rough total of over 93,000 dollars. Of this, two-thirds were set apart for distribution, in proportionate shares, to the soldiers, and one-third to the officers. Sir Hope Grant generously made over his share to the men, and, as a token of respect, the officers presented him with a claret jug, richly chased, one of the handsomest pieces of the booty."

A Convention, signed at Pekin on the 24th October, opened Tientsin to our trade, gave us a representative at the Court of Pekin, and added to our Eastern possessions Kooloon, a district at the mouth of the Canton River. Pekin was evacuated on the 5th November.

The North China Campaign was followed by the Maori War in New Zealand (1861-63) which arose from a dispute between the natives and the settlers about the purchase of land. So well did this brave race defend themselves in their pahs that our red-coats and blue-jackets suffered more than one repulse, but in the end the Maoris saw the futility of resistance, and, laying down their arms, sued for peace.

Next came the Bhotan War (1864–66). The natives of this district, which lies on the southern slope of the Himalayas, had made themselves very troublesome as marauders, and it was found necessary to annex their country. The European troops engaged in these operations were two batteries of the Royal Artillery, the 55th, and the head-quarters of the 80th.

CHAPTER XIX.

THE ABYSSINIAN EXPEDITION—1867-68.

The March on Magdala—Battle of Aroje—Release of the Abyssinian prisoner—Capture of Magdala, and Suicide of Theodore.

BY a strange succession of events, the year 1867-68 saw our troops in Abyssinia, the land of Prester-John, the Sheba of Scripture (according to the natives), whose emperors are the lineal descendants of David and Solomon. The Emperor of Abyssinia at this period was Theodorus, a name he had assumed because an ancient Abyssinian prophecy declared, that an emperor of that name should extend his power over all Ethiopia and Egypt, and deliver Canaan from the Moslems. His real name was Kussai, and he is said to have been the only son of a widow, who had been reduced by poverty to the humble calling of a kousso seller. Young Kussai received some education, probably in a convent, but at an early age he enlisted under the banner of his uncle, the governor of Dembea, and proved himself such a master of the art of war, that the governor gave him his favourite daughter in marriage, and appointed him to the charge of a district. These honours were not, however, sufficient for the aspiring mind of Kussai, who declared war against his kinsman, defeated his troops, proclaimed himself governor of the province, fought battle after battle with the neighbouring chiefs, and never rested until he became master of all Abyssinia. It was in 1851 that he assumed the name and title of "Emperor Theodorus by the Power of God." Theodore had many great and good qualities, but his life was embittered by the constant rebellions which harassed his empire, and his nature underwent a violent change. He became intemperate, and in his drunken fits his cruelties were absolutely diabolical. The mere mention of them makes the blood curdle : brands, stakes driven through the heart, the back flayed with the *courbach*, the stomach ripped open, shooting, and crucifixion. He began to be execrated by his subjects.

Theodore had a great desire to cultivate the friendship of England, and wrote a letter to the Queen, but Earl Russell, who was then Foreign Secretary, did not rate the importance of the Abyssinian Emperor nearly so high as he did himself, and the letter remained unanswered. This was unfortunate. Theodore's jealousy and anger were further excited by certain visits which Consul Cameron paid to some of the neighbouring provinces; for the viceroy of Egypt was his mortal enemy. "Your Queen," he exclaimed to Cameron, "can give you orders to visit my enemies and then return to Massowah ; but she cannot return a civil answer to my letter to her. You shall not leave me till that letter comes." So (July, 1863) Cameron became a prisoner. Cameron's servant and two belonging to a Mr. Stern, an English missionary, were beaten to death. Mr. Stern himself, who accidentally put his hand to his mouth in horror at the spectacle, was accused of biting his thumb at the Emperor, and he too was beaten till his life was despaired of. On the 22d November, a despatch came from the Foreign Office, borne by an Irishman named Kearns, but still no allusion to Theodore's letter to the Queen. This put him in a fresh rage. Captain Cameron was now put in chains, and the missionaries and other Europeans in the country were thrown into prison and tortured. Mr. Rassam was sent as ambassador to try and obtain the release of the prisoners, but he himself was seized and detained. So were his companions, Lieut. Prideaux and Dr. Blanc. Fresh efforts were made for the release of the captives, but in vain, and it was resolved to send an army to compel Theodore to deliver them up.

Then there were great preparations at Bombay, where the expedition began to embark in December, 1867. The landing was made at Zoulla, on the south side of Annesley Bay, an inlet of the Red Sea. Everything was on the most extensive scale and of the most complete character. The number of vessels employed in the transport of the army and its belongings was 291. Spain, Turkey, and other countries were ransacked for mules, horses were sent from various quarters, and elephants from India. The total number of animals landed at Zoulla was 36,094. The number of fighting men who went on the expedition was 13,164, of whom 4044 went to the front, and the camp followers, men of every race and calling, numbered 62,220. These figures show better than any laboured description the serious task which England had undertaken when she determined to release her captives from the hands of Theodore.

The leader of the expedition was Sir Robert Napier, Commander-in-chief of the Bombay army, an officer who had served in the campaign of the Sutlej, as senior engineer at the siege of Moultan, at Goojerat, at Lucknow, and in China. An engineer's war, there was much propriety in conferring the chief command on an engineer. Napier's second in command was General Sir Charles W. D. Stanley, C.B., an officer who had served with credit in the Crimean war. Colonel Merewether was appointed political agent, with the special duty of selecting a place suited for a base of operations, and obtaining carriage and supplies from the natives. Colonel Phayre, Quarter-master-general of the Bombay army, led the pioneer force. To Colonel Wilkins, of the Royal Engineers, was assigned the duty of erecting piers and floating wharfs at Zoulla, and advising upon positions to be selected during the march. The land transport train was under the command of Major Warden. The European troops that accompanied the expedition were the 3d, or Prince of Wales' Dragoon Guards, the 4th or King's, the Cameronians, the 33d or Duke of Wellington's Regiment, the 45th or Nottinghamshire, with a body of the Royal Artillery, two batteries of Armstrong guns, and a naval brigade to work the rockets, under Captain Fellowes of the *Dryad*. The rest were native Indian troops, including some Beloochees and a body of pioneers.

On the 3d January, 1868, Sir Robert Napier arrived at Zoulla in H.M.S. *Octavia*. Great progress had already been made. A convenient port had been established on a desert shore; a road for cart traffic had been formed through a difficult mountain pass to Senafe, 60 miles inland in the highlands of Abyssinia, and friendly relations had been struck up with the native chiefs. A few days afterwards, news arrived that Theodore had removed his prisoners from the capital, Debra Tabor, to the stronghold of Magdala, 400 miles inland, and Napier resolved to march thither. It was a most adventurous undertaking, only possible to the firmest resolution, the most heroic contempt of privation and danger, and the most advanced science; and after all it was very like to prove abortive, for nothing could be easier than for Theodore to remove the captives from stronghold to stronghold and lead the army a wild-goose chase, or to settle the matter at once by murdering them, as he had murdered so many others. The march commenced on the 22d January.

It would be tedious to follow the army day by day on its march of 400 miles from Senafe to Magdala—Zoulla to Addigerat, from Addigerat to Antalo, from Antalo to the front. Sometimes the road lay through plains full of immense herds of cattle; sometimes by steep conical mountains, on the top of which, perched like eyries, stood the strongholds of the robber-chiefs, moated and palisaded; sometimes by lakes and waterfalls, dotted with geese, heron, ibis, snipe, pelicans, and toucans, and surrounded with forests of tropical vegetation, the haunt of the jackal and the hyena; sometimes by terrible gullies and ravines, where roads had first to be made by the Royal Engineers and the Punjaub Pioneers. Everywhere the land had a war-wasted appearance, everything proclaimed the chronic disorder of the country. Watchful warders paced the ramparts of the robber chiefs, and the poorest class of peasants lived, like the ancient Troglodytes, in the cavernous recesses of the rocks. The chiefs and principal men always went abroad armed, with a numerous band of retainers. Their dress consisted of drawers, a cotton shirt, a syma or white cotton cloth cloak with a scarlet border, and a lion-skin tippet with long tails. Their arms were a curved sword, which hung at the right side in a red leather scabbard, a long spear grasped in the right hand, and a hide shield, ornamented with gold filagree bosses and silver plates, worn on the left arm.

On the 24th March, the army arrived at Dildee. At Dildee, says Mr. Henty, "we were told that it was only four marches distant. We have made three marches, and have sixty miles more to go! And yet Magdala is not more than twenty-five miles distant in a straight line, and is visible from a point four miles distant from this camp. It is found, however, that the country is perfectly impracticable, and that we must make a *détour* of sixty miles to get there. . . . We have scaled mountains and descended precipices, we have traversed along the face of deep ravines, where a false step was death; we are familiar with smooth slippery rocks and with loose boulders; and after this expedition it can hardly be said that any country is impracticable for an army determined to advance. I hear, however, that between this and Magdala there are perpendicular precipices which could scarcely be scaled by the most experienced cragsmen, much less by loaded mules." The sufferings and privations of the troops in marching over a country such as this may be faintly imagined. Each infantry-man carried 55 lbs. weight, more than half the load of a mule. In the low valleys they were scorched with heat and parched with thirst; frequently they were drenched with thunder-storms; and on the uplands the nights were piercing cold. All superfluous baggage was necessarily left behind, and the camp was destitute of everything that makes camp-life endurable. Tough beef and chupatties were the only rations. No spirits remained, and but a small quantity of tea and compressed vegetables.

On the 8th April, the army encamped on the Delanta plateau, in full view of Magdala. The army was divided into two brigades. The 1st brigade consisted of the 4th or King's Own, under Colonel Cameron, a company of the Royal Engineers, under Major Pritchard, two regiments of native Indian infantry—the Beloochees and 27th Punjaub Pioneers—and two companies of the 10th Native Indian Infantry. The 2d brigade consisted of the 33d or Duke of Wellington's Own, the 45th or Sherwood Foresters; Colonel Penn's 6-gun battery of Mountain Train Artillery (100 men), the Naval Brigade in charge of the rocket battery (100 men), and the Armstrong battery of six 12-pounders and two 8-inch mortars, manned by about 200 men. With incredible labour Theodore had formed roads across deep ravines, and up the steep sides of mountains, for the transport of his artillery, on which he mainly depended for success. Under his orders at Magdala were 6000 warriors, besides a few European workmen, Russians and Germans, and a host of camp-followers. Besides the British captives, he held 570 of the natives as prisoners, many of them chiefs.

Sir Robert Napier wrote a letter to Theodore demanding the surrender of the captives, but no answer was returned. Theodore was by this time little better than a madman. For days he took nothing but the Abyssinian beer called tej and drams of arachi. On the day before the arrival of the British army, he had all the European captives out, and, says one of the correspondents who accompanied the expedition, "before their eyes he put to death 340 prisoners, many of whom he had kept in chains for years. Among them were men, women, and little children. They were brought out chained, and thrown on the ground with their heads fastened to their feet. Among this defenceless and pitiable group the brutal tyrant went with his sword, and slashed right and left until he had killed a score or so. Then getting tired, he called out six of his musketeers, who continued to fire among the wretched crowd until all were despatched. Their bodies were then thrown over a precipice."

No answer being made to his demand, Sir Robert Napier determined to storm the fortress. By the night of the 9th April, all the preparations were made. On the morning of the 10th (Good Friday), the troops crossed the Bachelo, a muddy, swift river, fifty yards wide. Muddy as it was, the soldiers drank eagerly of it and filled their canteens, for they were dying of thirst. From the Bachelo a broad flat-bottomed ravine ran straight towards one of the peaks of Magdala. Theodore had made a road along the ravine, and it was determined that the mountain guns, rocket train, and baggage should proceed by this road, with Colonel Phayre's sappers marching in front. The infantry were ordered to climb the hills to the right, and scour them of the enemy should any be posted there. Sir Robert Napier and his staff galloped up to the head of the ravine. Right in front of them, more than 1000 feet high, "like a great ship among the surrounding billows," was Magdala; and they saw how difficult was the task before them. Magdala and the numerous peaks and saddles around it form a curve. Magdala is in the centre, and the peaks of Fahla and Selasse guard the approach to it, like pillars of Hercules. Between Magdala and the ridge where Sir Robert Napier and his staff stood, stretched the plain of Aroje. "Colonel Milward, the officer commanding the artillery, remarked to me," says one of the correspondents, "that in the hands of European troops Magdala would not only be impregnable but perfectly unattackable. Gibraltar is absolutely nothing to this group of fortresses. After capturing Fahla and Selasse—if such a thing were possible—an attacking force would still have Magdala to deal with; and Magdala rises from the end of the flat shoulder which connects it with Selasse in an unbroken wall, except at one point, where a precipitous road leads up to a gate."

Theodore had posted his army, consisting of 3000 soldiers armed with percussion guns, as many spearmen, and several pieces of ordnance, on the flat-topped hill of Fahla. What now ensued, we shall relate in the graphic words of Mr. Stanley, taking, however, the liberty of abridging them.

"About 3.30 P.M. two men were seen going from gun to gun on the salient of Fahla—the summit of which rose to the perpendicular height of 1000 feet above the ground on which Napier and his staff stood. It was supposed that they were loading them: and a critical survey, made through a field-glass, verified the supposition. With the exception of the sappers and miners, Sir Robert Napier and other chiefs of the crusade had no help at hand. And, 'Just God.!' the enemy were seen pouring down Fahla slope *en masse;* and a pearly wreath of smoke, a thundering report, and a chain-shot, shrieked the Emperor's defiance! In quick succession flashed the fire-flames from the rude mouths of his cannon—in quick succession rolled the white smoke—in quick succession a series of hideous wailing sounds were heard in the air; indubitably, Theodore was in earnest. 'Away you, sir,' Sir Robert commanded in sharp tones; 'bring up the King's Own on the double quick;' 'and you, sir,' to another aide-de-camp, 'order the naval brigade here instantly, and you, Sir Charles Stanley, let the Punjaubees deploy across that narrow plateau in front, but do not fire until the enemy are within 200 yards of you.'

"Nearer and nearer was the advent of the enemy, 3500 strong. They all appeared confident of the issue. Their war songs came pealing towards us. We could see their cavalry caracoling and bounding joyously along; the foot soldiers leaping and brandishing long spears, and swinging their black shields. With loud chorus all sang the death-doom of the invader. Onward, still onward they came, horsemen and foot soldiers vieing with each other. They flung away their flowing symas, their bezans, and many their loin clouts, and with lances and shields in rest they bore down the hill, reached the plateau, and inundated it with their dusky bodies. A clear open plain was before them, over which they rolled like a huge wave! Closer they drew, until we momentarily expected to see them launch their spears, and annihilate the sappers and miners. 'Here it is, general; the naval brigade has arrived!' said a smartish aide-de-camp. 'Very good!' responded Napier; 'let

Captain Fellowes take position on that little knoll in front.' Not a minute too soon did the little band of sailors appear on the scene. Quick as lightning and prompt as powder are sailors when they hear the well-known voice of their commander! No useless time was wasted here. 'Action, Front!' shouted the naval captain. 'Action, Front!' repeated the lieutenant and boatswain; and hardly had the words died away from their lips before the sailors had unstrapped rocket tubes and carriages, and had them arranged on the knoll; muleteers in the rear with their animals; rocket carriers with their ammunition; rocket men ready with their pry poles. 'Fire!' and, even in the act of launching their spears, a stream of fire darted along the enemy's ranks, ploughing its fiery way through their swaying masses. Another, and another, rushed through them; and cheer after cheer issued from the lips of the sailors and marines.

"The battle had begun! The cheers of the naval brigade were echoed fiercely behind; and as the general turned his head, he saw the King's Own coming up at the double quick, with cartridge-boxes rattling on the hips, and men's fingers manipulating cartridges, and fixing their Sniders for the strife as they ran. There were only 300 of the King's Own together; the others of the regiment were on duty as baggage guards; but they were pure Britons. A low ridge of ground rising but a few feet above the narrow plain and a hollow divided the enemy from the rocket battery. The sappers and miners had been withdrawn for the support of its flanks, and thus a clear space was left for the rocket guns to do good execution, and incessantly they vomited their fiery darts at the enemy, now but fifty paces from the battery. Without pause or hesitation the King's Own kept on their way, forming line the while. Into the little hollow in front of the battery they shook themselves, with their arms. Into, and through the scrub oak and underbush, and in a second almost, the head of the 4th foot crested the slope and confronted the enemy, a few of whom were on the rise on the other side. 'Commence firing from both flanks,' rang out clear as a silver bell from Colonel Cameron; and, instantaneously, two quick volleys of musketry were flashed in the faces of the dusky foe, and like a stream of fire volleys ran from side to side without a pause, raining such a storm of leaden hail, that for the second time the enemy halted from sheer astonishment. It was as if they were paralysed at the very moment they intended to launch their spears, and one could almost fancy that these weapons vibrated in their hands from the impetus they were about to give them. Slowly they seemed to regain consciousness, and horrified they gazed upon the awful result. Strangest sight it was to them, who had ever been victorious in the field of battle, to see their own men tumble by the dozen, by scores, by fifties, into the embrace of death. 'Retreat!' cried the chiefs. The enemy did retreat, but not fast enough. They broke out *en tirailleur*, and endeavoured to take vantage of boulders to escape the whizzing bullets; but the bullets found them out, searched out each bush and mound and rock, and stretched the men behind dead upon the ground. Here was one running for dear life for a copse, but suddenly you saw him leap into the air and fall on his face, clutching the ground savagely. Here was another one, with head bent low, in the vain thought that if his head escaped he would be safe, making all haste to get into a hollow, out of the reach of the leaden storm; but even as the haven dawned upon his frenzied eyes, a whirring pellet caught him, and sent him rolling down the incline. There was another one, just about to dodge behind a massive boulder, from where he could take slight revenge, but before he could ensconce himself the unerring ball went crashing through his brain; and there was another one about to plunge in hot haste down a ravine to the left, who had his skull shattered by a rocket, and with a dull sound the body fell down the precipice.

"Some chiefs there were who turned round to take a parting shot, and some who, not entirely panic-struck, strove to re-form the natives. They were partly successful, and under their leadership 1000 of them precipitated themselves down the steep sides of the narrow plain, and seemed determined to capture Penn's battery, isolated on their little knoll below Selasse. The guns of the mountain train artillery were ranged in a semicircle, and when the enemy were within 500 yards of them, Colonel Penn smilingly gave the word to 'Fire.' A sharp yelp-like report, and six shells flew through the clear air with a strange diapason, and directly burst among the advancing masses. Another astonished pause! Here were other strange things for the Abyssinians. Music like that of distant harps; while missiles were tearing and rending men to pieces. Simultaneously the enemy, instead of advancing, turned their faces upward to listen to the novel music, and seek the solution of what was a dark enigma to them; and while they were halting, and listening, and dubitating, they heard a concatenation of sharp cracks above their heads, and immediately afterwards a thousand pieces of iron were flying amongst them, laying whole groups of them level with the ground. They ascertained at last that the horrible hubbub proceeded from the little knot of men on the knoll. 'Forward!' yelled a bull-hearted chief, Dajatch Deris, using his spear freely among the most craven. Coerced into activity by gesture and example, they leaped downward like tigers, mad rage in each heart, up and across knolls and curves, and down again into a ravine choked with wild olive and tamarisk, until they were at the base of the hill on which the battery was posted. Just as the Abyssinians were coming up towards the battery, the Punjaub pioneers showed themselves to the enemy on each flank of the guns. 'Commence firing' was the command; and again rattling volleys were discharged in the faces of the sorely harassed natives—who had almost made sure of capturing the cannon—dashing them backward, and downward into the bottom of the ravine many times quicker than their advance. Against shell-vomiting cannon, and against a very wall of fire, discharging bullets by the hundred to their one, what could matchlocks and spears effect?

"Round the base of the battery knoll the ravine ran a serpentine course, emptying itself into the Aroje. It was overgrown with tangled brake and dense jungle. Along this ravine the baffled enemy crawled. 'They are going after our baggage, sir,' said an expostulating voice. 'Ah, are they indeed? so they are!' said Colonel Penn, after an examination. 'Right about! Left oblique! Forward, march!' were the sharp, firm, composed orders given at once and understood. The Punjaubees went sweeping across the knoll in an oblique direction towards the brow overlooking the Aroje. Up the Aroje were advancing long trains of baggage, ammunition, and commissariat stores, pell-mell, in confused masses and in straggling lines. Warned by the thousandfold echoes that the embosoming hills flung far and near, Captain Roberts, who was at the time commander of the baggage-guard, mustered a few companies of the Duke of Wellington's Own and two companies of the 4th, and stationed them at the head of the valley. No sooner had they done so than a confused noise was heard a little above, and presently a large body of men issued out of a narrow gloomy gully; and, as Captain Roberts said, 'By Jove!' the enemy was upon them. 'About face; fire!' and along the line of soldiers drawn across the Arojé ravine there ran a rattle of muskets, a clicking of triggers, and a sharp roar of musketry,—steady, deep-toned, like the thunder rush of an express train through a tunnel. Practised men were at work with the Snider rifle. The Punjaubees came directly upon the scene, looking down from the summit of the knoll, with their dusky faces as dark as the Ethiops'. They saw the enemy, and again the dreadful word for slaughter was given—a word that will be remembered by Abyssinians, and handed down to their posterity. The enemy dropped dead on all sides. Had they stopped ten minutes longer, not a man would have been left alive to tell of the grievous disaster that met them. Here, as elsewhere, they seemed to be too much astonished to fire in return. I did not hear a single Abyssinian musket fired; they seemed to wish to fight hand to hand, but the rapidity of the Sniders gave them no chance. Some six hundred—all that seemed left of the thousand —turned swiftly about, when they found no impression could be made. They dived back into the jungles whence they came; keen-eyed riflemen following them up, and 'potting' the fugitives unerringly.

"The Punjaubees, fleet of foot and prompt at command, swept to their old position near the battery, and deploying along the prolongation of the slope, calmly waited the flying foe to emerge out of the bushes. Not long had they to wait; as the dark forms bounded out of the recesses, the Punjaubees commenced their withering fire upon them once more, descending the slope as they fired. The position in which the Abyssinians now found themselves was a perilous one indeed. It was an open hollow, with clear slopes rising abruptly about a hundred feet from the bottom. On one side were the Punjaubees, 600 in number—up the opposite side, some fifty paces across, scrambled the Abyssinians, with the main desire now simply to get away as quickly as possible from the dangerous place. How easy to imagine the result of the unequal contest, where slope lined with cool riflemen fronted counter-slope clear and open as an artificial glacis. The fight became a *battue*—a massacre! Down the slope rushed the Sepoys, with bayonets fixed to their guns, and, fresher than the tired natives, they soon came up with them, as breathless they panted up the deadly steep. Out of that very despair which the most craven heart feels when hard driven they mustered new courage, and determinedly they turned round at bay. The fiery, hot-blooded, impulsive Sikhs came hand to hand with Ethiopian mountaineers, fierce and as impulsive as they. Now came the tug of a genuine contest! The Abyssinians launched their spears, drew their curved shotels, and charged down with loud cries. The Sikhs, undismayed, rushed up to meet them with their bayonets, and deftly crossed weapons with them. Blows were nimbly warded, stroke was met with counter-stroke, and murderous thrusts skilfully parried. Two companies of the 10th Native Infantry rushed down from the battery knoll to the support of the Sikhs. No mercy was asked; no high-toned sentiment found utterance; no puny blows were dealt; heads were chopped of, arms and limbs severed from trunks, and dead men lay stark and stiff plentifully. But they were all Abyssinians; very few of the Punjaubees were wounded."

While shells, rockets, and musketry were mowing down the Abyssinians, Theodore was belching his war thunder from the summits of Fahla and Selasse. A short, sharp storm of thunder and lightning, followed by torrents of rain, added to the uproar. The 4th, supported by the Beloochees, moved closer to Fahla, and picked the enemy out from every rock and bush. The rockets mounted the heights of Fahla, and destroyed some of the cannoneers. The last lingering group of the enemy was dispersed by Penn's guns. At 5.30 P.M. Theodore's guns ceased their fire, because, as he said, "The English are not afraid of my chain shot; they march up in spite of my big balls;" and because it was useless to fire any longer, as the guns could not be depressed enough to bear on men 1000 feet directly underneath.

One of the correspondents remarks of the battle of Aroje that, "It was a terrible slaughter, and could hardly be called a fight, between disciplined bodies of men, splendidly armed, and scattered parties of savages, scarcely armed at all. . . . Some had died instantaneously; others had fallen mortally wounded. Some of these had drawn their robes over their faces and died like Stoics. Some were only severely wounded, and these had endeavoured to crawl into bushes, and lay there uttering low moans. Their gaudy silk bodices, and the white robes with scarlet ends, which had flaunted so gaily but two hours since, now lay dabbled with blood, and dank with the heavy rains which had been pitilessly coming down for the last hour."

Through some blunder or other it was midnight before the baggage came up; "the tents could not be pitched, and the only resource left for us was to bivouac close to the smoky and uncomfortable fires. Sentries were posted plentifully around the camp, and soldiers slept with their arms ready for immediate use. Before rolling ourselves up in our rugs, and while thinking of the events that marked the day, our ears caught the sounds that betokened the presence of the beasts of prey. In ravenous packs the jackals and hyænas had come to devour the abundant feast spread out by the ruthless hand of war."

Next morning the doctor presented his report: one officer—Captain Roberts—and 31 privates, wounded; Captain Roberts and eight privates severely. Seventy-five wounded Abyssinians carried to hospital, 560 dead of the enemy buried by detailed party. But this did not nearly represent the loss of the Abyssinians. Hundreds of the wounded had crawled off to die, hundreds of the dead had been carried off during the night by their friends, and hundreds more had fallen where our burial parties failed to find them.

Bitter were the feelings of Theodore. When night came on he took to drinking arachi to drown his agony of spirit. Thrice he attempted suicide, but his attendants kept good watch and prevented him. He began to threaten that the English captives should pay for his defeat; but better counsels prevailed. On Saturday evening (April 11) all the captives, 61 in number, arrived in the British camp. Theodore hoped that would suffice, but Napier told him he still required the instant surrender of himself and the fortresses of Selasse, Fahla, and Magdala, assuring him of honourable treatment. "Rather than surrender," said Theodore, "I would fight to the death. Can you not be satisfied with the possession of those you came for, and leave me alone in peace?" Next day he sent 1000 beeves and 500 sheep to Sir Robert Napier, hoping that, as the day was Easter Sunday, the British soldiers would eat their fill, for were they not all Christians? But Napier sent an officer up to Magdala to say that he could not think of accepting anything from His Majesty, until himself, his family, and his fortresses were surrendered to the Queen of England. Napier almost implored him to surrender, but assured him that unless an affirmative answer was received by nine next morning he would move forward to the attack. Every preparation was made: scaling-ladders were constructed out of the long bamboo dhoolie poles, the rungs being the handles of the pioneers' pickaxes; powder charges and hand grenades were made ready for use; the elephants took the Armstrong guns to the front; and the mules were brought up from the Bachelo with two days' ration of grain.

Monday, 13th April—Easter Monday—the sun was shining brightly. At eight in the morning eight Abyssinian chiefs came into camp, and announced that they were ready to surrender Fahla and Selasse, on condition of being allowed to depart with their families and property unharmed. Sir Robert Napier gave them a solemn promise of protection until they crossed the Bachelo on their way home. Colonel Locke and Captain Speedy, with 50 of the 3d Dragoon Guards, were ordered to see them off. No signal of surrender having been received from Theodore, the troops were formed, and marched forward to the assault of Magdala. The 33d led the way, the band playing "Yankee Doodle;" the 4th followed, to the strains of "Garry Owen;" next came the 45th, marching to "Cheer, Boys, Cheer;" then came the Sepoy regiments, the Beloochees, the Punjaubees, two companies of the 10th Native Infantry, the sappers and miners, Penn's mountain train battery, with two mortars, the naval brigade in charge of the rocket battery, and two companies of the 3d Light Native Cavalry. All the rest of the cavalry were sent round into the valley, rearward of Magdala, to prevent Theodore's escape in that direction.

The heights of Fahla and Selasse were cleared by the 3d Light Cavalry and six companies of the 33d, and as the natives reached the foot of the hill they were disarmed by the 10th Native Infantry. While this operation was going on, some ten Abyssinians were seen careering about on the plateau of Islamgee, the saddle which connects Selasse and Magdala. One of these cavaliers rode a white horse, gaily caparisoned, and was clothed in gorgeous robes. Captain Speedy, who had been in Theodore's service, recognised this horseman as the Emperor, which was a great satisfaction, as it had been reported that he had escaped from Magdala. The object of the demonstration was quickly apparent when some of our people stumbled upon twenty guns and mortars, which Theodore had probably intended to convey into Magdala, but had been compelled to abandon. They were immediately taken possession of in the name of Her Majesty.

When the natives were cleared out, the British flag was hoisted on Fahla and Selasse, amid exulting cheers. A small guard was left in these fortresses, and the rest of the troops came down and took their places for the assault. The artillery was so posted as to give a convergent fire. At two P.M. Penn's battery piped for battle, and soon twenty guns of all calibres were thundering at the gates of Magdala. Covered by the fire of the artillery and rockets, the 33d formed columns at quarter distance, and advanced to storm, preceded by a small party of engineers and sappers deployed as skirmishers, and supported by the 45th. The 4th and the rest of the brigade formed in reserve. As the troops advanced along the plateau with trailed arms, signals for rapid firing were made to the artillery. When the storming party was within 50 yards of the rock, the artillery ceased firing, and the advancing column opened fire with their Sniders. Theodore had the men who still adhered to him posted at loopholes and along the cliff wall topped with wattled hurdles, and their fire wounded Major Pritchard and three or four of the most advanced of the engineers. The engineers rushed forward and made a dash upon the barbican, but found the gate closed, and the square tower blocked up with stones to the depth of ten feet. Most unaccountably the engineers had forgotten all their tools—powder, hammers, crowbars, pickaxes, and ladders. This mistake might have been a most unfortunate one, but Drummer M'Guire of the 33d found a way over the cliff wall topped with wattled hurdles, and the rest of the regiment followed, and cleared the plateau of Magdala with a few volleys. Theodore was found lying behind a haystack, scarcely dead, his right hand convulsively clutching a revolver, which in happier times he had received from Queen Victoria. The hoisting of the British flag, the hurrahs of the 33d, and the strains of the National Anthem, proclaimed that Magdala had fallen. During the assault there had been a thunderstorm, but now, as if in approbation, the sun shone forth in all his evening splendour.

All fighting ended with the life of Theodore. The greater part of his soldiers escaped down a path on the other side of the rock; the rest fled to their homes, and secreted the arms which had proved of so little avail against the strange weapons of the European invaders. The soldiers set to work with hammer and chisel and undid the fetters of the native prisoners, many of whom had lingered for years in ponderous iron chains. Some of them were so weak that they were unable to walk, and had to be borne by their friends. The booty was of the poorest description, though large sums were said to be buried somewhere. A few gold crosses and the brocade hangings of the king's tents were the only articles of value. A royal shield of Abyssinia and an ancient gold chalice were reserved for the British Museum.

On the 18th, Magdala was set on fire, and its thatched huts were in a few minutes one sheet of flame. The wind was blowing freshly at the time, and the whole plateau was covered with a fierce blaze, which suggested the burning of a gigantic farmyard of three-quarters of a mile, containing above 300 hayricks. The troops then commenced their return march. On the 20th May, when at Delanta, a general review was held; the division was formed into a hollow square, six deep, and the Adjutant-general (Colonel Frederick Thesiger) read aloud the following general order, reviewing the objects and incidents of the campaign :—

"SOLDIERS OF THE ARMY OF ABYSSINIA,—The Queen and the people of England entrusted to you a very arduous and difficult expedition—to release our countrymen from a long and painful captivity, and to vindicate the honour of our country, which had been outraged by Theodorus, King of Abyssinia. I congratulate you with all my heart on the noble way in which you have fulfilled the commands of our sovereign. You have traversed, often under a tropical sun, or amid storms of rain and sleet, 400 miles of mountainous country. You have crossed many steep and precipitous ranges of mountains, more than 10,000 feet in altitude, where your supplies could not keep pace with you. When you arrived within reach of your enemy, though with scanty food, and some of you for many days without either food or water, in four days you passed the formidable chasm of the Bachelo, and defeated the army of Theodorus, which poured down upon you from their lofty fortress in full confidence of victory. A host of many thousands have laid down their arms at your feet. You have captured and destroyed upwards of thirty pieces of artillery, many of great weight and efficiency, with ample stores of ammunition. You have stormed the almost inaccessible fortress of Magdala, defended by Theodorus with the desperate remnant of his chiefs and followers. After you forced the entrance, Theodorus, who never showed mercy, distrusted the offer of mercy held out to him, and died by his own hand. You have released not only the British captives, but those of other friendly nations. You have unloosed the chains of more than ninety of the principal chiefs of Abyssinia. Magdala, on which so many victims have been slaughtered, has been given to the flames, and remains only a scorched rock.

"Our complete and rapid success is due, first to the mercy of God, whose hand, I feel assured, has been over us in a just cause. Secondly, to the high spirit with which you have been inspired. Indian soldiers have forgotten the prejudices of race and creed, to keep pace with their European comrades. Never has an army entered on a war with more honourable feelings than yours: this has carried you through many fatigues and difficulties; you have been only eager for the moment when you could close with your enemy. The remembrance of your privations will pass away quickly, but your gallant exploit will live in history. The Queen and the people of England will appreciate your services. On my part, as your commander, I thank you for your devotion to your duty, and the good discipline you have maintained. Not a single complaint has been made against a soldier, of fields injured, or villagers wilfully molested in person or property. We must not forget what is due to our comrades who have been labouring for us in the sultry climate of Zoulla and the pass of Komaylee, or in the monotony of the posts which have maintained our communications. Each and all would have given all they possessed to be with us. But they deserve our gratitude.

"I shall watch over your safety to the moment of your re-embarkation, and to the end of my life remember with pride that I have commanded you.

"R. NAPIER,
"*Lieutenant-general, Commander-in-chief.*"

So ended this remarkable crusade, which Mr. Disraeli (Lord

Beaconsfield), speaking in the House of Commons, said, reminded him of the advance of Cortez into Mexico more than any other event of history. Sir Robert Napier was rewarded with a pension and the title of Lord Napier of Magdala, and medals were issued to the army. Theodore's queen, who had taken refuge in the British camp, died on the march homeward. Theodore's son and heir was consigned to the care of Captain Speedy, to be educated for service in our Indian cavalry.

CHAPTER XX.

THE ASHANTEE WAR—1873-1874.

Crossing the Prah—Skirmish at Borborassie—Battle of Amoaful—Capture of Becquah—Battle of Ordahsu, and March on Coomassie—Destruction of Coomassie and return of the troops—Treaty of Fommanah.

ON the west coast of Africa, between the Bight of Benin and Cape Palmas, are a number of forts. Some of these forts formerly belonged to the Danes, some to the Dutch, and some to the English, but at the period of the Ashantee war the English flag alone waved on the Gold Coast. The most important of the forts is Cape Coast Castle, and to the west of it is Elmina, ceded to us by the Dutch. The principal river in this part of Africa is the Prah, which, after running for some distance from the north-east to the south-west, makes a sudden bend, and taking a course almost due south, falls into the Atlantic about twenty miles west of Cape Coast Castle. The whole of the country through which it runs is covered by a dense scrub, except where the natives have made clearings for their villages, or noxious swamps prevent the growth of trees. During the rainy season especially, the climate is fatal to Europeans. The country between Cape Coast Castle and the Prah is inhabited by the Fantees, a tribe which seems to have lost all manly vigour, and will neither work nor fight. Beyond the Prah, to the north and west, the country is inhabited by the Ashantees, a brave and warlike people, but disgraced by incredible cruelty. Their chief delights are gold and blood. Thousands of victims annually perish at their "customs," and the graves of their chief people, kings, queens, and caboceers, are always watered with torrents of human blood. But with all their faults the Ashantees are the most vigorous and enterprising of the native races of that part of Africa, and their capital of Coomassie, which stands about 140 miles to the north of Cape Coast Castle, showed that they had made very considerable progress in many of the handicrafts and some of the arts of life. Their great ambition was to open up their territory to the sea, and this brought them in contact with the Fantees, who suffered terribly from their inroads and invasions. For obvious reasons, in all these quarrels our people at Cape Coast Castle sided with the Fantees, who, however, proved miserable allies. The bond was drawn closer in 1844, when a Protectorate was established over all the Fantee territory, the Fantees agreeing to acknowledge the jurisdiction of Queen Victoria, and obey the British laws, in return for British protection.

The recent transference of Elmina to the British gave great offence at Coomassie, the Dutch having been in the habit of paying the king of Ashantee £80 a-year; not, however, they alleged, as tribute or rent, but simply as a friendly gift. The war party at Coomassie professed to see in this transference an insult to the Ashantee name, and goaded King Coffee Calcallee on to war. They artfully insinuated that the young king, who took his seat upon the stool of royalty in 1868, had not yet equalled the warlike achievements of his distinguished ancestors, and that such another opportunity might never occur again of proving the invincibility of the Ashantee arms. King Coffee was young, rash, and ambitious of military renown, and on the eve of a grand custom, when the whole people were mad with drink and the sight of torrents of human blood, he arose, and in presence of his nobles, knights, and courtiers, swore by "Meminda Coromantee," the sacredest of oaths, that he would carry his golden stool of royalty to Cape Coast Castle, and there wash it in English blood. He then caused to be brought to him the skull of Sir Charles M'Carthy—slain in battle with the Ashantees in 1824—and this ghastly drinking-cup he drained to the toast of victory, and to the conquest of all lands and peoples between Coomassie and the sea.

King Coffee began his invasion of the Fantee and other territories nominally under British protection in January, 1873, with an army of 60,000 men. Colonel Harley's entire force at Cape Coast Castle at this time was only 600 men, consisting of 167 West Indian troops, divided between five or six forts, 200

Houssa police—negroes like the Ashantees themselves, imported from the lower Niger—and 200 local volunteers. The Fantees could have brought into the field a force equal to that of the invaders, but they had no stomach for fighting, and after a double defeat at Yancommassie, their levies dispersed. The Ashantee invasion now swept on, meeting with little or no resistance, and the Ashantee army sat down at Dunquah, 25 miles from Cape Coast Castle. But Cape Coast Castle itself was secured, chiefly by the exertions of Lieutenant Gordon, who raised and drilled a body of Houssas, and formed a redoubt at the village of Napoleon, 5 miles inland. The native town of Elmina showed a disposition to side with the invaders, and on the refusal of the chiefs to give up their arms, the place was bombarded and set on fire. While the bombardment was going on, a force of 2000 or 3000 Ashantees emerged from the forest, and, attacking the loyal part of Elmina, were about to burn it, when the Houssas. the royal marines, under Colonel Festing, and a party of blue-jackets, under Captain Fremantle of the *Barracouta*, came to the rescue. Taking cover under a garden wall, our people poured such a fire upon the Ashantees that they retreated into the bush, leaving two or three hundred dead on the field.

Several other affairs occurred—among others the bombardment of Chamah, by the guns of the *Rattlesnake*, on account of the treachery of the natives, who agreed to an amicable conference, and then fired from an ambuscade upon our boats, wounding Commodore Commerell, commanding on the West African station in H.M.S. *Rattlesnake*, Commander Percy Luxmoore of H.M.S. *Argus*, Captain W. Helden, 2d West India regiment, and six seamen. By this time it was clear to all the officers acquainted with the country, that if peace was to be restored on the Gold Coast, a small army must be despatched from England to strike a decisive blow. But the Government was not yet convinced of the necessity of what must prove so expensive an undertaking, and appointed Sir Garnet Wolseley, who had given proofs of high ability as leader of the Canadian Expedition, in 1870, to proceed to Cape Coast Castle, and report. Sir Garnet and his staff landed at Cape Coast Castle on the 2d October. He first endeavoured to form an army of Fantees, but after a month's experience gave up the attempt as hopeless, and wrote home requesting that the regiments which had been selected for the expedition, should they be found necessary, might be immediately sent out.

Pending the arrival of the troops from England, Sir Garnet set himself to work to free the Protectorate from the Ashantee invaders. The forces at his disposal consisted of only 20 royal marine artillery, under Lieutenant Allen; 169 royal marine light infantry, from H.M.S. *Simoom*, under Captain Crease; 500 blue-jackets and marines, under Captain Fremantle; 200 West India negro troops, under Captain Forbes and Lieutenant Eyre; 20 Kroomen and 126 Houssas, under Lieutenant Richmond; besides a few armed police, and 300 labourers with axes to clear the path. His efforts were admirably seconded by Captain Rait and Lieutenant Eardley Wilmot, of the royal artillery, who drilled a number of Houssas for Gatling guns and rockets; and by Lieutenant-Colonel Wood and Major Russell, who raised two efficient regiments of between four and five hundred men each, from the bravest tribes. After sweeping the Ashantees from their positions near Cape Coast Castle and Elmina, and so preventing them from continuing to obtain smuggled supplies of arms from foreign traders at the sea-coast villages, Sir Garnet commenced his march inland, about the end of October. The Ashantees made an effort to arrest his progress by besieging Abrakrampa, the chief town of the province of Abra, of which the native king was our staunch ally. The place was defended by—besides the native king and his people—Major Baker Russell of the 13th Hussars, with 50 marines and seamen, and 100 Kossohs and other natives, under Captain Bromhead and Lord Gifford of the 24th, and one or two more English officers. After a three days' ineffectual leaguer, during which the Ashantees sustained heavy losses, while not so much as one Englishman was wounded, the Ashantees crossed the Prah at Prahsu, and retreated to Coomassie. While pressing the pursuit, the gallant Lieutenant Eardley Wilmot was shot through the heart. On the 15th December, 1873, Sir Garnet Wolseley was able to report —"That the first phase of the war had been brought to a satisfactory conclusion, by a few companies of the 2d West India regiment, Rait's artillery, Gordon's Houssas, and Wood's and Russell's regiments, admirably conducted by the British officers belonging to them, without the assistance of any other troops except the marines and blue-jackets, who were on the station on his arrival."

This task accomplished, Sir Garnet sketched out the plan of the campaign, and made every preparation for it in his power. The main body of the army, consisting of the European troops, the naval brigade, Wood's and Russell's regiments, and Rait's artillery, was to advance from Prahsu on the main road to Coomassie. On the extreme right, Captain Glover was to lead a native force across the Prah somewhere at Assum; and, as a connecting link between him and the main body, a column composed of natives, under the command of Captain Butler, of the 69th, author of the "Great Lone Land," was to cross the river lower down. On the left, another column of natives, under Captain Dalrymple of the 88th, was to march on Coomassie by the Wassaw road. The real difficulties of the campaign lay in the nature of the country and the climate. First, a road had to be pierced into the very heart of the Ashantee kingdom, through a country of marshes and matted forests, forming an almost impenetrable ambush to an enemy who knew how to take advantage of it. In the second place, the health of the soldiers had to be preserved in every possible way, to enable them to hold out against the pestiferous climate. And lastly, the final blow must be struck and the campaign finished by a certain day, because, if our white troops were caught by the sudden downpouring of the usual rains at the end of February, their return would be stopped, and half of them sick of fever. As Lord Derby remarked, it was to a large extent an engineers' and doctors' war. As to the Ashantees themselves, they were no contemptible enemies, but neither in weapons nor discipline were they any match for our troops. In his "Notes" for the use of the army, Sir Garnet Wolseley says:—"Each soldier must remember that, with his breechloader, he is equal to at least twenty Ashantees, wretchedly armed as they are with old flint muskets, firing slugs or pieces of stone that do not hurt badly at more than forty or fifty yards' range. Our enemies have neither guns nor rockets, and have a superstitious dread of those used by us."

With the aid of native labourers, the royal engineers cleared and widened the forest path for the passage of the troops and stores, flooring the marshy parts with a "corduroy" of tree trunks laid side by side. Bit by bit as the road was made they erected an electric telegraph, to flash the latest news to Cape Coast Castle. They constructed pontoon bridges over the Prah and other smaller rivers, and they provided huts for the men at the nightly halting places. These huts were constructed of bamboo framework, thatched with palm leaves, and furnished with raised bedsteads made of bamboo wattle. Each hut was some 80 feet long by 18 feet wide, and large enough to lodge half a battalion.

The troops sent to the Gold Coast consisted of the 42d Royal Highlanders, with 135 volunteers from the 79th Highlanders, the rifle brigade, a detachment of the royal engineers, the 23d Welsh fusiliers, and a detachment of the royal artillery — in all 2504 men. The disembarkation took place on the 1st day of January, 1874, and by seven o'clock that evening the whole force was at Inquabim, six miles from Cape Coast Castle. Several days were occupied in making the march to Prahsu, 84 miles inland, where Sir Garnet Wolseley and his staff had arrived on the 2d, and the naval brigade on the 3d. The British troops were accompanied by 350 men of the 2d West India regiment, Rait's artillery, 50 men, and Wood's and Russell's regiments, numbering together 800 men. The land transport service had great difficulties to contend with. Nearly 5000 of the Fantee porters and roadmakers deserted when ordered to carry their burdens to the front. This caused some delay at Mansu, 35 miles inland, and as idleness in such a climate is utterly prostrating to white men, this short period of inaction did more harm to our soldiers than all the hard work of the campaign. Another vexation consequent on the desertion of the Fantees was that the Welsh fusiliers and the royal artillery had to re-embark, all but 200, as there was no conveyance for their stores. The 42d volunteered to act as their own porters, and actually performed this unusual service for a day or two.

Seventy medical officers accompanied the expedition, most of them volunteers, and everything was done to preserve the health of the soldiers that medical science and untiring devoted zeal could do. Instead of the regimental uniforms, which were left behind in the transports, all wore a suit of grey tweeds, light and easy, with pockets, and a pith helmet to protect the head from the rays of a tropical sun. The men were allowed to march with their jackets off, but had orders to put them on the instant they halted, and when on sentry or at rest to court the shade as much as possible. The food supplied was wholesome in quality and sufficient in quantity; fresh meat and bread at every second road station, tins of Australian beef, with biscuits, served out on alternate days, with preserved vegetables, potatoes, and rice. Every soldier had chocolate in the morning, and tea with sugar at night; but latterly, instead of tea at night, a little rum. A dose of quinine was administered daily to prevent sickness, and a potion of lime-juice several times a week.

Prahsu was reached in the early part of January. During the stay here ambassadors arrived from King Coffee, with letters expressive of a desire for peace. Sir Garnet told the ambassadors that he would only grant peace, on condition, first, that the king must sign a treaty securing the British Protectorate from future aggression; second, that he must release all European captives—for two German missionaries and their families, named Kuhne and Ramseyer, M. Bonnat, a French merchant, and one or two others, had been captives at Coomassie for four years, having been sent thither in irons after a treacherous invitation to a friendly conference at the Ashantee camp; and lastly, that he must pay 50,000 ounces of pure gold, or nearly a quarter of a million sterling, towards the expenses of the war. As security for the performance of these articles, Sir Garnet demanded as hostages the Queen Dowager and the king's brother, Prince Mensah, the heir apparent to the throne. One of the Ashantee ambassadors came to a melancholy end at Prahsu. The ambassadors were shown the practise of the Gatling guns, and this one told his colleagues that it was vain to fight against foes so armed. They threatened to accuse him of cowardice to the king, and the miserable man, dreading the fate which awaited him on his return to Coomassie, shot himself in the night.

But, from the intelligence brought him by Lord Gifford and Major Russell, in their scouting expeditions across the Prah, Sir Garnet had no faith in the king's overtures for peace; and on the 20th January, the engineers having put the last touches to the bridge over the Prah, the troops intended for the attack on Coomassie crossed over. The advance was preceded by Lord Gifford and his native scouts. The army passed the Adansi hills, the natural barriers of the Ashantee kingdom on the south, and on the 24th occupied Fommanah, a town about 30 miles from Coomassie. Messrs. Kuhne, Ramseyer, and Bonnat now arrived with further overtures for peace, but as the king had not delivered up the hostages, Sir Garnet answered that he meant to go on to Coomassie. Every day it became more plain

that King Coffee was concentrating his forces, and on the 29th
the naval brigade and some other troops had a skirmish with a
party of the enemy at Borborassie. Captain John Nicol
(formerly of the 13th, and late adjutant of the Hants militia),
who led the advance with his dark-skinned Annamboes, was
unfortunately shot dead while explaining to the Ashantees that
if they did not fire they would not be fired on. Captain Nicol
was the first officer who fell north of the Prah. On the night of
the 30th our advanced guard was at Quarman, within two miles
of Amoaful, where the Ashantees were stated to be some 20,000
strong, under their greatest General, Amanquatiah. The position
was admirably adapted for their peculiar mode of fighting.
The ground was covered with a mass of vegetation almost solid,
intersected by lanes seldom above 8 feet wide, and, hollowed by
rains, so uneven and steep at the sides as to afford but scanty
footing. Between Quarman and Amoaful was the hamlet of
Egginassie, on the bank of a stream that flowed through the
densest forest.

Sir Garnet Wolseley adapted his tactics to the peculiar exi-
gencies of an engagement in the bush. He divided his forces
into four columns, so disposed that when they closed up they
would form a square; the side columns to take in ground to the
line of advance, so as to prevent any flank attack on the advancing front centre. Paths through the jungle were cut for
each column by large parties of native labourers.

On the morning of the 31st January, the army advanced to
the attack in the following order:—The front column, which
was to extend in line as it advanced, was commanded by Brigadier-general Sir Archibald Alison, C.B., and consisted of the
42d Royal Highlanders, under Major Duncan Macpherson and
Major Scott; two 7-pound guns, commanded by Captain Rait
himself; and a detachment of royal engineers under Major
Home. The left column, under the command of Colonel J. C.
M'Leod, C.B., consisted of the right wing of the naval brigade,
under Captain Luxmore of the *Druid;* Major Russell's regiment
of native allies, part of Rait's Houssa artillery, two rocket detachments, and a detachment of royal engineers under Captain
Buckle. The right column, under the command of Lieutenant-
Colonel Evelyn Wood, V.C., 90th Light Infantry, consisted of
the left wing of the naval brigade, under Captain Grubbe of

the *Tamar;* Wood's native allies, a detachment of Rait's Houssa artillery, two rockets, and a detachment of the royal engineers. The rear column consisted of the 2d battalion of the rifle brigade, under Lieutenant-Colonel A. F. Warren. Each column was followed by a number of Fantee porters, bearing the reserve ammunition and thirty or forty hammocks for the wounded. The Fantees were carefully guarded by soldiers lest they should run away. The whole force numbered 2500 men. Sir Garnet was borne aloft in a Madeira cane chair, mounted on the shoulders of four Fantee porters.

The battle commenced at 8.5 A.M., when Lord Gifford and his scouts carried the village of Egginassie. The front column then extended into the thick bush on each side of the road, which, says Sir Garnet Wolseley, "was cut and widened by labourers under the royal engineers, so as to admit of the advance of the guns. As the leading column advanced northward, the left column, according to orders previously issued, cut a path diagonally to the left front, with a view of protecting the left flank of the front column; and as it moved along this path, the right column, closing up, cut a path diagonally to the right to protect the right flank, while the rear column extended, so as to gain touch of the right and left columns, and, should it be outflanked, to face east and west outwards. My intention was to fight in the form of a square, and so oppose the invariable flanking tactics of the enemy, which their superior numbers would probably allow them to carry out against any line which I could form."

The advance of the front column is thus described by Mr. Stanley:—"The front column, pushing on to occupy the village of Egginassie close after Gifford's scouts, had swept across the open ground of the clearing and deployed into position in the jungle. Reserving their fire until they encountered the enemy, the Highlanders had continued advancing until they had penetrated about 200 yards beyond the village, when the concealed enemy suddenly revealed himself by firing into their faces from cleverly-contrived ambuscades. Henceforward the Highlanders continued to sweep the bush in front of them with steadily-poured volleys, until they had silenced the enemy's fire, during which pause the engineer labourers were pushed forward to cut the bush for a farther advance. When the labourers had succeeded in clearing a space of ground in front, the Highlanders moved forward until they discovered the enemy again. The road to Amoaful from Egginassie served as a guide to the wings spread out on each side of Rait's artillery, which continued to move down in line with the infantry. Whenever a favourable opportunity presented itself, Captain Arthur Rait with his brave Houssas sent telling shots. Thus artillery and Highlanders slowly marched down the sloping ground, driving the foe steadily out of his numerous hiding-places, which he had constructed of bush, with a skill which almost defied detection by the eye. The best means of discovering his whereabouts were found to be telling volleys from Sniders, and booming rounds from the tiny 7-pounders, which sent their shot with disastrous effect through the forest.

"At the bottom of the slope ran a lazy stream, which coursed sluggishly through expanses of morass, and over depths of black slime. A hundred yards beyond this stream were seen the silvan huts which the Ashantees had constructed out of tree boughs and plantain leaves. These huts numbered hundreds, spread out far on each side of the road. Such was the place the Ashantees chose to defend, which they did with a pertinacity that won high praise and admiration from the Highlanders. The soldiers were put to their mettle, and the Houssas, as if catching the fierce enthusiasm which animated the Scotch Highlanders, laboured with a vigour and energy not eclipsed by any on the field. Captain Rait, halting at the same altitude above the stream below as the Ashantee camp was on the other side of it, aimed his guns with such good effect at the huts that, on passing them, the ghastly heaps that met the sight, of rent bodies and disfigured dead, bore a silent but significant testimony to the important service the Houssa artillery had contributed on this day towards crushing the pride of the enemy.

"When the front column had dislodged the Ashantees from their several positions, and finally driven them with fearful loss from their camps, Sir Archibald pushed it forward; and while bagpipes blew their most strenuous notes, and the wild Highland cheers for victory pealed through the forest, the whole line surged across the stream, and swept up the opposite slope until the outskirts of Amoaful were reached. Here Highlanders and Houssas, now animated to the highest pitch of valour, rushed forward at the top of their speed, to the entrance of the broad avenue which divides the town into two equal portions. As they appeared within the town at the foot of this avenue, they saw several excited groups of natives hurrying away from it, some bearing away wounded chiefs, others transporting their household property. One group specially attracted the attention of Lieutenant Saunders, R.A.—that of four slaves carrying on their shoulders the wounded body of their master, with two others following closely behind. Aiming a shell at them, the missile exploded but a few inches above their heads and in the centre of the group, killing every soul instantly. After a few more desultory shots, the capture of the town of Amoaful was complete."

In the meantime, the other columns were not idle. "The left column," says Sir Garnet Wolseley, "advancing under a heavy fire, by which Captain Buckle, R.E., was killed while urging on his labourers, occupied the crest of a hill, where a clearing was made, and the enemy was driven away from this position of their camp by an advance of the naval brigade and Russell's regiment. Colonel M'Leod, having cleared his front, and having lost touch of the left of the front column, now cut his way in a north-easterly direction, and came into the main road in rear of the Highlanders about the same hour that the advance occupied Amoaful. I protected his left rear by a detachment of the rifle brigade. Our left flank was now apparently clear of the enemy."

Very hot was the contest which the right column was called upon to sustain. "At 11.30," says Stanley, "the right column was rudely awakened from apparent inactivity into a fierce blaze of excitement, and as the village of Egginassie was situated on the slope of the long low forest-clad hill, the enemy when he crested it and bore down on the right column in force, visited ourselves (with the head-quarters in the centre of the square at Egginassie) with a hail of slugs, which caused the trees around and the branches above us to shed their leaves over us as thick as flakes in a snow-storm. A few seconds after this tremendous firing in our vicinity began, Colonel Wood, commanding the right column, was brought in with an iron slug in his chest; then his aide-de-camp followed, disabled with a slug in his hip; then we find that in a short time fourteen blue-jackets have been assisted into the village, some of them grievously wounded. The firing at such close quarters to us waxes terrific. The line of the fighting right column, now hotly engaged with a persisting foe, who crawls serpent-like closer and closer to them, is not fifty yards away from us, and we are plentifully touched and tapped, lightly it is true, by a hail of slugs. Men with whom I am conversing abruptly spin round as they feel the blows. Lieutenant Maurice, sitting on a log, listening to the thunder of the unceasing, ear-splitting fusilade, is struck in the back. Doctor Fegan, of the *Active*, while conversing for a moment with Commodore Hewett and myself, is violently struck on his scarf-pin, and others have similar experiences to relate. Every man of the right column feels that this is a critical moment, and that he must roll back the tide of attack, or be driven himself in hot haste to infamous flight, and so he plies his faithful Snider with that nervous rapidity born of desperate necessity. Probably Sir Garnet feels that it is a critical moment also, considering that Wood's regiment of native allies only lies between his head-quarters and the enemy, and he orders the 23d Royal Welsh Fusiliers forward to the support, to advance in a north-easterly direction.

"The firing rises to a deafening pitch, there is not a break or pause in the thick volume of sound, lazy clouds of gunpowder-smoke enwrap the forest tops as with a curtain. Things proceed at this rate for a short interval, wounded combatants drop in rapidly; there are about 100 wounded, dying, and dead in the village, though several of the wounded, having had their wounds dressed, have been borne to Quarman, when Sir Garnet orders up a second support of two companies of the rifle brigade, with emphatic orders to push on and drive the stubborn enemy from his coverts. We, waiting to hear the support of fresh men, can tell the very minute they commence firing, can mark the progress which they make through the thick jungle by the diminishing volume of the musketry, can almost reckon the rate at which they advance, and feel very much relieved when at 12.30 the wild cheers which the Apoboes utter tell us of the rapid retreat of the Ashantees.

"But while we are congratulating ourselves that the important battle of Amoaful is ended, loud and continuous musketry is heard in our rear along the road to (the entrenched post of) Quarman, whither the wounded have been taken for safety, and the entrance to the village from Quarman is choked by the forms of the frightened Fantee carriers. Sir Garnet thought of this possibility, and prepared his plan of battle for such a contingency. The four companies of the rifle brigade, hitherto unemployed in the battle, are ordered to take the back track and defend the line of communication, and they are soon engaged.

with the Ashantees in vigorous earnestness, until 1.45 P.M., when a cessation of the musketry announces that the enemy, having attempted the power of the Europeans on the left, the front, the right and rear columns, is convinced that he has been defeated, and is unable to withstand the strange weapons which the white men use in war."

During the afternoon and evening the enemy made several partial attempts on Quarman, and on a large convoy of baggage which had been packed at Insarfu during the action, but were everywhere repulsed. It was 5 P.M. when Sir Garnet arrived at Amoaful. As all the baggage had been left behind at Insarfu, the troops kindled large bonfires, and bivouacked on the avenue in the open air. The loss in the battle of Amoaful was 1 officer (Captain Buckle) and 3 men killed, and 15 officers and 193 men wounded. The greater part of this loss fell on the 42d, which had 2 men killed, and 9 officers and 106 men wounded. The naval brigade had 34 men wounded.

The loss of the Ashantees was estimated at from 800 to 1200 killed, and as many more wounded; but it was difficult to judge, as it was the invariable custom of the enemy to bear his dead and wounded from the field, for fear of decapitation. This fearful fate occurred to one of our men, a Highlander, who fell back to Egginassie to have his wound dressed, but lost his way, and unfortunately fell in with a body of Ashantees, who overpowered him and cut his head off. His body was afterwards found by some men of Russell's regiment, and buried at Amoaful. The slashed hands and almost severed fingers showed what a terrible struggle the poor man had made for his life. The Ashantees lost many of their best leaders at Amoaful. The king of Mampon, who commanded the right, was mortally wounded; and Amanquatiah, who commanded the left, and Appia, one of the great chiefs engaged in the centre, were killed.

Next day (February 1) the village of Becquah, about a mile and a half to the left front, was captured by Colonel M'Leod, with the naval brigade, a gun and rocket trough, Rait's artillery, Russell's regiment, Lord Gifford's guides, and a detachment of Major Home's engineers, supported by detachments of the Welsh fusiliers and the 42d. On the 2d, leaving the baggage behind, the army resumed its march to Coomassie, preceded by Russell's regiment and Gifford's scouts. The ground was everywhere bestrewed by native accoutrements, silk-cotton bolsters, stools, and scores of corn rations in neatly plaited corn leaves, which the enemy had dropped in their hurried flight. The air was filled with a peculiar odour of death. "Each village had its human sacrifice lying in the middle of the path, for the purpose of affrighting the conquerors. The sacrifice was of either sex, sometimes a young man, sometimes a young woman. The head, severed from the body, was turned to meet the advancing army, the body was evenly laid out with the feet toward Coomassie. This laying out in this manner meant no doubt, 'Regard this face, white men, ye whose feet are hurrying on to our capital, and learn the fate awaiting you.'" On the evening of the 3d the army reached the left bank of the Ordah, the last natural barrier between them and the capital of the Ashantee kingdom. The engineers immediately set to work to throw a bridge over the river, and the troops encamped for the night; but their rest was broken by a tornado and a tremendous downpour of rain that drenched the bivouac. But no one thought much of these discomforts, for the enemy were reported to be in force at Ordahsu, a village a mile and a half beyond the northern bank of the river; and if all went well to-morrow—and who could doubt it?—they might make their next bivouac in Coomassie. During the course of the day (the 3d) Sir Garnet had received a letter from King Coffee, imploring him to halt and give him time to collect the indemnity, promising to give up the hostages; to which Sir Garnet had replied that he would halt only when the money and the hostages were in his power, and if they were not in the camp by next morning, he would march on Coomassie and burn it to the ground.

Next morning, no money or hostages having arrived, the army crossed the bridge which the engineers had hastily thrown over the Ordah. Scarcely were the troops in motion when, at 7.40 A.M., the advanced guard, consisting of Gifford's scouts, the rifle brigade, Russell's regiment, and Rait's artillery, found itself fiercely engaged with large numbers of the enemy, who had crowded into the village of Ordahsu, and manned the huts on each side of the road with great bravery and no little skill. King Coffee Calcallee directed the battle in person, from the village of Akkanwassi, about a mile and three-quarters farther on. Here, seated on his golden stool, under his red umbrella, sheltered by the plantain fronds, with a number of his chiefs around him, he waited for that special intervention which the fetish ulemas had promised him, but waited in vain, for as the day wore on, and the tide of war rolled slowly forward, a Snider bullet sang past his ears, and he was fain to be borne away by his slaves.

But not without a fierce struggle did the Ashantees give way. For hours they kept our troops at bay; but at length the rifle brigade gained the village of Ordahsu. Immediately its capture was reported, Sir Garnet ordered forward the baggage. Thus secured between the advanced guard and the main column, a panic flight of the Fantee porters was impossible. It was a happy inspiration, for no sooner were the Ashantees driven away in front than they surged round on the right flank, expectant of plunder, but were disappointed.

"Sir Garnet," says Mr. Stanley, "now did that which he ought to have done before, but which done even at noon, half an hour before the battle ended, shows better than anything, in my opinion, the audacity of his character, and the quick intelligence of the active and capable General who is prompt to conceive and ready to execute. He ordered up the 42d Highlanders, and gave orders to Colonel M'Leod to carry the positions in front, and march straight into Coomassie. Captain Rait's artillery was to cover the attack. No man is more cool than Colonel M'Leod in action. He drew up his men in double file from one end of the village (Ordahsu) to the other. The famous Black Watch appeared, though greatly reduced in numbers (340 on this day), to be fit followers of their colonel. Both colonel and soldiers mutually understood one another. There was no doubt or hesitancy in either commanding officer or men. During the brief halt, Colonel M'Leod surveyed his men, and then said, 'The 42d will fire volleys by companies, according to order. Forward!'

"Then began the sublime march to Coomassie, the most gallant conduct, and most impressive action, of the Ashantee campaign. It was on the 'fast fire' and 'advance fast' principle. The Highlanders marched out of the village, from the garish sunlight of the open into the gloomy chasm of the forest, by a road beset by ambuscades, with a proud military bearing, full of determination and a joyous courage. Soon after they advanced into that fearful gaping pass in the forest, the enemy opened on them from his coverts. Colonel M'Leod shouted out clear and loud, 'Company A, front rank fire to the right, rear rank fire to the left. Forward!' The companies fired in succession, according to order, front ranks firing to the right, rear ranks firing to the left, and, halting not even to deliver their volleys, marched past the ambuscades, the bagpipes playing, and the wild Highland cheers echoing as loud as the musketry; Captain Rait, with his hard-striking artillery, hurling his shot and rockets to the right and left of the enemy.

"This was a new game of war which the white man inaugurated in Ashantee, and which the Ashantees did not understand. It was out of all precedent. The custom used to be to lie down and adhere to the earth, and fire away for hours until one party or the other expended all his ammunition, or got tired of the tedium of this kind of fighting to try in another part of the field. But this marching past ambuscades with salutes of bullets they did not understand; they became anxious, and then panic-stricken, and within half-an-hour after the Highlanders had departed, the impression that something unusual had happened in the front seemed to have been transmitted throughout the ranks of the enemy on all sides. A loud blowing of horns on our right and in our rear seemed to announce, 'To your tents, O Ashantees! Coomassie is fallen, the battle is lost!' and subsiding notes heard at a distance, sounded like a wail of despair, as the gentle breeze bore them through the forest to our ears. At last the sounds of the battle of Ordahsu died away, and the last clod of earth was thrown over the remains of the young and gallant gentleman (Lieutenant Eyre, of Wood's native allies) who had fallen in the early part of it.

"Then the native regiments were ordered to advance, the porters carrying the reserve ammunition and medical stores were driven after them; the staff followed, then came the rifles, and finally the naval brigade. It was in this manner we followed the road which the 42d Highlanders had cleared for us but half an hour before. A few of the results of their volleys we saw in dead men lying across or on the side of the road. We saw one man who had evidently taken shelter behind a thick cotton-wood buttress. A Snider bullet with great penetrative force had gone clean through the five inches of cotton-wood, and had slain the man behind it. . . .

"But the Highlanders continued their march past Karsi, meeting with flags of truce on the way—Sir Archibald Alison on his white mule, and Colonel M'Leod on foot, leading them across the fetid deadly swamp which insulates Coomassie. While crossing this place, Sir Archibald's mule stumbled, and the gallant brigadier fell under the animal into the nauseous liquid, which reeked with human putrefaction. As Sir Archibald has but one arm, it would have been difficult for him to have extricated himself from his dangerous position, had not his brigade major, Captain Robinson, immediately relieved him.

"In the meantime the main body, consisting of the 23d Royal Welsh Fusiliers, Wood's and Russell's regiments, rifles and naval brigade, were toiling on hard and fast after the 42d. On the road Sir Garnet received a cheery despatch from Sir Archibald Alison to this effect—'We have taken all the villages but the last before entering Coomassie. The enemy is flying panic-stricken before us. Support me with half the rifles, and I enter Coomassie to-night.' Then came, by two different flags of truce, letters from Dawson the missionary, begging in piteous terms for delay for the sake of his life and that of his fellow-captives. A bearer of one of them informed us that the king had left Coomassie the night before for the battle-field, and had not returned to his capital since, but he and his army were known to be in full flight towards Amineeha, a country residence of His Majesty. Still marching past we came through and passed by Karsi, and at 6 P.M. the staff and head of the main body of the column had crossed the swamp and entered a long broad avenue flanked on each side by pretentious-looking edifices of porticoed and alcoved houses. We were at last in Coomassie!

"As we arrived in the market-place, we saw hundreds of wondering Ashantees, with their weapons in their hands, regarding us most curiously. It was attempted at first to disarm them, but the general, doubtless thinking that at this late hour of the day it was bad policy to begin hostilities, ordered them to be treated kindly and to be left alone. Turning to the left when we arrived at the market-place, we saw another wide and noble street, half a mile long, where the 42d Highlanders were drawn quietly in line, awaiting the arrival of the general. As the general arrived in front of them, the Highlanders uttered their victorious cheers; and soon every straggler and new arrival of the main body caught up the hearty cries, and announced to those far behind, not yet arrived in the capital, as well as to the wondering citizens regarding us, and the advancing fugitives from the battle-field, the certain FALL OF COOMASSIE, the dread capital of the Ashantee kingdom."

Sir Garnet spent the next day in Coomassie, in the hope that the king would arrive and come to terms; but King Coffee did not make his appearance, and a heavy downpour of rain made the general apprehensive that the rainy season was coming on, in which case the health of the troops would suffer, and his retreat to the coast be interrupted by the flooding of the rivers. He resolved therefore to destroy Coomassie, and set out for the coast at once. Accordingly, early on Friday morning (February 6, 1874) the streets were cleared of people by detachments of the naval brigade, and as the troops marched out on their homeward route, the engineers passed from house to house with fiery torches, the rear guard, composed of the 42d, moving slowly on before them. Scarcely had they left the town when several explosions were heard, proclaiming that the stone palace of King Coffee Calcallee had become a shapeless ruin.

Sir Garnet was at Fommanah (February 13) when King Coffee sent, with an urgent request for peace, 1000 ounces of gold as the first instalment of the war indemnity. The humbled king's tardy submission was accepted, and a treaty of peace was drawn up, by which the war indemnity was fixed at 50,000 ounces of gold; the king of Ashantee confined himself strictly to his own kingdom, and withdrew all pretentions to Elmina; freedom of trade was established between the sea-coast and Coomassie, the king guaranteeing that the roads from Coomassie to the river Prah should always be kept open and free from bush to a width of 15 feet; and, lastly, the king would use his best endeavours to check the practice of human sacrifice, with a view to putting an end to it altogether.

Glover's force reached Coomassie on the 12th. The day before, Captain Reginald Sartorius, of the 6th Bengal Cavalry, had ridden into the capital with 20 men. Captain Butler's and Captain Dalrymple's forces had ere this deserted them.

By the 22d February the troops had nearly all arrived at Cape Coast Castle, and were immediately embarked for England —the rifle brigade in the *Himalaya*, the Welsh fusiliers in the

Tamar, the Black Watch in the *Sarmatian*, and the general and his staff in the *Manitoban*. On their arrival in England, officers and men were received with the greatest enthusiasm, and honours were showered on the successful warriors. Sir Garnet Wolseley received a baronetcy and a pension, and the Grand Cross of St. Michael and St. George. Most of the surviving officers—many, alas! had succumbed to the climate and the slugs of the enemy—were promoted. The Victoria Cross—the most coveted distinction of the soldier—was conferred on Lord Gifford and Sergeant M'Gaw of the 42d.

On the issue of the Ashantee war medals to those who had distinguished themselves during the campaign, Sir John M'Leod of the 42d penned the following Regimental Order, which tells of many a deed of valour done in the gloomy depths of the African forest:—

"MALTA, 24*th May* 1875.

"Sir John M'Leod considers the Ashantee war medals, now received in full and issued to the regiment, will be worn with satisfaction by the men. He thinks that, although the expedition for which it is granted was only a little war, the medal may take its place, not unworthily, beside the other decorations on the breast. Though little, the war had a magnitude and audacity about it to awaken the interest of the civilized world, and to exhibit in a marked degree those same qualities, latent in you, which sustained the corps of old in the Savannah, in Flanders, and in other unhealthy places; where, be it remembered, they were not cared for as you were on the Gold Coast by a beneficent government. Men who can act as you acted—and the Bush has terrors of its own—altogether as though the honour of the regiment was committed to each individual member of it, has given evidence of a standard of character blending a perfect obedience with a just self-reliance. There is no page of your regiment's annals brighter than that which tells of your encounter with your savage foe in the murky bottoms of Amoaful; of the valour and discipline which carried you into the gaping chasm of the forest at Ordahsu; through the fetid Soubang swamp — headed by Colour-sergeant Barton, who, though wounded at Amoaful, continued working hard, hardly missing a shot—never halting until you had set your foot in the market-place of Coomassie. And on this day it is fitting to remember the distinguished conduct of Privates Alexander Hodge and

John Arthur, carrying Major Baird, more desperately wounded than themselves, to a place of safety; and the noble heroism of Private W. Thomson, one of the party, sacrificing himself rather than see his captain fall into the hands of the enemy; how Sergeant M'Gaw won the Victoria Cross; the sustained gallantry throughout of Privates Thomas Adams and George Ritchie; the cheerful disregard of personal danger of Sergeant-instructor-of-musketry Street, though badly wounded in the thigh; of Quarter-master-sergeant Patterson running the gauntlet of fire upon the road, for a hammock to carry the dangerously wounded Sergeant-major to the rear, assisted by Paymaster-sergeant Bateman; of Pioneer-sergeant Gairns's look of scorn when, disabled in the right arm, he was advised to fall to the rear! how was the flame of battle to be fed if he was at the rear and not there to serve out the ammunition? how Sergeant Butters, shot through the leg at Amoaful, marched with his company till again struck down in the gloomy pass of Ordahsu; of Sergeant Graham Gillies, and Privates Jones and John Grant, of B Company, always to the front; how wounded Piper Weatherspoon, taking the rifle and place of dead Corporal Samuel, fought till overpowered with wounds; of Sergeant Milne and Private Hector White, and gallant Privates W. Bell, Imray, and M'Phail, fighting with remarkable bravery. But the space I would allow myself is more than filled, and I have before me Sergeant John Simpson, Colour-sergeant Farquharson, and Privates Calderwood, W. Armstrong, J. Miller, Peter Jeffrey, Colour-sergeant Cooper, and Piper Honeyman, 'tangled in the bush,' and lost to his company; Surgeon-major Clutterbuck, your old doctor, using few hammocks, how he marched all the way—his own recipe for surmounting all difficulties—and defended successfully his wounded, on the roadside, with his revolver; and Hospital-orderly M'Cudden—the hammock-men hesitating to follow the regiment into the dread Ordahsu Pass, encouragingly he threw aside his sword and revolver, placed himself at their head, led thus into Coomassie; and Quarter-master Forbes—unsurpassed—how, in the hottest of the fray, you had your ammunition always handy, your rations—sometimes more—ready. The first to swim the Dah on your return, few will forget the hot tea he welcomed you with at your bivouac on that wet dreary night; Private Johnston, the last to pass over, how he lost his clothes in the dark, and was sandwiched by the doctor in two hammocks, faring not so badly. And others unmentioned, generous men, and remembered. Scattered as you are in detachments over Cottonera, I regret I have been unable with my own hand, and the fever on me, to give to each of you his well-earned medal. But I address you on this the Queen's birthday, that you may be sure your good conduct is not forgotten. Wear the medal with its ribbon, yellow and black, significant colours to you."

We have had no fighting since the Ashantee War, with the exception of another Kaffir outbreak at the Cape. But our Redcoats and Bluejackets are still made of the same stuff as in the days of Waterloo and the Alma, of the Nile and Trafalgar. This was shown, only the other day, so to speak, when complications arose in the East, and it seemed likely that Britain would have to draw the sword to defend her honour and her interests. Everything portended war. There was a great stir in the dockyards at Chatham and Portsmouth, the Mediterranean fleet was ordered first to Besika Bay and then to the Sea of Marmora, a contingent from the native Indian Army was conveyed to Malta to be in readiness, and the Reserves were ordered to join the colours. The ready and eager spirit which pervaded all ranks of the service was extremely gratifying. The soldiers of the regular army and the seamen of the fleet were, of course, elated at the prospect of a brush with their old enemies of Russia; but more remarkable was the pride of the native Indian troops at serving under the British flag in Europe, and the alacrity of the Reserves in leaving their peaceful occupations to obey the call of duty. Happily the war-cloud passed over, and the sword remained in its scabbard; orders were therefore issued for the re-conveyance of the native troops to India, and the discharge of the Reserves. But before these orders took effect, the Duke of Cambridge reviewed the native Indian troops at Malta (June 17, 18, 19, 1878), and the Reserves at Aldershot (July 24). Of both he gave the most favourable reports. Telegraphing to the Viceroy of India, he says:—"Having completed the inspection of the Indian forces assembled at Malta, I beg to now congratulate you, and the Indian armies, on the admirable appearance and efficiency of the troops. Their health is excellent, and their conduct admirable." In terms not less gratifying does he speak of

the Reserves. In a general order of the 29th July, he says:—
"His Royal Highness, the Field-Marshal commanding-in-chief, has received the Queen's commands to convey to the non-commissioned officers and soldiers of the army and militia reserves, who are now about to return to their homes, Her Majesty's entire approbation of the manner in which they performed their duties whilst serving with the colours. The cheerfulness and alacrity with which they responded to the call made upon them at a period of national emergency has made a deep and most favourable impression upon Her Majesty."

Regarding the navy, the Right Honourable W. H. Smith, First Lord of the Admiralty, spoke as follows at the Banquet at the Mansion House, after the freedom of the City of London had been conferred, in the Guild Hall, upon the Earl of Beaconsfield and the Marquis of Salisbury, August 3, 1878:—"It is usual on occasions like this to speak of the events of the remote past, and to say that the proud history of the navy will be repeated in the future; but I prefer on the present occasion to speak of the services of the navy at the present time—to speak of the services rendered to this country within the last six months, that most eventful period in the history of this country and of the world. It will be recollected that some five months ago the order was given by Her Majesty's Government to Admiral Hornby to advance up the Dardanelles and to anchor in the Sea of Marmora. On that occasion the weather was so severe, a snowstorm was falling so dense and so thick, that it was impossible for one ship to make out the vessel that was leading immediately before it. But that duty was, nevertheless, discharged to the full—the fleet arrived at its anchorage. . . . But this service has not been performed without strain, without anxiety, and without an exhibition of qualities which are far higher, in my estimation, than those which are required to fight a battle or to engage an enemy. Day after day, night after night, the boats and men of the fleet have kept watch and ward. They observed the proceedings of those whom, I would not say they feared, but who might have become their enemies at any moment. They were in a state of constant preparation and constant preparedness. They knew not when the blow would fall, or when it would become their duty to maintain the honour and interests of England. And during all this period of strain, a period of anxiety, a period of great difficulty on the part of those who had to command—of great self-denial and great self-control on the part of those who had to be commanded—not one single breach of discipline so far as I know has occurred, not one single error has been committed. We have remained at peace with him who might have been our enemy. Fortunately no mistake has been made, and now, after this long period of watching and waiting, we look forward with confidence to the blessings of rest and peace. I venture to think that those brave men who have endured this period of waiting and watching, of care and anxiety, who have not known what leave, or liberty, or rest is, deserve the expression of the confidence of the people of this country. I think we may well be proud, not only of the power and strength of the navy, as it is exhibited by guns and ships, but we may also be proud of the self-reliance, of the patience and the self-control, which is exhibited by the officers and sailors. Fortunately it has not happened that they have been called upon to engage in active war. . . . They have not been called upon to draw a sword or fire a gun. But I can assert with confidence that if it had been so—if it had been their duty to engage in a conflict, there never was a time when England was so worthily represented as she has been during the last twelve months in the Mediterranean, and during the last six months still nearer the theatre and the scene of war."

While such a spirit continues to be manifested, there is little fear of England losing her proud position among the nations. We are at peace with all the world; but just at this moment there come rumours of threatened war from the Afghan frontier. Shere Ali, the Ameer of Afghanistan, has long been deeply offended with what he considers our encroaching border policy, with our expeditions against the hill-tribes—although they are scarcely even in name subjects of the Ameer—and with the occupation of Quettah; and it does not seem to have soothed his irritation when he learned that the Indian Government were intending to send him a Mission, comprising contingents of horse and force, and mustering, all told, more than a thousand persons. On the 21st of September this Mission set out from Peshawur, under the command of Sir Neville Chamberlain. The first stage of the journey was a place named Jumrood, on reaching which Major Cavagnari rode forward, attended by the friendly Khyberees, to the first Afghan fort, Ali Musjid, to ask a safe passage through the Khyber Pass. To this demand a resolute negative was returned. A three hours' interview terminated in the officer in charge assuring Major Cavagnari that any attempt to advance would be resisted by force; and that this threat was not an empty one the troops which lined both sides of the Pass made too clear. Only one course remained for the representative of the Indian Government; the inexorable officer was warned that Shere Ali would be held responsible for the refusal, and word was sent by telegraph to Lord Lytton, the governor-general of India, who ordered the Mission to return to Peshawur.

Just on the back of this news, as was to be expected, we were informed of prompt military measures taken by the Indian Government. Orders had been issued for the concentration of British troops on the Afghan frontier, with the view of undertaking immediate ulterior operations should circumstances render military action necessary. A force of 8000 men was to assemble at Moultan, and be prepared to advance through the Bolan Pass to Quettah, where a large force is already assembled, and whence, if necessary, a forward movement could be made on Candahar, so as to separate Cabul from Herat. A second force, 6000 strong, was to proceed to Kohat, and enter Afghanistan by the Koorum Valley, the occupation of which would separate Cabul from Chuznee. A third column was to proceed along the famous Khyber Pass. War was regarded by all parties to be inevitable, unless the Ameer came to his senses and made acknowledgment of his error. The insult offered to the conquerors of India was witnessed by two eminent Indian Princes, and, unless wiped out by firm and resolute action, all India would ring with it.

An Anglo-Indian correspondent gives the following account of the famous Khyber Pass, through which it was intended that the Mission should advance :—

"It is six and thirty years since the dreaded name of the Khyber Pass was familiar in the mouths of our fathers as a household word; and now that the ominous Afghan war-cloud is reappearing over the Suffed Koh, it is brought back to the minds of a generation which only associates it dimly with the annihilation of Elphinstone's unfortunate army. Nevertheless, that holocaust to official mismanagement of 4500 armed men, and from 12,000 to 13,000 camp followers, was not offered up in the Khyber at all, but in the Khurd-Cabul and Jugdulluck Passes, more than 100 miles distant from it. Formidable as the 'Iron Gate of India' appears to be and really is, it has been successfully passed by armies, great and small, whether descending from the 'Roof of the World' or ascending from the valley of the Indus. From the time of the great Macedonian down to that of Shah Zemaun, Suddozai ruler of Cabul and brother to our whilom *protégé*, Shah Shoojah, in 1796, it has offered no serious impediment to a long roll of conquerors, who have poured through it in their invasions of India. Seleucus, Mahmoud of Ghuznee, Muhammed Ghoori, Timour Leng, Baber, Nadir Shah, and Ahmed Shah Doorance, have all passed and re-passed it with or without the leave of its jealous janitors. Nearer to our own times the defile was forced by Sir Claude Wade in July 1839, who captured the fort of Ali Musjid, situated in the centre of the pass at the point where the northern and southern branches of it, coming from Peshawur, converge. In the following year Lord Keane retired through it with a portion of his army, after placing Shah Shoojah on the throne of Cabul. Brigadier Wild, who formed the advance portion of Sir George Pollock's avenging army, certainly came to grief in a premature attempt to force a passage in January 1842, when he knocked his head against Ali Musjid; but in the April following the famous old Field-Marshal himself wiped out the failure by his brilliant campaign. Taking the simple precaution to line the heights with his infantry before pushing through his guns and baggage with his cavalry, he led his relieving force, in spite of all opposition, not only through the Khyber, but also through the Khurd-Cabul and Jugdulluck to the Afghan capital, and back again to the Indus, with consummate skill and trifling loss. General Nott, who brought up the rear of the retiring army with his 'Glorious Candahar Brigade,' and who did not trouble himself to adopt the wise example of his leader, suffered in consequence from the murderous jezails of his despised enemy. Since our Sepoys of the plains have been quartered in Peshawur this once dreaded portal of Afghanistan has become familiarised to them, and the traditions of Elphinstone's retreat to Gundamuck have lost much of their old demoralising effect from lapse of time. . . . Thirteen miles from the cantonment of Peshawur stands the old fort of Jumrood, our frontier post towards the Khyber. Two miles further we cross the border and enter the defile, but we do it at the peril of our lives without a safe-conduct from the head man of the neighbouring district, and without an escort of his truculent clansmen. The entrance to the gorge is between two cliffs about 1200 feet in height, and for the first few miles there is a good road, constructed by our sappers in 1841, and flanked on each side by cindrous-looking rocks, piled in interminable confusion, without a sign of vegetation, and as brown and forbidden-looking as the cut-throats that clamber over them. These worthies, clad in poshteens swarming with vermin, of the true Khyberee breed, with greasy puggarrees round their matted locks, and a complete arsenal of murderous weapons disposed about their persons, may be seen any day about the fort of Jumrood, when not otherwise engaged against each other. Their sole formula of existence is 'an eye for an eye and a tooth for a tooth.' If one of them is killed his family or friends carry on a vendetta that would appal even a Corsican. They acknowledge no law or no rule, except that of their head man, as long only, however, as it suits them, and are as independent of Shere Ali as they are of the Kaiser-i-Hind."

A CHRONOLOGICAL LIST OF THE NAVAL AND MILITARY ENGAGEMENTS OF ENGLAND.

1793.

Feb. 3. France declares war against Great Britain and Holland: first coalition against France headed by England: a British army, under the Duke of York, joins the Allies.
May 8. Coldstream Guards at St. Amand.
 ,, 25. British at the storming of Valenciennes.
Aug. 18. The guards at Lincelles.
 ,, 28. Toulon declares for Louis XVII., and surrenders to Lord Hood's fleet.
Dec. 19. English evacuate Toulon, and burn the French fleet there.

1794.

April 24. The 15th Hussars at Villiers-en-Couche.
 ,, 25. British cavalry at Caudry.
 ,, 22. Surrender of Bastia to the British.
June 1. Lord Howe's great victory over the French fleet off Ushant.
 ,, 1. Surrender of Calvi to the British, and temporary conquest of Corsica.

1795.

Jan. End of the war in the Low Countries, and return of the British troops.
Mar. 13, 14. Admiral Hotham's action.
June 8. Admiral Cornwallis's masterly retreat.
„ 22. Lord Bridport's victory.
„ 27. Landing of the emigrants in Quiberon Bay.
Sep. 16. First capture of the Cape of Good Hope.
Oct. The Directory established in France.

1796.

Aug. 17. Capture of a Dutch fleet in Saldanha Bay.
Oct. 2. Spain declares war against Great Britain.
Dec. Failure of a French expedition against Ireland.

1797.

Feb. 14. Battle of Cape St. Vincent: defeat of the French fleet by Sir John Jervis.
„ 22. Landing of the French in Fishguard Bay.
July 3. Bombardment of Cadiz.
„ 24. Nelson's attempt on Santa Cruz.
Oct. 11. Battle of Camperdown: Admiral Duncan defeats the Dutch.

1798.

Aug. 1. Battle of the Nile: Nelson destroys the French fleet.
Sep. 8. General Humbert, sent to help the rebels in Ireland, surrenders at Mayo.
Oct. 11. Defeat of a French squadron in Killala Bay.

1799.

May 4. Siege of Seringapatam, and fall of the Kingdom of Mysore.
„ 20. Sir Sidney Smith foils Napoleon at Acre.

NAVAL AND MILITARY ENGAGEMENTS. 375

Aug. 27. Sir Ralph Abercrombie lands at the Helder: capture of the Dutch fleet.
Sep. 10. Defeat of General Brune at Zype.
 ,, 19. Battle of Alkmaar.
 ,, 30. Captain Louis of the *Minotaur* at Rome.
Dec. 25. Napoleon declared First Consul.

1800.

Sep. 4. Surrender of Malta to the British.
Dec. 16. Maritime Confederacy formed against Great Britain by Russia, Sweden, and Denmark.

1801.

Mar. 21. Battle of Alexandria.
April 2. Battle of the Baltic.
Aug. 15. Threatened Invasion of England: Nelson attacks the Boulogne flotilla.

1802.

Mar. 27. Treaty of Amiens signed.

1803.

May 12. Rupture between France and Britain.
Aug. 29. The Mahratta War: Lord Lake captures Allyghur.
Sep. 11. Lord Lake routs the Mahrattas at Delhi.
 ,, 21. Battle of Assaye.
Nov. 1. Battle of Leswaree.
 ,, 29. Battle of Argaum: the Mahratta power utterly broken.

1804.

May 18. Napoleon declared Emperor of the French.
Oct. 5. Capture of the Spanish treasure-frigates.
 ,, 12. Spain declares war against England.

1805.

July 22. Sir R. Calder engages the French fleet off Cape Finisterre.
Oct. 21. Battle of Trafalgar and death of Nelson.
Nov. 4. Sir Richard Strachan's action off Cape Ortegal.

1806.

Jan. 8. Second Capture of the Cape of Good Hope.
Feb. 6. Sir John Duckworth's victory at St. Domingo.
June 28. Buenos Ayres capitulates to Sir Home Popham.
July 6. Battle of Maida.

1807.

Feb. 2. Sir Samuel Achmuty takes Monte Video.
 ,, 19. Sir John Duckworth forces the Dardanelles: retreats March 3.
July 7. General Whitelocke capitulates at Buenos Ayres.
Sep. 7. Surrender of the Danish fleet to Admiral Gambier and General Lord Cathcart.

1808.

June 6. Joseph Buonaparte proclaimed king of Spain.
July 30. Wellington lands in Portugal.
Aug. 17. Battle of Roliça.
 ,, 21. Battle of Vimiero.
 ,, 23. Convention of Cintra: the French evacuate Portugal.

1809.

Jan. 16. Battle of Corunna, and death of Sir John Moore.
April 11. Lord Cochrane in the Basque Roads.
May 12. Wellington crosses the Douro.
July 28. Battle of Talavera.
Aug. 16. The Walcheren expedition: capture of Flushing.

1810.

Sep. 27. Battle of Busaco: Massena invades Portugal, and Wellington retires within the lines of Torres Vedras.

1811.

Mar. 13. Naval action off Lissa.
May 3–5. Battle of Fuentes d'Oñoro: deliverance of Portugal.
„ 16. Battle of Albuera.
Sep. 26. Surrender to the British of Java, the last remnant of the Colonial Empire of France.
Oct. 28. Hill surprises Girard at Arroyo dos Molinos.

1812.

Jan. 19. Storming of Ciudad Rodrigo.
April 6. Storming of Badajos.
May 19. Hill surprises the bridge of Almaraz.
June 18. Outbreak of the American War.
„ 22. Battle of Salamanca.
Aug. 12. Wellington enters Madrid.
Oct. 21. Wellington retreats from Burgos.

1813.

June 1. Sea-duel between the *Shannon* and the *Chesapeake*.
„ 21. Battle of Vitoria.
July 25–Aug. 2. Battles of the Pyrenees.
Aug. 31. Storming of San Sebastian, and liberation of Spain.
Sep. 7–9. Wellington forces the passage of the Bidassoa, and invades France.
Nov. 10–12. Passage of the Nivelle.
Dec. 9. Passage of the Nive.
„ 10–13. Battles before Bayonne.

1814.

Feb. 27. Battle of Orthes.
April 10. Battle of Toulouse.
May 10. Peace of Paris signed.

1815.

Feb. 26. Napoleon escapes from Elba: Wellington and Blucher proceed to Belgium.
June 16. Battle of Ligny: Napoleon defeats Blucher.
  ,,   ,, Battle of Quatre Bras: Wellington defeats Ney.
  ,, 18. Battle of Waterloo.
July 7. British and Prussian armies enter Paris.
Aug. 7. Napoleon sails for St. Helena.
Nov. 30. Second Peace of Paris.

1816.

Aug. 27. Bombardment of Algiers.

1824.

May 11. Bombardment of Rangoon.

1827.

Oct. 27. Battle of Navarino: destruction of the Turkish fleet.

1839.

July 23. Expedition to Afghanistan: storming of Ghuznee.
Aug. 7. British enter Cabul.

1840.

Sep. 27. Bombardment of Sidon.
Nov. 2. Bombardment of Acre.

1841.

Nov. 2. Outbreak at Cabul, and murder of Sir Alexander Burnes.

1842.

Jan. 6. Commencement of the retreat from Cabul.
July 21. First Chinese War: storming of Chin-Kiang-Foo.
Aug. 29. Peace signed with China.
Sep. 15. Enter of the Army of Retribution into Cabul.

1843.

Feb. 17. The War in Scinde: battle of Meeanee.
Mar. 24. Battle of Dubba, and annexation of Scinde.
Dec. 29. The Gwalior Campaign: battle of Maharajpore.

1845.

Dec. 18. First Sikh War: battle of Moodkee.
 ,, 22. Battle of Ferozeshah.

1846.

Jan. 28. Battle of Aliwal.
Feb. 10. Battle of Sobraon.

1849.

Jan. 13. Second Sikh War: battle of Chillianwalla.
Feb. 13. Battle of Goojerat.
Mar. 30. Annexation of the Punjaub.

1851.

April 5. Second Burmese War: storming of Martaban.
 ,, 11. Second bombardment of Rangoon.

1852.

June 30. Peace concluded with Burmah.

1853.

Mar. 12. Peace concluded with the Kaffirs.

1854.

Mar. 27. War declared by France and England against Russia.
April 22. Bombardment of Odessa.
Aug. 16. Bombardment and surrender of Bomarsund.
Sep. 20. Battle of the Alma.
Oct. 17. First bombardment of Sebastopol.

Oct. 25. Battle of Balaclava.
Nov. 5. Battle of Inkerman.

1855.

Jan. 26. Sardinia joins the Anglo-French alliance.
Feb. 15, 18. Omar Pasha defeats the Russians at Eupatoria.
April 9. Second bombardment of Sebastopol.
May 27. Capture of Kertch.
June 3. Bombardment of Taganrog.
 ,,   6. Third bombardment of Sebastopol : capture of the Mamelon.
 ,, 17, 18. Fourth bombardment of Sebastopol : unsuccessful assault on the Malakoff and the Redan.
 ,, 28. Death of Lord Raglan.
Aug. 9. Bombardment of Sveaborg by the Anglo-French fleet.
 ,, 16. Battle of Tchernaya : Russians defeated by the French and Sardinians.
Sep. 6-8. Last bombardment of Sebastopol : the French capture the Malakoff ; the British are repulsed from the Redan : in the night of the 8th the Russians evacuate Sebastopol.
Oct. 17. Bombardment and surrender of Kinburn.

1856.

Mar. 30. Treaty of Paris : peace with Russia.
Dec. 10. War with Persia : bombardment of Bushire.

1857.

Feb. 8. Battle of Khooshab : defeat of the Persians.
May 2. Treaty of Bagdad : peace with Persia.
 ,, 10. The Indian Mutiny : outbreak at Meerut.
June 1. Second Chinese War : action with Chinese war-junks at Fatshan Creek.
 ,, 5. The Indian Mutiny : outbreak at Cawnpore.
 ,, 27. First massacre at Cawnpore.

June 30. English besieged in the Residency at Lucknow.
July 12. Sir Henry Havelock on his march to the relief of Lucknow defeats the rebels at Futtehpore.
 ,, 15. Havelock gains two victories, at Aong and Pandoo Nuddee.
 ,, ,, Second massacre at Cawnpore.
 ,, 16. Havelock defeats Nana Sahib at Aherwa.
Aug. 16. Havelock defeats the Nana at Bithoor.
Sep. 14. Storming of Delhi.
 ,, 25. Havelock relieves Lucknow.
Nov. 17. Rescue of Lucknow by Sir Colin Campbell.
Dec. 6. Battle of Cawnpore.
 ,, 28, 29. Second Chinese War: bombardment and storming of Canton.

1858.

Mar. 21. Capture of Lucknow by Sir Colin Campbell.
April 2. Sir Hugh Rose takes Jhansi.
May   5. Battle of Bareilly.
 ,, 20. Second Chinese War: capture of the forts at the mouth of the Peiho.
June 19. Sir Hugh Rose takes Gwalior.
 ,, 26. Treaty of Tientsin: peace with China.
Sep.   1. The government of India transferred from the East India Company to the Queen.

1859.

June 25. Third Chinese War: Admiral Hope repulsed before the Taku forts.

1860.

Aug.   1. Anglo-French expedition to China lands at Pehtang.
 ,, 12. Defeat of the Chinese at Sinho.
 ,, 13. Defeat of the Chinese at Tangku.
 ,, 21. The Taku forts stormed.
Sep. 18. Seizure of Messrs Parkes and Loch at Ching-chai-wan: defeat of the Chinese.

Oct. 8. The allies take possession of the Summer Palace of the Emperor of China.
,, 12. The allied troops enter Pekin.
,, 24. Convention of Pekin: peace with China.

1867.

Nov. 19. Parliament sanctions the Abyssinian expedition.

1868.

Jan. 3. Sir Robert Napier lands at Zoulla.
,, 21. March on Magdala commences.
April 10. Battle of Aroje, in front of Magdala.
,, 11. Theodore releases the captives.
,, 13. Capture of Magdala, and suicide of Theodore.
July 10. Elevation of Sir Robert Napier to the peerage as Lord Napier of Magdala.

1873.

Jan. The Ashantees invade the Protectorate.
Oct. 2. Sir Garnet Wolseley arrives at Cape Coast Castle.
Dec. 15. Sir Garnet Wolseley reports that the Ashantees have been driven across the Prah.

1874.

Jan. 1. Disembarkation at Cape Coast Castle of the troops sent from England.
,, 20. The army crosses the Prah.
,, 29. Skirmish at Borborassie.
,, 31. Battle of Amoaful.
Feb. 4. Battle of Ordahsu, and march on Coomassie.
,, 6. Destruction of Coomassie.
,, 13. Treaty signed at Fommanah: peace with Ashantee.

Small crown 8vo, 384 pages, cloth, price 5s.,

THE SECRET OF SUCCESS;
OR,
HOW TO GET ON IN THE WORLD.

With some Remarks upon *True and False Success*, and the *Art of making the Best Use of Life*.

INTERSPERSED WITH NUMEROUS EXAMPLES AND ANECDOTES.

By W. H. DAVENPORT ADAMS,

Author of "English Party Leaders," "The Bird World,"
"Memorable Battles in English History," &c.

"The talent of success is nothing more than doing what you can do well."
—*H. W. Longfellow.*

WOOD ENGRAVINGS BY THOMAS BEWICK.

THE PARLOUR MENAGERIE:

Wherein are exhibited, in a Descriptive and Anecdotical form, the Habits, Resources, and Mysterious Instincts of the more interesting portions of the Animal Creation. With upwards of 300 Engravings on Wood, chiefly by BEWICK and two of his Pupils. Dedicated by Permission to the Right Hon. the BARONESS BURDETT-COUTTS (President), and the Members of the Ladies' Committee of the Royal Society for the Prevention of Cruelty to Animals.

Large crown 8vo, handsomely bound, gilt edges, price 7s. 6d.

From Professor OWEN, C.B., F.R.S., D.C.L., L.L.D., &c. (Director of the Natural History Department, B. Museum).
To the Editor of the "Parlour Menagerie."

"The early love of Nature, especially as manifested by the habits and instincts of animals to which you refer, in your own case, is so common to a healthy boy's nature, that the 'Parlour Menagerie,' a work so singularly full of interesting examples, culled from so wide a range of zoology, and so fully and beautifully illustrated, cannot fail to be a favourite with the rising generation—and many succeeding ones—of juvenile naturalists. When I recall the 'Description of Three Hundred Animals' (including the cockatrice and all Pliny's monsters), which fed my early appetite for natural history, I can congratulate my grandchildren on being provided with so much more wholesome food through your persevering and discriminating labours.
"RICHARD OWEN."

From the Right. Hon. JOHN BRIGHT, M.P.
To the Editor of the "Parlour Menagerie."

"I doubt not the 'Parlour Menagerie' will prove very interesting, as indeed it has already been found to be by those of my family who have read it. I hope one of the effects of our better public education will be to create among our population a more humane disposition towards what we call the inferior animals. Much may be done by impressing on the minds of children the duty of kindness in their treatment of animals, and I hope this will not be neglected by the teachers of our schools. . . . I feel sure what you have done will bear good fruit.
"December 13, 1877."
"JOHN BRIGHT.

"The 'Parlour Menagerie' is well named. Full as an egg of information and most agreeable reading and engravings, where before was there such a menagerie?"
—*Animal World.*

London: JOHN HOGG, Paternoster Row.

"Decidedly, this life of De Quincey is the best biography of the year in the English language."—*Vide Critical Notices.*

In Two Volumes, crown 8vo, cloth, with Portrait, price 21s.,

THOMAS DE QUINCEY:
HIS LIFE AND WRITINGS.
WITH UNPUBLISHED CORRESPONDENCE.
By H. A. PAGE,

Author of "Memoir of Hawthorne," "Golden Lives," "Fables for Old and Young," &c.

*** THE LETTERS IN THE TWO VOLUMES COMPRISE NEARLY ONE HUNDRED, FROM MR. DE QUINCEY TO HIS FAMILY, THE WORDSWORTHS, AND OTHERS; AND TO HIM FROM MR. THOMAS CARLISLE, PROFESSOR WILSON, AND OTHERS.

PRESS NOTICES.—SOME LONDON PAPERS.

"The work is enriched by letters which his two surviving daughters have brought out of long-closed repositories. . . . In taking leave of this creditable book, we thank Mr. Page for his labour of love, and congratulate him on the collaboration that he has been favoured with. We should add that there is, as frontispiece, an excellent likeness of De Quincey, from a chalk drawing by Mr Archer. It is far superior to any other published portrait of him."—*Times.*

"An interesting record of a remarkable writer, and still more singular individuality, is presented in these volumes. . . . Mr Page has succeeded in giving a vivid portraiture of an original and striking intellect. . . . De Quincey was by no means the least among a very noteworthy set of men who cast a light over English literature in the first half of the present century; . . . but the man himself was perhaps more interesting than his books. . . . The reminiscences of Mr. Hogg, the publisher, are very interesting; and Dr. Eatwell's 'Medical View of Mr. De Quincey's Case' is curious and instructive."—*Daily News.*

"A carefully and temperately-written biography."—*Spectator.*

"A welcome addition to the library. . . . The reminiscences of Mr. Hogg are new and interesting; so are those of Mr. Francis Jacox. Dr. Warburton Begbie's account of De Quincey's last days is really valuable. . . . If ever there was a man of genius, Thomas de Quincey was one. His position in our literature is perfectly unique."—*Athenæum.*

"One of the most interesting and well-written biographies which we have read for some time."—*Standard.*

"At last we are indulged with a life of De Quincey, . . . and we are mistaken if the result be not to set Thomas de Quincey on a higher pinnacle as a man with conduct and conscience, a man with responsible family relations, a true gentleman as well as cultivated scholar, than he had hitherto reached. . . . The author is one practised in kindred pursuits, and has had the great advantage of Mr. James Hogg's reminiscences of De Quincey, as well as free access to De Quincey's daughters, and the papers and documents in their possession."—*Academy.*

"Here we at last find a full picture of De Quincey's life, with all the lights and shades so deftly touched in as to leave no canvas uncovered."—*Globe.*

London: JOHN HOGG, Paternoster Row.

www.ingramcontent.com/pod-product-compliance
Lightning Source LLC
Chambersburg PA
CBHW032028220426
43664CB00006B/403